October 13, 1999

To Ane, with many good wishes and thanks. May the spirit always be with you. *[signature]*

The Lehmann-Prins Pirkei Avoth

The Lehmann-Prins
PIRKEI AVOTH

By Rabbi Dr. Marcus (Meir) Lehmann
and completed by
Rabbi Eliezer Liepman Philip Prins

Translated and adapted from the German
by C.H. Moore, M.A., Ph.D.

FELDHEIM PUBLISHERS Jerusalem / New York

First published 1992
Copyright © 1992 by the estate of C.H. Moore

Feldheim Publishers
POB 35002/Jerusalem, Israel

Feldheim Publishers
200 Airport Executive Park
Spring Valley, NY 10977

Library of Congress Cataloging-in-Publication Data

Mishnah. Avot.
    The Lehmann-Prins Pirkei Avoth / by Marcus Lehmann
and completed by Eliezer Liepman Philip Prins; translated
and adapted from the German by C.H. Moore.
    496 p. 23cm.
    ISBN 0-87306-589-1. — ISBN 0-87306-593-x (pbk.)
    1. Mishnah. Avot—Commentaries. I. Lehmann, Marcus,
1831-1890. II. Prins, Liepman Philip, 1835-1915. III.
Mishnah. Avot. English. 1992. IV. Title.
BM506. A2E5 1992
296. 1'23—dc20   91-39597
                                         CIP

Printed in Israel

Foreword

RABBI MARCUS (MEIR) LEHMANN ז״ל, was born on 25 Teveth, 5591 (January 10, 1831) to Roeschen (Shoshanna) and Lemuel Aharon Lehmann in the town of Verden, province of Hanover, Germany. He was their eighth and youngest child, and he showed early promise of having a gifted intelligence. Young Meir was encouraged in his Torah studies by his father, who was an outstanding disciple of the renowned *Noda Biyehudah*, Rabbi Ezekiel Landau. He studied for two years at the yeshivah of Rabbi Ezriel Hildesheimer in Halberstadt and then attended the lectures (*shiurim*) of Chief Rabbi Solomon Loeb Rappaport and Rabbi Samuel Freund in Prague, from whom he received a rabbinic diploma. In Berlin, he studied with Rabbi Michael Landsberger, who also awarded him a rabbinic diploma in 1854.

While in Prague and Berlin, Rabbi Lehmann founded talmudic societies for young intellectual Jews in order to encourage them to study Jewish tradition. He also studied at the Universities of Prague and Berlin and earned a doctorate from Halle University. In September 1854, having decided to devote his life to the rabbinate, he accepted a position offered by a small group of Orthodox Jews in Mainz. This group of people, under the leadership of the outstanding talmudic scholar, Rabbi Samuel Bondi, separated from the large Jewish congregation in that city when an organ was brought into the synagogue.

In 1856, Rabbi Lehmann married Theresa (Tirza) Bondi. They had three children: Asher, Emma-Rosalie and Jonas. In December 1856, Rabbi Lehmann opened his own synagogue and school, where both secular and Jewish subjects were taught. In 1858 his school finally received official recognition from the Jewish Community Council, and by 1878 the size of his congregation had increased to such an extent that they moved into a larger building. He helped to found similar Orthodox communities in other cities, such as Darmstadt, Wiesbaden and Bingen.

Another milestone in Rabbi Lehmann's life was when he founded *Der Israelit*, a traditional Jewish weekly newspaper, in May 1860. It was soon read eagerly throughout Germany, and was published continuously for many years until Hitler banned all Jewish publications. Rabbi Lehmann also wrote stories and novels for the popular magazine section of the newspaper, all with Jewish religious and historical themes. One of his novels, *Rabbi Yosselmann von Rosheim*, was based on original historical documents and his book, *Akiva*, was drawn from the Talmud and Midrash. In addition to newspaper stories, editorial articles and novels, Rabbi Lehmann also wrote a great many important religious works. Two books on Tractate Zera'im of the Jerusalem Talmud, with the commentary of Rabbi Salomon Sirillo and his own notes on it, were published in 1878 under the title *Meir Nethiv*. When he died on Nissan 23, 5650 (April 13, 1890), Rabbi Lehmann left two unfinished manuscripts: *The Pesach Haggadah* (later completed by Rabbi H. Ehrmann and other students) and *The Commentary on Pirkei Avoth*, up to chapter 4, mishnah 5. Rabbi Eliezer Liepman Philip Prins ז״ל completed the *Commentary*.*

Rabbi Eliezer Liepman Philip Prins (1835-1915) was born in Arnhem, Holland. His family was widely known for its activities on behalf of the Jewish community. Rabbi Prins first studied Torah under the tutelage of Rabbi Yoel Frankfort and his son, Naftali, in Arnhem; even then he showed his outstanding abilities and noble character. He married Henrietta Jacobson, the daughter of a distinguished Jewish Amsterdam family, and they had six children. His eldest son, Maurits (Moshe Meir) married Rabbi Lehmann's only daughter, Emma. After the death of his first wife, Rabbi Prins married Sara Lob-Federman (Emma's cousin) and they had four children.

Although at first he joined the family carpet business, Rabbi Prins never stopped studying Torah; indeed, עשה תורתו קבע, he made his study of the Torah a regular activity. At the age of forty, he left the business and devoted the rest of his life to learning, teaching, writing and public service. By the age of forty-five he

* See his introduction, pp. 289-291.

was already well known in the Jewish communities of both Europe and Eretz Yisrael as a *talmid chacham*, a philanthropist, a community leader, a bibliophile and an author. He corresponded with the greatest Torah scholars of his time, and as a *mohel*, he circumcised hundreds of Jewish children without remuneration.

When he agreed to complete Rabbi Lehmann's commentary on Pirkei Avoth, Rabbi Prins wrote: "The editorial board of this journal has honored me by requesting that I continue the commentary to Pirkei Avoth...presented...by the unforgettable Dr. Lehmann... I venture to respond to the call...in the awareness that it is a privilege to work on a journal which has contributed so much that is good and great. Furthermore, I believe that I could not pay greater homage to the memory of the founder of this newspaper than by continuing the explanations in his style..." Rabbi Prins fulfilled his commission admirably. *The Commentary on Pirkei Avoth* first appeared in serial form in the weekly *Der Israelit*. Both Rabbi Lehmann and Rabbi Prins cited widely from Talmud and Scriptures, particularly Mishlei and Midrash, but Rabbi Lehmann especially favored the authoritative commentaries of Rabbi Shemuel of Ozedah (the *Midrash Shemuel*) and Rabbi Shimon ben Tzemach Duran (the *Rashbatz*).

This translation of the original serialized commentary was put into a condensed format for the English edition and the language was modernized. I tried, however, to remain completely faithful to the spirit, if not the letter, of the original text, and in the course of my work, I corrected a considerable number of printing errors and misquotations.

ואלה יעמדו על הברכה:

I am grateful to Mrs. Dvora Kiel for editing the English text.

Special thanks are due to: Rabbi S. D. Sassoon ז"ל, and ילח"ט the Sassoon family of Jerusalem, Mozelle and Abraham Gubbay of London and Els and Charles Bendheim of New York, descendants of the authors, for their generous contributions which have made this publication possible. In addition, Mrs. Els Bendheim gave a considerable amount of helpful advice which is very much appreciated. I also wish to thank Rabbi D. Freilich שליט"א, for lending a helping hand; Dayan C.D. Kaplin שליט"א, for his valuable advice; Yaakov Feldheim נ״י, for undertaking to publish the English edition; my sons, Joel, Michael, Jonathan and Benjamin Moore שיחי׳, for assisting me in so many ways; Mr. J. Schijveschuurder נ״י, for kindly providing me with the original German text; and my daughter-in-law, Helen Moore, for her technical assistance.

It is my hope that בס״ד the English edition of this most learned and instructive commentary to Pirkei Avoth will be widely read and studied, להגדיל תורה ולהאדירה.

C. H. Moore, M.A., Ph.D.
Nissan 5746/1986

Unfortunately, my father ז״ל did not live to see the publication of his translation. He passed away on *Rosh Chodesh Elul*, 5746 (September 5, 1986). I would like to thank Mrs. Dvora Kiel and also the editorial staff at Feldheim Publishers for ably assisting me in preparing the manuscript for publication. I am especially indebted to Mrs. Els Bendheim both for her meticulous proofreading of the galleys and for her invaluable editorial comments.

May my father's wish, that this edition be widely read and studied, be fulfilled, and may the Torah that is learned from this work be a merit for his *neshamah*.

ת.נ.צ.ב.ה

B.S. Moore
Adar I 5752/1992

Preface

WHEN NATURE AWAKENS from its winter sleep, field and meadow reflect the beauty of spring, the stately fruit trees gladden the eyes and the heart with their splendid blossoms, then man, too, feels a stirring of new life and hidden desires. In this season, therefore, as a way of restraining those awakening passions, the Sages enjoin us to read the *Chapters of the Fathers*, a remarkably fine collection of ethical teachings which contains the five chapters of Tractate Avoth and a sixth, the *baraytha* called *Kinyan Torah*. These ethics differ considerably from those of other nations, for the latter are man-made, whereas Jewish ethics emanate from God. That is why the tractate begins with the words משה קבל תורה מסיני, "Moshe received the Torah from Sinai," that is, from the One Who revealed Himself to His people on Mount Sinai, from the almighty, the omniscient, and the only God.

When God gave His people the 248 positive and 365 negative commandments, He ordered Moshe to write them down concisely, along with an account of the creation of the world, the first man, and the history of our forefathers—the people of Yisrael, down through the death of our teacher Moshe. God Himself taught Moshe the understanding of every individual commandment and the manner of its observance. After Moshe taught his brother Aharon all that he had learned from God, Aharon's sons, Elazar and Ithamar, came to Moshe and he repeated his discourse. Then the seventy Elders of Israel, the members of the Great Sanhedrin, entered, and Moshe taught for the third time all that he had learned from God. The fourth time, he recited it to all the people of Yisrael. Then Aharon and his sons repeated what they had learned three more times, until all Yisrael under-

stood every positive and negative commandment to the last detail. That is the Oral Law, which was not written down at that
time, and which was verbally passed on from generation to generation.

Moshe received God's Torah from Sinai exactly as God had
taught it to him "and he handed it down to Yehoshua." But
Yehoshua was not able to absorb it entirely, and therefore the
text reads ומסרה ליהושע, "handed it down to Yehoshua" and not
ויהושע קבלה ממשה, "Yehoshua received from Moshe." Our Sages
relate in the Talmud:

> When the hour approached for Moshe to depart from this
> world, he said to Yehoshua, "My faithful disciple, to whom I
> entrust the flock that I have tended carefully for forty years,
> do you wish further instruction on any point?" Yehoshua
> replied, "How should anything not be clear? After all, I have
> never left your side, beloved teacher; you have taught me
> the whole Torah and have not withheld anything from me."
> Nevertheless, during the thirty days of grief and deep
> mourning for Moshe, many commandments were forgotten,
> and it was only through the ingenuity of Othniel ben Kenaz
> that the forgotten laws were completely recalled.
>
> (*Temurah* 16a)

This account in the Talmud teaches us an important lesson
—in order to preserve our Tradition intact, we cannot rely
merely on our own understanding or memory; we must study the
Oral Law, the Talmud, with great diligence. We must try to
penetrate the meaning of the text, comparing one section with
another to clarify and resolve apparent inconsistencies. That is
our task when we study Torah today, just as it was in the days of
Othniel ben Kenaz.

The short introduction to the *Chapters of the Fathers* found in
every prayer book is the beginning of chapter 10 of Tractate
Sanhedrin:

כָּל יִשְׂרָאֵל יֵשׁ לָהֶם חֵלֶק לְעוֹלָם הַבָּא, שֶׁנֶּאֱמַר
וְעַמֵּךְ כֻּלָם צַדִּיקִים לְעוֹלָם יִירְשׁוּ אָרֶץ נֵצֶר מַטָעַי
מַעֲשֵׂה יָדַי לְהִתְפָּאֵר:

All Yisrael have a portion in the World to Come, as it is
said: "And your people, all of them righteous, shall inherit the Earth forever, the flower of My plantings, the
work of My hands, to glorify Me" (*Yeshayahu* 60:21).

The *Chapters of the Fathers* do not contain actual legal regulations but rather, ethical doctrines which man can use to raise his
personal moral standards. Indeed, the desirable standards are so
high that they may seem to be beyond some people's capabilities.
"Raise up many students!" (*Avoth* 1:1), is one such example. How
can a person who has barely learned anything himself meet this
obligation? Or, "Do not be like servants who serve their master
for the sake of receiving a reward!" (*Avoth* 1:3). For many people
it is only the prospect of receiving a reward or the fear of punishment which keeps them on the right path. Someone who finds it
too hard to meet all these demands might decide not to meet any
at all, so our Sages preface their lessons by saying, "All Yisrael
have a share in the great World to Come, in eternal happiness."
The size of one's share, however, depends on the individual
himself, and the higher he will rise in the fulfillment of his moral
and religious duties, the greater will be his share in eternal life.

Now, you might think that "all Yisrael" without exception has
a share in the World to Come. However, the final sentence of
mishnah 1, chapter 10 in Tractate Sanhedrin speaks of Jews who
will not have a share in the World to Come, such as those who say
that the Torah does not teach about resurrection, or those who
deny the divine origin of the Torah. The words כל ישראל mean
that every Jew who strives to live wholly as a Jew will have a share
in the next world. The continuous happiness of eternal life does
not fall into a Jew's lap like a ripe fruit; he has to reach for it. You
might also think that the words כל ישראל exclude everyone except
Jews from immortality and the World to Come, but such exclu-

siveness is not compatible with Jewish belief. Our Sages teach, "As it is said, 'All the nations that forget God shall return to the lowest world' (*Tehillim* 9:18). Rabbi Yehoshua taught, 'It does not say, "all the nations" (without resurrection), but "all the nations that forget God." From this we conclude that even among non-Jews there are pious people who will have a share in the World to Come' " (*Tosefta* on *Sanhedrin*, ch. 13 and *Sanhedrin* 105a). Rabbi Yehoshua's lesson was accepted as the Law.

In his commentary to the Mishnah, the Rambam remarks, וזכר בלעם והוא אינו מישראל לפי שחסידי אומות העולם יש להם חלק לעולם הבא והודיעו שבלעם מרשעי אומות העולם ואין לו חלק לעולם הבא. "The Mishnah mentions Bilam, who was a non-Jew, because pious non-Jews also have a share in the World to Come, but Bilam was wicked and therefore lost his eternal happiness." Pious non-Jews are those who keep the seven Noachide commandments: to refrain from murder, idolatry, immorality, robbery and blasphemy, to love right, justice and virtue, and to avoid cruelty not only to human beings but also to animals. The words כל ישראל do not exclude non-Jews from eternal happiness but do suggest that everyone fortunate enough to be born a Jew finds a ready path which leads upward to the abode of our Heavenly Father.

Perek One

אָ מֹשֶׁה קִבֵּל תּוֹרָה מִסִּינַי וּמְסָרָהּ לִיהוֹשֻׁעַ
וִיהוֹשֻׁעַ לִזְקֵנִים וּזְקֵנִים לִנְבִיאִים
וּנְבִיאִים מְסָרוּהָ לְאַנְשֵׁי כְנֶסֶת הַגְּדוֹלָה: הֵם אָמְרוּ
שְׁלֹשָׁה דְבָרִים, הֱווּ מְתוּנִים בַּדִּין וְהַעֲמִידוּ
תַלְמִידִים הַרְבֵּה וַעֲשׂוּ סְיָג לַתּוֹרָה:

1 Moshe received the Torah from Sinai and handed
it down to Yehoshua and Yehoshua to the Elders and
the Elders to the prophets and the prophets handed it
down to the Men of the Great Assembly. They said
three things: Be cautious in judgment, raise up many
disciples, and make a fence around the Torah.

*　　*　　*

The Torah was handed down in one unbroken chain from the
revelation on Sinai to the present day. The Elders were "the
Elders who outlived Yehoshua" (*Shoftim* 2:7). Among them were
Kalev ben Yefuneh, Othniel ben Kenaz, the first judge in Yisrael,
and all the judges thereafter who led the people, until the last
one, Shemuel, who was also a prophet. He was followed by all the
other prophets of Yehudah and Yisrael down to Yirmeyahu, who
lived at the time that the Holy Temple in Yerushalayim was
destroyed. Then, during the Babylonian captivity, Yirmeyahu's
disciples handed down the Oral Law to the Jewish people and
eventually led them back from Exile to the Holy Land. Three of
them, the prophets Chaggai, Zecharyah and Malachi, later be-

came members of the Great Assembly as well.

MEN OF THE GREAT ASSEMBLY. In the time of the Second Temple, God allowed the great men of Yisrael to write down the Law in the Mishnah. One hundred and twenty of the most outstanding of them formed the Great Assembly, led by Ezra, Nechemyah, Zerubbavel, Serayah, Re'elayah, Mordechai, Bilshan, Chaggai, Zecharyah and Malachi. They established the practices and traditions that we still enjoy today, and they were the authors and arrangers of our prayers. The Talmud explains, "Yehoshua ben Levi said, 'Why were they called Men of the Great Assembly? Because they restored the crown of Divine attributes to its ancient completeness.' Moshe said, 'God the great, the mighty, and the feared' (*Devarim* 10:17). Yirmeyahu said, 'God the great and mighty' (*Yirmeyahu* 32:18), leaving out 'the feared,' for the heathens are devastating His Sanctuary—where, therefore, is the fear of Him? Daniel said, 'God the mighty and the feared' (*Daniel* 9:4), leaving out 'the great,' for the heathens are enslaving His sons—where, then, is His power? Then came the Men of the Great Assembly and placed at the beginning of our *Shemoneh Esreh* prayers all the original words of Moshe, saying, 'On the contrary! This is His might—that He can suppress His wrath and tolerate the wicked. And, but for the fear of Him, how could one nation survive among all the nations?' " (*Yoma* 69b).

If we ourselves could but feel Yirmeyahu's sorrow when he saw the House of God, the residence of the Creator of Heaven and earth, in ruins, if we could but suffer Daniel's sadness at the sight of the sons of a free nation, the chosen people, being led into slavery, we might then appreciate the great achievement of the Men of the Great Assembly. They understood that eternal truth is not linked to the physical existence of the Holy Temple nor to the political independence of Yisrael.

BE CAUTIOUS IN JUDGMENT, RAISE UP MANY STUDENTS AND MAKE A FENCE AROUND THE TORAH. Three fundamental principles were laid down by the Men of the Great Assembly, which we can paraphrase: Learn, teach and do! To judge wisely, one must know the Law extensively and thoroughly. The Jewish judge shall not rely on his own intelligence; he should apply the relevant precepts of our holy Torah, כי המשפט לאלהים הוא, "For the judgment is God's" (*Devarim* 1:17). Targum Yonathan uses the word מתון (cautious) to mean "be slow to judge" (commentary on *Bemidbar* 15:34). This verse tells of a man whom *bnei Yisrael* found gathering sticks on the Shabbath day. When they took him and brought him to Moshe because they were not sure which punishment he deserved—Moshe in turn, asked the Lord for advice. In this way, Moshe set an example for all future teachers in Yisrael: It is not demeaning to ask for advice when judging a difficult case.

Rashi says that מתון means the same as קשה (hard, difficult). Then הוו מתונים בדין means "Investigate carefully before you come to a decision"; nothing is too insignificant to question. Indeed, the principles of thorough research, deep learning and careful reflection are closely linked to our nation's existence. Rabbi Ovadyah of Bertinoro explains that מתונים means "reflective." When called upon to judge a case that is similar to one that you have judged once, twice or even three times before, do not say, "I have already investigated this matter on one, two or three previous occasions and it would be superfluous to examine it again." On the contrary—be even more careful in your judgment, examine the case again and again before you make a decision.

RAISE UP MANY STUDENTS. Teaching is as important as learning! The more we disseminate knowledge of the Torah, the greater and more illustrious our people become. A genuine Sage does not keep great pearls of wisdom to himself, as a miser who buries his gold in the ground. *Rabban* Gamliel was a great teacher in Yisrael, but he was criticized for being too severe in testing his students. Teach many students even if there may be some among them who do not devote themselves to learning with a pure purpose, but out of ambition or greed. Let them learn as they like, but let them learn. The light of the Torah will purify their thoughts and its truth will protect them in spite of their petty concerns. If a master has only a few apprentices, he can devote a great deal of attention to each of them, whereas with a large number, his attention will be splintered. The Men of the Great Assembly therefore caution us to be wary of careless instruction.

Students must be able to stand on their own feet, for some day, God willing, they will also be teachers in Yisrael.

Furthermore, teaching the Torah's wisdom only when you are young, and then doing nothing in your old age, is not acceptable. Certainly not! You must never stop teaching, as it is said: בבוקר זרע את זרעך ולערב אל תנח ידך, "In the morning [of your life] sow your seed and in the evening withhold not your hand" *(Koheleth* 11:6). There was probably no scholar who gathered more disciples around him than Rabbi Akiva, yet in the "evening" of his life he saw many of the fairest flowers of Israel's youth wither and die in a terrible epidemic, and the rest fall in Bar Kochva's rebellion. All his work seemed to have been in vain, but he did not lose heart. In his old age, he once more gathered disciples around him and these men—Rabbi Meir, Rabbi Yosei, Rabbi Yehudah, Rabbi Shimon, Rabbi Nechemyah and Rabbi Yochanan Ha-Sandlar—became the fathers of Yisrael and the guardians of our Torah.

AND MAKE A FENCE AROUND THE TORAH. The Torah can be compared to a magnificent garden, full of the most beautiful flowers and precious fruit trees. Without a protective fence, this magnificent garden would be exposed to destruction by either wicked people or wild animals. Therefore our Sages built a protective fence around the garden of the Torah; the fence consists of the Shabbath laws, which are very strict indeed, and the laws on marriage, morality, and family purity, and all the laws which teach us how to observe the commandments properly. These laws became the fence which effectively protected the Jewish nation in the days of Ezra and Nechemyah, as they continue to protect all the generations of Yisrael—past, present and future.

שִׁמְעוֹן הַצַּדִּיק הָיָה מִשְׁיָרֵי כְנֶסֶת הַגְּדוֹלָה. הוּא הָיָה אוֹמֵר, עַל־שְׁלשָׁה דְבָרִים הָעוֹלָם עוֹמֵד, עַל הַתּוֹרָה וְעַל הָעֲבוֹדָה וְעַל גְּמִילוּת חֲסָדִים:

2   Shimon *Ha-Tzaddik* was among the last of the Men of the Great Assembly. He would say: The world is based on three things: the Torah, serving God and acts of lovingkindness.

*   *   *

Shimon *Ha-Tzaddik* was one of the youngest members of the Great Assembly. Scholars cannot agree about when he lived. According to Jewish tradition, only forty years elapsed between the return from Babylonian captivity and the conquest of the Persian empire by Alexander the Great, while secular historians adduce a gap of more than two hundred years. The Talmud tells us that Shimon *Ha-Tzaddik*, the High Priest, led all the priests to meet the Macedonian conqueror and impressed him so favorably that Alexander became a friend of the Jews (*Yoma* 69a). Yehoshua ben Sira, a contemporary poet, calls Shimon one of the most outstanding Jewish leaders from the period between Avraham and Nechemyah. During the forty years that Shimon was High Priest, many miracles took place in the Holy Temple on his account (*Yoma* 39a). Shimon's maxim contains three great concepts about the origin, the final purpose and the maintenance of the world. It also describes the three areas of moral responsibility for a Jew—to himself, to God, and to his fellowman.

TORAH. It is the duty of a Jew to perfect his mind. Man's intellect is unformed and insignificant at birth, but with painstaking effort and training he may eventually comprehend the most sublime thoughts. The Torah signifies the highest form of spiritual knowledge attainable by man; it teaches extremely advanced concepts. To study the Torah, therefore, is the Jew's paramount obligation. God created the world because of the Torah, as it is written, "Thus says the Lord, but for My covenant (the Torah) I would not have instituted night and day, the ordinances of Heaven and earth" (*Yirmeyahu* 33:25). The Sages say, "At the creation of the world the existence of Heaven and earth was closely linked to the acceptance of the Torah by Yisrael" (*Shabbath* 88a), and also "He who occupies himself with the study of the Torah with a pure purpose is comparable to a partner of God in the work of Creation" (*Sanhedrin* 99b).

SERVING GOD. The second obligation of a Jew is taught at the end of Tractate Kiddushin: "Man was created only to serve his God" (*Kiddushin* 82a). While the Holy Temple was still standing, we were able to serve God actively (see also *Ta'anith* 27b and *Megillah* 31b). Since the Holy Temple was destroyed, however, the order of prayers has taken the place of the sacrificial service.

LOVINGKINDNESS. A Jew also has a duty to his fellowman. This is best expressed in the true practice of charity. "And you shall love your fellowman as yourself" (*Vayyikra* 19:18), the Talmud says, is the all-embracing principle of the Torah (*Yerushalmi, Nedarim* 9:4). Man and the universe will be perpetuated by love and kindness, as it is said, "The world is built on kindness" (*Tehillim* 89:3). The practice of lovingkindness (*gemiluth chasadim*) does not merely consist of giving alms. The Sages said, "Our Rabbis taught that *gemiluth chasadim* is superior to charity in three respects: charity can be performed only with one's money, but *gemiluth chasadim* can be practiced both with one's person and with one's money; charity is given only to the poor, but *gemiluth chasadim* benefits both the rich and the poor; charity can be given to the living only, while *gemiluth chasadim* can be done for the living and the dead" (*Sukkah* 49b).

The Sages tell us that when God deliberated with the angels about the creation of man, the Angel of Peace and the Angel of Truth advised against it, but the Angel of Love stepped in front of the Almighty's throne and said, "Create him, gracious God, for he will carry out deeds of love on earth." And God created man so that, through him, love would be practiced. In the Talmud Yerushalmi (*Megillah* 3:6), the maxim of Shimon *Ha-Tzaddik* is joined to the words of the prophet (*Yeshayahu* 51:16) who says:

‏ואשם דברי בפיך ובצל ידי כסיתיך לנטע שמים וליסוד ארץ ולאמר לציון עמי אתה.‏
"And I shall put My words in your mouth"—that is, the Torah; "and I shall cover you with the shadow of My hand"—that is, the practice of charity (that is done with the hand); "that I may plant the heavens and lay the foundations of the earth"—that is, the sacred sacrificial service for the sake of which the world was created (as we have seen above); then (when you make Torah, *avodah* and *gemiluth chasadim* your maxims) "I shall say to Tzion, 'You are My people.' "

In the Midrash, these three concepts are joined to a saying from the Torah (*Shemoth* 15:13): ‏נחית בחסדך עם זו גאלת נהלת בעזך אל נוה‏ ‏קדשך–נחית בחסדך, זה החסד, נהלת בעזך, זו תורה כד"א יי עוז לעמו יתן, אל‏ ‏נוה קדשך זו עבודת המשכן והמקדש.‏ , " 'You in Your kindness have led forth this people'—that is *gemiluth chesed*; 'You have guided them in Your strength'—that is the Torah, as it is written, 'God will give His people power'—'unto Your holy Habitation'—that is the Divine service in the Temple" (*Yalkut Shimoni* 251, from the *Pesikta of Rabbi Kahana*).

In each reference the three principles are mentioned in a different order. In this mishnah the order is that of a man's lifetime: early in life the child must start learning Torah; at the age of thirteen he becomes duty-bound to serve God; and he can practice *gemiluth chasadim* only when he earns his own living.

The Midrash arranges the principles in the order in which they came into the world. Before the revelation on Mount Sinai, the world was solely preserved by love; then it was given the Torah through Yisrael, and finally the Divine service was instituted in the Holy Temple. In the Talmud Yerushalmi they are arranged according to their importance. *Avodah* is mentioned last, as it only encompasses duties toward God. *Gemiluth chasadim* is second because works of love are a source of joy for both God and man. The Torah is foremost, for it is written ‏תלמוד תורה כנגד כלם,‏ "But the study of the Torah excels them all," that is to say, is greater than all the other sacred duties (*Pe'ah* 1:1).

אַנְטִיגְנוֹס אִישׁ סוֹכוֹ קִבֵּל מִשִּׁמְעוֹן
הַצַּדִּיק. הוּא הָיָה אוֹמֵר, אַל־תִּהְיוּ
כַּעֲבָדִים הַמְשַׁמְּשִׁין אֶת־הָרַב עַל־מְנָת לְקַבֵּל פְּרָס,
אֶלָּא הֱווּ כַּעֲבָדִים הַמְשַׁמְּשִׁין אֶת־הָרַב שֶׁלֹּא עַל־
מְנָת לְקַבֵּל פְּרָס וִיהִי מוֹרָא שָׁמַיִם עֲלֵיכֶם:

3 Antigenos of Socho received [the Tradition] from Shimon *Ha-Tzaddik*. He would say: Be not like servants who serve their master for the sake of receiving a reward, but rather be like servants who serve their master without thought of a reward; and let the fear of Heaven be upon you.

*   *   *

The most outstanding disciple of Shimon *Ha-Tzaddik* was Antigenos of the Judean town, Socho. His maxim teaches us not to be selfish and to do good for its own sake—not for a reward. We should do so from a sense of duty since God has created us to serve Him and to observe His commandments. But maxims are sometimes confusing. Because of their brevity and precision they are often effective as teaching devices, but these same qualities must not conceal their meaning. In a later mishnah, the Sage Avtalyon warns us, "Scholars, be careful with your words!" (*Avoth* 1:11; see Bertinoro's commentary). This maxim was grossly misinterpreted soon after Antigonos' time, we are told, for this very reason.

The fifth chapter of *Avoth of Rabbi Nathan* tells of Antigenos' disciples, Tzadok (or Saduc) and Baytos (Boethos) who taught their disciples the master's maxim without careful and adequate explanation, and their disciples did the same. Thus a generation arose saying, "What might have induced our fathers to establish such a principle? 'Be like servants who serve...not for the sake of [receiving] a reward'—Is it imaginable that a worker should work all day without obtaining his wages in the evening? If our fathers really believed in another world, a future life, they would not have made up such a principle! They obviously did not really believe in the World to Come." Based on this kind of ill-founded thinking, a sect was formed, whose members were called Sadducees or Boethusians, after these two misguided disciples of Antigenos. They abandoned the Torah, sought to enjoy life as much as possible and mocked those who remained faithful to the Law—those who, to their way of thinking, rendered life more difficult through the observance of the commandments.

The attitude of those disciples seems historically plausible when we consider the older, and probably more correct, reading of the maxim: אלא הוו כעבדים המשמשין את הרב על מנת שלא לקבל פרס, "but rather be like servants who serve their master for the sake of not receiving a reward." Rabbi Shimon ben Tzemach Duran (Rashbatz) comments, "Some have changed the reading, saying, 'Why shall we serve the Lord with the intention of not receiving a reward and what harm is there when the Lord grants a reward? It is only the intention that matters and this was not directed to the reward.' However, there is no need to change the correct reading on that account; for the perfect servant will say, 'My Master has already bestowed many kindnesses upon me, and I am duty-bound to serve Him therefor.' "

This is the kind of service commanded by God, Who says, "And you shall love the Lord your God." In this way Avraham served his Creator and he is therefore called אוהב (he who loves), as we read: זרע אברהם אוהבי, "The seed of Avraham who loved Me" (*Yeshayahu* 41:8). And we further read (*Avodah Zarah* 19a): אשרי איש ירא את ה', במצותיו חפץ מאד-אמר רבי אליעזר, במצותיו ולא בשכר מצותיו, " 'Happy is the man that fears the Lord...that delights greatly in His commandments' (*Tehillim* 112:1). Rabbi Eliezer said: 'in His commandments,' but not in the reward of His commandments." Yet our Sages teach that it is permitted to give charity with the express intention of obtaining a reward from God. Thus we are allowed to say, "I am dedicating this sum to the poor so that God may keep my son alive," or "so that I may have a share in the World to Come." This apparent contradiction is solved by Tosafoth in the following way: Many people serve God in order that He may grant them everything good—good health, life, honor, riches—but if everything does not turn out as they wish, they resent it, saying, "How could such a thing happen to me? Why do I deserve this?" But that is how heathens treat idols when their wishes are not granted.

Antigenos therefore warns us: Do not be like servants who serve their master for the sake of receiving a reward, and who stop serving their master if the reward is a long time coming. One may hope for a reward, certainly, but he must not make his service to God conditional upon the receipt of a reward. Yeshayahu explains עין לא ראתה אלהים זולתך יעשה למחכה לו, "No eye has seen, oh God, beside You, what He will do for one who waits for Him" (*Yeshayahu* 64:3).

LET THE FEAR OF HEAVEN BE UPON YOU. Though the first part of the maxim recommends the purest and most devoted love of God, the Sage believes that love of God must be accompanied by fear of God. The Sage does not mean fear of punishment, but rather fear in the sense of awe, as it is written, השמים מספרים כבוד אל, "The Heavens tell the glory of God" (*Tehillim* 19:2). There is an apparently truer, though perhaps less commonly cited, explanation that translates these words as: "And the fear of God will be upon you." That is, when we serve God with a pure heart and devoted love, without secondary objectives, without expectation of a reward, solely guided by the thought that He, the Almighty, the All-Merciful, the All-Wise, is our loving Father Who has created us for His glorification and for His service, then the awe of Him will rule over us to such an extent that we never think of sinning. We shall be so thoroughly aware of His greatness, sublimity and omnipresence, that we will resist any form of enticement and will successfully overcome temptation.

יוֹסֵי בֶּן־יוֹעֶזֶר אִישׁ צְרֵדָה וְיוֹסֵי בֶּן־יוֹחָנָן
אִישׁ יְרוּשָׁלַיִם קִבְּלוּ מֵהֶם. יוֹסֵי בֶּן־יוֹעֶזֶר
אִישׁ צְרֵדָה אוֹמֵר, יְהִי בֵיתְךָ בֵּית וַעַד לַחֲכָמִים
וֶהֱוֵי מִתְאַבֵּק בַּעֲפַר רַגְלֵיהֶם וֶהֱוֵי שׁוֹתֶה בַצָּמָא
אֶת־דִּבְרֵיהֶם:

4 Yosei ben Yoezer of Tzeredah and Yosei ben
Yochanan of Yerushalayim received [the Tradition]
from [those preceding] them. Yosei ben Yoezer of
Tzeredah says: Let your house be a meeting place for
sages, cover yourself with the dust of their feet, and
drink their words thirstily.

* * *

A new period in Jewish history began with these disciples and
successors of Antigenos of Socho, the *Tannaim* Yosei ben Yoezer
and Yosei ben Yochanan. Until this period one individual was
always looked upon as the leader of Yisrael; his decisions were
authoritative and binding and no one dared oppose him. Moshe
was followed by Yehoshua and he by each of the judges, then the
prophets in turn. Ezra, who brought them back to Eretz Yisrael
from captivity in Bavel, was followed by Shimon *Ha-Tzaddik* and
Antigenos. The two Yoseis initiated a long period during which
two equally great men shared the mantles of spiritual and political leadership of Yisrael. They were called the זוגות (pairs). The
more powerful of the two was the נשיא (prince or president) and
the other was the אב בית דין (dean or head) of the Great *Sanhedrin*
which convened in the Hall of Hewn Stone of the Holy Temple.
Yosei ben Yoezer at first held both offices, but later Yosei ben
Yochanan rose to the rank of אב בית דין.

The Mishnah (*Sotah* 47a) says of them: משמת רבי יוסי בן יועזר
איש צרידה ויוסי בן יוחנן איש ירושלים בטלו האשכולות, "When Yosei
ben Yoezer of Tzeredah and Yosei ben Yochanan of Yerushalayim
died, the *eshkoloth* were no more." מאי אשכולות, "What are *eshkoloth*?" אמר רבי יהודה אמר שמואל איש שהכל בו, "Rabbi Yehudah said

in the name of Shemuel, 'Men who combined within them everything' " (ibid. 47b), who taught the Torah in the way it was handed down to Moshe from Sinai.

RECEIVED FROM THEM. The plural antecedent "from them" is confusing, since only Antigenos of Socho is mentioned as the preceding link in the chain of Jewish tradition. There is, in fact, another reading: ממנו from him, instead of מהם from them. The Rashbatz says that this would be a better reading if it were authentic, but it is not. It is merely an old correction made by someone who found מהם incomprehensible. We therefore must accept the traditional reading, and look further for an explanation. Some commentators say that מהם refers to Antigenos and another colleague not mentioned in this mishnah, since we do not know for sure that the two Yoseis received their knowledge of the Law from Antigenos alone. This explanation, however, is contradicted by the use of the root קבל in this phrase, just as it is used in the phrase משה קבל תורה מסיני. In Tractate Avoth קבל means "to receive a knowledge of the Torah from the highest authority."

Rabbi Shemuel of Ozedah, the author of *Midrash Shemuel*, gives a different explanation, as follows. Shimon *Ha-Tzaddik* defines the three pillars on which the world rests (the Torah, serving God, and acts of lovingkindness). Each of his three successors makes one of these three principles the subject of his maxim. Antigenos teaches us how to serve God: "Do not serve for the sake of a reward"; Yosei ben Yoezer teaches us how we can best acquire knowledge of the Torah: "Let your house be a meeting place for sages"; Yosei ben Yochanan teaches how to practice lovingkindness: "Let the poor be members of your household." Since the two Yoseis as well as their teacher Antigenos expand on the maxim of Shimon *Ha-Tzaddik*, the latter may also be regarded as their teacher, and that is what the plural מהם means.

LET YOUR HOUSE BE A MEETING PLACE FOR SAGES. Rabbi Yosei ben Yoezer teaches that you must always increase your knowledge through association with sages—not only when you are a pupil at school, but even when you are a man and have acquired an important station in life. Make your house a meeting place for sages, for this association will give you continual mental stimulation. The words of sages will enrich your mind until it becomes like a spring, small at its source, but which has absorbed so many tributaries that it expands into a mighty river. Anyone who is not fortunate enough to be able to turn his house into a meeting place for sages should regard the *beith ha-midrash* as his own house and spend the greater part of his time there; for all his business is unimportant in comparison with his duty to learn Torah.

COVER YOURSELF WITH THE DUST OF THEIR FEET. Yosei ben Yoezer also says, "There are three prerequisites for learning Torah: industry, humility and thirst for knowledge." The all-merciful God has been gracious and has bestowed upon us His most precious jewel, the Torah, which only becomes our own property when we dedicate ourselves to learning it. Industry is therefore mentioned first. Humility is the second requirement. It was principally on account of his humility that Moshe was chosen to become the first teacher of Yisrael. A proud, conceited man cannot teach properly. His haughtiness prevents him from penetrating the depths of the sages' thoughts. Yosei ben Yoezer therefore recommends: Sit at the feet of the sages, acknowledge their superiority; do not think, "What can they teach me? I know more than they." Although you are the master of your house and the sages are your guests, approach them humbly and regard them as your lords and masters. We can also understand these words to mean: When the sages leave your town for some reason, when they move from Yerushalayim to Usha, from Usha to Yavneh and from Yavneh to Teveryah (Tiberias), follow them and do not mind the dust they raise in front of you with their feet.

DRINK THEIR WORDS THIRSTILY. The third requirement for learning Torah is a strong thirst for knowledge. The Avoth of Rabbi Nathan mentions Rabbi Akiva as an example of one who had an unquenchable thirst for knowledge. The son of a converted heathen, he remained an ignorant shepherd until, at the age of forty, a thirst for knowledge was awakened in him. Though he was poor and had to support a wife and children by selling pinewood, he made Torah study his main occupation; he studied indefatigably and comprehensively. At first, the Torah seemed to him hard to penetrate as a rock, but he did not desist; he approached it with his intelligence, which was as sharp as a chisel, and mastered it. Just like the rock which provided Moshe with an endless supply of water, the Torah provided for Rabbi Akiva a refreshing spring from which he drank continuously.

God also blessed him with earthly goods. He eventually became very rich and adorned his loving wife, who had gladly shared his poverty, with precious jewels. Rabbi Akiva did not acquire these riches by improving his trade in pinewood, but through the gracious providence of God from Whom all blessings come. Know, then, that your livelihood is not endangered by devoting time to the study of Torah. Invite sages to be members of your household and you will not be the poorer for it; sprinkle upon yourself the dust from their feet, as it were, and it will not dishonor you; drink in their words, for the thirst for Torah will bring you wealth both in this world and in the World to Come.

ה יוֹסֵי בֶּן־יוֹחָנָן אִישׁ יְרוּשָׁלַיִם אוֹמֵר, יְהִי
בֵיתְךָ פָּתוּחַ לָרְוָחָה וְיִהְיוּ עֲנִיִּים בְּנֵי
בֵיתֶךָ וְאַל־תַּרְבֶּה שִׂיחָה עִם הָאִשָּׁה, בְּאִשְׁתּוֹ אָמְרוּ
קַל וָחֹמֶר בְּאֵשֶׁת חֲבֵרוֹ. מִכַּאן אָמְרוּ חֲכָמִים כָּל־
הַמַּרְבֶּה שִׂיחָה עִם הָאִשָּׁה גּוֹרֵם רָעָה לְעַצְמוֹ
וּבוֹטֵל מִדִּבְרֵי תוֹרָה וְסוֹפוֹ יוֹרֵשׁ גֵּיהִנֹּם:

5 Yosei ben Yochanan of Yerushalayim says: Let
your house be open for relief and let the poor be
members of your household, and do not engage in
idle talk with women. They said this applies to one's
own wife; how much more then, to a neighbor's wife!
The Sages therefore would say: Whoever engages in
much talk with women harms himself, neglects the
study of Torah and will in the end inherit *Gehinnom*
(eternal destruction).

* * *

The teachings of the fourth and fifth mishnayoth are as closely
linked in thought as their authors were in friendship. Yosei ben
Yoezer emphasized the acquisition of תורה while Yosei ben
Yochanan here explains the performance of דרך ארץ, that is, the
proper behavior of man toward his fellow.

LET YOUR HOUSE BE OPEN FOR RELIEF. The finest expression of general human kindness is what we usually call hospitality. A
perfect model of this trait is our ancestor Avraham. It is written,
ויטע אשל בבאר שבע, "And Avraham planted an *eshel* (tamarisk) tree
in Be'ersheva" (*Bereshith* 21:33). ואמרו חכמינו ז"ל אשל זה פונדק, "And
our Sages said, 'An *eshel* means an inn' " (*Sotah* 10a). Avraham
turned his home into an inn. Any passing traveler received a most
cordial reception, food, drink and lodging. He did not differenti-
ate between rich and poor, old and young, noble or subordinate—even though most of his guests were idol-worshipers! Our
father Avraham received everyone with love and kindness; in-

deed, he ran to meet them and begged them to avail themselves of his hospitality. The Sages relate that his home had doors opening on all four sides, in all four directions, so that travelers had no need to search for an entrance; a door was always open to receive them. Yosei ben Yochanan recommends that we emulate this.

AND LET THE POOR BE MEMBERS OF YOUR HOUSEHOLD. It is not sufficient, however, to open your house to the poor and feed them; you must also treat them as kindly and cordially as if they were members of your own family. Earthly wealth is not permanent; the sons or grandsons of a wealthy man may one day fall upon hard times and have to depend on the charity of others. You should regard the poor as members of your own family, so that God may turn such a sad fate away from your sons and grandsons.

The interpretation of this maxim given in the Avoth of Rabbi Nathan juxtaposes the word עניים (poor) with ענוה (humility) so that we say not only, "Let the poor be members of your household," but also, "Let your household regard itself as poor"; that is, cultivate the attribute of humility. What a valuable lesson this is even in our own day!

AND DO NOT ENGAGE IN IDLE TALK WITH WOMEN. THEY SAID THIS APPLIES TO ONE'S OWN WIFE; HOW MUCH MORE THEN, DOES IT APPLY TO A NEIGHBOR'S WIFE! Opinions differ on how much of this maxim may be attributed to Yosei ben Yochanan. Some commentators maintain that the words, "They said this applies..." were added by later Sages and that Rabi, the arranger of the Mishnah, added the final phrase, "The Sages therefore would say...." But others say that all the words are Rabbi Yosei's and that his use of the plural אמרו (they said), is easily explained. All the maxims repeated in Tractate Avoth are based on the Tradition, but the Sages to whom they are attributed were accustomed to repeating them so often that they became like personal mottoes. We know that this maxim is, in any case, very old and that Yosei ben Yochanan received it from his teachers.

We see that Yosei ben Yochanan first enjoins us to practice

unrestricted human kindness, especially through generous and cordial hospitality; at the same time, he warns us that we may easily commit a transgression as a result of this very hospitality, that is, the lighthearted kind of conversation which our Sages called שיחה (small talk). Small talk stirs desire and may lead people to sin. The sensible man will restrain himself from purely frivolous conversation even with his own wife, especially בעת נידתה, "in her period of ritual separation" (*Nedarim* 20a) lest he overstep the bounds of the Law. How much more circumspectly, then, should he behave toward other women!

Man's strongest passion is sexual desire. Even though this emotion is God-given for the preservation of mankind, its effect can also be destructive if it arouses man to lose his self-control and incites him to transgress Divine laws. How many people have suffered for that reason, how many families have been destroyed that way! It is extremely difficult, nay, almost impossible, to overcome a passion that burns like a bright flame. Wild passion breaks through all barriers; the soundest principles yield to it. The fire of passion blinds a man so that he does not hesitate to sacrifice his honor, his life and even his eternal happiness. It is therefore essential to prevent it at its source, to divest the fire of its energy, and that is why Yosei ben Yochanan admonishes us not to indulge in seemingly innocent small talk with a woman!

יְהוֹשֻׁעַ בֶּן־פְּרַחְיָה וְנִתַּאי הָאַרְבֵּלִי קִבְּלוּ
מֵהֶם. יְהוֹשֻׁעַ בֶּן־פְּרַחְיָה אוֹמֵר, עֲשֵׂה לְךָ
רַב וּקְנֵה לְךָ חָבֵר וֶהֱוֵי דָן אֶת־כָּל־הָאָדָם לְכַף
זְכוּת:

6 Yehoshua ben Perachyah and Nittai of Arbel received [the Tradition] from them. Yehoshua ben Perachyah says: Provide yourself with a teacher, get yourself a colleague, and judge all men favorably.

*　　*　　*

Yehoshua ben Perachyah and Nittai of Arbel were the disciples who succeeded the two Yoseis. This mishnah is continued in the following mishnah and the sayings of these two Sages complement one another. Yehoshua ben Perachyah teaches, "Provide yourself with a teacher." Nittai warns us, "If the lord or official in your city indulges in evil, then keep away from him." Yehoshua teaches, "Get yourself a companion." Nittai warns us, "Be cautious in your choice of a friend and do not associate with a lawless man." Yehoshua teaches, "Judge all men favorably." Nittai says, "Do not let too much kindness convince you that there is no retribution." It is probable that Nittai issued his warning because of the Sadducees, a growing sect which rejected both the Oral Law and the principle of the immortality of the soul.

PROVIDE YOURSELF WITH A TEACHER. Learning is the Jew's primary vocation, from early childhood until he draws his last breath. No matter how influential a man may become, he should always recognize someone who is greater than himself from whom he can learn and who will correct him. No one was greater than David, "man of God," gallant warrior, inspired singer, disciple of the prophet Shemuel, who was compared to Moshe and Aharon! And yet David chose a younger man as his teacher, Mefibosheth, Yonathan's son, one of the most outstanding scholars of his time (*Berachoth* 4a). David discussed everything with his teacher and when he was asked to make a judgment, he first consulted

Mefibosheth and was not ashamed to have his opinion corrected.

Sometimes exceptional men tend to have too great an opinion of themselves, an error that is often compounded by admirers and flatterers who agree with whatever these men say or do. This is another reason that Yehoshua ben Perachyah tells us: עשה לך רב. If you have little knowledge or ability, choose someone who can teach you; if you are educated and famous yourself, do not be ashamed to accept good advice from someone who knows more than you do.

GET YOURSELF A COLLEAGUE. find a friend with whom to study Torah. The exchange of opinions between equals leads to the discovery of the truth, as our Sages teach, "Only through joint study can knowledge of the Torah be acquired" (*Berachoth* 63b). Besides, every man needs a real friend. The Rambam says that this is the meaning of the maxim. A true friend will not only help you in life, but he will also try to prevent you from doing an injustice and will encourage you to do good. A truly unselfish friendship is a blessing to both sides.

JUDGE ALL MEN FAVORABLY. This is how you will keep a good teacher and a good friend after you have acquired them. By imputing evil motives to them, you will soon estrange your teacher and fall out with your friend. Judge your companion's behavior favorably, even when circumstances seem to condemn him. Our Sages tell us (*Shabbath* 127b), "Once a servant wished to leave service after three years and when he demanded his wages, his rich master answered him, 'I have neither money nor goods to give you.' The servant left with a heart full of sorrow. A few weeks later, the master called on the servant and gave him his wages plus many gifts as well. 'And now tell me, did you not think poorly of me when I refused to pay you your wages?' the master asked. 'Certainly not,' the servant replied, 'for I never doubted your word.' 'As a matter of fact,' the master said, 'at that time I had nothing. My son refused to occupy himself with the Torah, and I had consecrated all my wealth to the Sanctuary for his sake. Now I have been absolved of my vow, since it was too hastily made, and as soon as the ownership of my property was returned to me I hurried to pay my debt to you. As you have judged me favorably, may God also be gracious in judging you.' "

ז נִתַּאי הָאַרְבֵּלִי אוֹמֵר, הַרְחֵק מִשָּׁכֵן רָע
וְאַל־תִּתְחַבֵּר לְרָשָׁע וְאַל־תִּתְיָאֵשׁ מִן־
הַפּוּרְעָנוּת:

7 Nittai of Arbel says: Keep away from an evil neighbor and do not associate with a lawless man, and do not doubt eventual retribution.

* * *

In this saying there are a few difficult expressions that call for explanation. Nittai says ואל תתחבר, "and do not associate," so why does he not say תתרחק, "keep away"? The word רשע (a lawless man or criminal) is stronger than the general term רע (evil) so why does Nittai not say: Keep away from a criminal and do not associate with an evil man? Rabbi Yosef Ya'avetz raised this question in his commentary on the Chapters of the Fathers about five hundred years ago and he answers with the passage from the Talmud (*Kiddushin* 40a): "As it is said, 'Say to the righteous man when he is good that it shall be well with him, for he shall eat the fruit of his doings. Woe unto the wicked man, it shall be ill with him, for the reward of his hands shall be given him' (*Yeshayahu* 3:10-11). Are there then righteous men who are good and righteous men who are not good? Are there wicked men who are evil and those who are not?" The Talmud answers that a צדיק (righteous man) is one who observes his duties toward God, and an איש טוב (good man) is one who is kind to his fellowman. A רשע (lawless man) fails in his duties to God and an אדם רע (an evil man) is wicked to his fellowman. Yeshayahu's words, then, should be translated like this: "Tell the philanthropist that he will enjoy the benefits of his good works; woe to the malefactor, he will suffer the punishment of his own deeds."

We learn from this commentary that there are people who carefully observe those commandments which prescribe their duties to God, but not those that regulate their social relationships. There are men who don prayer shawls, kiss their phylacteries, observe the proper interval between eating meat and dairy food, but who are without compassion for their neighbor and malicious and quarrelsome in their behavior; these are friends to be avoided. It is those who are attracted by such apparent piety, whom Nittai warns: Keep away from an evil neighbor. And conversely, lest anyone think that a lawless man who disregards God's commandments by not putting on *tallith* and *tefillin,* by not observing the dietary laws and the Shabbath, is acceptable as a friend as long as he is pleasant, kind and friendly to all, Nittai cautions: Do not associate with a lawless man, for you cannot become friends without learning from him, without imitating his actions, without being influenced by his views.

DO NOT DOUBT EVENTUAL RETRIBUTION. Even if a lawless acquaintance seems to be flourishing, enjoying riches or good health, know that his transgressions will certainly be punished one day, as will yours if you follow his lead. Nittai lived at the time when the Sadducees were gaining influence. They transgressed God's commandments, did not believe in reward and punishment in the World to Come, and their main purpose in life was the enjoyment of earthly goods. Those who joined the Sadducees were chiefly rich and well-known public figures. Because it is human nature to wish to associate with rich and popular people, the Sage was forced to raise his voice in warning.

As we know, Yehoshafat was a pious king who walked in God's ways; and God was gracious to him, saving him from his enemies and greatly blessing his rule. However, when Yehoshafat formed an alliance with Achazyahu, an idol-worshiper, God's prophet came to Yehoshafat and said: כהתחברך עם אחזיהו פרץ יי את מעשיך, "Since you have formed an alliance with Achazyahu, God has frustrated your plan"—and so it happened (*Divrei Hayyamim* II, 20:37).

Rashi explains this part of the maxim thus: Do not put your trust in reputation, power and riches, as if you could thereby escape misfortune, as we read, "Fortunate is the man who is always afraid" (*Mishlei* 28:14). However, when you do meet with misfortune, אל תתיאש, "Do not despair!" Almighty God will soon bring you good fortune, as it is said, "Behold, the Lord's hand is not too short to save" (*Yeshayahu* 59:1).

ח יְהוּדָה בֶּן טַבַּאי וְשִׁמְעוֹן בֶּן שָׁטַח קִבְּלוּ
מֵהֶם. יְהוּדָה בֶּן־טַבַּאי אוֹמֵר, אַל־תַּעַשׂ
עַצְמְךָ כְּעוֹרְכֵי הַדַּיָּנִין וּכְשֶׁיִּהְיוּ בַּעֲלֵי הַדִּין עוֹמְדִים
לְפָנֶיךָ יִהְיוּ בְעֵינֶיךָ כִּרְשָׁעִים וּכְשֶׁנִּפְטָרִים מִלְּפָנֶיךָ
יִהְיוּ בְעֵינֶיךָ כְּזַכָּאִין כְּשֶׁקִּבְּלוּ עֲלֵיהֶם אֶת־הַדִּין:

8 Yehudah ben Tabbai and Shimon ben Shatach received [the Tradition] from them [Yehoshua and Nittai]. Yehudah ben Tabbai says: While sitting as a judge, do not act as counsel. As long as the parties [in the lawsuit] stand before you, consider them equally guilty, but once they leave and accept the verdict upon themselves regard them as innocent.

*   *   *

When Yehoshua ben Perachyah and Nittai of Arbel died, their two most prominent disciples, Yehudah ben Tabbai and Shimon ben Shatach, took their places. Jointly they restored the *Sanhedrin*; Shimon became the dean of the *Sanhedrin* and Yehudah the president. One of the most ·sacred principles in Judaism is justice, and that is what our great teacher Moshe conveyed to the first judges, saying, "And I gave your judges their duties at that time saying, 'Hear [the arguments] between your brethren and judge righteously between a man and his brother and between him and a stranger. You shall recognize no person in judgment, you shall hear the petty cases just like the big ones, you shall not stand in awe before any man, for the judgment belongs to God' " (*Devarim* 1:16-17).

DO NOT ACT AS COUNSEL. These words have been explained in different ways, but Bertinoro's translation of עורכי הדיינים as "lawyers" (*Shabbath* 139a) seems correct because Yehudah ben Tabbai does not speak here of halachic transgression. His warning is intended as ethical guidance for judges in their personal moral behavior. A judge must be absolutely impartial and avoid even the slightest suspicion that he is acting for one of the parties (as a lawyer). At the time of Yehudah ben Tabbai, there ruled a king who was apt to act with violence. The Sadducees, who held powerful and important positions in the realm, followed his example and were fond of taking vengeance upon a judge who decided against them; it was therefore tempting for a judge to be lenient when judging a person who might threaten or even harm him afterwards. The Sage's warning was not only necessary in his time, but valid for all time. We find many examples throughout history of judges who became the advocates of powerful and influential people and made biased judgments. On the other hand, we also find many incorruptible judges who suffered hatred, persecution and revenge for passing honest verdicts.

AS LONG AS THE PARTIES STAND BEFORE YOU, CONSIDER THEM EQUALLY GUILTY. The commentators question why a judge should not regard both parties as not guilty, and still be considered impartial. When two people engage in a lawsuit against one another, one party must be in the wrong to some extent. Since both parties have to be judged equally, both therefore, should be regarded as guilty until the case has been decided.

REGARD THEM AS INNOCENT. After the sentence has been passed, and the guilty party has accepted the decision, then the judge must regard both sides as equals before the law, treating both parties kindly in case an error has been made unintentionally. The Sage's concluding words reveal a great difference between Jewish Law and the law of other nations. Woe to the man who is brought before a contemporary gentile court for the second time, for cases of unjust convictions due to judicial prejudice are common. According to Jewish Law, however, every case must be judged on its own merits; previous convictions should not be considered at all. One who has fully atoned for his crime regains his integrity (Rambam, *Hilchoth Sanhedrin* 23:10, *Choshen Mishpat* 17:10).

שִׁמְעוֹן בֶּן שָׁטַח אוֹמֵר, הֱוֵי מַרְבֶּה **ט**
לַחֲקוֹר אֶת הָעֵדִים וֶהֱוֵי זָהִיר בִּדְבָרֶיךָ
שֶׁמָּא מִתּוֹכָם יִלְמְדוּ לְשַׁקֵּר:

9 Shimon ben Shatach says: Examine the witnesses thoroughly and be careful with your words, lest they learn from them to falsify.

* * *

Shimon ben Shatach was an ardent advocate of truth and justice. Neither social pressure, royal power, bribery nor pity could divert him from his principles; neither for riches nor even for the love of his son would he waver in his duty as it is taught in the Torah. According to Jewish Law, an accused person can only be sentenced when two irreproachable witnesses attest to the crime. Inductive proof, which so often leads to the conviction of innocent people in the criminal courts of other nations, is disallowed in Jewish Law.

The story is told that once Shimon ben Shatach saw one man pursue another man. Shimon ben Shatach ran after them both and caught up to them amid some ruins. The pursued man lay dying on the ground and the other man held a bloody sword in his hand. Shimon said, "You villain! Who has killed this man, you or I? But what shall I do? Your punishment was not given into my hand, for the Torah said that the statement of two witnesses is required to kill a man who deserves death. He Who knows man's thoughts will punish the murderer!" Shimon had hardly spoken these words when a snake came along, wound itself around the murderer's body, sank its poisonous fangs into his flesh and the criminal died (*Sanhedrin* 37b).

BE CAREFUL WITH YOUR WORDS. When two irreproachable witnesses accuse someone of a crime, it is the judge's sacred duty to question the witnesses in great detail, supposing every possible combination of circumstances, to find out whether the witnesses do not contradict themselves or whether one man's statements do not conflict with those of the other. A case in which the statements of the witnesses agree to the minutest detail is also held to be suspicious, for identical statements indicate the likeliness of collusion. The judge, therefore, has to question the witnesses again and again, and in a different manner each time, until he determines the truth or falsity of their statements. But this multiple questioning also bears a danger; the witness, if he is a dullard, may be so confused by the many questions that he thinks he must give answers which would please the judge. If he is cunning, he may learn to deduce the answers from the questions put to him. The Sage therefore adds, "Be careful with your words lest they learn from them to falsify."

Shimon ben Shatach's saying can also be interpreted in a more personal way. Even a good person, who is trying hard to reach the highest state of moral perfection, must examine himself scrupulously before the tribunal of his own conscience. It is too easy to see one's own actions in a favorable light, to use one's own virtue and good deeds as witnesses for the defense, as it were, to imagine that if you have a good character you will not succumb to temptation. The Sage therefore warns us to examine witnesses again and again; that is, inquire into your own motives and find out whether you have not sinned simply because you have not had the opportunity to do so. Perhaps the reason for your industry is attaining honor, perhaps you really help the poor so that your friends will praise you. When you judge yourself, take care that your thoughts do not disguise themselves in a cloak of deceit.

Shimon ben Shatach instituted several enduring *takanoth* (rulings or regulations). The first one was intended to render divorce more difficult. In former days, the wealth assigned to a wife in the כתובה (marriage contract) was held by her parents so that lack of money would be no obstacle to divorce. Later, a husband was allowed to invest the wealth of the *kethubbah* in such a way that it was readily available. Shimon ben Shatach, however, gave a husband the right to fully dispose of his wife's portion, but he had to guarantee it with all his own property. Since a husband is allowed to use the *kethubbah* portion in his business, the money is not so readily available and so divorce is rendered more difficult. This is the way the *kethubbah* is written still.

Of even greater importance to the Jewish people, indeed for

the future of Yisrael, was his setting up of schools for the instruction of children. The Torah commands us, "And you shall teach them (the words of the Torah) diligently to your sons"—a commandment that we recite in *Keriath Shema* twice a day. A father's sacred duty is to instruct his child in the Torah, but over the years this duty had been more and more neglected. Shimon ben Shatach established a system to appoint teachers and to organize schools where children were taught together. It is true that there were always academies of learning, adult schools where learned men assembled groups of disciples and taught without remuneration, but instruction for groups of children by salaried teachers was introduced by Shimon ben Shatach.

The third *takanah* of the great Sage was of an entirely different nature. The Torah states that utensils made of metal and wood, earthen vessels, and cloths made of linen, wool or hair are susceptible to impurity (מקבלים טומאה) in different ways. No similar statement concerning glass vessels is found in the Torah because glass was invented years later. "And he (Shimon ben Shatach) established that glass utensils are susceptible to impurity and a fence for the Torah was made." Now, Yosei ben Yoezer and Yosei ben Yochanan had already established that glass vessels were subject to the laws of impurity (טומאה) as soon as people began to use them, but the people did not comply with the law. Shimon ben Shatach succeeded in getting the *takanah* accepted generally, and that is why it is attributed to him. From this we learn that the great men of Yisrael observed those very commandments, which nowadays are disparagingly called "ceremonial laws," with the same devotion as they observed the great principles of morality and education. As it is said, נותנין את נפשם עליהם, "They give their lives for them" (*Yerushalmi, Kethubboth*, 8:11; cf. *Bavli, Shabbath* 15a).

שְׁמַעְיָה וְאַבְטַלְיוֹן קִבְּלוּ מֵהֶם. שְׁמַעְיָה ❡
אוֹמֵר, אֱהַב אֶת־הַמְּלָאכָה וּשְׂנָא אֶת־
הָרַבָּנוּת וְאַל־תִּתְוַדַּע לָרָשׁוּת:

10 Shemayah and Avtalyon received [the Tradition] from them [Yehudah and Shimon]. Shemayah says: Love work, hate lordship (public office) and do not seek to become intimate with the authorities.

*   *   *

Shemayah and Avtalyon were the disciples and successors of Yehudah ben Tabbai and Shimon ben Shatach. Shemayah was the *Nasi* and Avtalyon was the *Av Beith Din*. There is a difference of opinion among scholars about the origins of these two men; several passages in the Talmud indicate that they were born heathens and converted to Judaism later. Avtalyon is sometimes said to have been a famous teacher of law in Rome before he converted to Judaism. The Rashbatz holds the view that the two Sages were non-Jews by birth. This concurs with the Rambam's commentary to Eduyyoth 1:3 where he says that, as foreigners, they could not pronounce the letter "H". Those who dispute this, cite the law that permits only sons of Jewish parents to fill the two highest offices. The Maharal and many other scholars therefore hold the view that the fathers of these great men were proselytes who married Jewesses, making Shemayah and Avtalyon born Jews.

The Rashbatz solves the difficulty by assuming that even proselytes were admitted to the highest offices when there was no one equal to them in prestige and scholarship. That was certainly true in their cases. The Talmud calls them גְּדוֹלֵי הַדּוֹר (the greatest men of their time). In a sad and stormy period, they were responsible for keeping alive the study of Torah, the life-source of the nation. It was indeed a sad time, a time of fraternal strife and civil war. Shemayah and Avtalyon, however, kept clear of all political strife, both the civil war between the Jewish princes, Hyrkanus and Aristobulus, as well as the struggle between the Roman emperors, Caesar and Pompey. They lived solely for their sublime vocation of learning and teaching, and they preserved the Torah even though the State and the holy Sanctuary were destroyed.

LOVE WORK. The Sage does not say, "Work, for that is your duty." He says, "Love work" for its own sake; do not regard it as a burden. Find satisfaction and joy in the work itself and do not seek a reward for doing it. The Sages tell us (*Avoth of Rabbi Nathan*) that work has been man's appointed vocation since the creation of the world, when he was instructed to continue the work God had begun. It is written, "...from all His work which He had done..." (*Bereshith* 2:2); "...and *Hashem Elokim* took the man and placed him in the Garden of Eden, to work it and to guard it" (*Bereshith* 2:15).

Many passages in the Torah and the Talmud teach us how and why man should work. We are told in the Ten Commandments, "Six days shall you labor and do all your work" (*Shemoth* 20:9). The Sages comment: If a person is industrious during the week, earning his living through his work, he can hope to rest undisturbed on the day of the Lord. However, if he does not work honestly, but appropriates the fruit of someone else's labor, he will land in prison and be forced to work even on the Shabbath. Many people tend to regard work as a burden of which they would like to be relieved. How foolish they are! Only one who is usefully occupied finds real inner satisfaction. Useful activity stimulates further activity and strengthens both body and mind. Idleness does the opposite, it either leads to mental illness or to immorality (*Kethubboth* 59b).

HATE LORDSHIP (PUBLIC OFFICE) AND DO NOT SEEK TO BECOME INTIMATE WITH THE AUTHORITIES. We are not asked to hate the ruler, but the office. Man has an inborn desire to govern. It seems so attractive, so pleasant to be able to rise above the next fellow and make him do as you wish. Beware! Not only people of outstanding capabilities are dominated by this passion; even unimportant and ordinary men are tempted to seek "connections" with the powerful of this earth. How despicable it is to be obsequious on the way up, and then to become a tyrant in office. The dire consequences of acting against the advice of this mishnah are clearly seen in the destruction of the Jewish nation at the time of Shemayah and Avtalyon.

י**אַ**בְטַלְיוֹן אוֹמֵר, חֲכָמִים הִזָּהֲרוּ
בְּדִבְרֵיכֶם שֶׁמָּא תָחוּבוּ חוֹבַת גָּלוּת
וְתִגְלוּ לִמְקוֹם מַיִם הָרָעִים וְיִשְׁתּוּ הַתַּלְמִידִים
הַבָּאִים אַחֲרֵיכֶם וְיָמוּתוּ וְנִמְצָא שֵׁם שָׁמַיִם
מִתְחַלֵּל:

11 Avtalyon says: Scholars, be careful with your
words, for you may incur the penalty of exile and be
sent to a place of evil waters, and the disciples who
follow you may drink from them and die, and the
Heavenly Name would be profaned.

*   *   *

Shemayah's friend and companion was Avtalyon. His name has
puzzled the commentators; it is neither Hebrew or Aramaic, and
apparently not Greek, despite the Greek ending. It seems to be a
compound of the Hebrew אב (father), and the Aramaic word טלי
(child), which is frequently used in the Talmud, meaning "father
of the children," i.e., benefactor of orphans. It is a surname that
the Sage apparently acquired through his beneficent activities. In
Avtalyon's time Yehudah was rent by civil war. The victorious
Sadducees punished the opposition with death or exile, usually to
Alexandria in Egypt. The large and wealthy Jewish community
there enjoyed complete equality with the ruling Greeks. Jewish
writers, poets, and philosophers flourished and wrote in the
Greek language. It was there that the Tanach, the Scriptures, was
first translated into Greek. A Jewish coterie known as "the allego-
rists" began to interpret the names and laws of the Torah symbol-
ically (allegorically) for their contemporaries, and this encouraged
the Jews of Alexandria to lapse in their strict observance of the
commandments.

   In Yerushalayim, the great Sages of Yisrael still met in the
Hall of Hewn Stone of the Temple and watched over the people's
correct interpretation and performance of the commandments,
"for out of Tzion shall go forth the Torah and the word of God

from Yerushalayim" (*Yeshayahu* 2:3). The Sages were, in fact, so strict that when a scholar made careless statements or expressed himself in a way that might have been misinterpreted, he was sent into exile to Alexandria, "a place of evil waters," where the integrity of the Torah was no longer maintained. Thus the Sages wanted to prevent careless words from leading to apostasy, which is, as Avtalyon warned, tantamount to death, and, Heaven forbid, the profanation of God's Name.

יב הִלֵּל וְשַׁמַּאי קִבְּלוּ מֵהֶם. הִלֵּל אוֹמֵר,
הֱוֵי מִתַּלְמִידָיו שֶׁל אַהֲרֹן אוֹהֵב שָׁלוֹם
וְרוֹדֵף שָׁלוֹם אוֹהֵב אֶת־הַבְּרִיּוֹת וּמְקָרְבָן לַתּוֹרָה:

12 Hillel and Shammai received [the Tradition] from them [Shemayah and Avtalyon]. Hillel says: Be of the disciples of Aharon, loving peace and pursuing peace; loving your fellowmen and bringing them near to the Torah.

*   *   *

Hillel and Shammai were the most outstanding disciples, but not the immediate successors, of Shemayah and Avtalyon. Hillel's was a noble family, descended from King David, which stayed behind in Bavel (Babylonia) when the Jews returned from captivity there. Hillel, filled with passionate enthusiasm for Torah learning and attracted by the reputation of the two great academic authorities in Yerushalayim, traveled to the holy city to quench his thirst for knowledge at the feet of Shemayah and Avtalyon. He lived in extreme poverty, cutting wood and drawing water to earn a few pennies a day, half of which he used to support himself and his family. The other half he gave to the doorkeeper of the *beith ha-midrash* to hear the words of God from the mouths of Shemayah and Avtalyon. One day he could not find work, and because he could not pay, the doorkeeper refused him entry. Hillel then leaned against the window of the *beith ha-midrash* to hear the words of Shemayah and Avtalyon. It was the day before the Shabbath in the middle of winter and snow was falling.

At dawn the next day Shemayah said, "My brother Avtalyon, what may be the reason that daylight does not enter through the window?" They investigated and found that a man, frozen and completely covered with snow, was preventing the daylight from coming in through the window. They immediately extricated him from the snow, washed and annointed him, and warmed him by the fire. "To be sure," they said, "he is worthy of having the Shabbath laws be transgressed for his sake."

Erev Pesach fell on the Shabbath one year, and the sons of Betheira, who succeeded Shemayah and Avtalyon as *Nasi* and *Av Beith Din*, did not know whether they were therefore allowed to offer the Pesach sacrifice. They summoned the Babylonian scholar Hillel, the most brilliant disciple of Shemayah and Avtalyon, and he proved to them that the Pesach offering over-rules the Shabbath. They found objections to all his proofs until he declared that it was a tradition that he had received from Shemayah and Avtalyon, going back to the revelation at Sinai (*Pesachim* 66a). The sons of Betheira submitted to Hillel's author-ity, resigned from their high office, and Hillel was then ap-pointed *Nasi*. Hillel's patience, gentleness and humility were by then well-known, but on that occasion he became angry. He told the Sages of Yisrael, "It is your fault that I, a Babylonian, had to be appointed *Nasi* over you. You did not study zealously enough with your great teachers, Shemayah and Avtalyon!" Anger, how-ever, even the anger of a righteous man like Hillel, was unwise. As a result of his anger, he was unable to respond to a question, forgetting for the moment the appropriate *halachah*. Soon after Hillel was appointed *Nasi*, Shammai was appointed *Av Beith Din* and together they led the nation as the last, and most influential, of the pairs.

BE OF THE DISCIPLES OF AHARON. Of him it is said, "The law of truth was in his mouth, and iniquity was not found on his lips; he walked with Me in peace and dignity and turned many away from iniquity" (*Malachi* 2:6). The priests were appointed by God to bless His people, and peace is the vessel containing the blessing. "The Holy One, blessed is He, could not find any other vessel to hold and preserve blessing as well as peace, for it is written, 'God will grant power to His people, God will bless His people with peace' " (*Tehillim* 29:11; *Oktzin* 3:12). Aharon, the first High Priest of Yisrael, embodied the ideal of peace and of peacemaking.

In the *Avoth of Rabbi Nathan* we are told how concerned Aha-ron was with peace, as is shown in this example of his behavior: When Aharon learned that two people had quarreled, he would visit one of them and tell him how much his opponent regretted having wronged him; he entreated him until the sting of hatred was gone from his heart, and good humor restored. He then went to the other man and did the same, and so succeeded in turning two enemies into good friends again. When it became known that a married couple was quarreling, Aharon would go to their tent and induce them to be indulgent and to forgive each other. Who could resist the kind words of the High Priest? He thus preserved the happiness of many marriages.

And when Aharon learned that someone had committed a sin, he would go to see him, greet him kindly and converse with him in a most friendly fashion. Afterwards, the sinner would say to himself, "Woe is me! If this great and holy man were to know what I did, he would not speak to me any more." This thought was usually enough to bring the sinner back from the path of iniquity. When Aharon died, it is said, "They wept for Aharon for thirty days, all the House of Yisrael" (*Bemidbar* 20:29), even the women; whereas when Moshe died, "the sons of Yisrael wept for Moshe in the plains of Moav for thirty days" (*Devarim* 34:8)—just the sons of Israel, not the women (*Pirkei of Rabbi Eliezer*, ch. 17).

Man is by nature dependent upon others. A human child needs the support and maintenance of his parents for much longer than any other creature. When the child achieves full control of his body, he still needs teachers to train his mind. In early times, families joined together into clans; later, national entities were formed to protect common interests. It was inevitable, then, that the interests of one group came into conflict with the interests of other groups, and so the blessings of communal organization degenerated into the curse of conflict and war. Only peace can permit man to develop as he was meant to. It is therefore not enough just to love peace; you also have to pursue it.

LOVING YOUR FELLOWMEN. To desire peace continually and to restore it despite all obstacles, you must acquire the attribute of love, which is kindness in its purest and noblest form. Now, there is a kind of love that arises from selfish motives, such as a man's love for a woman. He loves her, first of all, for his own sake because he believes she will make him happy. Love for a friend also may be selfish in character, for human association promises the advantages of mutual support and the pleasures of companionship. The love of parents and children, brother and sister, is normally not completely free from selfish motives either. Even one's love of God can be attributed to personal need, and that is not pure love. We should love our Father in Heaven, not from fear of punishment, not in the hope of receiving a reward, but for His own sake because He is the most perfect being, the essence of the universe. A pure love for God also encompasses all His creatures because they are the work of His hands; it prevents us from hurting anyone else's feelings and lets us actively participate in each other's joys and sorrows.

AND BRINGING THEM NEAR TO THE TORAH. The way Hillel himself followed this principle is related by our Sages (*Shabbath* 31a, and the *Avoth of Rabbi Nathan*, ch. 15). A heathen came to Shammai and he asked to be converted to Judaism, saying, "I will acknowledge the Written Law but I cannot believe in the Oral Law." Shammai turned him away and he went to Hillel with the same request. "Have you learned to read Hebrew already?" Hillel asked him. He answered, "Yes." Hillel wrote an *aleph* on a slate. "Do you know this letter?" he asked. "Certainly. It is an *aleph*." "No," said Hillel, "it is a *beith*." Hillel did the same with a few more letters, then asked, "How do you know that the letters are really called by these names?" "Oh," was the reply, "it is a generally acknowledged tradition which sons have learned from their fathers since ancient times." "You see," explained Hillel, "without the Tradition we could neither read nor understand the Written Law. The Oral Law is the interpretation and explanation of the written word of God." The man was circumcised and became a pious and God-fearing Jew.

Another heathen presented himself to Shammai saying, "I would like to be converted to Judaism so that I can become a High Priest," because he had heard what splendid clothes the High Priest wore. Shammai only laughed and sent him away; Hillel, however, received him, listened to his request and told him, "If you wanted to enter the service of the king, would you not have to learn first how to appear before him and how to serve him? Now that you wish to become a servant of the King of kings, the Holy One, blessed is He, you must first learn how the High Priest must behave and what tasks he must perform in the Temple." This man also began to learn, but when he read the verse, "And the stranger that draws near shall be put to death" (*Bemidbar* 1:51), he asked his teacher who this stranger was that was forbidden to approach the Sanctuary upon threat of death. His teacher explained that the sacrifices on the sacred altar could only be offered by a descendant of Aharon, and that even David, king of Yisrael, would be called a stranger in this respect. The man thought to himself: "If all Israel, of whom it is said 'You shall be unto Me a kingdom of priests and a holy nation' (*Shemoth* 19:6), are called strangers in relation to the service in the Sanctuary, how can I expect to become a High Priest?" He returned to Hillel and asked to be admitted into the Covenant as a simple Jew.

A third would-be proselyte asked to be taught the whole Torah while standing on one foot. Shammai drove him away angrily, but Hillel said, "What you do not like, do not do to another; that is the essence of the Torah. All the rest is commentary—go and learn!" The lesson continues, when these three proselytes later met and spoke of their experiences. Shammai's hasty decision, they agreed, would have caused them to miss out on the happiest times of their lives; Hillel's patience led them under the wings of God's majesty. What can we learn from this lesson? First of all, we see how important it is for us to learn the Tradition in order to understand the meaning of the Law. Second, we learn that Divine service is not wholly dependent upon the High Priest—he is only needed for the sacrifice in the Sanctuary—and every Jew, and even the stranger that joins us, can serve God. The humblest man who is learned in Torah is held in higher esteem than an ignorant priest.

Finally, we learn that the most important principle of Judaism is to love one's fellow man. The Midrash says (*Shemoth Rabbah* 28:1) that the angels only agreed to surrender the Torah to Moshe when God reminded them of Avraham's lovingkindness. Hillel teaches, therefore, that lovingkindness is an all-important principle for us, indeed it is one of the three pillars of the world (see *Avoth* 1:2), but it can only be achieved and preserved together with the other two pillars—knowledge of the Torah and service to God.

יג הוּא הָיָה אוֹמֵר, נְגִיד שְׁמָא אֲבַד שְׁמֵהּ
וּדְלָא מוֹסִיף יָסֵף וּדְלָא יַלִּיף קְטָלָא חַיָּב
וְדְאִשְׁתַּמַּשׁ בְּתָגָא חֲלָף:

13 He [Hillel] would say: He who seeks fame destroys his name; he who does not increase [his knowledge] decreases it; and he who does not study deserves to die; and he who makes worldly use of the crown [of the Torah] shall perish.

*   *   *

When a person achieves something in life and his name becomes known, it is hard for him to keep his heart free of ambition and pride. It feels wonderful to be respected and famous, but there is always a danger that ambition will take over, that the passion for glory and fame will lead to unworthy and foolish behavior and result in the loss of that good name. Lest you think that restraining your ambition also entails reducing your efforts, the Sage adds further admonitions.

HE WHO DOES NOT INCREASE [HIS KNOWLEDGE] DECREASES IT. In nature, everything is constantly changing; there is a continual process of growth and decay. The same applies to moral endeavor, to spiritual perfection. If you are not constantly increasing the measure of your devotion to God and perfecting your moral achievements, you are regressing. Man's natural inclination is toward evil and so he must cultivate his love of virtue; otherwise he will slip back from whatever heights he may have reached. This becomes even more evident in connection with training his spiritual faculties, with acquiring knowledge of Torah. Our Sages say: אם תעזבני יום יומים אעזבך, "If you desert me one day, I will desert you two days. If someone goes north and he meets a man going south, they will be two hours away from each other one hour after they met" (*Yerushalmi, Berachoth* 9:5). The same applies to the student and the Torah. Do not think that the knowledge of the Torah which you have acquired will remain with you if you stop learning. You are moving and it is moving but you move in different directions so that within a short time you will be far away from each other. There is no let-up in spiritual life, only progress or regression, only steady increase or gradual forgetting.

HE WHO DOES NOT STUDY DESERVES TO DIE. Knowledge of the Torah is difficult to obtain and easy to forget. If a Jew allows himself to rest at any time, from earliest childhood to his last days, he may decide it is too difficult to catch up and he will stop trying. The Sage therefore uses the very strong words, "deserves to die." The Torah endows our lives with true value; to put it aside, therefore, is to commit spiritual suicide. When you cling to the Torah and cherish it, as you do to the wife of your choice, you will enjoy true life in this world and ineffable happiness in the World to Come. During the reign of Hadrian (117-138 C.E.), the Jews suffered fierce persecution. Torah study and the observance of God's commandments were crimes punishable by death. The greatest men in Yisrael secretly assembled in the attic of Nitza to determine which was more important for the preservation of Yisrael: to carry out the commandments or to study the Torah (*Yerushalmi, Shevi'ith* 4:2). They unanimously decided that the study of Torah was the indispensable prerequisite of Jewish life, because תלמוד גדול שהתלמוד מביא לידי מעשה, "He who studies Torah is induced, through his learning, to obey its holy commandments" (*Kiddushin* 40b).

HE WHO MAKES A WORLDLY USE OF THE CROWN [OF THE TORAH] SHALL PERISH. As important as the study of the Torah is to us, it may nevertheless be studied for the wrong reasons. The Torah is pure and so must be the lives of its devoted students. The correct goals of its study are learning and teaching, obeying and doing. Students who seek, through Torah study, money and possessions, honor and esteem, or power and influence, soil the holy crown and tarnish its Heavenly radiance. It is true that they cannot harm the Torah—which is immortal and whose glory cannot be destroyed through the unworthy actions of its unfaithful custodians—but they will destroy themselves!

To paraphrase the maxim: When you have earned a good

name, try to preserve it with humility and modesty; when you have already amassed great treasures of knowledge, do not slacken, for then you will stagnate and your knowledge will diminish. Relinquishing the goal and essence of Jewish life—study of the Torah—is tantamount to committing suicide. The constant search for knowledge will earn you the most splendid crown, for the learned man walks among his fellowmen like a king in this life, and the radiance of that crown will transfigure him in the World to Come.

יד הוּא הָיָה אוֹמֵר, אִם אֵין אֲנִי לִי מִי לִי
וּכְשֶׁאֲנִי לְעַצְמִי מָה אָנִי וְאִם לֹא עַכְשָׁו
אֵימָתַי:

14 He [Hillel] would say: If I am not for myself,
who will be for me? And if I am only for myself, what
am I? And if not now, when?

* * *

In this short sentence, the great Sage has condensed three basic
ethical principles: man's obligation to himself, man's obligation
to society and man's duty to utilize well his time on earth.

IF I AM NOT FOR MYSELF WHO WILL BE FOR ME? Man, as
an individual, is a microcosm, a world in himself. The impulse of
self-preservation is implanted in him even as a small child and he
tends to shape his life according to his own desires and inclinations. He must be taught to restrain these desires and instincts
when they are directed to evil and danger, and to develop them
when they are directed toward good. Education, good examples
and environmental factors notwithstanding, the final determi-
nant of man's behavior is man himself. Each of us has received
the precious gift of free will. It is therefore not surprising that the
most careful education does not always produce favorable results;
sometimes children of the most pious parents become wastrels,
and children of neglectful and undisciplined parents become
capable, fine adults with high morals. Sometimes even children
of the same parents reveal widely contrasting personalities in
later life.

Ya'akov and Esav were twins, begotten by the same father and
born to the same mother. In childhood the same grandfather
watched over them, the most pious and distinguished man of the
time, for they were fifteen years old when Avraham died. Yet
what contrasts were already evident in their characters! Ya'akov
was a scholar and constantly tried to improve himself, while Esav
was devoted to the sensual things in life—he liked to hunt and to
kill the beasts of the field. Esav disavowed the immortality of the

soul in order to enjoy this world with no restraint, and even
longed for his father's death so that he might murder his brother
unhindered. He worshiped idols, married idol-worshiping
women and became the ancestor of a heathen people that dishon-
ored the traditions of its fathers. Ya'akov, however, remained
faithful to those traditions, seeking even to surpass his father and
grandfather in piety and holiness.

Then what determined their characters? In each case the
determining factor was their own free choice. And just as it was in
their time, so it has remained until today. Parents and teachers
can provide guidance, but the decision of whether to do good or
bad deeds, whether to live a life agreeable to God or a criminal
life, is made by each individual. This is also true of man as part of
a group. The natural human tendency is to try to dominate
others in order to impose one's own way. The true leader, however, is the man who is master of himself, who restrains his
passions, controls his instincts, subordinates his whims and does
not try to dominate others. Such a man will be happy even in
poverty and illness and will manage to overcome his suffering;
his good deeds will fashion a king's throne for him in the World
to Come.

Another way of expressing the thought behind the words
אם אין אני לי מי לי is, "If I do not belong to myself, who and what
does belong to me?" All things on earth are transitory; people
who pride themselves on their wealth only too often live to see it
disappear. A man enjoys good health today; tomorrow he is ill
and near death. A person is proud of his wisdom and knowledge;
suddenly he suffers a breakdown and he is more to be pitied than
the poorest beggar. As the prophet Yirmeyahu says, "Let not the
wise man pride himself on his wisdom, let not the strong man be
proud of his strength and not the rich man of his riches"
(*Yirmeyahu* 9:22). Nothing belongs exclusively to you; it can be
taken away at any moment.

AND IF I AM ONLY FOR MYSELF, WHAT AM I? The strong
sense of individuality recommended in the first part of the
maxim must not degenerate into egotism and selfishness. Man's
life depends on other people to a great extent. He is bound in

different relationships to his parents, his siblings and others. He chooses a wife and is, hopefully, blessed with children; he joins fellow Jews in forming a congregation and fellow citizens in furthering their common interests. Even towns, villages and larger political units must join forces, being dependent on one another for mutual protection and stability. There is yet another bond which connects the whole of mankind: all human beings are the children of one Father and they should regard each other as brothers. How foolish is the man who only thinks of himself, who only lives for himself. "And if I am only for myself, what am I?" The answer is: Nothing—nothing at all! A truly worthy person, a truly good Jew, loves and cares about his fellowmen, participates in their joys, tries to alleviate their pain and sorrow and brings up his children to practice virtue, fear God and fight against evil.

AND IF NOT NOW, WHEN? Behind us lies the past, before us stretches a future that we cannot foresee, and the present is becoming part of the past at every moment. Yet this moment is the actual time of our existence, of our thinking, our doing and our creating. Hillel admonishes us to use this moment to advantage. Youth is the time of building, the time when foundations must be laid. אשרי איש ירא את יי, "Blessed is the man who fears God" (*Tehillim* 112:1), the Gemara tells us, refers to a man in his full vigor (*Avodah Zarah* 19a). The Sages tell us in a similar vein that the verse: מפני שיבה תקום והדרת פני זקן ויראת מאלהיך אני יי, "Rise up before the hoary head and honor the face of the old man, and fear your God" (*Vayyikra* 19:32), means that before your hair whitens, you should pluck up the courage to fear God; then you will honor your own old age (*Zohar*, part 3, p. 87b).

Yet even the aged must spend their remaining time on earth usefully. This is the nature of the world, that it is a time of action—what we fail to do in this life cannot be made good in the World to Come. The World to Come resembles the Shabbath, and the time we spend on earth resembles the week. One who works throughout the week can peacefully enjoy the results of his efforts; similarly, one who is active in this world may expect his appointed reward in the World to Come. There is yet another great truth contained in these words. The almighty God has created man to glorify and serve Him; He has given us a Law of truth and ordinances of love and goodwill, according to which we are to live and work. If someone wastes his time with useless activities, if he sits in public houses playing cards, carrying on purposeless conversation or slandering people, he not only commits a great wrong, he also loses precious time that is irretrievable. A wrong that is done can perhaps be rectified, but it is impossible to retrieve lost time. Therefore, always ask yourself: If not now, when?

שַׁמַּאי אוֹמֵר, עֲשֵׂה תוֹרָתְךָ קֶבַע אֱמוֹר **טו**
מְעַט וַעֲשֵׂה הַרְבֵּה וֶהֱוֵי מְקַבֵּל אֶת־כָּל־
הָאָדָם בְּסֵבֶר פָּנִים יָפוֹת:

15 Shammai says: Make your study of the Torah a fixed activity, say little but do much, and receive all men with a friendly countenance.

*   *   *

Hillel's worthy friend and companion was Shammai. They were both scholars of the highest rank and both founded great academies of learning which bore their names. Both upheld the Torah and both were concerned with the strict observance of God's commandments. Although their tenets were at variance in a number of matters, it was always a מחלוקת לשם שמים, a difference of opinion "for the sake of Heaven" based on the purest motives on both sides. Our contemporaries mistakenly speak of religious differences between Hillel and Shammai, or rather between their schools, in order to justify their own differences, but there were no "religious" conflicts between them. Both Sages were of one opinion on Torah principles, both acknowledged the divinity of the Written and the Oral Law, and both recognized the obligation to live in accordance with God's Law. Their opinions differed only in the interpretation of and the approach to certain halachic precepts. Shammai's disciples were usually stricter than Hillel's in the use of logic and insisted on consistency in the practical applications of the Law. Hillel's disciples, who distinguished themselves by great modesty, were in the majority and therefore the *Halachah* was settled in accordance with Hillel's school in most cases.

MAKE YOUR STUDY OF THE TORAH A FIXED ACTIVITY. The love of consistency, exemplified by Shammai's school, is seen in the first part of the master's maxim. According to Bertinoro, this means: Act as you teach, and do not be severe with yourself and lenient with others or vice versa. Shammai stresses here strict consistency of practice for oneself and for others. This principle

has great advantages. The multitude is not misled when everything is measured according to one standard and when the same
behavior is expected of everyone. בית אבא של רבן גמליאל]שהוא מבית
ישראל היו מחמירין על עצמן ומקילין לכל ישראל הלל] (Beitzah 2:6; Eduyyoth
3:10), Hillel's school held that it was correct to be more severe
with themselves, as scholars, than with others.

Since the Law follows Hillel's school in this practice and renders the observance of religious duties somewhat easier for the
multitude of ordinary men, most commentators give another and
more satisfactory explanation of Shammai's saying. In this
maxim, Shammai is telling us in a very special way to confirm
Shimon *Ha-Tzaddik*'s three pillars of the world. The first of the
three pillars on which the world stands is the study of Torah. God
has blessed us above all the nations of the earth by giving us the
Torah, and it is the specific task of our lives to study the Torah
and learn it. Make this study the main occupation of your life and
regard everything else, even earning a living, as secondary. If you
are forced to devote the greater part of your time to earning the
necessities of life, however, then you should fix a (certain) few
hours daily for Torah study and ensure that these hours will
remain undisturbed; nothing should induce you to shorten the
appointed time or fill it up with other activities.

Rabbi Shemuel of Ozedah pointed out that the word תורתך
(your Torah) is used instead of לימודך (your studies). Tehillim
opens with the verse, "Happy is the man who has never walked in
the counsel of the lawless, never stood in the path of the frivolous,
and who has never sat where the scornful sit, but the Torah of the
Lord is his delight and he will meditate in his Torah day and
night" (*Tehillim* 1:1-2). At first the Torah is called תורת יי, "the
Torah of the Lord," and then it is called תורתו, which we may say is
"his (the pious man's own) Torah." The verse reads: בתורת יי חפצו,
"the Torah of the Lord is his delight," ובתורתו יהגה יומם ולילה, "he
will meditate in his Torah day and night." The Sages conclude:
בתחילה נקראת תורת יי ומשעמל בה נקראת תורתו, "As long as a man
only finds delight in the Torah it is called 'the teaching of the
Lord,' but as soon as a man eagerly works at it, it is called his
own, תורתו" (*Avodah Zarah* 19a). Thus the Mishnah says that
when your studies, לימודך, become a fixed activity, קבע, they

are transformed into your own Torah, תורתך.

The meaning of תורתך can also be explained in a different way. The Torah given to us by God contains, in its simple meaning, the sacred knowledge of the Kabbalah which even our great teacher Moshe was unable to understand completely. This part of the Torah is therefore called תורת יי (the Torah of the Lord). The revealed part of the Torah, which man is capable of absorbing through continual hard work and unflagging perseverance, can therefore be called תורתנו (our Torah), תורתו (his Torah), תורתך (your Torah), etc. It belongs to the man who has worked at it. And so when Shammai teaches: עשה תורתך קבע, "Make [the study of] your Torah a fixed activity," we can understand: Do not devote the greater part of your time to searching into the secrets of the Torah. You may occasionally devote yourself to these studies, but your regular efforts should be applied to the revealed Torah.

SAY LITTLE AND DO MUCH. The wicked speak a lot and do little. When Avraham wanted to acquire the cave of Machpelah as a resting place for Sarah, Efron the Hittite said he would give it to him as a present, but ultimately charged an excessively high price for it. Avraham, on the other hand, not only ran to meet three strangers and invited them into his home to drink a little water, to wash their feet and to taste a morsel of bread, but also ordered fine cakes to be prepared and a good calf to be slaughtered. He himself also fetched curd and milk to refresh them while they waited. The pious say little but do a great deal. The following verses on this subject come to mind:

> It is a good thing not to give a solemn promise, for you could so easily fail to carry out your promise.
>
> *(Koheleth 5:4)*

> What your lips have uttered, that you must keep.
>
> *(Devarim 23:24)*

> Like a loose tooth and a sprained ankle is the promise of a faithless man on his day of need.
>
> *(Mishlei 25:19)*

When a man does not know yet that his tooth is bad, and he suddenly bites on it, a dreadful pain grips him. When someone tries to stand on a sprained ankle, he not only feels pain but he will also fall down. A man who says, or promises, a great deal and does little can be relied upon to the same extent as a bad tooth or a sprained ankle; he is not only defective, but he may cause harm to others as well.

AND RECEIVE ALL MEN WITH A FRIENDLY COUNTE-NANCE. If you learn a great deal and also do a great deal, will you then have any time left for simple friendliness and concern for others? The third pillar on which the universe rests, lovingkindness towards your fellow, is no less significant than the other two. A great scholar often suffers material want, for he devotes time, that others use for earning a living, to Torah study. In addition, he usually has community responsibilities thrust upon him, which he accepts for the benefit of others. This, too, consumes a great deal of his time. Yet he does not allow the time he sets aside for Torah study to be shortened by any other obligations, and so his time for sleep and recreation is thus curtailed.

Also, many unimportant people come to him either to make the acquaintance of a great and famous man or to request advice or favors. Could one blame him if he harshly refused such burdensome visits? But you will find that the sincerely pious man receives them all with patience and gentleness. Shammai's behavior toward the three proselytes does not contradict his maxim (*Shabbath* 31a, cited above in *Avoth* 1:12). Shammai surely received them in a friendly manner at first and only chased them away, when, in his opinion, they demanded unseemly things of him. The Sage teaches: Receive graciously everyone who comes to you, even the most humble, for he, like you, was created in the image of God and so you will be honoring God.

טז רַבָּן גַּמְלִיאֵל אוֹמֵר, עֲשֵׂה לְךָ רַב
וְהִסְתַּלֵּק מִן הַסָּפֵק וְאַל־תַּרְבֶּה לְעַשֵּׂר
אֲמָדוֹת:

16 Rabban Gamliel would say: Provide yourself with a teacher, and free yourself of doubt, and do not give an excess tithe through guesswork.

*   *   *

Hillel and Shammai were the last of "the pairs." Thereafter, only one great name is mentioned as the head of Yisrael's Sages. Even though Shimon ben Hillel followed his father in the office of *Nasi,* the actual successor to the Tradition of Hillel and Shammai was Rabbi Yochanan ben Zakkai. Hillel lived to an extremely old age and as long as he was alive, his son could not assert himself as leader; that explains why Shimon's name is not mentioned in any mishnah and why the Talmud hardly refers to him. Shimon probably outlived his father but was in office for only a short time. Shimon's son and successor, *Rabban* Gamliel, called the Elder to distinguish him from his grandson of the same name, was one of the greatest of our Sages.

The title of *Rabban,* our teacher, was first given to Gamliel. The prophets and the great men of Yisrael before his time were known simply by their first names and גדול מרבן שמו, no title was needed (*Tosefta Eduyyoth* 3:4). When the two great academies began to vie with one another for leadership, it became necessary to choose one leader whom all would follow. Thus the *Nasi* came to be called *Rabban,* and his learned contemporaries, such as Akavyah ben Mahalalel and others, were not given any titles. The custom of calling every ordained Torah scholar "Rabbi" (*Rabi,* my teacher), arose only later.

PROVIDE YOURSELF WITH A TEACHER AND FREE YOURSELF OF DOUBT. The first part of *Rabban* Gamliel's saying is identical to that of Yehoshua ben Perachyah. Why does he repeat the words of the Sage who preceded him by more than a century? While the academies of Hillel and Shammai flourished, though each group of disciples was actively involved in the defense of its own methods of interpretation, the Tradition was always accepted with no outstanding differences of opinion between scholars. Disciples generally never left their teachers, following the example of Yehoshua who never separated himself from Moshe. A teacher was thus able to correct any possible misinterpretation immediately, and during that period doubts and differences of opinion never arose. משרבו תלמידי הלל ושמאי שלא שימשו כל צרכן רבו מחלוקת בישראל–שלא למדו כל צרכן לא אמרו אלא שלא שימשו כל צרכן "When the number of disciples of Hillel and Shammai who did not attend their teacher['s discourses] often enough increased, the [amount of] disagreement in Israel also increased" (*Sanhedrin* 88b)—the text does not say, "[those] who did not learn enough," but "[those] who did not attend enough."

The later disciples of Hillel and Shammai, however, did not have sufficient contact with their teachers and that is how doubts and differences began to emerge. *Rabban* Gamliel therefore warns: Do not rely too much on your own perceptive faculty, on your memory or wisdom, for it is likely that you do not perceive the whole, that your memory is faulty, that your wisdom is in error. Stay near your teacher and free yourself of doubt.

AND DO NOT GIVE AN EXCESS TITHE THROUGH GUESS-WORK. When an experienced farmer sees a heap of grain in front of him he will know approximately how much it weighs and will easily separate one-tenth of it as the tithe. But he may be wrong by a small quantity either way, and if he separates too much or too little he has not done his duty. That is what happens with all things based on guesswork. You might therefore think that you can remove all doubt by deciding to follow the stricter way, but that is not always so.

Our Sages teach: הרואה טרפה לעצמו עליו הוא נאמר יגיע כפיך כי תאכל אשריך וטוב לך (*Tehillim* 128:2; *Chullin* 44b). Rashi says that this means that one who has to decide a doubtful case will apply the strict rule in his own house. *Rabbenu* Nissim refutes this (ibid.), saying that there is no special merit in taking the stricter view. One who has not learned much, when in doubt, has to declare even permitted things as not permitted; however, one who has applied himself to Torah study diligently can, as a result of his wide knowledge, declare as permitted that which from all appearances, seems not to be so. Of such a person we are told: יגיע כפיך כי תאכל אשריך וטוב לך, "When you eat the labor of your hands," that is, when a question arises in your own house and, because of your wide knowledge you know that the food being questioned may indeed be eaten, then "happy shall you be, and it shall be well with you." You will be happy in this world, for you can enjoy what would seem not to be permitted, and it will be well with you in the World to Come because you have proven conscientious in studying the Torah and therefore you will also acquire eternal happiness. The surest way to achieve this goal, *Rabban* Gamliel advises, is to provide yourself with a teacher and remain with him.

יז שִׁמְעוֹן בְּנוֹ אוֹמֵר, כָּל־יָמַי גָּדַלְתִּי בֵּין הַחֲכָמִים וְלֹא מָצָאתִי לַגּוּף טוֹב מִשְּׁתִיקָה וְלֹא הַמִּדְרָשׁ הָעִקָּר אֶלָּא הַמַּעֲשֶׂה וְכָל־הַמַּרְבֶּה דְּבָרִים מֵבִיא חֵטְא:

17 Shimon, his son, says: All my life I have grown up among the Sages, and I have found that nothing is better than silence for the physical welfare of man, study is not the most important thing, but practice, and too much talk causes sin.

*   *   *

Rabban Shimon ben Gamliel succeeded his father as *Nasi*, yet it seems that he was in office for only a short time. *Rabban* Gamliel lived to a very old age, but *Rabban* Shimon probably died a violent death during the war which preceded the destruction of the Holy Temple. His maxim dates from his most vigorous years, before he became the *Nasi*, when he was still known as his father's son, as was the custom in Talmudic times.

ALL MY LIFE I HAVE GROWN UP AMONG THE SAGES. One may suppose that as a child, the son, grandson and great-grandson of *nesi'im* freely associated with the wisest men then living. His words indicate, however, that even as a grown man he was still eager to learn from them.

NOTHING IS BETTER THAN SILENCE. The Rambam mentions four kinds of ordinary speech: the first kind comprises slander, lies, curses, immoral and obscene talk, and is completely reprehensible; the second kind consists of talk that is apparently good but easily leads to evil, such as insincere praise— לעולם אל יספר אדם בטובתו של חבירו שמתוך טובתו בא לידי רעתו, "A person should never speak [to someone else] about the good qualities of his friend, for through speaking about his good qualities, they will come to speak of his bad qualities" (*Bava Bathra* 164b)—such talk is equally reprehensible; the third type includes whatever talk a man uses in his daily living, which is the ordinary speech of most people. The fourth is usually trivial and pointless and its only purpose is to pass the time. According to the Rambam, it is from this type of speech that the maxim urges us to refrain. Maintaining silence is not so simple. You should try to keep silent when you really have nothing to say, and try to hold your tongue when someone attempts to provoke you, and not answer in the face of outright calumny. A person who manages to keep silent when he is slandered and gossiped about is not only wise, but spares himself much aggravation.

Rabban Shimon's words chiefly refer to the physical benefits of silence; aggravation, annoyance, excitement and anger have an unhealthy effect on the body. Someone who answers his slanderers only provokes them to increase their calumny; the one who keeps silent disarms them, as the Wise King said: אל תען כסיל כאולתו, "Do not answer the fool in accordance with his foolishness!" (*Mishlei* 26:4). We also say in the daily *Shemoneh Esreh*: אלהי נצור לשוני מרע ושפתי מדבר מרמה, ולמקללי נפשי תדום, ונפשי כעפר לכל תהיה "My God, guard my tongue from evil and my lips from speaking falsehood. Let my soul be silent to those who curse me, and let my soul be as dust of the earth to all things." We all stamp our foot in anger, and there is no harm in that; but by holding our tongues in the face of all kinds of provocation, we guard our good health.

The Sages, moreover, pay great tribute to a person who holds his tongue before slanderers: עלובין ואינן עולבין שומעין חרפתם ואינן משיבין עושין מאהבה ושמחין ביסורין, עליהן הכתוב אומר ואוהביו כצאת השמש בגבורתו, "Those who let themselves be put to shame but do not put others to shame, those who listen to slander and do not reply, who do this out of love of God, and cheerfully accept the wrong done to them, of them we read, 'Let them that love Him be as the sun that rises in its might' " (*Shoftim* 5:31, *Shabbath* 88b; see also *Yoma* 23a, *Gittin* 36b, *Bava Bathra* 8a). The radiance of the pious man who keeps silent will cut through clouds of slander, just as the morning mist is dispersed by the rising sun.

STUDY IS NOT THE MOST IMPORTANT THING, BUT PRACTICE. Our Sages teach, "Rabbi Yitzchak said, האמנם אלם צדק תדברון וגו', 'Is it true that you are silent? Justice should you speak!' That is to

say, there is nothing more praiseworthy in this world than silence, but this refers to ordinary matters, whereas in regard to
Torah, speaking is imperative" (*Tehillim* 58:2 cited in *Chullin* 89a).
We say in our prayers: ותלמוד תורה כנגד כלם, "But the study of the
Torah excels them all (*Pe'ah* 1:1), so we know that Torah study is
the Jew's most desirable occupation, and you cannot learn without talking. The teacher must talk, students must discuss, pupils
must ask questions, and even the person learning on his own
ought to learn aloud. The ear must hear that which the mouth
speaks. And yet studying, learning or teaching are not the
main things, but doing. The Sages place learning before doing,
התלמוד גדול שהתלמוד מביא לידי מעשה (*Kiddushin* 40b), because only
learning renders doing possible, but doing remains the goal.

We read (*Shemoth* 15:26), "And He said, 'If you will only
hearken diligently to the voice of the Lord, your God, and will do
that which is right in His eyes and will give ear to His commandments and keep all His laws, then all the illness with which I have
afflicted the Egyptians, I will not afflict you, for I, the Lord, am
your Healer.' " If we are not to be afflicted, why do we need a
healer? The Almighty is not the kind of healer on whom you only
call to cure sickness, but a healer by virtue of His preventive
instructions which can keep us whole and healthy. These instructions are of course His holy commandments, which we may not
comprehend but which nevertheless safeguard our temporal and
eternal well-being. This can be compared to good medical advice;
it is useless if not heeded. Study and learn, therefore, but do not
forget to act.

The Sages teach, "Whoever occupies himself with the study of
the Torah without carrying out God's commandments will not
succeed in acquiring a knowledge of the Torah, as it is said,
ולמדתם אתם ושמרתם לעשותם, 'that you may learn them, and observe to do them'" (*Devarim* 5:1, *Yevamoth* 109b). Experience
confirms this, for proper study of the Torah absolutely requires
observance of the commandments. If you regard the Torah as
mere knowledge, like any other science, you will never learn
anything; you will be able to penetrate the profound depths of
the Torah only if you study with the honest intention of conscientiously observing its sacred commandments.

AND TOO MUCH TALK GENERATES SIN. *Rabban* Shimon ben Gamliel does not repeat the same phrase that appears in *Mishlei* 10:19, ברב דברים לא יחדל פשע, "Where there is much talk, evil will not cease," which refers to the useless talk and vain gossip which cause so many sins every day. The Sage wishes to teach us something else here, namely, that even in those cases when speaking is necessary, such as in prayer and the observance of the commandments, superfluous words are to be avoided. Because of a superfluous word, the first mother caused her descendants untold harm. God had forbidden the first human couple "to eat of the tree of knowledge." Chavah, however, told the serpent, "God has said, 'You shall not eat of it and you shall not touch it,' " adding her own words, "and you shall not touch it" (*Bereshith* 3:3). This is what caused the transgression of God's commandment, for the snake was able to prevail upon her to touch the fruit first, and when no punishment was forthcoming, the snake easily induced her to partake of the fruit.

Similarly, in the case of Channah, the mother of the great prophet Shemuel, two superfluous words shortened her son's life. She said, וישב שם עד עולם, "And he shall be dedicated to the Lord's service in the Holy Temple forever" (*Shemuel* I, 1:22). She should not have said "forever." Channah's prayers were answered in all respects, so she could not have meant that Shemuel was to live "forever," because man is destined to die. Therefore her words must be compared to the verse (*Shemoth* 21:6): ועבדו לעולם, which refers to a servant who voluntarily gives up his freedom and whose ear is then pierced, and who must "serve his master forever," meaning of course עולמו של יובל, "until the end of the fifty-year period before the *Yovel* (Jubilee) year" (*Kiddushin* 15a). The *Levi'im* also served in the Temple for fifty years (*Bemidbar* 8:25); Shemuel was a *Levi*—the superfluous two words spoken by his mother caused him to die early, at the end of his fifty years of service!

יח **רַבָּן** שִׁמְעוֹן בֶּן גַּמְלִיאֵל אוֹמֵר, עַל־
שְׁלֹשָׁה דְבָרִים הָעוֹלָם קַיָּם עַל הַדִּין
וְעַל הָאֱמֶת וְעַל־הַשָּׁלוֹם שֶׁנֶּאֱמַר אֱמֶת וּמִשְׁפַּט
שָׁלוֹם שִׁפְטוּ בְּשַׁעֲרֵיכֶם:

18 *Rabban* Shimon Ben Gamliel says: By virtue of three things does the world endure—justice, truth and peace, as it is said, "You shall administer truth, justice and peace in your gates" (*Zecharyah* 8:16).

*   *   *

Rabbenu Ya'akov Ba'al Ha-Turim begins the Tur Choshen Mishpat, containing the judicial precepts of the Torah, with this saying of *Rabban* Shimon and relates it to the maxim of Shimon *Ha-Tzaddik*, "The world is based on three things: the Torah, serving God and acts of lovingkindness." To show how the two maxims agree, *Rabbenu* Ya'akov cites *Rabbenu* Yonah's explanation, which notes the difference between the words עוֹמֵד (is based) and קַיָּם (endures). The pillars that support the world, it is explained, are also the purposes of Creation: the Torah, Divine service and the practice of lovingkindness; but the world order continues to exist because of justice, truth and peace. Without justice, the strong would suppress the weak; without truth, trusting human relationships would be impossible; and without peace, war would destroy human society.

Rabbi Yosef Caro, in his commentary, Beith Yosef, rightly objects and says that the three things mentioned by Shimon *Ha-Tzaddik* as the reasons for the creation of the world would also suffice to maintain the world. He therefore explains that during Shimon *Ha-Tzaddik*'s lifetime, the Temple was still standing. When it was destroyed, the *avodah* (the service in the Holy Temple) was no longer possible, and only 270 of the 613 commandments could actually be performed. Also, the organized practice of charity waned without the infrastructure of a Jewish state to support it. Different pillars were therefore required to maintain the universe, namely: justice, truth and peace. Objections can also be found to this explanation, for even justice, truth and peace will only be practiced to perfection when God gathers in the dispersed of Yisrael and rebuilds His Holy Temple. Rabbi Shemuel of Ozedah, following Rabbi Caro's fundamental idea, is probably more correct. He says that all three values of *Rabban* Shimon ben Gamliel are needed to replace the missing pillar, sacrificial service. The sacrifices prescribed by the Torah are: חטאות ואשמות (sin- and guilt-offerings), נדרים ונדבות (vows and voluntary gifts) and שלמים (peace offerings). Justice, to punish wrongs, replaced the sin- and guilt-offerings, truth replaced the vows and voluntary gifts, and peace between Yisrael and God should continue to be practiced even without access to the Temple. We can no longer bring חטאות ואשמות (sin- and guilt-offerings), but if we try to be always just, God will forgive our sins and pardon our offences. We can no longer offer vows and voluntary gifts in the Temple, but if we are ever truthful and faithfully keep promises, God will consider it equal to an offering in the Holy Temple. We bring peace offerings no more, but if we always seek to uphold peace, wherever and however we can, God will grant peace to His people.

JUSTICE, TRUTH AND PEACE. When mankind became so corrupt that only one person in the whole world respected the Law of God, spoke the truth and shunned violence, the flood was sent to exterminate the race. When our nation became a nation of thieves and bribers and did not pity the poor, our Holy Temple was utterly destroyed.

Redemption, however, may be brought about through a return to right and justice. "Tzion shall be redeemed with justice and her penitents with righteousness" (*Yeshayahu* 1:27). "Seek justice, relieve the oppressed, judge the fatherless, plead for the widow. Come now, and let us reason together, says the Lord; though your sins be like scarlet they shall be as white as snow; though they be red like crimson they shall be [as white] as wool" (*Yeshayahu* 1:17-18).

TRUTH is most important and, to a certain extent, the only possession of Yisrael. To acknowledge truth, our ancestors gladly and happily surrendered their lives by the thousands, and even in our time there are countless Jews and Jewesses prepared to live and die for truth. What is truth? God himself is truth, as we read: יי אלהים אמת, "The Lord, God, is truth" (*Yirmeyahu* 10:10). And just as God is truth, He has also given us a teaching of truth, for which we daily thank him in the words: ונתן לנו תורת אמת, "Who has given us the Torah of truth."

There is only one kind of truth, the pure and absolute truth, but in its application to the human condition it sometimes has to adapt itself to circumstance, and thus we read: אמת מארץ תצמח, "Truth will grow up from the earth" (*Tehillim* 85:12). This truth, adapted to human limitations, can be called veracity, and is the one mentioned in the Sage's maxim. Sincerity in thought, speech and action is a fundamental tenet in a stable human society. The human heart easily lends itself to evil and falsehood, but the prevalence of only falsehood would soon ruin all human life. As our Sages teach (*Shabbath* 119b), לא חרבה ירושלים אלא בשביל שפסקו ממנה אנשי אמונה, "Yerushalayim was destroyed only because completely truthful and trustworthy men ceased therein." Be truthful to yourself, be a strict judge of your own thoughts, words and deeds, and don't try to justify your motives. Be truthful to your fellowmen. Do not allow, even in unimportant matters, a word of untruth, of exaggeration or diminution of fact, to cross your lips. When you have promised something, keep you word and do not depart from it. When you have done a wrong, do not try to conceal it through a lie. Admit it and feel shame; that is the best way to avoid repeating it. It is certainly very hard to do, but consider that the future of human society depends on people who love truth more than anything. Do not speak differently from the way you think; do not simulate love and friendship for those whom you feel justified to dislike or hate. Speak the truth and you will gain the confidence of your fellowmen. Even the ordinary trade and communication of human society cannot exist without mutual confidence.

Be truthful toward God. Know that He is omniscient and that you cannot conceal anything from Him. God's seal is truth (*Shabbath* 55a). God hates those who talk differently from the way they think (*Pesachim* 113b); he who equivocates, trying to deceive his fellow, is guilty of a sin as serious as idol-worship, since by behaving like that he denies God's omniscience (*Sanhedrin* 92a). God loathes falsehood even if it is presumably for a good cause, for Judaism teaches that the end does not justify the means (see *Shabbath* 149b).

Look at the shape and position of the letters of the words אמת (truth) and שקר (falsehood): the א stands firmly on two feet, the מ rests on a broad foundation, the ת also stands on two feet—the truth cannot be shaken. The ש is broad at the top but narrow at the bottom, the ק and the ר each stand on one foot, and the ק is even suspended on a breath of air—so falsehood must collapse. And these letters have one more peculiarity: in the Hebrew alphabet the first letter is א, at midpoint is the letter מ, and the last letter is ת. The three letters are therefore as distant from each other as possible—truth resists all separation of space and outlasts all time. On the other hand, the letters of the word שקר are quite close together in the alphabet—no part of falsehood can stand alone and it is easily unmasked. קושטא קאי שיקרא לא קאי, "Truth can stand, falsehood cannot" (*Shabbath* 104a). Any evil that destroys the world order finds its source in falsehood; truth is the base of all that is good and straight. Even the longed-for redemption will be brought about by truth, as it is said, כה אמר יי שבתי אל ציון ושכנתי בתוך ירושלים ונקראה ירושלים עיר האמת והר יי צבאות הר הקודש "Thus says the Lord, 'When I am returned unto Tzion, and will dwell in the midst of Yerushalayim, then Yerushalayim will be called the City of Truth, and the mountain of the Lord of hosts, the Holy Mountain" (*Zecharyah* 8:3).

PEACE. The Sages teach that when there is peace between husband and wife, the reflection of God's majesty rests upon them; when there is peace within the entire family, just as in the wider reaches of community, society and nation, then peace can preserve the world. Peaceful competition advances man's endeavors, while war destroys everything in its path and its disastrous effects spread far in space and time. Justice, truth and peace are all principles which preserve and bring blessing to the world. They often are interdependent, however, and even overlap, so that sometimes one may have to be put aside for another. It can happen, for instance, that justice cannot be enforced because truth demands that justice should temporarily be ignored. Our Sages call this הוראת שעה, a temporary decision required by a specific set of circumstances and running counter to the Law. When the prophet Eliyyahu was prevailed upon to stand up for eternal truth, he erected an altar on Mount Carmel and brought a sacrifice to the Lord there, although the Law states that a sacrifice is only permitted in the Holy Temple in Yerushalayim. In this case, the Law had to give way temporarily before eternal truth.

On the other hand, truth is sometimes secondary to justice. When Shimon ben Shatach clearly had witnessed a murder, the truth could not be heard because the Law requires two witnesses in order to convict a murderer. There have been times when the Law as well as the truth have been put aside for the sake of peace. Shimi ben Gera had cursed and blasphemed the fleeing King David, the anointed of the Lord; however, for the sake of peace, the returning victorious king was not allowed to claim justice. Yoav, the mighty general, had committed a double murder; for the sake of peace, King David was unable to sentence him. As we know, Aharon, the first High Priest, did not speak the exact truth in order to make peace. מותר לשנות בדבר השלום, "It is permitted to deviate from the truth in order to restore peace" *(Yevamoth* 65b).

Peace is, so to speak, the vessel suited to hold everything that is good; but when the greater good of mankind is endangered, we must not refrain from breaking this vessel—indeed, peace itself demands it. When the *bnei Yisrael* had illicit relations with the daughters of Midyan, Pinchas, in his zeal for truth and justice, disturbed the peace by killing a prince of Yisrael and the Midyanite woman. For that, God gave him His covenant of peace, for real peace can only be maintained by preserving the truth and the Law. Man is thus charged with the difficult task of balancing justice, truth and peace.

Perek Two

אַ רַבִּי אוֹמֵר, אֵיזוֹ הִיא דֶרֶךְ יְשָׁרָה שֶׁיָּבוֹר
לוֹ הָאָדָם כָּל־שֶׁהִיא תִּפְאֶרֶת לְעֹשָׂהּ
וְתִפְאֶרֶת לוֹ מִן הָאָדָם, וֶהֱוֵי זָהִיר בְּמִצְוָה קַלָּה
כְּבַחֲמוּרָה שֶׁאֵין אַתָּה יוֹדֵעַ מַתַּן שְׂכָרָן שֶׁל־מִצְוֹת,
וֶהֱוֵי מְחַשֵּׁב הֶפְסֵד מִצְוָה כְּנֶגֶד שְׂכָרָהּ וּשְׂכַר
עֲבֵרָה כְּנֶגֶד הֶפְסֵדָהּ. הִסְתַּכֵּל בִּשְׁלֹשָׁה דְבָרִים וְאֵין
אַתָּה בָא לִידֵי עֲבֵרָה, דַע מַה־לְמַעְלָה מִמְּךָ עַיִן
רוֹאָה וְאֹזֶן שׁוֹמַעַת וְכָל־מַעֲשֶׂיךָ בַּסֵּפֶר נִכְתָּבִים:

1 Rabi says: Which is the right course for a man to
choose? One which reflects credit on him who does it
and which also reflects glory on him [in the eyes] of
men. Be as careful with a light precept as with a
weighty one, for you do not know the reward for
[doing] the commandments; and balance the loss incurred in the performance of a commandment
against its reward, and the gain from a sin against the
loss it entails. Consider three things and you will not
come into the grip of sin: Know what is above you: a
seeing eye, and a hearing ear, and that all your deeds
are recorded in the book.

*   *   *

Rabbi Yehudah *Ha-Nasi* was the son of *Rabban* Shimon ben
Gamliel the Second. His greatness was such that he came to be
known simply as "Rabi" or "our holy Rabbi." Rabi's saying is very

difficult to understand and is full of apparent contradictions.

WHICH IS THE RIGHT COURSE FOR A MAN TO CHOOSE? The Midrash Shemuel asks: Why does Rabi ask this question when the answer is clearly given in the Torah? והודעת להם את הדרך, "And you will make known to them the way in which to go" (*Shemoth* 18:20). The word דרך (way), it is explained, indicates that Rabi is talking about the practice of human kindness. How do we know that? The Sages said, את הדרך זו גמילות חסדים, "the way, that is the practice of lovingkindness" (*Bava Metzia* 30b, *Bava Kama* 100a).

The word ישרה can mean either "right" (*Shoftim* 7:16), "honest" (*Tehillim* 11:7), or "straight" (*Iyyov* 33:27). The verse, "If you will do that which is right (ישר) in His eyes" (*Shemoth* 15:26), the Sages say, "refers to business relations; from this we learn that one who is honest in business relations earns the goodwill of his fellowman, and the Torah values it as greatly as if he had fulfilled all the *mitzvoth* in the Torah" (*Mechilta* on *Shemoth*, ibid.).

When Rabi alludes to man's choice of direction in life, he refers to man's relationship with his fellowman, and in this respect everybody has the right and the duty to choose the manner best suited to his abilities. The addition of the word ישרה widens the concept of the word דרך to include not only acts of lovingkindness, but also all aspects of man's dealings with his fellowman. We must, however, distinguish between דרך ישרה and מצוה. In regard to *mitzvoth*, the commandments of God, the pious Jew is not given a choice. He must try to observe them all with equal care, whether they appear to him as minor or major. The many precepts which are not commandments, which are only recommended to us, are the ones Rabi suggests we choose to do, for our own benefit and for the good of our fellowman.

ONE WHICH REFLECTS CREDIT ON HIM WHO DOES IT. Since the reading לעושיה, "on him who does it," does not really agree with דרך in gender, Rashi's reading: לעושהו, "on his Creator," seems more accurate. The meaning is then: Which is the right course? One that reflects glory on his Creator and on him in the eyes of man. This is the sense of the phrase as it is used in Iyyov 31:15, הלא בבטן עשני עשהו ויכוננו ברחם אחד, "Did not my

Creator also create him in the womb, and did He not fashion us in the same way in the womb?"

AND WHICH ALSO REFLECTS GLORY ON HIM [IN THE EYES] OF MEN. The word תפארת is difficult to translate. One meaning can be found in the words of the wise King Shelomo: שכל אדם האריך אפו ותפארתו עבר על פשע, "A man's good sense induces him to show patience, but true glory will induce him to overlook an insult" (*Mishlei* 19:11). To overcome your desire for revenge, to pardon your fellow as though he had not offended you—that is glory, that is the selfless love we are commanded to practice.

Rabbi Naftali Hertz Wessely, in his commentary on Pirkei Avoth (*Yain Levanon*), explains תפארת in the sense that it expresses God's wondrous direction of the world by the light of prophecy and by the Divine control of the laws of nature. תפארת is also related to the vocation of Yisrael as a kingdom of priests with a holy mission to perform. The Torah connects these two concepts, said Rabbi Akiva, and is therefore called *tifereth*: והתפארת זו מתן תורה (*Berachoth* 58a). When Yisrael fulfills its holy mission, then the world will recognize and glorify God. ועמד כלם צדיקים לעולם יירשו ארץ נצר מטעי מעשה ידי להתפאר, "And your people shall all be righteous, they shall inherit the land forever; the branch of My planting, the work of My hands, that I may be glorified" (*Yeshayahu* 60:21). Any course is the right one which leads to the fulfillment of Yisrael's mission as an instrument of God's direction of the world, and also influences humanity to recognize this. But what can we individual Jews do when we face so many alternatives, each of which appears good in itself and yet contradicts the others? We must rise above bias and self-interest and base our lives on the great, comprehensive principles that God has given us, asking ourselves always, "Is this the right course?" Especially in matters neither specifically commanded nor yet prohibited, our high vocation should direct us. Rabi himself, in his own life and work, exemplified this splendid maxim. He not only chose the path that led to the realization of God's purpose, but he even caused the powerful emperor of Rome, Antoninus, to appreciate Yisrael's high vocation.

The Talmud mentions a variation of this maxim which implies yet another path leading to תפארת, true glory before God and man. "Rabi said, 'Which is the right course that a man should choose?—Let him love reproof, for when there is reproof in this world, ease of mind comes to it, and goodness and blessing, and evil departs from it, as it says, "To them who admonish shall come delight, and a good blessing shall come to them" (*Mishlei* 24:25).' Some, however, say, 'Let him be scrupulously honest, as it says, "My eyes are upon the faithful of the land that they may dwell with Me" (*Tehillim* 101:6)' " (*Tamid* 28a). In this passage Rabi gives a different answer to the same question, and Rashi explains that "man has to make many choices and Rabi here mentions only one of them." The Maharshah asks why, then, if this explanantion of Rashi is correct, do others differ with Rabi on this point? The answer is that Rabi's maxim in Avoth is actually identical with the one in Tamid. The full verse reads: אמר לרשע צדיק אתה יקבהו עמים יזעמוהו לאמים: ולמוכיחים ינעם ועליהם תבוא ברכת טוב, "When you praise the wicked you will be cursed and condemned, but when you reprove [evil] you will be blessed" (*Mishlei* 24: 24, 25). History shows us that evil rulers have always found flatterers to make excuses for them and fools to praise them, yet eventually they earned only curses and maledictions from the people. When a ruler had courageous advisers who reproved his evil and admonished him for his errors, and he listened to them and acted on their advice, then he earned the blessings of his people and the nations.

When the political and social barriers that existed between Jew and Gentile were gradually eliminated nearly two centuries ago, the tide of fashion and assimilation carried away many Jews. Increased commercial opportunities endangered Shabbath observance, and easier travel regulations encouraged violation of the dietary laws. Young Jewish students became acquainted with non-Jewish ideas in the universities newly opened to them and they neglected their Torah studies. At first, the lawbreakers were well aware that their sins stemmed from laziness, carelessness or greed, but soon the apostles of the so-called Reform appeared and assured them that the violation of God's commandments was really progress—that the Laws of God were antiquated and that their abolition was necessary for the advancement of the human mind! Anyone who dared to admonish them was persecuted. Many pious people came to believe, therefore, that it was laudable to observe the commandments carefully themselves, but closed their eyes to violations of the Law by their children, friends and employees. A misunderstood version of Rabi's maxim was even used to justify this: the right course is the one which reflects glory on you before God and man, so you should above all seek the approval of your peers. The elucidation of Rabi's maxim in the Talmud, however, teaches clearly that only reproof and admonition will lead to glory, the true glory before God and man. It is important to remember, though, that only one who is himself righteous should reprimand others.

The four parts of Rabi's mishnah can also be read as four separate admonitions which have been compared to the four different degrees of service to God (*Toledoth Yehoshua*). The highest degree, לפנים משורת הדין, is the observance of more than what is commanded and the avoidance of that which has even a semblance of wrong. This highest degree of service necessitates our choosing the right course—that is, the one that reflects true glory before God and man. The second degree of service is the observance of only that which has been commanded and the avoidance of only that which is prohibited. This degree requires us only to be equally careful to observe both a minor precept and a weighty one. The third degree of service consists of the intention to do good, but includes the inability to resist strong temptation and results in the ultimate loss of the rewards that might have been enjoyed. The fourth and least sophisticated degree of service to God is service which stems from fear of punishment. Rabi is simply saying in this case: Do not give in to your passions, for even in the darkest night, even in the loneliest place, a seeing eye will observe you, a hearing ear will hear you, and all your deeds will be recorded in a book for all time.

Even the most dedicated person, who usually tries to do more than the commandments strictly require, may occasionally be tempted to neglect those that appear minor to him; and passion may sometimes overpower even the best of men. The Sages tell of the pious Rabbi Amram, who, in the heat of passion, was about to commit a great wrong. Nobody saw him, but at the last moment, by calling out, "Fire! Fire!" he roused his neighbors and was saved from sin. A pious life is an everlasting struggle, not only against hostile forces from without, but even more so, against the enemy within, the foe that nestles in man's heart and tempts him.

BE AS CAREFUL WITH A LIGHT PRECEPT AS WITH A WEIGHTY ONE, FOR YOU DO NOT KNOW THE REWARD FOR [DOING] THE COMMANDMENTS. This admonition invites the questions of what Rabi means by the word "commandments," and which commandments he regards as less or more stringent. The opinions of the commentators vary greatly on this point. Bertinoro, following the Rambam, declared that Rabi means to say that the positive commandments are the lighter ones and the negative commandments are the weightier ones, because no rewards are specified in the Torah for the observance of the positive commandments, but various degrees of punishment are mentioned for specific transgressions, ranging from no punishment at all, to death, according to the severity of the crime. Many outstanding men have raised objections to this explanation because the term מצוה (commandment), without any further qualification, includes both the positive and the negative ones; the person who avoids transgressing a negative precept is therefore also obeying a commandment and may expect a reward for it. For example, with regard to the *mitzvah* of sending away the mother bird, our Sages teach: ומה אם מצוה קלה שהיא כאיסר אמרה תורה למען ייטב לך והארכת ימים קל וחומר על מצות חמורות שבתורה, "If so light a precept, dealing with a subject of little value, is rewarded with blessing and a long life, how much more reward must there be for observing the more difficult precepts of the Torah" (*Chullin*, last mishnah). Since sending away the mother bird is also a negative commandment, לא תקח האם על הבנים, "you shall not take the mother bird together with her young" (*Devarim* 22:6), we learn that sometimes a negative commandment is also called a מצוה קלה.

The mishnah in Tractate Chullin, then, conflicts with the Rambam's explanation and apparently also with Rabi's saying. Rabi tells us to be equally careful with a light precept and a

weighty one because we do not know the reward for the commandments, but Tractate Chullin draws a conclusion from minor
to major (קל וחומר) in the case of a light precept. Another explanation is therefore given by Rabbi Chayyim ben Betzalel, brother
of the Maharal of Prague, in his work Derech Chayyim (see
Tosafoth Yom Tov on this mishnah). He writes that the criterion for
a major *mitzvah* is the sacrifice entailed, whether financial or
physical. After all, the mishnah in Tractate Chullin adds at once
that sending away the mother bird is called a light *mitzvah* because
only a minor loss is incurred. The Gemara elsewhere mentions
that a light precept is one which can be observed without financial sacrifice: ולמה נקראה מצוה קלה מפני שאין בה חסרון כיס (*Avodah
Zarah* 3a).

There are sacred duties which can only be fulfilled with the
greatest sacrifice in time, energy or money, such as פדיון שבויים
(the redemption of hostages). We know that the patriarch
Avraham took the greatest possible care both in the difficult
military expedition to redeem Lot from captivity, as well as in
the relatively easier act of receiving the three travelers. And
who knows which of Avraham's actions was rated higher? The
conclusion drawn by the mishnah in Tractate Chullin is therefore: If God promises well-being and long life for sending away
the mother bird, which has only a lesser financial value, He
will surely give an even greater reward, for example, to someone who foregoes large sums of money in order to observe the
Shabbath rest.

AND BALANCE THE LOSS INCURRED IN THE PERFOR-
MANCE OF A COMMANDMENT AGAINST ITS REWARD, AND
THE GAIN FROM A SIN AGAINST THE LOSS IT ENTAILS. This
statement not only seems to contradict the previous one (Rabi
said that the rewards for the *mitzvoth* are not known, and now he
asks us to calculate the reward and to balance it against any loss),
but also seems to refute Antigenos (*Avoth* 1:3) who told us not to
be like servants who serve their masters with the intention of
receiving a reward (meaning that we are to love justice for its own
sake and refrain from evil for its own sake) and so any calculation
of reward or loss is wrong. A simple explanation might compare

the loss in time, money and effort incurred by the observance of one commandment with the great reward granted by God in this world and that reward which will be granted in the World to Come; likewise, the consequences suffered in this world for the pleasure or gain acquired through a transgression ought to be compared with the consequences we will suffer in the World to Come. But Rabi says: כנגד שכרה (against the reward), and not כנגד מתן שכרה (against the reward granted), as he did above, which leads us to quite a different interpretation.

A later mishnah (*Avoth* 5:1) will remind us that God created the world in ten locutions when He might just as well have done it in one. This shows us the extent to which righteous men can preserve the world and lawless men can destroy it, as we shall learn. The same principle is stated in Mishlei 10:25, וצדיק יסוד עולם, "And the righteous man is the foundation of the world." If a righteous man is one who observes God's positive command-ments and refrains from transgressing God's negative command-ments, while a lawless man is one who does the opposite, we see that it is only the observance of God's Law that preserves the world. The Sages teach, "We read in the Torah, 'And you shall love the Lord your God.' How does one show love for God? The Torah tells us, 'And these words which I command you today shall be upon your heart.' We show our love of God and our desire to help preserve His creation only by taking His com-mandments to heart and observing them" (*Sifrei* on *Devarim* 6:5-6). How man's behavior influences the preservation or destruction of the world, and the link between this and the Torah is a vast subject in itself. The Written and the Oral Law only allude to it, but the Kabbalah deals with it in more detail. Suffice it to say that man is merely a particle in almighty God's great creation, though a highly important one. He alone, among all God's creatures, has been endowed with freedom of will, and it is man's will that ultimately helps to preserve the world or contrib-utes to its destruction!

The distinction between שכר and מתן שכר then, must be that מתן שכר is the reward we eventually receive from God, while שכר is the beneficent results that are accomplished when we perform the *mitzvah*, as it is said: שכר מצוה מצוה, "the reward of a good deed is a good deed" (*Avoth* 4:2). And now Rabi's admonition reads this way: Calculate the harm you do to the whole world order by neglecting a *mitzvah*, compared with the great things you accomplish for the whole world by observing even one of God's commandments; likewise calculate the pleasure you gain from committing a sin, compared with the harm you do thereby to the world order. Rabi's saying, therefore, does not at all contradict that of Antigenos, for Rabi recommends, like Antigenos, that we do good for its own sake and that we refrain from evil for its own sake. The calculation which he enjoins upon us is only intended to encourage us to aim for the highest degree of observance.

CONSIDER THREE THINGS AND YOU WILL NOT COME INTO THE GRIP OF SIN: KNOW WHAT IS ABOVE YOU: A SEEING EYE, AND A HEARING EAR, AND THAT ALL YOUR DEEDS ARE RECORDED IN THE BOOK. This section of the mishnah inspires a number of questions: Why does Rabi add the word ממך, which seems to be superfluous, and why does he ask us to consider these particular three things? Also, Rabi begins with the verb הסתכל (consider) and he continues with דע (know), which makes the grammar awkward. Furthermore, the word לידי (into the hands [grip]) seems unnecessary. Rabi could just as well have said, ואין אתה בא לעבירה, "and you will not come to sin."

We have already learned that it is not enough to love God above all else and to observe His sacred commandments for their own sake; we must also fear Him. That is what King David means in the verse: סמר מפחדך בשרי וממשפטיך יראתי, "My flesh shuddered from the dread of You, and I was afraid of Your judgments" (*Tehillim* 119:120).

During his life on earth, man sometimes endures anxieties, worries, hardship, pain and affliction; at times his mind is clouded and the light of the soul is obscured. Just as black clouds cover the moon, passion obscures the light of his intellect and even worthy people stumble and fall. The only way to overcome the power of the evil inclination is to develop a constant awareness of God's presence. The Sages tell us that Yosef was at the point of yielding to the enticements of his master's beautiful wife when the image of Ya'akov appeared to

him and he ran away, leaving his garment in his seducer's hand.
If just the thought of his revered father was able to save Yosef
from sin, how much more does the constant awareness of God's
presence prevent us from sinning. הסתכל! King David expresses
this thought: אברך את יי אשר יעצני אף לילות יסרני כליותי, "I will bless
the Lord Who has given me counsel, even in the nights (that is,
in life's dark and sad hours) my intellect rebuked me." How?
שויתי יי לנגדי תמיד כי מימיני בל אמוט, "I have always set the Lord
before me," that is, I am always aware that "He is at my right
hand, I shall not falter" (*Tehillim* 16:7-8). In your hour of danger
"sin lies in wait at the gate" (*Bereshith* 4:7), stretching out its
"hands" to seize you, as it were. Nothing can save you unless you
have acquired the habit of seeing God's presence with your spiritual eye at all times.

Rabbi Shemuel of Ozedah gives a different but equally instructive explanation of the expression לידי. It means not only
"the hands," but also "the handles" of a vessel by which we can
hold or lift it. The "handles" of sin are those transgressions which
seem light and insignificant to man: an untruth, an indecent jest,
slander, partaking of milk or cheese not prepared under supervi-
sion, and similar things. Man avoids severe sins more easily than
transgressions that seem light and insignificant to him. Only
rarely is a man tempted to commit a murder, but he is frequently
induced to tell a "white" lie, or cheat just a little bit, or eat
forbidden food once in a while. When you consider, however,
that God's eye can see you anywhere, that God's ear hears you
always, and that all your deeds are recorded by Him, you will not
be tempted to grasp even the "handles" of sin.

Rabbi Shemuel of Ozedah says that the word ממך is employed
to draw our attention to the fact that though God is enthroned in
Heaven, He is still always present with us. Even if you hide in the
most secret room, even if you move to a place that is in deep,
impenetrable darkness, if you go down into the depths of the
earth, do not think that you will be unseen, unheard or unno-
ticed. דע מה למעלה ממך, know that above you there is a seeing eye
that penetrates the blackest darkness, a hearing ear that hears the
softest word, and that all your deeds will be recorded for eternity.

Another highly ingenious explanation of the word ממך is

given by Rabbi Wessely in the commentary Yain Levanon. David, the poet-king, says, "Consider, you ignorant ones among the people, and you fools, when will you understand? He that forms the ear, should He not hear? He that shapes the eye, should He not see?" (*Tehillim* 94:8-9). Since man, the creature, can see and hear, it is self-evident that the Creator can see and hear, but man is a finite and limited being with limited faculties, and so his seeing and hearing are limited, whereas the seeing and hearing of the Infinite, the Almighty, must be unlimited and infinite. The meaning is therefore דע מה למעלה, "Know what is above," ממך, "your capability." That is to say, you must extrapolate from your known and circumscribed abilities the unbounded omniscience of your Creator. The expressions "eye," "ear" and "book" are to be understood allegorically.

The Torah, both the Written and the Oral Law, resembles an inexhaustible source which incessantly refreshes us and which never dries up; it resembles, too, the radiant sun which casts its pure light on different objects in different ways, and this leads us to a different explanation of Rabi's saying. Rabi recommends that we choose the right course and, though we have a standard to measure ourselves against, we may still misunderstand the true weight of a *mitzvah*. Rabi therefore warns us to be careful with all *mitzvoth* and to beware of the consequences of all our actions. Ever since human beings have lived on earth, the sages of all nations have been searching for the right course but have not found it; their teachings even contradict one another. What one calls good seems bad to another, what one proclaims as truth, another regards as a lie. How is that possible? Because man's eyes do not see far enough and his thinking is imperfect. Only Divine revelation, only God's Law, which is a product of the highest wisdom, can mark the right course for us. Rabi therefore explains that three things will keep us from the clutches of sin: a constant awareness of God's presence, the knowledge of our own fallibility and the understanding that our own behavior has transcendental significance in the world order.

We can add another explanation as to why Rabi particularly mentions these three things. What differentiates between man and beast? Thoughts, words and deeds. No other creature is capable of thinking, no other creature can express its thoughts in words, and no other creature is capable of turning its thoughts and words into deeds. Be pure in your thoughts, be true in your speech, be perfect in your deeds; then your gracious Father's eyes will look upon you with mercy, He will hear your heart's entreaty and He will remember eternally all the good that you have accomplished on earth, so that one day you will reap your reward.

בַּ רַבָּן גַּמְלִיאֵל בְּנוֹ שֶׁל־רַבִּי יְהוּדָה הַנָּשִׂיא
אוֹמֵר, יָפֶה תַּלְמוּד תּוֹרָה עִם דֶּרֶךְ אֶרֶץ
שֶׁיְּגִיעַת שְׁנֵיהֶם מְשַׁכַּחַת עָוֹן, וְכָל תּוֹרָה שֶׁאֵין עִמָּהּ
מְלָאכָה סוֹפָהּ בְּטֵלָה וְגוֹרֶרֶת עָוֹן, וְכָל הָעוֹסְקִים
עִם־הַצִּבּוּר יִהְיוּ עוֹסְקִים עִמָּהֶם לְשֵׁם שָׁמַיִם שֶׁזְּכוּת
אֲבוֹתָם מְסַיַּעְתָּם וְצִדְקָתָם עוֹמֶדֶת לָעַד וְאַתֶּם
מַעֲלֶה אֲנִי עֲלֵיכֶם שָׂכָר הַרְבֵּה כְּאִלּוּ עֲשִׂיתֶם:

2 *Rabban* Gamliel, the son of Rabbi Yehudah *Ha-nasi*, says: Excellent is the study of Torah together with a worldly occupation, for the pursuit of both of these causes sinful thoughts to be forgotten. And any study of Torah not combined with some kind of work must fail in the end and be conducive to sin. Let all those who occupy themselves with the community do so only for the sake of Heaven, for the merit of their fathers will sustain them, and their righteousness will endure forever. But as for you, I credit you with great reward, as if you had accomplished it.

*   *   *

Very little is known of the life of *Rabban* Gamliel ben Yehudah, except that his father, Rabi, appointed him *Nasi* and that he was a pious, saintly man. We learn that he was an אוכל טהרות, that is to say, that he observed the priestly precepts of purity even when partaking of ordinary food (*Chullin* 106a). And just as he carried out his duties toward God with the greatest strictness and care, his disposition toward his fellowman and even toward animals was extremely kind. In Tractate Shabbath 151b we find another of his sayings: "One who is merciful toward all creatures will have mercy shown to him by Heaven, but one who is not merciful to others will not have mercy shown to him by Heaven."

EXCELLENT IS THE STUDY OF TORAH TOGETHER WITH A WORLDLY OCCUPATION. This mishnah has also inspired the commentators to ask many questions and give many explanations. If דרך ארץ is "work, or a worldly occupation for the purpose of earning a living," as Rashi, the Rambam, Bertinoro and other commentators explain it, then why does *Rabban* Gamliel need to say both דרך ארץ and מלאכה? If Torah study together with a worldly occupation is only "excellent," perhaps it is not really vital to our well-being, yet *Rabban* Gamliel goes on to say that the combination of both is definitely necessary "lest we fail in the end" or lest we "sin." And surely כל תורה, "any study of Torah" at all, without work, is an exaggeration, for we can think of many cases where a student does not absolutely have to work. Finally, why does *Rabban* Gamliel call sin עון when his father, in the last mishnah, calls it עברה? An ingenious interpretation by Rabbi Shemuel of Ozedah, which is different from all the other explanations, answers most of these questions. To understand it, we must first grasp the differences between דרך ארץ and מלאכה, between עברה and עון. While מלאכה is work in the ordinary sense, the concept of דרך ארץ includes the idea of courtesy and civility in our relations with other people. עברה is any kind of transgression, irrespective of the cause; עון, on the other hand, is a sin committed by intention.

The Midrash tells us of two fundamentally different actions for the sake of which God will not punish even for the most grievous sins: As it is said: ואתי עזבו ואת תורתי לא שמרו, "And they have forsaken Me and have not kept My Torah!" (*Yirmeyahu* 16:11). [Is this not a tautology? Forsaking God means not keeping the Torah, that is, God's commandments. No, the Sages say] it is as if God were to say, "I would not punish them even had they forsaken Me, even had they grieviously sinned by transgressing My commandments, if only they had continued to study the Law; for its light will finally lead them back on the right path." To keep the Torah, in this case, means to study it (beginning of *Eichah Rabbah*).

We read in Hoshea, חבור עצבים אפרים הנח לו, "Efraim is joined to idols, let him alone" (4:17) and חלק לבם עתה יאשמו, "As soon as their heart is divided, they shall be found guilty" (10:2), that is to say, that God will not punish Yisrael's sins as long as there is unity and peace in the nation (Rashi on *Hoshea* 10:2 in the name of *Midrash Aggadah*).

So we see that if the study of God's Law, on the one hand, and good manners and peace among men, on the other hand, will prevail, then God will not punish His people for their sins. Since each of these deeds separately can achieve so much, both of them together must surely be protection from punishment. *Rabban* Gamliel is therefore telling us: Study the Torah and be polite and peaceable in pursuing your worldly occupation and God will somehow forget, as it were, to punish your sins.

This explanation solves all the difficulties of the first two sentences. Nevertheless, the simple interpretation of the mishnah seems more to the point. Yisrael is the people chosen by God, and it is our mission as a people to study God's Law, to live in accordance with its precepts and to pass it on to each succeeding generation. The existence and survival of our people depends upon it! On the other hand, every Jew bears the responsibility to earn his livelihood, to provide for himself and his family. The way in which he does this is called, דֶּרֶךְ אֶרֶץ, as Rabbi Yishmael clearly states: הנהג בהן מנהג דרך ארץ, "You must study the words of the Torah and also do whatever is necessary to sustain yourself" (*Berachoth* 35b).

Rabban Gamliel assumes here that our worldy occupation, that is, earning a living, is our main concern, and so he tells us, therefore, that it is an excellent thing when, in addition to all the efforts expended on that, we do not neglect our mission to study the Law. The farmer, the artisan, the merchant, the public servant, before starting his day's work and after completing it, should devote some hours of the day and the night to the study of the Torah. That is excellent! It is even better when he is modest in his requirements and devotes less time to his work and more time to Torah study, or even when he divides his time equally between the two. Then he will have neither the time nor the desire to sin. It is better still if he can restrict his work to that which is absolutely vital and spend the greater part of his time in increasing his knowledge of the Torah. Then his worldly occupation is no longer called דרך ארץ, as is the case with most people, but מלאכה, work which is limited to acquiring only the absolutely necessary minimum.

It is true that Rabbi Shimon bar Yochai teaches (*Berachoth* 35b) that the truly pious person who is exclusively occupied with learning Torah does not need to provide for his own livelihood; that is quite the opposite of Rabbi Yishmael's teaching, but the Talmud adds, "Many have acted according to Rabbi Yishmael and have been very successful, and many have followed Rabbi Shimon bar Yochai and have failed" (ibid.). *Rabban* Gamliel goes even further than Rabbi Yishmael, however. "Any Torah study not combined with work will cease in the end and is conducive to sin." Even the rich man who does not have to work, should do so. While he has no need to chop wood or carry water or walk behind the plow, he should nevertheless devote himself to the affairs of the community and to the public welfare, finding a useful occupation apart from his Torah studies.

LET ALL THOSE WHO OCCUPY THEMSELVES WITH THE AFFAIRS OF THE COMMUNITY DO SO ONLY FOR THE SAKE OF HEAVEN. *Rabban* Gamliel is well aware of the dangers inherent in a life devoted to public service. Even a person who is neither ambitious nor fond of power, who perhaps wishes to avoid the disagreeable aspects of public office in the belief that he cannot achieve anything useful anyway, should be encouraged to hold public office. *Rabban* Gamliel therefore says: Let all those who occupy themselves with the affairs of the community do so only for the sake of Heaven (*i.e.*, with pure intentions) "for the merit of their fathers will sustain them." Even lacking these incentives for public activity, their work can be useful because God will further their efforts for their ancestors' sake. And, in the event that a community leader might relax his own efforts and rely on the merits of great ancestors, to him *Rabban* Gamliel answers: As for you, I will reward you as if you had accomplished it by yourself and the community will prosper through your efforts.

As in the previous mishnah, there is a reminder here, too, of man's greatest gift—freedom of choice—which he can use to overcome the dangers placed in his path by the evil inclination. In this mishnah, the hint lies in the juxtaposition of Torah study and *derech eretz*. *Rabban* Gamliel wishes to caution you to exercise your will to overcome the dangers that lie in your path: the danger of becoming arrogant—though you may be a great Torah scholar, treat those who know less than you with respect and courtesy; the danger of becoming proud—do not become so proud of your knowledge that you forget to put it into practice and neglect your obligations; the danger of status-seeking and the temptation of wielding power when you hold public office.

BUT AS FOR YOU, I CREDIT YOU WITH GREAT REWARD, AS IF YOU HAD ACCOMPLISHED IT. Bertinoro explains this in three ways: The success of a community leader in his work for the public good can only be achieved with God's help, and this is something that only the merit of his ancestors has really earned for him, yet the reward will accrue to him as though he had done it all by himself; his success in inspiring many others to make great sacrifices for good causes, while he seeks neither honor nor advancement for himself, will also earn him a reward as though he had done it all by himself. In Bertinoro's third explanation, which follows the Rambam, a sincere and honorable public servant will merit a full reward even when he neglects other obligations due to the demands of his office.

GREAT REWARD. Only a man who works for the public welfare can achieve the highest degree of good. Not only will the virtue and good deeds of all those whom he has trained be credited to him by God as if they were his own, but the good he has accomplished will continue even after his death. The seed he has sown will sprout again and again like fruit which is replenished by its own seed. Thus his great deeds on earth will earn שכר הרבה, the ever-multiplying reward that God provides for the righteous souls who serve Him.

אֶ הֱווּ זְהִירִין בָּרָשׁוּת שֶׁאֵין מְקָרְבִין לוֹ
לְאָדָם אֶלָּא לְצֹרֶךְ עַצְמָן, נִרְאִין כְּאוֹהֲבִין
בִּשְׁעַת הֲנָאָתָן וְאֵין עוֹמְדִין לוֹ לְאָדָם בִּשְׁעַת דָּחֳקוֹ:

3 Be cautious with the ruling authorities, for they befriend a man only for their own interests; they appear as friends when it is to their advantage, but they do not stand by a man in times of distress.

*   *   *

Both sayings of *Rabban* Gamliel are obviously an elaboration on Avoth 1:10. "Shemayah said: Love work, hate lordship (public office) and do not seek to become intimate with the authorities."

LOVE WORK! *Rabban* Gamliel has just told us to love work even when we dedicate our lives to learning Torah, for the study of the Torah together with a worldly occupation is an excellent thing. If you concentrate on both of these you will forget about sin, but if you concern yourself with one, and not with the other, you will surely be led to sin.

HATE LORDSHIP (PUBLIC OFFICE)! Shemayah meant to say that we must not hate the office itself but hate the way it is used. *Rabban* Gamliel develops this idea further: Let all those who occupy themselves with the affairs of the community do so only for the sake of Heaven, with pure intentions, then God will enable them to succeed.

AND DO NOT SEEK TO BECOME INTIMATE WITH THE AUTHORITIES! Shemayah's words were spoken at a time when the Jewish state was still in existence. At that time Yehudah (Judea) was torn by party quarrels; two hostile brothers were fighting each other for supremacy. Anyone who loved his people and the Torah was compelled to keep clear of the party leaders in order to save what could be saved. But in the time of *Rabban* Gamliel ben Yehudah, the Jewish state was extinct and the Jews were Roman subjects. Those who led the people had to be in contact with the Roman despots in order to protect the people and to ease their tax burden. Both Shemayah and *Rabban* Gamliel use the word רשות and not מלכות. *Malchuth* refers to a government that rules with law and justice, but *reshuth* implies despotism unfettered by law and justice.

BE CAUTIOUS WITH THE RULING AUTHORITIES. In Roman times, just as in later periods, the official representatives of despotic rulers extorted taxes from the people both to satisfy the ruler and to enrich themselves. *Rabban* Gamliel, as a community leader, knew that the avarice of such officials can never be satisfied and so warns us never to rely on their good will. Rabbi Shemuel of Ozedah bases his interpretation of this mishnah on the word רשות, which may also mean "permission." He explains the text: Beware of those things that you are allowed to do but which have no inherent higher purpose; in other words, be careful when you enjoy even permitted pleasures. Eating your favorite dishes and drinking wine may well help you to celebrate the Shabbath and Festivals, but if you derive merely physical pleasure and delight from them, do not overindulge. Rich food and stimulating drink may seem beneficial while you are enjoying them, but they can be unhealthy and cause you to waste precious time. In time of trouble or danger or real need, these transitory pleasures will be of no use to you. Enjoy the permitted joys and pleasures, therefore, only sparingly, and devote most of your time and strength to serious and sacred things which will stand you in better stead throughout your life.

ד הוּא הָיָה אוֹמֵר, עֲשֵׂה רְצוֹנוֹ כִּרְצוֹנֶךָ
כְּדֵי שֶׁיַּעֲשֶׂה רְצוֹנְךָ כִּרְצוֹנוֹ. בַּטֵּל רְצוֹנְךָ
מִפְּנֵי רְצוֹנוֹ כְּדֵי שֶׁיְּבַטֵּל רְצוֹן אֲחֵרִים מִפְּנֵי רְצוֹנֶךָ:

4 He would say: Do His will as you would do your
own will, so that He may do your will, just as He does
His will. Set aside your will for the sake of His will, so
that He may set aside the will of others before your
will.

*   *   *

There are four great principles implied in these few impressive
words, each one of them a fundamental principle in our holy
faith. The first is the freedom of the human will; the second is the
existence of a free, personal God Who directs and guides the
world at His own discretion; the third is the positive or negative
influence of man's deeds, his commissions and omissions, on the
direction of the world in general, and on his own destiny in
particular; the fourth is an educational one, one that parents and
teachers alike should heed well—the need to strengthen the
human will when it is directed toward good things and to break it
when it inclines toward evil. There is also a direct correlation
between these four principles and *Rabban* Gamliel's previous
sayings: If our leaders shy away from contact with the authorities,
people whose friendship is superficial and whose motives are
selfish, then who will ward off dangers to the Jewish community,
and who then will appear before kings and princes to defend and
protect our people? Moreover, what is the use of gaining favor
with officials who will not stand by us in times of distress? This
mishnah tells us: If we must deal with despots, if we must try to
gain favor with the authorities, then we must also remember not
to rely on the good favor of people in power. Try, rather, to
invoke the grace of the Almighty, King of kings, Who can move
the hearts of princes, mold their designs and thwart their machi-
nations according to His own judgment.

Apply the same zeal and joy in doing God's will that you use in pursuing your own heart's desires, and the Holy One, blessed is He, will pay you in the same measure. "All that which the Lord willed, He has done in heaven and on earth, in the seas and in the deep places" (*Tehillim* 135:6). Set aside your own evil inclinations "for the sake of His will" and God will not fail to grant you His almighty help and destroy the will of your enemies. Obviously, to succeed in doing this, you must be able to control your own will fully. If man's will were not free, if in all his activities he had to yield to a strict determination, there would be no sense in commandments or prohibitions; there would be neither virtue nor vice, neither merit nor crime, neither reward nor punishment, and consequently we could assume that there would be nothing following after physical death. Murderers and robbers and adulterers would merely be yielding to predetermination in committing crimes, just as virtuous people would be doing good instinctively. The state would not be able to enact laws and directives, to punish crime nor reward merit. That is the dreadful philosophy of pessimism, the theory of the philosopher Schopenhauer and his ilk, spread by anarchists who aim to destroy all religious, social and political order. That is the teaching of modern science which would have us believe that the functioning of the entire world is rigidly controlled and restricted by unalterable, natural laws.

Science has gone astray in denying man's free will and in considering nature a god which is fettered by its own laws. If this were true, there would be no point to prayer, to trust, to hope. The world would take its course, obeying necessary and unalterable laws of nature. But our holy religion teaches us that man's will is free; it is the highest privilege that God has bestowed on man. It is this freedom which gives value to all the other privileges that man enjoys and it sheds its glow on the great deeds of heroes, of sages, and of benefactors of mankind.

It is not clear, however, how the second principle, the free will of God, to which all creation bows, is compatible with the third principle, the influence that man may have on the direction of the world and on his own fate. How can we human beings presume to give an omnipotent and omniscient God directions by praying? How can we venture to ask Him to heal our afflictions when He in His wisdom has caused them? How can we beg His blessing for the fruit of the field when He allows a bad harvest? How can we demand that He should redeem us from all evil, since both good and evil occur according to His wise plans?

The first principle answers all these questions. Since God bestowed freedom of will upon man, He has set bounds, as it were, to His own omnipotence. As our Sages teach: הכל בידי שמים חוץ מיראת שמים, "Everything is in God's hands, except the fear of God" (*Berachoth* 33b). Man can fear God or not fear Him; he can do good or evil deeds after his own choice. Since that is the case, our whole appreciation of the direction of the world gains a very different construction. We pray that God may help and assist us to make use of our freedom for our own benefit, that God may help us to return to the right path if we have gone astray, that God may facilitate our choice of the just and good by freeing us from disease and protecting us from evil. It is our choice, however, whether to consolidate or destroy the world order. Free will thus makes life a constant struggle, and one man's freedom limits that of another. Men constantly fight one another, and since a good person will not bend justice and truth in order to fight his battles, one would expect the virtuous person to succumb and the wicked to triumph. *Rabban* Gamliel tells us, however: If you will use the freedom given you for doing only that which is right and good, then you will be in constant harmony with God's will and He will protect and guard you. רצון יראיו יעשה ואת שועתם ישמע ויושיעם, "He does the will of those who revere Him; and he hears their cry and saves them" (*Tehillim* 145:19).

The fourth principle of this maxim relates to the training of man's will. Infinite, devoted love for our Father in Heaven has to be implanted in a child's heart early in life. Your child cannot be told too often about God's infinite love for His people, how He chose our forefathers above all the nations, how He saved and protected our people in miraculous ways, how He has given us his Laws for our own benefit. Man's worst enemy lurks in his own heart: the impulse to do evil. A parent, an educator, must seek to humble this impulse, to overcome it—not through excessive strictness, but through sensible instruction and loving care of the child. Excessive strictness, just as excessive indulgence, is dangerous. Excessive strictness will introduce the child to hypocrisy when he does the forbidden thing and tries to elude punishment. Indulgence will corrupt his character by fostering the bad qualities latent in him.

Most parents want to educate their children well, but do not know how. *Rabban* Gamliel makes it simple: "Do His will as you would your own; set aside your will for the sake of His will!" Do not teach your child to refrain from forbidden foods because he will get sick from them, but because his Father in Heaven forbids it. Train him from early youth to set aside his own inclinations when they run counter to God's teachings, when they are inconsistent with the precepts of our holy faith. Then your child's character will be strong enough to withstand the greatest temptations. The Sages teach us: ברצות יי דרכי איש גם אויביו ישלם אתו, " 'When a man's ways please the Lord, He will grant him peace against his enemies' (*Mishlei* 16:7), זה יצר הרע, that is, against his evil inclinations" (*Bereshith Rabbah* 54:1).

ה הִלֵּל אוֹמֵר, אַל־תִּפְרוֹשׁ מִן־הַצִּבּוּר וְאַל־
תַּאֲמִין בְּעַצְמְךָ עַד יוֹם מוֹתְךָ וְאַל־תָּדִין
אֶת־חֲבֵרְךָ עַד שֶׁתַּגִּיעַ לִמְקוֹמוֹ וְאַל־תֹּאמַר דָּבָר
שֶׁאִי אֶפְשָׁר לִשְׁמוֹעַ שֶׁסּוֹפוֹ לְהִשָּׁמֵעַ וְאַל־תֹּאמַר
לִכְשֶׁאֶפָּנֶה אֶשְׁנֶה שֶׁמָּא לֹא תִפָּנֶה:

5 Hillel says: Do not ,set yourself apart from the community; and do not trust yourself until the day of your death; and do not judge your fellowman until you have been in his situation; and do not say of anything that it cannot be understood, for in the end it will be understood; and do not say: "When I have leisure [from my business] I shall study," for you may never have leisure.

*   *   *

There has been some disagreement among the commentators as to which Hillel was the author of this mishnah—Hillel the Elder, the Babylonian scholar who became *Nasi* of Yisrael and head of the academy in Yerushalayim, or his descendant, Hillel the Younger, grandson of Rabbi Yehudah *Ha-Nasi*. Although both views are well-documented by the highest authorities, and both of these great men lived according to the principles laid down here, the generally accepted view is that Hillel the Elder said this.

DO NOT SET YOURSELF APART FROM THE COMMUNITY. Hillel, it seems, is addressing anyone who imagines himself superior to others in scholarship, piety or other virtues. Overweening pride in your own excellence is a dangerous trait, for there are likely to be others among the multitude who are more talented. Overconfidence is also a risky virtue, for you never can be sure that you will not some day succumb to temptation. Virtuous people are often severe and unkind in judging their erring and sinful fellowmen. O virtuous man, you who condemn the sinner! Have you considered how powerful were the temptations that ruined him? O rich man, you who despise the poor man who robbed his neighbor! Have you ever experienced hunger? O beloved child, you who have been given a proper education! Can you judge the unfortunate person who has grown up neglected and abused? Do not, therefore, judge your fellow until you have been in his position!

Rabbi Shemuel of Ozedah connects this mishnah to the previous one which drew attention to the risks of holding public office. It is all too understandable, he says, that a capable person would try to evade community reponsibility in order to immerse himself more deeply in Torah study, to serve God more devotedly, or perhaps simply to isolate himself from the evils and immorality he sees within the community. Yet we are commanded to pray together. We must sanctify God's name in public and we should study with others so that there will be someone to correct our errors. Furthermore, one whose concern for the community brings him into contact with undesirable influences may, with God's help, be able to counteract these influences on society.

The Torah abounds in illustrations of the benefits of obeying Hillel's maxim and the consequences of ignoring it. When God threatened to destroy the entire community, our teacher Moshe offered to be destroyed in their place; "Oh, this people have sinned a great sin, and have made themselves a god of gold; yet now, if You will forgive their sin; and if not, I pray You, blot me out of Your book which You have written" (*Shemoth* 32:31-32). And we know, of course, that the faithful shepherd's plea was granted.

The righteous Mordechai also served his community well. When Mordechai asked Esther to intercede with the king to save her people, and Esther was reluctant to appear unbidden before the king, Mordechai asked, "Why do you refuse to help your fellow Jews? Do you think that because you are the king's wife you will escape their fate? Will you not risk your life along with them? If you keep silent now, freedom and salvation will arise for the Jews from another quarter, but you and your father's house will perish!" (*Esther* 4:13-14). Conversely, Elimelech of Beith Lechem (Bethlehem), a rich man from a noble family, separated himself from the community when famine afflicted the land.

Elimelech, although pious and God fearing, feared the demands of his poor, hungry countrymen even more and he went abroad with his family. We know that God's punishing hand caught up with him, and he and his sons died within ten years.

The Men of the Great Assembly composed our prayers in such a way that a Jew never prays for himself alone, but always for the community as a whole. An individual Jew does not pray, "Give me intelligence, understanding and reason, lead me back to your Torah, pardon me for I have sinned...." No, we pray for ourselves and for all our brethren. It is not proper to request something from the Almighty without thinking of all those who are in a similar position. Anyone who does not feel the distress of the community and does not share its plight will not experience the community's salvation nor share in its joy, as it is said: שישו אתה משוש כל המתאבלים עליה, "Rejoice for joy with her all you that mourn for her" (*Yeshayahu* 66:10). Only those who have mourned the destruction of Yerushalayim will rejoice with her when she is rebuilt (*Ta'anith* 30b).

The principle אל תפרוש מן הצבור can only be applied, however, when we are not induced to do some wrong together with our congregation. A wrong can never become right just because it is sanctioned by a multitude. On the contrary, the tribe of Levi was given special privileges because they segregated themselves from the congregation and did not participate in making the golden calf. A Jew is obligated to belong to a congregation which enables him to serve God in accordance with the Torah. The *beith kenesseth, talmud Torah, shechitah, mikveh, beith kevaroth* and any other community institution must be maintained in accordance with the Laws of the Torah. If the majority of a congregation decides to make forbidden additions or deletions to the synagogue service, or perhaps, to employ a rabbi belonging to the Reform movement, which ignores sacred laws like *shechitah*, then it is the duty of all faithful Jews to part from such a community and to form a community of their own. שנאתי קהל מרעים, "I have hated every gathering of evildoers" (*Tehillim* 26:5).

DO NOT TRUST YOURSELF UNTIL THE DAY OF YOUR DEATH. In Tractate Berachoth 29a, our Sages tell us about

Yochanan the High Priest, who faithfully attended to his office for eighty years, but in his old age became a Sadducee. His father was assassinated when Yochanan was a young man, and he became both High Priest and king. He immediately struck back at the assassin and set siege to his castle. The murderer brought Yochanan's captive mother out onto the wall of his castle and threatened to kill her before her sons's eyes. Although the valorous lady encouraged her son to continue the siege regardless of her plight, he abandoned the siege in order to save her. In later years, Yochanan was privileged to hear the Divine voice in the Holy of Holies on the Day of Atonement. How tragic then, that toward the end of a conscientious and pious life, Yochanan in effect repudiated all that he had accomplished by joining those who were ultimately responsible for the final dissolution and destruction of the Jewish state. The actual reason why Yochanan joined the Sadducees is unknown, but it is easy to understand the attraction of their permissive ideas, the promise of this world's pleasures without fear of retribution. The Sadducees disavowed the immortality of the soul and rejected the idea of reward and punishment.

Our Sages say that one should never intentionally expose oneself to a test (*Sanhedrin* 107a). David, king of Israel, said, "Examine me, O Lord and try me" (*Tehillim* 26:2). Unable to stand up to His testing, David brought unspeakable sorrow upon himself. If David, the Heaven-inspired singer, the noble hero, a man after God's own heart, was unable to stand the test, how shall we insignificant and unimportant human beings be able to do so? Therefore, never be so self-satisfied in your piety nor so confident of your character that you open yourself to spiritual temptation.

Why did the prophet Eliyyahu literally run away when Izevel sent her messengers to him with an invitation? He had already stood up to the severest moral and physical tests inflicted upon him by her husband, King Achav, his soldiers and the priests of Ba'al. But "when he saw that (Izevel's message), ויֵּלֶךְ אֶל נַפְשׁוֹ, he arose and went to his soul" (*Melachim* I 19:3). The Zohar on *parashath* Vayyigash 80 explains, "What do the words mean, 'and he went to his soul'? He went to save his soul, to the tree of life to cling to it." Izevel did not threaten God's prophet with death when

she sent him the message: כי כעת מחר אשים את נפשם כנפש אחד מהם,
"...for I shall make your soul as the soul of one of them by
tomorrow at this time" (*Melachim* I 19:2). She wanted to draw him
to her court and ensnare him by her magic so that his soul would
become like that of the priests of Ba'al. וירא, Eliyyahu recognized
this danger, ויקם, then he arose, וילך אל נפשו, and decided to
escape so that he could cling to the tree of life, as before. Even a
man of Eliyyahu's great moral stature was afraid of the enticements of a bewitching, wanton woman! We should not, therefore,
rely on our own firmness of character. We should pray that our
Creator will protect us from temptation and enticement until the
day of our death and in that way, our soul will cling to the tree of
life eternally.

DO NOT JUDGE YOUR FELLOWMAN. This is similar to
Yehoshua ben Perachyah's saying (*Avoth* 1:6), "Judge all men
favorably." That is to say, if someone is not clearly in the wrong,
then give him the benefit of the doubt. Hillel says: Even if there
is no doubt that someone has committed an evil deed, still you
should not be harsh and unkind in your judgment. Consider all
the circumstances before you condemn anyone. The Sages tell us
that when King Shelomo finished building the Holy Temple, he
retired to his chamber, taking the keys with him. His wife,
Pharaoh's daughter, intentionally caused him to sleep late into
the morning. Since the keys were with the king and the king was
asleep and no one dared to wake him, the early morning sacrifice
in the Holy Temple was not offered until ten o'clock in the
morning (*Yalkut Shimoni* II:320). This was unthinkable! So young
Yarovam assembled eighty thousand men from the tribe of
Efrayim and spoke angry words against the negligent king, even
though Shelomo had only been a שוגג, one who unintentionally
does wrong. How ironic it was that when Yarovam himself became king, the sweetness of power turned his head and he became an apostate for political reasons, a מזיד, a wanton sinner, an
idol-worshiper and a demagogue (see Rashi on this mishnah).

UNTIL YOU HAVE BEEN IN HIS SITUATION. עד שתגיע למקומו
may also be taken literally to mean "in his geographical position,
his locale." A man's attitude is much influenced by his surround-

ings. When we hear from afar that someone behaves in a certain manner, does one thing or another, let us withhold our judgment until we understand the local circumstances really well. Perhaps we would see it in a different light if we were on the spot. Does Hillel mean that we should never judge our fellowman under any circumstances? If so, how can we obey God's commandment: לא תשנא את אחיך בלבבך הוכח תוכיח את עמיתך ולא תשא עליו חטא, "Do not hate your brother in your heart, but surely rebuke your neighbor, and do not bear sin because of him" (*Vayyikra* 19:17). How may we rebuke anybody without first making a judgment? To find an answer, let us delve further into the meaning of this saying and compare it with another saying. In Tractate Shabbath, the Sages tell us that once a heathen came to Hillel and asked to be taught briefly the main principles of the Jewish faith. The great teacher of Israel answered, "What you dislike, do not do to another person" (*Shabbath* 31a). He was really saying: Most people use one standard to judge themselves and a different one to judge others—but you ought to apply the same standard to judge others as you would like them to use in judging you.

This mishnah is an extension of that thought. Do not criticize your friend without first asking yourself how you would have acted in his position. If you still think he has done something wrong, call him to account for it frankly and honestly, but reprimand him gently, taking care not to offend or shame him. In fact, your judgment of him need not yet be fixed when you rebuke him, and you may thus be able to lead him back to the right path. In the light of this explanation, the maxim complements the two preceding ones most beautifully: Do not set yourself apart from the community, but live and work in it; do not be sure of yourself until the day of your death; and since you cannot be sure how you yourself will bear testing, do not judge your fellowman until you can put yourself exactly in his position.

DO NOT SAY OF ANYTHING THAT IT CANNOT BE UNDERSTOOD, FOR IN THE END IT WILL BE UNDERSTOOD. Rashi explains this in two ways. When you have an opportunity to learn something, seize it at once. The sooner you learn something, the sooner you will be able to make use of it. The other explanation is: Never speak of anything (even when you are alone) if you wish it to remain a secret, for as soon as one other person knows of it, it will become general knowledge. A commonly accepted interpretation, according to the reading of the Rambam and others, is: Never say anything that cannot be understood at once, that only careful examination and profound reflection will clarify. Hillel is repeating what Avtalyon said: "Scholars, be careful with your words"(*Avoth* 1:11). This explanation, however, refutes itself. If Hillel were warning the Sages not to permit their words to have multiple interpretations, he would not have presented his own saying in a form that provokes diverse interpretations.

The most likely explanation is: Never say that a subject is incomprehensible, because if you try hard enough you will understand it. The verb שמע not only means "to hear" but also "to understand." You will inevitably encounter deep and apparently unfathomable subjects in your studies, but do not reduce your efforts, thinking that these matters are too deep for you. The Sages say, "When someone says to you, 'I have not taken trouble and yet I have found'—do not believe him; but when someone says, 'I have taken trouble and have found'—then believe him" (*Megillah* 6b). In God's Torah there are many things that seem incomprehensible at first glance, but insistent determination and steadfast application allow us to penetrate deeply the most difficult material.

Another meaning of the word שמע is "to obey." This meaning gives us yet another interpretation of Hillel's saying. Tractate Shabbath 14b relates that Shammai and Hillel never desisted in their efforts to see that a *halachah* was introduced even in the face of widespread popular disagreement, and in the end, they saw their efforts rewarded. Hillel's saying could therefore mean: When you know that something is good and just, do not say to yourself that nothing you can do will help in any case, and so give up; keep trying and in the end you will be heard.

This can also be applied to the lesson of admonition: Do not assume you will fail, and therefore refrain from rebuking a sinful neighbor; keep trying and in the end your words will make an impression.

Our Sages tell us that God once commanded the angel of

death to kill the wicked and to spare the pious (*Shabbath* 55a). Then the Accuser stepped in front of God's throne, saying, "Lord of the Universe, why do You wish me to spare these and punish those?" And God answered, "These are completely pious and those are wholly scoundrels." The Accuser replied, "The pious ought to have warned, rebuked and stopped the wicked." God said, "It is obvious and clear to Me that the admonitions would have remained ineffective." But the Accuser retorted, "It is obvious and clear to You, but they could not know that and they should at least have done their duty and tried." God heeded the Accuser's advice, and the pious were also punished because they failed to rebuke their sinful brethren. A good word may be compared to a fruit pit that has fallen amongst brushwood and stones and therefore does not sprout. But somehow the fruit pit works its way down into the earth and eventually grows into a beautiful tree bearing the finest fruit.

DO NOT SAY, "WHEN I HAVE LEISURE [FROM MY BUSINESS] I SHALL STUDY," FOR YOU MAY NEVER HAVE LEISURE. We are told of Shammai the Elder that on all the weekdays he made preparations in honor of the Shabbath meals. When he purchased a fine animal, he kept it for the Shabbath; when he found a finer animal, he had the first animal slaughtered straight-away, keeping the finer one for the Shabbath (*Beitzah* 16a). Shammai's school teaches: Prepare for the Shabbath from the very first day of the week. Hillel the Elder, however, had a different habit, for all his actions were dedicated to the Lord's service. He used to say, ברוך יי יום יום, "Blessed be the Lord day by day" (*Tehillim* 68:20).

When Hillel dismissed his pupils after a lesson, he used to leave with them. "Rabbi," they once asked, "where are you going?" "I am going to fulfill one of God's commandments," Hillel answered. "Which one?" his disciples asked. "I am going to the baths, to bathe, to tend, to honor, to strengthen the being created in the image of God." Another time he answered that he was going out to go shopping in honor of his guest, and when the disciples inquired about this guest, he said, "That is the immortal soul that has been allotted a temporary place in my body by God.

I must look after its residence, and procure all that is necessary for it, so that the heavenly guest may feel at home in it." We learn from this that Hillel regarded everything, even the satisfaction of bodily needs, as the fulfillment of God's commandments. He ate and drank only to strengthen his body in the service of God; he enjoyed the pleasure of bathing only to honor his body as the dwelling place of a soul emanating from God. It is a great *mitzvah* to honor the Shabbath with better food and drink; but it is also a *mitzvah* to strengthen the body on weekdays through eating and drinking in the service of God. Hillel did not want to defer a *mitzvah* or to dispense with it, even in order to do a greater *mitzvah* later on. He was not anxious about the Shabbath, for he trusted in the Almighty's care; יעמס לנו האל ישועתנו, סלה, "He will supply us [with what we need], the God of our salvation, *selah*" (*Tehillim* 68:20; Rashi on *Beitzah* 16a).

It was Hillel's principle never to put off doing a *mitzvah*, even when he might have been able to do it better at a later date. It is therefore a good practice to devote an hour or longer to the study of the Torah early in the morning, when the mind is still fresh after a night's rest and still undisturbed by other matters. ואתהלכה ברחבה כי פקדיך דרשתי, "And I will walk at ease, for I have (first) studied Your Laws," (*Tehillim* 119:45), and not the reverse, "When I have first attended to my business then will I study Your laws." There are very good reasons why Hillel stressed Torah study above all the other *mitzvoth*. Torah study is a perpetual occupation; "This book of the Law shall not depart from your mouth, but you shall meditate on it every day and night that you may observe and do according to all that is written in it; for then you shall make your way prosperous, and then you shall be wise" (*Yehoshua* 1:8). Torah study is so easily cast aside— the slightest excuse suffices for most people—but one who accustoms himself to learn continually whenever and wherever he can, will always find spare time for it; and though his study is fragmented, he will in the end achieve something great. "And I will walk at ease, for I have studied Your Laws: I will speak of Your testimonies before kings and will not be ashamed" (*Tehillim* 119:45-46).

And so it is clear that this part of the mishnah, too, is linked to

the parts preceding it. Before judging your neighbor, judge yourself; do not hesitate to rebuke your neighbor if it is warranted;
even if the rebuke is likely to be ignored at first, it will somehow
be a good influence; be as strict with yourself as with others and
do not say, "When I have leisure from my business I shall occupy
myself with the Torah." Cling to the "tree of life," that is, to the
word of God, as it is said, עץ חיים היא למחזיקים בה ותמכיה מאשר, "It
is a tree of life to those who hold on to it and those who follow it
will be happy" (*Mishlei* 3:18).

ו הוּא הָיָה אוֹמֵר, אֵין בּוּר יְרֵא חֵטְא וְלֹא
עַם הָאָרֶץ חָסִיד וְלֹא הַבַּיְשָׁן לָמֵד וְלֹא
הַקַּפְּדָן מְלַמֵּד וְלֹא כָּל־הַמַּרְבֶּה בִסְחוֹרָה מַחְכִּים
וּבַמָּקוֹם שֶׁאֵין אֲנָשִׁים הִשְׁתַּדֵּל לִהְיוֹת אִישׁ:

6 He would say: An uncivilized man cannot fear sin,
an ignorant man cannot be truly pious, nor can a
timid man learn, nor a hot-tempered man teach, and
one who is too deeply involved in business cannot
make others wise, and in a place where there are no
men, strive to be a man.

*   *   *

According to *Rabbenu* Menachem Azaryah de Fano, the accepted
reading הוא היה אומר, "he would say," was erroneously tran-
scribed and should read instead הלל אומר, "Hillel says," because
this mishnah was a saying of the elder Hillel. Most commentators
hold the view, however, that הוא היה אומר is correct, and that both
sayings are from the mouth of the elder Hillel. In subject as well,
this mishnah follows the sense of the previous mishnah. After his
warning never to postpone Torah study, Hillel characterizes six
different types of men, from the lowest to the highest, in relation
to their devotion to study.

The word בור is derived from the Aramaic word meaning "to
lie fallow" (see *Bava Metzia* 104a) and refers to the simplest type
of intellect, possessed by a man who neither learns nor works,
who has neither worldly nor Torah knowledge and is completely
unproductive. Such a person does not fear sin. The next type,
עם הארץ, literally "[one of] the people of the land," refers to an
ordinary man who has little or no knowledge of the Torah but is
a well-meaning, law-abiding citizen. The בישן, "the timid one," is
a falsely modest person who may learn, indeed wishes to learn,
but is so terrified of being laughed at and so concerned for his
dignity that he does not admit his failure to understand, and so
never learns anything properly. We must clearly distinguish be-

tween the בישן and the בוש פנים in this lesson, however. The בוש פנים is a bashful and modest man; of him we read, "The בוש פנים has his share in the Life to Come" (*Avoth* 5:23). The בישן harbors a false sense of shame and because of it, he remains ignorant.

Neither a קפדן, "a hot-tempered person," who lacks patience with his pupils and therefore cannot successfully transmit his knowledge to them, nor a מרבה בסחורה, a scholar who is too concerned with the business world, will ever be able to train scholars of importance. Ilfa and Yochanan were two disciples, equally gifted and equally poor. Ilfa entered into business and sought worldly profits; although he was a great scholar, his name is only rarely mentioned in the Talmud. Yochanan, however, persevered through years of hardship, became a great rabbi and raised up many famous disciples.

Only a man who takes it upon himself to train other men to grow in wisdom deserves to be called איש (man) as it is said: והאיש משה, "and the man Moshe." If your town contains no "men" except the uncivilized, the ignorant, the unlearned, those who cannot teach, or even scholars who devote themselves to other occupations and do not find enough time for students, then endeavor to be a "man" yourself so that your generation does not become barren; for every individual in Yisrael has the duty to see to it that the Torah is preserved and passed on to future generations.

FEAR SIN. "Rabbi Chanina ben Dosa said: He in whom the fear of sin goes before his wisdom, his wisdom will endure" (*Avoth* 3:11). Hillel tells us that an ignorant man must first acquire wisdom and so learn to fear sin. Rabbi Chanina ben Dosa's lesson seems to contradict Hillel's; yet both teach that fear of sin is the more important value. This is reminiscent, too, of Rabbi's saying (*Avoth* 2:1), "If you calculate the harm you do to the world by committing a sin, you will surely fear sin." Hillel not only enumerates these six categories of men, but at the same time characterizes their potential growth in terms of יראת חטא (fear of sin), חסידות (true piety), and השתדלות (great striving).

Let us see what is said in the Gemara about fear of sin:

> Rabbi Pinchas ben Ya'ir said: Diligence in the service of the Creator (זריזות) leads to cleanliness; cleanliness (נקיות) leads

to purity; purity (טהרה) leads to abstinence; abstinence
(פרישות) leads to holiness; holiness (קדושה) leads to humility;
humility (ענוה) leads to fear of sin; fear of sin (יראת חטא)
leads to true piety; true piety (חסידות) leads to possession of
the Divine spirit; the Divine spirit (רוח הקודש) leads to the
resurrection of the dead; and the resurrection of the dead
(תחיית המתים) comes through Eliyyahu of blessed memory,
amen.

(Sotah, last mishnah)

Fear of sin and true piety are ranked high in this lofty grada-
tion. Thus Hillel's words must actually mean that a בור, even
though he may be diligent in the service of the Creator, clean in
his relations with his fellow men, pure, abstinent, holy and humble, but still unlearned, cannot attain the grade of יראת חטא.
Similarly, an עם הארץ might reach the level of יראת חטא, but he
cannot achieve true piety. The simple translation of both expressions, however, does not entirely explain this mishnah.

Most commentators understand בור to mean a man who is
untutored in every respect and עם הארץ to mean a man who has a
general education but no Torah knowledge. Tractate Berachoth
47b concludes: אחרים אומרים אפילו קרא ושנה ולא שמש תלמידי
חכמים הרי זה עם הארץ אמר רב הונא הלכה כאחרים, "An *am haaretz* is a
person who may be well-versed in Bible and Mishnah but has not
advanced to the study of Gemara" (see Rashi on this passage). In
those days, knowledge of Gemara could only be acquired
through continuous association with the Sages. Through this
association, a man learned two things: to comprehend both the
actual sense and the deeper meaning of the Written and the Oral
Law, and to observe the behavior of the Sages with regard to
things like *derech eretz* and *lefanim mishurath ha-din*, things that are
not strictly prescribed by the Law.

Thus the עם הארץ was one who had not learned to think and
to study, while the בור had not even observed the behavior of the
Sages. The passage in Tractate Sotah teaches us how many levels
of moral and intellectual attainment we must master before attaining יראת חטא. A man who has not eagerly studied the Torah
and associated with sages (and thus cannot ponder on the direc-

tion of the world) is called a בור by Hillel. Hillel's saying, therefore, does not contraditct that of Rabbi Chanina (*Avoth* 3:11).
Such a person can be God-fearing and honest, can walk humbly
on earth, but he cannot truly fear sin because he does not comprehend the calamitous significance of a man's sin in the world
order.

TRULY PIOUS. In the passage in Tractate Sotah we have
recalled, חסידות is a grade higher than יראת חטא. Just as fear of
sin denotes the correct appreciation of transgression, true piety
embodies the right appreciation of *mitzvoth*. When you consider
what you will accomplish for yourself and for the community by
obeying a commandment, when you consider that you are con-
tributing to the preservation of the world, you will love God's
commandments more than anything else and you will be a *chasid*,
a truly pious person. King David was called a *chasid* because, first
of all, he gave up his own comfort in order to be able to praise
God; second, he undertook many difficult tasks in the service of
God willingly and at the cost of his own prestige; and third, he
never relied wholly upon his own opinion in sacred matters, but
asked the advice of his teacher (*Berachoth* 4a). To acquire these
virtues and perfect them in ourselves, we must search deeply into
the truths of the Torah and work hard to train ourselves. The
best method of doing so is to associate with sages.

IN A PLACE WHERE THERE ARE NO MEN, STRIVE TO BE A
MAN. איש is not only "man" but "master" (see *Tosafoth Yom Tov* on
Avoth 1:3, also Bertinoro on *Yoma* 1:3). These final words of the
mishnah may be explained in the following way: In a place where
there is a shortage of suitable leaders, brush aside all your scru-
ples and become a leader yourself. If you feel that you are better
able to work for the common good than others, try to become the
head of the community. If there are other equally qualified—or
even more qualified—men, then gladly leave it to them. There
was a time when the gentle Hillel himself became passionately
angry because there was a shortage of suitable men and he felt
constrained to take over the leadership of his people (see
Pesachim 66a).

On a deeper level, Hillel's words can be taken to mean: Even in a place where there are no men to equal you in Torah knowledge, do not be satisfied with what you have achieved, but endeavor to become ever wiser, ever more perfect. Indeed, this last part of the mishnah is reminiscent of Hillel's saying (*Avoth* 1:13): ודלא מוסיף יסיף "One who does not increase [his knowledge] decreases it." Another explanation of this mishnah reminds us that many people are only virtuous and God-fearing when they are observed by others, but they are not strong enough to resist temptation when they believe that their actions will not be found out. Hillel calls out to such people: Even where there are no other men and you are alone, be a man, stand up to and resist temptation.

ז אַף הוּא רָאָה גֻּלְגֹּלֶת אַחַת שֶׁצָּפָה עַל־
פְּנֵי הַמָּיִם. אָמַר לָהּ, עַל דְּאַטֵּיפְתְּ
אַטִיפוּךְ וְסוֹף מְטַיְּפָיִךְ יְטוּפוּן:

7 Moreover he saw a skull floating on the surface of
the water, [and] he said to it: Because you drowned
[others], they have drowned you, and in the end those
who drowned you, will themselves be drowned.

*   *   *

The commentators ask a number of questions. To begin with,
how did Hillel know that the man, whose skull he saw floating
on the water, had been drowned? Secondly, how did Hillel
know that the man whose skull he saw had been a murderer
and had thrown another man in the water? Furthermore, why
does Hillel say that murderers are punished by their own
methods? Experience teaches us that many criminals die in
their beds calmly and peacefully, without being punished for
their crimes in this life. Why does Hillel assume that several
people cast this person into the water? "Because you have
drowned, they have drowned you." If Hillel deduces the principle that a murderer is always punished by his own method, it
must be asked: How can this principle be proven in a direct
line back to Adam, the first man? The Torah, too, tells of many
men who were murdered who did not themselves commit murder—the best known example is Hevel (Abel). Even the first
word of this mishnah, אף (moreover), seems to refer to something else that we do not know about.

All these problems, as Rashi informs us, have induced many
people to reject this mishnah and not to include it in the Chapters
of the Fathers. This is an extreme view, for the difficulties mentioned can be resolved and there is no doubt that this saying
originates from the pen of the great man to whom it is attributed.
It is, in fact, confirmed in Tractate Sukkah 53a and in chapter 12
of Avoth of Rabbi Nathan. The latter reference also gives us some
commentary on the unusual form of the mishnah and on the use

of the word אף. There, another incident precedes this one. The first incident was not included in this mishnah because no maxim was attached to it, but the second event, the one that inspired Hillel's remark, was included and was logically introduced by the word אף.

In Tractate Sukkah, Rashi explains that Hillel recognized the skull floating on the water as that of a notorious murderer who had been in the habit of severing the heads of victims from their bodies and throwing the heads into the water. So Hillel told him: Retribution has already caught up with you, but those others who murdered you have not yet been judged and will not escape their just deserts either. We must realize that Hillel lived in a time of the most dreadful party rivalry and civil war. The Idumean slave, Herod, had usurped the throne of Yehudah with the help of the Romans. The people rebelled, Herod fought them, defeated them and took bloody revenge. In addition to party warfare and civil strife, robber bands roved about, burning towns and villages, murdering and robbing peaceful citizens. Hillel the gentle one, the peaceful one, stayed far away from the party conflict and also sought to keep his disciples away from it. He lived solely for the study of the Torah and the observance of God's commandments and taught his disciples to do the same. When he spoke to the skull on the water, he was actually saying to his disciples: See, that is the fate of men of violence. The punishment for their deeds will suit their crimes. This principle is also expressed in Tractate Sotah 8b and 9b: במדה שאדם מודד בה מודדין לו, "The measure with which a man measures is used to measure him."

AND IN THE END THOSE WHO DROWNED YOU, WILL THEMSELVES BE DROWNED. Rabbi Shemuel of Ozedah (among other commentators), found the key to this statement in the word וסוף, "and in the end." This word seems superfluous, since Hillel could easily have said ומטיפיך יטופון, "And those who have drowned you will be drowned as well." Commentators think that Hillel wanted to refer to the doctrine of transmigration of the soul, גלגול הנשמות, by using the word וסוף. When a murderer dies without his misdeed having been punished in this world, his immortal soul will pass over into another human or animal body until he suffers the same cruel death as he once inflicted on someone else. Nevertheless, Rabbi Heller, in Tosafoth Yom Tov, does not accept this explanation. He says: כמו שאין המקרא יוצא מידי פשוטו כך אין המשנה יוצאת מידי משמעה המובנת לכל, "Just as with a verse of the Bible, the simple sense is the right one, so also with the Mishnah; only the simple, generally comprehensible sense may be applied."

ח הוּא הָיָה אוֹמֵר, מַרְבֶּה בָשָׂר מַרְבֶּה רִמָּה, מַרְבֶּה נְכָסִים מַרְבֶּה דְאָגָה, מַרְבֶּה נָשִׁים מַרְבֶּה כְשָׁפִים, מַרְבֶּה שְׁפָחוֹת מַרְבֶּה זִמָּה, מַרְבֶּה עֲבָדִים מַרְבֶּה גָזֵל, מַרְבֶּה תוֹרָה מַרְבֶּה חַיִּים, מַרְבֶּה יְשִׁיבָה מַרְבֶּה חָכְמָה, מַרְבֶּה עֵצָה מַרְבֶּה תְבוּנָה, מַרְבֶּה צְדָקָה מַרְבֶּה שָׁלוֹם. קָנָה שֵׁם טוֹב קָנָה לְעַצְמוֹ, קָנָה לוֹ דִבְרֵי תוֹרָה קָנָה לוֹ חַיֵּי הָעוֹלָם הַבָּא:

8 He would say: The more flesh, the more worms; the more property, the more worries; the more women, the more superstition; the more maidservants, the more lewdness; the more manservants, the more larceny. The more Torah, the more life; the more study, the more wisdom; the more counsel, the more understanding; the more justice/charity, the more peace/perfection. One who has acquired a good name has made an acquisition for himself; one who has acquired the words of Torah has acquired eternal life.

* * *

Hillel's remarks about the skull he saw floating on the water are regarded by most commentators as an introduction to this mishnah. The fundamental idea of the last mishnah is that Divine justice governs the earth, that man can expect retribution for his deeds, that there is no such thing as chance, that Divine providence directs and guides everything. Every human being therefore decides his own fortune; his fate is but the fruit of his own deeds. But when daily experience seems to teach us the very opposite, when we see that some righteous people suffer greatly and others who are wicked enjoy wealth, good health and strength, then this mishnah tells us that all these things are externals and do not signify real happiness. The wise Hillel instructs us to reflect on what we do and evaluate the consequences of our deeds with an eye to our eternal happiness.

THE MORE FLESH, THE MORE WORMS. It is a Divine commandment to guard your life and maintain a healthy body. Hillel fulfilled this duty with great care. He went to the baths regularly to preserve the residence of his immortal soul. But the baths, eating, drinking and other bodily satisfactions were not an end in themselves to him—they were only a means to make his body an appropriate instrument for his immortal soul to attain a greater spiritual level. Some commentators say that מרבה רמה (the more worms) refers to the time after death when the body is in the grave and becomes food for worms; but if so, what does that matter to the soul? Others, therefore, say that these words refer to the time between death and burial when the immortal soul can still suffer because of the condition of the body. (See Tosafoth Yom Tov on this mishnah.) Yet others, like Rabbi Wessely, explain that the body begins to decay even during a man's lifetime—an observation which has been confirmed by the discovery of viruses and germs and the modern pathology of internal disorders. Many people die in the prime of life because they eat too much, and Hillel therefore phrases his warning in terms of bodily overindulgence, מרבה בשר, which leads to early death, מרבה רמה.

THE MORE PROPERTY, THE MORE WORRIES. Ponder carefully the great Sage's words. He does not say: One who has a large fortune has great worries. He says rather: One who increases his property has more worries. Riches granted through God's blessing may be regarded as a means to an end—a pleasant life and good deeds. The constant preoccupation with increasing one's possessions, however, creates anxieties which prevent the peaceful enjoyment of prosperity. Continual striving after riches draws a man away from the Torah and distracts him from the careful performance of the commandments. It overrides his concern for the well-being of his family, banishes peaceful slumber from his couch, and stifles his feeling for the community. Moreover, if he succeeds in increasing his fortune he will still not be at peace. The more he has, the more he will want to possess. As it is said: אהב כסף לא ישבע כסף...גם זה הבל, "One who loves money will not be satisfied with money...this is also futility" (*Koheleth* 5:9), or as Rashi explains, "One who loves money for itself, regarding it not as a means but as an end in itself, will never be satisfied no matter how much he amasses."

THE MORE WOMEN, THE MORE SUPERSTITION. The most powerful and dangerous of all earthly pleasures is the satisfaction of sensual love. As we have learned, the teachings in Chapters of the Fathers do not deal with the details of the Law itself, but rather reflect on the highest range of morality possible within the parameters of the Law; that is, refraining from doing even that which is permitted and doing more than that which is commanded. We know, for instance, that polygamy is not prohibited either in the Bible or in the Talmud, and it is specifically permitted in some cases to oriental Jews. However, *Rabbenu* Gershom, called the Light of the Diaspora, together with ninety-nine colleagues, revoked the legality of polygamy for occidental Jews more than one thousand years ago. Furthermore, although it was originally permitted, we find several restrictions on it which suggest that it was never wholly recommended.

Indeed, the Sages found a hint in the Torah that warns against marrying more than one wife: they placed side by side the two verses in which the short word ולו occurs. One states ולו שתי נשים, "and he had two wives " (*Shemuel* I, 1:2), and the other reads ולו היכן כלי מות, "and he prepared for himself the weapons of death" (*Tehillim* 7:14). The meaning is evident: A person who marries two wives will destroy himself. When God created the world He gave the first man only one wife; that is the model for all time. Therefore when Hillel equates women (plural) with superstition, he is referring to the conflict between man's nature and his obligations. It is impossible for a husband to allot an equal measure of love to two or more wives. The natural inclination is to favor one wife over the others, and this must not only have a most harmful effect on the children's education but must also cause quarrels between the wives. Since the feminine temperament is more inclined to superstition, the inevitable rivalry and jealousy in a plural household will result in the practice of superstitious rites.

THE MORE MAIDSERVANTS, THE MORE LEWDNESS; THE MORE MANSERVANTS, THE MORE LARCENY. Hillel's adage gives us a natural sequence of events. First the sensualist looks after himself, after his own body, מרבה בשר; then he seeks to procure the permanent means of good living, מרבה נכסים; if he succeeds in doing that, he marries many wives for the satisfaction of his passions, מרבה נשים; the women need female servants to serve them, מרבה שפחות; when the household is large, male servants are needed to do heavy work, מרבה עבדים; but the female servants do not usually have high morals, מרבה שפחות מרבה זמה, and they will introduce immorality into his house and dishonor his name. A profusion of male servants encourages dishonesty and pilfering from the master, מרבה עבדים מרבה גזל, and, according to another explanation, the dissipation of his wealth on vanities instead of help for the poor, thus indirectly stealing from them.

THE MORE TORAH, THE MORE LIFE. There are, on the other hand, pleasures which man can never have enough of, and the great Sage enumerates them in this half of the mishnah, in a sequence which corresponds to those listed in the first half. Do not think, Hillel says, that painstaking occupation with the Torah is unhealthy for you. It cannot be compared with other indulgences which weaken the body and paralyze the will when you invest all your strength in them. As we read in Mishlei 3:8, "It (the Torah) will bring health to your body and refreshment to your bones," and in Tehillim 19:9, "The mandates of the Lord are upright, rejoicing the heart," and man's heart is the source of his life. Similarly we read, "For with You is the fountain of life, in Your light we see light" (*Tehillim* 36:10). The Torah is, after all, a means to acquire fear of God, to recognize His path, His love, His justice, and the fear of God in turn leads to a prolongation of life. "The fear of God adds days, but the years of the wicked shall be shortened" (*Mishlei* 10:27); "The fear of God grants life" (ibid. 19:23); "the fear of the Lord is a fountain of life, which teaches how to depart from the snares of death" (ibid. 14:27). And in the Torah itself we are taught: "For it (the Torah) is not a vain thing for you, but it is your life and the length of your days" (*Devarim* 32:47).

What is actually meant by the word "life"? The German poet Goethe rightly said, "A useless life is an early death," and we are taught in the Talmud that an idler can be compared to a person who is always asleep. To be really alive therefore means to fill your days and hours with good and useful activity. There are people who reach the age of eighty or ninety or more and all the achievements of their lives are equal to zero; there are others who fill their lives with evil and wicked deeds whose achievements total to a negative number. On the other hand, there are men and women who achieve such great things during the comparatively short period of their lives that their beneficial influence is felt for decades and even centuries. A life of sorrow is also an empty life. "And Ya'akov lived in the land of Egypt for seventeen years" (*Bereshith* 47:28). Only during those years did he really live; the twenty-two years before were not worthy of being called life because, sunk in grief for his lost son, he thought only of going down to his grave.

To enjoy a meaningful life, one requires both a useful occupation and tranquillity. Both are provided by occupation with the Torah. "The more Torah, the more life" is precisely the opposite of the saying, "The more flesh, the more worms." Sensual pleasures are transitory; they give momentary enjoyment but their aftermath is harmful. The pleasures of Torah study are enduring, for they ennoble the heart, expand the spirit and give the body long life and joy.

THE MORE STUDY, THE MORE WISDOM. The original meaning of the word ישיבה (*yeshivah*) was "sitting." Then it came to mean "sitting in a place where the Sages teach." The way to increase wisdom is by sitting and listening to words of knowledge directly from the mouths of the Sages. We are told in Avoth 1:1 that Moshe received the Torah from Sinai and handed it down to Yehoshua and the latter to the Elders and these to the Prophets and so forth. That is the *Mesorah*, the Tradition, the Oral Law, and it will always be considered Oral Law, that is, it will always retain the character of Tradition, even though it was eventually written down in the Mishnah and the Talmud. The character of the Oral Law can best be transmitted through oral instruction by sages. In the *yeshivah*, when the teachers instruct, the students do not always immediately understand, but by their questions they force the teachers to express themselves more clearly. Intellectual dispute between companions, between defenders and opponents of a particular viewpoint, becomes an instrument for discovering the truth, for mistakes are refuted and competent criticism is appreciated.

"The more sitting/study, the more wisdom" parallels Hillel's second phrase, "the more property, the more worry." "Who is like the wise man and who knows what things mean? A man's wisdom lights up his face and transforms his countenance" (*Koheleth* 8:1). Wisdom teaches a man to walk the straight path and to know that he has chosen correctly. The Sages tell of a wise man, a Talmudic scholar who was forced to leave his homeland and travel on a ship together with many merchants. One had gold and silver utensils, another precious stones and jewelry, a third, garments of silk and purple, a fourth, spices and so on. "Where are your goods?" the others asked him. "I have gathered my goods at the *yeshivah*," he replied, "and I carry them all with me in my head." They laughed at him. The ship was eventually captured by a pirate, all their goods were appropriated and they were taken to be sold as slaves. The merchants cried and lamented, but the scholar preserved his composure. Later, at the slave market, a man came to look at them and said to the scholar, "Wisdom shines from your eyes. Are you a scholar?" "I have learned at the *yeshivah* in my town," he replied modestly. The man bought him, set him free and took him home. He was later elected Rabbi and teacher of that congregation and was able to purchase the freedom of his traveling companions as well (*Yerushalmi, Berachoth*).

THE MORE COUNSEL, THE MORE UNDERSTANDING. What is עצה and what is תבונה? The basis of this saying is probably a verse of the Bible where these two terms are used together: לו עצה ותבונה, "He [God] has counsel and understanding" (*Iyyov* 12:13). The word עצה has about the same meaning as "counsel" in English. An intelligent man prefers not to give counsel because it is so difficult to give the right kind and he will probably not be thanked for it. The one who does act upon another's advice will wonder if he should, perhaps, have done the opposite, and of course he will blame his counselor for any difficulties he encounters. Apparently it is better to withhold one's counsel.

Hillel's maxims, however, teach just the opposite. Giving wise counsel is the practical application of all that has gone before: more study of Torah, deeper examination of the Oral Law, evermore sharpening of the mental faculties and acquisition of more and more wisdom—all this raises a man to a level from which he can eventually give good counsel, and so he should! His counsel will of course be drawn from the live fountain of Torah, which is also called "counsel" (*Mishlei* 1:30), and he will attain for himself still more clarity of thought and exactitude in judgment by being asked frequently for his advice. The word תבונה denotes a higher stage of wisdom than חכמה; it is the practical application of knowledge learned in theory. In Kantian terminology, חכמה is pure reason and תבונה is practical reason, and the latter can only be acquired through experience. בישישים חכמה וארך ימים תבונה, "With the aged is wisdom, and understanding [is] in a long life" (*Iyyov* 12:12).

THE MORE JUSTICE/CHARITY, THE MORE PEACE/PERFECTION. Each of these terms, *tzedakah* and *shalom*, expresses a comprehensive concept found only in the Hebrew language and cannot be directly translated by a single word. In Biblical usage, the term *tzedakah* comprehends all the excellent virtues man can acquire and the one who practices them is called a *tzaddik*. They are also used in reference to God, the most perfect Being: לך יי הצדקה, "to you, O Lord, is righteousness" (*Daniyyel* 9:7), and צדיק יי בכל דרכיו, "The Lord is righteous in all his ways" (*Tehillim* 145:17). In the usage of the Sages, *tzedakah* means both doing good deeds and, in particular, giving alms to the needy. Where the word *tzedakah* occurs in the Bible we usually translate it as "justice" or "righteousness," but sometimes as "virtue" or "benevolence." The word *shalom* (שלום) is usually translated as "peace" but it also denotes completion, wholeness or perfection and is therefore also used as one of the names of the Almighty.

Knowing the Talmudic usage of the words illuminates Hillel's saying for us. The goods of this world are very unevenly distributed: one person is born in luxury, surrounded by love and care from his earliest youth, and has his heart's desires easily fulfilled; another person is born in poverty and distress and grows up hungry and full of worries. The contrast is even more obvious when a wealthy person suddenly becomes poor or a lowly one rises to a privileged position. We therefore tend to doubt the perfect justice of Divine providence. So Hillel teaches us that earthly goods are not valuable in themselves, that the joys and pleasures of this world, tremendous wealth, the satisfaction of every desire, power, honor and reputation, are not only worthless in themselves but also bear within them the seeds of evil and wickedness. He contrasts these with things that can be obtained by anyone, including the poor and humble, things which are a source of true happiness and eternal blessing. The Torah is a gift of the Almighty and it is available to everyone; yet we must often see to it that the boy born in poverty receives our help to enable him to learn.

Although the root of the word *shalom* (שלום) means "perfection," since war, conflict and dispute destroy perfection, the word *shalom* can also mean "peace," the opposite of "war." The concept of peace has two aspects: peace between God and man, and peace between human beings. *Tzedakah* promotes peace in both directions. Justice and peace are also associated in the case of Pinchas. When Yisrael, toward the end of their wanderings in the desert, were encamped at Shittim, many were seduced to prostitution and idolatry by the daughters of Midyan. A prince, the chief of the tribe of Shimon, acted with unspeakable impudence and brought his Midyanite woman before Moshe and the Elders as they stood in the entrance to the Tabernacle weeping. Pinchas arose and stabbed both the man and the woman. This bold action is called *tzedakah* by the Psalmist: ותחשב לו לצדקה, "And that was counted to him for righteousness" (*Tehillim* 106:31) and God spoke, "Behold, I bestow upon him My covenant of peace [for it]" (*Bemidbar* 25:12). Because of his *tzedakah* (righteousness), Pinchas restored peace between our Father in Heaven and His people. Had Pinchas not immediately punished the crime, immorality and idolatry would have destroyed the perfection, and with it the peace, of Yisrael.

ONE WHO HAS ACQUIRED A GOOD NAME HAS MADE AN
ACQUISITION FOR HIMSELF. Most commentators do not add a
word of explanation to this saying of Hillel. It seems so simple, so
self-evident: No earthly possession is secure—however large a
fortune may be, it can be lost; thrones can topple and power and
glory disappear; the soundest constitution is vulnerable to disease; the deepest love is vulnerable to death. And even if a man
enjoys many worldly possessions, in peace and health to the end
of his life, he will still have to leave them behind when he dies.
This is not so with a good name.

"Rabbi Shimon says, 'There are three crowns: the royal
crown, the priestly crown and the crown of the Torah; but the
crown of a good name surpasses all three' " (*Avoth* 4:17). And
likewise God prophesies through the prophet's mouth, "Let not
the childless say,'Behold, I am a dried-up tree.' For thus says the
Lord to the childless who observe My Shabbaths and live in
accordance with My will, keeping to My covenant. And I will give
them in My house and within My walls strength and a name
better than sons and daughters; I will give them an eternal name
that will not be destroyed"(*Yeshayahu* 56:3-5).

Although this explanation seems logical and clear, something
remains to be said. It is not quite correct to say that a good name
cannot be lost. Sometimes slanderers destroy the good name of a
perfectly innocent person. Sometimes a good name will outlive a
truly pious person for only a short time. There are also cases
where a good name is not authentic. The Sages teach: It is better
for you to be regarded as a fool by everyone all your life, than to
be a malefactor before your Creator for one hour. Striving after a
good name is not praiseworthy in itself. We should walk with our
God in all modesty, not seeking outward glory; we should do
good privately and not make a show of our charity; fear of God
should dwell in our heart and should not attract the eyes of the
multitude through peculiar, conspicuous actions. What then do
Hillel, Rabbi Shimon and Yeshayahu mean?

We read in the Torah: והיה עקב תשמעון את המשפטים האלה ושמרתם
ועשיתם אתם ושמר יי אלוהיך לך את הברית ואת החסד אשר נשבע
לאבותיך: ואהב וברכך..., "And it shall come to pass if you listen to
these judgments and keep and do them, that the Lord your God

shall keep for you the covenant and the kindness which He swore unto your fathers; and He will love you and bless you..." (*Devarim* 7:12). The least analytical reader will notice that the first part of this passage is addressed to the whole of Yisrael while the second part of the verse is addressed to the individual. God demands of all Israel obedience to His word. In this respect, one man is not to be distinguished from another. It is only the normal state of affairs when all Jews fear God and keep His commandments, and no one individual can earn a name better than any other. But when God grants rewards every single individual is taken into account, as if he alone were virtuous and just and had walked in fear of God on earth.

The point, therefore, is that we must try to acquire a שם טוב with our Father in Heaven. That name cannot be ruined by a slanderer, and can never fade away, since there is no oblivion before His throne; such a name becomes a possession that can never be lost; it will outlast life on earth. Your fellowmen may call you a fool when you place the observance of God's commandments over the acquisition of external advantages, but if you acquire a good name with God, שם עולם אשר לא יכרת that will be "an everlasting good name, inalienable and indestructible."

ONE WHO HAS ACQUIRED THE WORDS OF TORAH HAS ACQUIRED ETERNAL LIFE. This final passage contains the essence of the whole mishnah. Hillel contrasts five earthly assets with five spiritual concepts, the central one of which is מרבה תורה, "the more study of Torah." Here, in the final passage, however, we do not read, "One who has learned words of Torah," but "One who has acquired words of Torah." When you have made the words of the Torah completely your own, in that they become the yardstick for all your thinking and behavior and you apply them in every situation, then you have also acquired eternal life.

Further, והמשכילים יזהרו כזהר הרקיע ומצדיקי הרבים ככוכבים לעולם ועד, "And the learned ones will shine as the brightness of the firmament, and those who make many righteous, [will shine] as the stars, forever and ever" (*Daniyyel* 12:3). Those who have absorbed the words of the Torah so thoroughly that those words have become completely their own, will not wish to keep them only to themselves. They will endeavor to pass them on, to spread the knowledge everywhere. That is the task of our people as a whole and the duty of every individual Jew on earth—to spread the light of Divine knowledge. He who fulfills this task will shine. Can such a small thing be compared with something so vast? Behold, we read in the holy Zohar (at the beginning of *Bereshith*) that the light-giving spark slumbers in a secret place; its beam is like a small dot, but then it spreads, erecting a palace of splendor and glory. Thought can be compared to light. Thought slumbers in a secret place, and the Torah is the instrument that awakens it. The teaching of our omniscient God strengthens the spark and it becomes a flaming sun that lights up the universe, and this light can never be extinguished. The soul ignited by it acquires eternal life in the World to Come.

"And this secret," explains the Zohar, "is indicated in the prophet's words, '...the holy seed shall be the stock [of the nation of Yisrael]' (*Yeshayahu* 6:13)." The prophet Yeshayahu foresaw a very sad period in our history, when even the tenth of the nation that would survive the destruction and devastation would be in danger. With the terebinth and the oak, so long as a tiny stem remains, a seed will replenish their stock; in the same way Yisrael cannot be destroyed—a new seed will always flower and grow and thrive. But the young stem needs the hand of the gardener, the teacher, the מצדיקי הרבים, those who make many righteous. As they maintain our people, so they maintain the world. They will therefore shine as the stars, forever, and having given light to this world, they will continue to do so in the next.

Hillel teaches: sensuality, avarice, passion, immorality, immoderate ambition—they lead a man to ruin, not only destroying life in this world but depriving him of eternal bliss. Studying the Torah, understanding spiritual values, using wisdom in everyday life, dispensing charity, all these earn the good name that is recorded in God's eternal book. What are worldly joys compared with the delights of beholding Divine glory, which no man can relate or describe, of which we read, "No eye has seen it but You, God alone!" (*Yeshayahu* 64:3).

ט רַבָּן יוֹחָנָן בֶּן־זַכַּאי קִבֵּל מֵהִלֵּל וּמִשַּׁמַּאי.
הוּא הָיָה אוֹמֵר, אִם לָמַדְתָּ תּוֹרָה הַרְבֵּה
אַל־תַּחֲזִיק טוֹבָה לְעַצְמְךָ כִּי לְכָךְ נוֹצָרְתָּ:

9 *Rabban* Yochanan ben Zakkai received [the Tradition] from Hillel and Shammai. He would say: If you have learned a great deal of Torah, do not pride yourself on it, for this is the purpose for which you were created.

*   *   *

The Mishnah now continues to enumerate the line of those who passed on the Tradition. *Rabban* Yochanan ben Zakkai was the youngest disciple of the great Hillel and he outlived all three of Hillel's descendants: Shimon, his son, *Rabban* Gamliel the Elder, his grandson, and his great-grandson Rabbi Shimon ben Gamliel. *Rabban* Yochanan ben Zakkai was a merchant, but from the age of forty he devoted himself exclusively to the study of the holy Torah and became a member of the great *Sanhedrin*. At the age of eighty he opened an academy of learning in Yerushalayim and devoted the rest of his life to teaching and leading the community. Our Sages describe his universal scholarship and prodigious zeal, saying, "Rabbi Yochanan ben Zakkai never in his whole life uttered profane talk nor walked four cubits without Torah or without *tefillin*. Because his thoughts were always occupied with Torah, he was careful not to pass through filthy alleys. He was always the first to arrive at the academy in the morning, never slept or dozed there, and was the last to leave at night. He was never to be found sitting idle, no one but himself ever opened the door to his disciples, and he never in his life said anything that he had not heard from his teachers.

"Only on the eve of Passover and on the eve of the Day of Atonement would he ever say, 'It is time to leave the academy.' His knowledge comprised everything worth knowing, both the Written and the Oral Law and all the ramifications, explanations and interpretations as they are contained in the holy Torah,

Mishnah and Gemara. His scholarship extended to astronomy and geometry, botany and metaphysics, and he knew how to present his deep thoughts clearly to his disciples through allegories both from the lives of great men and from the animal kingdom. Nothing was hidden from him, neither the greatest nor the smallest matters—the greatest: metaphysical truths; the smallest: the dialectical discussions of Abbaye and Rava. In him was fulfilled the promise, 'That I may cause those that love Me to inherit substance, and that I may fill their treasures' " (*Mishlei* 8:21, *Sukkah* 28a).

Rabbi Yochanan ben Zakkai lived through some of the saddest events in Jewish history, the destruction of the Holy Temple and the dissolution of the Jewish state, but his life amply illustrates the teaching, "Almighty God always sends the cure ahead of the illness" (*Megillah* 13b). Picture this scene:

It is dawn. A funeral procession moves through the streets of the old city of Tzion—disciples, they say, burying their beloved teacher. Everyone gives way in awe and reverence, even the guard at the gate. Outside the city, the procession stops; the disciples lay the coffin down, open the lid, and the revered *Rabban* Yochanan ben Zakkai emerges and enters the Roman camp unchecked and unharmed.

He approaches Vespasian, the Roman conqueror, who is so impressed by the venerable teacher that he permits him to ask for the fulfillment of a wish. The Rabbi does not beg for mercy for his people, nor special favor for the holy city nor even the Temple. He only asks, "Let me found a school at Yavneh."

With a smile, the proud Roman grants his request, not realizing the transcendental importance of his act to a people whose existence is dependent upon the preservation of its Torah, though its state lies in smouldering ruins. Mighty Rome would one day perish, many nations would be swept away in the storm of history; but Yisrael would survive wholly and solely through that seed of the tree of Torah which Yochanan ben Zakkai carried from the burning city of Yerushalayim and replanted about sixty miles away, in the small town of Yavneh.

(*Gittin* 56a,b)

Rabban Yochanan ben Zakkai reached the age of 120, outliving the Holy Temple only by a few years. Yet in this short period he assembled disciples around him at Yavneh and set firmly in motion the task of preserving the Torah without the support of a Jewish state. He established a *beith din* and a number of other institutions which served the transplanted community and bolstered its hope for the reestablishment of the Jewish state and the rebuilding of the Holy Temple.

IF YOU HAVE LEARNED MUCH TORAH DO NOT PRIDE YOURSELF ON IT, BECAUSE FOR THIS PURPOSE YOU WERE CREATED. *Rabban* Yochanan's great modesty is transmitted to us in this lesson about the strict performance of duty. We are not entitled to regard ourselves as something special when we have merely fulfilled our duty. Our wise men also said this: "Who is destined for the World to Come? The one who walks meekly and humbly on earth, a constant student of the Torah who claims no merit [for his study]" (*Sanhedrin* 88b).

Nechemyah, one of our greatest leaders, was reproached for saying זכרה לי אלהי לטובה, "Remember me, my God, for good," because this statement reveals a small amount of pride in his own good deeds (*Sanhedrin* 93b). For the same reason the Talmud raises an objection to Rabbi Shesheth's custom of reviewing his learning every thirty days and exclaiming: "Rejoice, O my soul, for your benefit have I studied the Law." They said that we must learn Torah to fulfill the wider purpose of the world, for is it not written, "If not for My covenant (the Torah) I would not have appointed day and night, the ordinances of heaven and earth!" (*Yirmeyahu* 33:25)? The answer is, however, that the first object of learning Torah is the ennoblement of your own soul; the purpose of Creation is thereby fulfilled automatically (*Pesachim* 68b).

The *Midrash Shemuel* gives an ingenious explanation of this mishnah through a parable.

A man had two sons, let us call them Reuven and Shimon, to whom he left a considerable fortune when he died. After the two brothers had divided their inheritance, the younger brother said, "I am content with my father's inheritance. It will suffice to provide for myself and my family, and I shall therefore devote my life to the study of the holy Torah." The elder brother, however, said, "It is true, my father has left me a large fortune, but I wish to increase it." And so it happened. The elder brother founded a big business; consequently, he often had to undertake long journeys, while the younger brother stayed at home, devoting all his time to the study of the Torah.

Once Reuven, the elder brother, was returning from a journey in the middle of winter. Some miles away from his home, his carriage broke down. While the coachman ran to a neighboring village for help, Reuven decided to return home on foot, in spite of the deep snow. He arrived there exhausted, at midnight. Everyone was fast asleep but there was a light in his brother's study. "Rabbi Shimon," Reuven called. His brother opened the window. "Is it you, my brother? I will open for you at once." He took the exhausted man to his well-heated room, gave him dry clothing and while Reuven changed, he prepared a warm nourishing drink for him. He also fetched bread and butter and then filled a pipe for his brother. While Reuven gradually recovered, ate and drank, and lit the pipe, Shimon resumed his interrupted studies. After a while he said, "You have come home at the right time, my brother; I have just solved a contradiction in the Talmud, which the greatest scholars have tried in vain to explain."

"Listen, my dear brother," Reuven thereupon said, "rightly and justly, I am more entitled than you to the bliss of the World to Come. You are already enjoying this world, sitting at home in a well-heated room, eating and drinking when you are hungry and thirsty, all the time occupied with studies that give you great joy. But I have to drudge and toil, in storm and snow, in heat and cold, only too often occupied with unpleasant things, frequently cheated of the fruits of my hard work by malevolent debtors. I am not enjoying my life; I therefore, have the higher claim to the joys of the World to Come." Then the younger brother smiled, saying, "Just listen to your own words, my beloved brother! All your endeavors are only directed to acquiring the possessions of this world, and you do not succeed in them—how can you lay claim to the assets in the World to Come, for which you do not strive at all?"

Our Sages teach, at the end of Tractate Kiddushin, that he who completely lives up to the purpose of the Creation will find his subsistence on earth painlessly, through the grace of God. It is the highest purpose of human life to know God through the study of the Torah and to observe His holy commandments, and that is also taught by *Rabban* Yochanan ben Zakkai in the Chapters of the Fathers: If you learn much Torah, אל תחזיק טובה לעצמך, then you will not need to cling to the good things by force, then you will not need to work so hard for good fortune, for then God will keep you and bless you, since you are fulfilling the purpose of Creation.

DO NOT PRIDE YOURSELF ON IT. Another explanation of this mishnah points to the significance of transmitting the Tradition, as we learned in the first mishnah of Avoth. *Rabban* Yochanan ben Zakkai says אל תחזיק טובה לעצמך, which may also be translated, "Do not reserve the good [only] for yourself," the good being the Torah, as it is said: אין טוב אלא תורה, "*Good* implies Torah" (*Avoth* 6:3). We have an obligation to transmit to our descendants that which we have learned from our teachers. *Rabban* Yochanan himself was a shining example of this, being the crucial force at that point in our history, who was able to save the Torah and the Tradition of the Jewish people from utter destruction, and preserve them for all future generations.

י חֲמִשָּׁה תַלְמִידִים הָיוּ לוֹ לְרַבָּן יוֹחָנָן בֶּן־
זַכַּאי. וְאֵלוּ הֵן: רַבִּי אֱלִיעֶזֶר בֶּן־
הֻרְקָנוֹס, רַבִּי יְהוֹשֻׁעַ בֶּן חֲנַנְיָה, רַבִּי יוֹסֵי הַכֹּהֵן, רַבִּי
שִׁמְעוֹן בֶּן נְתַנְאֵל, וְרַבִּי אֶלְעָזָר בֶּן עֲרָךְ:

10 *Rabban* Yochanan ben Zakkai had five disciples, namely, Rabbi Eliezer ben Hurkanos, Rabbi Yehoshua ben Chananya, Rabbi Yosei *Ha-Kohen*, Rabbi Shimon ben Nethanel and Rabbi Elazar ben Arach.

*   *   *

This mishnah implies that *Rabban* Yochanan ben Zakkai had only five disciples. This is not true; we know that he had thousands. It might then be supposed that these five men were his most outstanding disciples, who transmitted the Tradition which the master himself had received from Hillel and Shammai. This would indeed apply to three of those named: Rabbi Eliezer ben Hurkanos, Rabbi Yehoshua ben Chananya and Rabbi Elazar ben Arach. But Rabbi Yosei *Ha-Kohen* and Rabbi Shimon ben Nethanel were equalled in importance, if not surpassed, by others like *Rabban* Gamliel the Second, Rabbi Eliezer ben Tzadok, Abba Shaul, Rabbi Chanina ben Antigenos, and others. Rabbi Yosei *Ha-Kohen* is mentioned in the Mishnah once more (*Eduyyoth* 8:2) and only rarely mentioned in the Gemara, and Rabbi Shimon ben Nethanel even more rarely. Why have just these five disciples been given special mention? *Rabban* Yochanan ben Zakkai's greatest achievement was a knowledge of מעשה המרכבה, "the understanding of the unrevealed truth," compared with which, abstruse Talmudic reasoning is called דבר קטן, "a small thing." In the Talmud Bavli, Chagigah 14a, we are told that Rabbi Elazar ben Arach, Rabbi Yehoshua ben Chanina and Rabbi Yosei *Ha-Kohen* were instructed in this deep wisdom.

Rabban Yochanan ben Zakkai was once going somewhere and Rabbi Elazar ben Arach followed him. On the way the disciple requested, "Rabbi, teach me a chapter from *Ma'aseh Ha-*

Merkavah." The teacher answered, "Have I not taught you that one should not lecture to an individual on the *Merkavah?*" "Then permit me to tell you something that you have already taught me," Rabbi Elazar said. The teacher gave his permission and sat down on a stone under an olive tree to listen to his disciple. When Rabbi Elazar had finished his discourse, the teacher kissed him and praised almighty God for the fact that there lived on earth a man who was capable of such discernment, such insight and such clarity of thought as Rabbi Elazar ben Arach.

The same passage mentions both Rabbi Yehoshua ben Chananya and Rabbi Yosei *Ha-Kohen* in similar stories, while still another names these two together with Rabbi Shimon ben Nethanel (*Yerushalmi* ibid. 2:1). Although the Talmud does not expressly state it, we may infer from two other passages that Rabbi Eliezer ben Hurkanos was also initiated into the secret knowledge by his teacher (*Yerushalmi, Sotah,* end of tractate). Rabbi Yochanan apparently taught only these five disciples the lessons of *Ma'aseh Ha- Merkavah,* and this glimpse into the deepest secrets of Divine wisdom is what differentiated them from all his other disciples.

יא הוּא הָיָה מוֹנֶה שִׁבְחָם: רַבִּי אֱלִיעֶזֶר
בֶּן הֻרְקָנוֹס בּוֹר סוּד שֶׁאֵינוֹ מְאַבֵּד טִפָּה,
רַבִּי יְהוֹשֻׁעַ בֶּן־חֲנַנְיָא אַשְׁרֵי יוֹלַדְתּוֹ, רַבִּי יוֹסֵי הַכֹּהֵן
חָסִיד, רַבִּי שִׁמְעוֹן בֶּן־נְתַנְאֵל יְרֵא חֵטְא, וְרַבִּי
אֶלְעָזָר בֶּן־עֲרָךְ כְּמַעְיָן הַמִּתְגַּבֵּר:

11 He [*Rabban* Yochanan ben Zakkai] would enumerate their merits: Rabbi Eliezer ben Hurkanos resembles a cemented cistern which loses not a drop;
Rabbi Yehoshua ben Chananya—happy is she who
bore him; Rabbi Yosei *Ha-Kohen* is truly pious; Rabbi
Shimon ben Nethanel is sin-fearing; and Rabbi Elazar
ben Arach is like a spring which steadily increases its
flow.

* * *

RABBI ELIEZER. In the Holy Land and in many other Mediterra-
nean countries, rainwater is collected during the rainy season in
well-cemented tanks called cisterns, to be available in time of
drought when the wells dry up. The teacher compares his disciple, Eliezer ben Hurkanos, to such a cistern, in which all the
religious precepts and all the Heavenly knowledge that Rabbi
Eliezer received from his teachers remained safe and unchanged.
This does not mean that *Rabban* Yochanan intended to extol his
disciple for his excellent memory. There are people who have a
naturally retentive memory—for all kinds of useless information;
on the other hand there are people whose memory is not particularly good by nature, but they know how to strengthen it splen-
didly with their love of learning. Thus, contemporaries of the
world famous Rabbi Moshe Sofer used to say of him that he had
זכרון עשוי, "a worked-on memory," that is to say, he strenghtened
his natural memory with the aid of his infinite willpower. The
praise bestowed on Rabbi Eliezer ben Hurkanos must be similarly interpreted. Because Rabbi Eliezer loved wisdom and because the Torah was dearer to him than any treasure, he received

all his teacher's lessons with such great love and undivided attention, both those which interested him and those which did not,
that everything he learned remained stamped upon his memory.

This concept is also expressed by King David: פלאות עדותיך
על כן נצרתם נפשי, "Your testimonies are wonderful, therefore does
my soul keep them" (*Tehillim* 119:129). When someone sees a
miracle with his own eyes, he will not forget it; that is also why
Rabban Yochanan says: מאבד rather than אובד. The former implies loss by utter annihilation while אובד can be loss by simple
misplacement. Ordinarily, memory is a mental faculty, independent of willpower; one person has a good memory, another a
weak one; one person firmly retains that which he has learned,
while the other quickly forgets it again. Certain things, however,
make such an impression that even someone with a weak memory can never forget them. When you love the Torah with an
ardent, infinite love, every word of it will leave its mark. Someone who learns Torah and forgets it proves he has definitely not
given it his full attention. He believes that small details of the
holy wisdom have slipped from his memory inadvertently, but he
himself has really blotted them out.

RABBI YEHOSHUA. "Happy is the mother who bore him!"
There can hardly be greater praise of a man than this! In fact,
Rabbi Yehoshua ben Chananya seems to have been a person of
wide-ranging accomplishments and a well-rounded personality.
His understanding encompassed the whole of the Torah and all
other human disciplines as well. His own people revered him as a
teacher and even the Emperor Hadrian frequently sought his
instruction. In a learning competition, Rabbi Yehoshua defeated
the sages of Alexandria and the sages of Athens. With all that, he
was gentle and kind to everyone and so unselfish that he worked
as a needle-maker to support himself even in his old age. He
helped his people in time of trouble; he was humble and modest
and patiently suffered insults. Truly, the mother who gave birth
to such a son must be happy! Yet why has *Rabban* Yochanan
called only his mother happy and not his father, too? It is known
that Rabbi Yehoshua's mother merits particular praise for her
son's education. When the child was still in his cradle she took

him to the *beith ha-midrash* so that the boy's first impressions would be of Torah and nothing but Torah. Some commentators say that this remark of *Rabban* Yochanan teaches that it is chiefly the mother who exerts an influence upon the child with regard to his religious and moral education. Also, the Sages say that sons will resemble their mother's brothers, meaning that the mother naturally gives her sons the type of education which she saw her parents give to her own brothers.

Rabban Yochanan valued his disciple's pure morals, sincere piety and vast scholarship, and he attributes his appreciation of these qualities to his mother's influence. This opinion is supported by a mishnah in Eduyyoth 2:9 which states that the father's influence upon his son relates to the realms of beauty, strength, wealth, wisdom and life span, and from this it has been inferred that the qualities of the heart and of the character chiefly come from the mother. This division, however, does not preclude the father of an outstanding son from feeling happy. We read, "A wise son gladdens a father, but a foolish son is the grief of his mother" (*Mishlei* 10:1). The meaning of this passage can be traced to the commandment which obliges a man to marry and be fruitful, but allows a woman to refuse to marry if she does not wish to. The father of a wicked son will suffer, but his suffering is somewhat relieved by the knowledge that he has fulfilled God's commandment. A mother whose child does not turn out well has no comfort whatever, and her grief will therefore be greater than her husband's. On the other hand, if the son turns out well, the father's joy is greater, for the mother married only with the purpose of having such children, while the father was obligated to marry in any case. When the son is so outstanding that even his mother has special reason to be happy, all the more so will his father be happy. *Rabban* Yochanan ben Zakkai therefore says, אשרי יולדתו, "Happy is the mother" who bore Rabbi Yeshoshua! The world must be more grateful to the mother for such a son than to the father, for the father was obliged to produce children while the mother was not. May all the mothers in Yisrael be blessed both by their contemporaries and by posterity for the children they raise.

RABBI YOSEI *HA-KOHEN* is called a *chasid* (truly pious person) by his teacher. The very inclusion of this tribute in the mishnah indicates the importance of the concept of *chasiduth* to *Rabban* Yochanan. A *chasid* is one who ceaselessly endeavors to do more than his duty, to improve his piety, to increase his knowledge of God and to do good selflessly, without expecting reward or gratitude.

RABBI SHIMON BEN NEṬHANEL is called sin-fearing and it is understood that fear of sin for its own sake indicates a high degree of piety. When the Sages teach אהב את השמא ושנא את המה בכך, "Love the 'perhaps' and hate the 'what does it matter?'" (*Masecheth Derech Eretz Zuta* 1), they are teaching us that both important and seemingly unimportant things could lead to situations in which sin is unavoidable. There are many things that seem to most people small and insignificant, such as spending money on the Shabbath, carrying on the Shabbath, drinking milk that was not supervised, eating and drinking with an uncovered head, etc. They say, "What does it matter?" Yet these apparently insignificant sins are the beginnings of apostasy. Rabbi Shimon ben Nethanel, because he feared sin for its own sake, avoided most carefully any incident that might lead to it.

RABBI ELAZAR BEN ARACH received the highest praise of *Rabban* Yochanan ben Zakkai—he was called "a spring that steadily increases its strength." Some philosophers believe the human soul is "an empty slate" on which cognition and experience impress themselves, or a hollow vessel that receives its contents from the outside. Others, however, maintain that the soul has an inner substance which may be acted upon by external phenomena to produce beautiful and splendid things. This latter view is shared by our Sages who describe the soul in a beautiful image. Before the soul is united with the body, that is, before the child's birth, an angel of God leads the unborn soul through all the spaces of the world, showing it everything, teaching it everything; nothing remains hidden from it, not on high in Heaven, nor below in the depths of the abyss. But as soon as the child is born, he forgets it all.

Whatever he learns during his whole lifetime is only a partial recollection of what he has seen before his birth. Unknown to himself, therefore, every man contains hidden treasures of knowledge and ability, which only need to be stimulated into activity. Just as the spring brings forth a continual flow of clear, refreshing water from deep in the earth, in the same way the human soul draws upon its own resources; and just as the well-spring in the earth is replenished by Heaven-sent rains, the soul is also replenished by forces from above. Spring water, however, tastes better than rainwater because the rocks and the soil purify it. The fruitful outpouring of a genuine artist, a scientific genius or a true sage is like a natural spring that wells up from deep within his soul, shaped by the knowledge he has acquired along the way, but inspired by his soul's treasure of Heavenly wisdom, once glimpsed and then forgotten.

Rabbi Elazar not only received that which his teacher taught him, but drew forth inspiration from his own Heaven-inspired soul; thus he assimilated the precepts of the Torah and was then able to wholly reproduce them, much like Moshe who actually brought them down from Sinai. The genius of our Sages makes the Torah accessible to us, and no generation can do without such a key to the Torah. Rabbi Elazar's wisdom streamed out into the world, refreshing and stimulating it, like an ever-replenished spring.

יב הוּא הָיָה אוֹמֵר, אִם יִהְיוּ כָל־חַכְמֵי
יִשְׂרָאֵל בְּכַף מֹאזְנַיִם וֶאֱלִיעֶזֶר בֶּן־
הֻרְקָנוֹס בְּכַף שְׁנִיָּה מַכְרִיעַ אֶת כֻּלָּם: אַבָּא שָׁאוּל
אוֹמֵר מִשְּׁמוֹ, אִם יִהְיוּ כָל־חַכְמֵי יִשְׂרָאֵל בְּכַף
מֹאזְנַיִם וֶאֱלִיעֶזֶר בֶּן־הֻרְקָנוֹס אַף עִמָּהֶם וְאֶלְעָזָר
בֶּן־עֲרָךְ בְּכַף שְׁנִיָּה מַכְרִיעַ אֶת־כֻּלָּם:

12 He [*Rabban* Yochanan ben Zakkai] would say: If all the Sages of Yisrael were in one scale of the balance and Eliezer ben Hurkanos in the other, he would outweigh them all. Abba Shaul said in his name: If all the Sages of Yisrael, including Eliezer ben Hurkanos, were in one scale of the balance, and Elazar ben Arach in the other, he would outweigh them all.

*　　*　　*

How do the commentators explain the apparent contradiction in this mishnah? The simplest explanation is that *Rabban* Yochanan ben Zakkai makes only one of the statements himself, while Abba Shaul adds the second. This solution is simple indeed, but hardly satisfactory. Bertinoro tries to adjust the disparity this way, saying, "I found the opinion expressed in a manuscript, that *Rabban* Yochanan ben Zakkai made both statements and that they were both in accordance with the truth. With regard to wealth of knowledge and memory, Rabbi Eliezer was the greater, while Rabbi Elazar ben Arach surpassed him in sagacity and dialectic ability."

The question appears to be: Which has priority—breadth of knowledge or sharpness of intellect? The question was once submitted to the Sages in the following form: איזהו עדיף סיני או עוקר הרים, "Who should be given precedence—one who resembles Mount Sinai [which encompasses the whole Torah, as it were], or one who uproots mountains [with profound dialectics]?" The answer was: "Sinai takes precedence" (*Horayoth* 14a). According to this view, we see that Rabbi Eliezer clearly has precedence, for as a "well-cemented cistern," he had absorbed the whole Tradition without losing a drop. Some commentators therefore concluded that the master gave him priority in public, but privately, to his closest disciples, he admitted the superiority of the dialectics of Rabbi Elazar ben Arach. The objection to this explanation, of course, is that Rabi, the arranger of the Mishnah, would then not have included Abba Shaul's statement at all.

The answer must lie elsewhere. We read in the Avoth of Rabbi Nathan, ch. 14, "And [*Rabban* Yochanan ben Zakkai] called Elazar ben Arach a flowing stream and a spring, ever gaining in strength, the waters of which became invigorated and are dispersed abroad, to fulfill that which is written, 'Your fountains will be dispersed abroad, through the streets like streams of water' (*Mishlei* 5:16)." The scholarship of Rabbi Elazar ben Arach was like a burgeoning stream that swelled and grew throughout his lifetime. At the beginning of his career his knowledge was probably less than that of the great Rabbi Eliezer ben Hurkanos, and later he probably equalled Rabbi Eliezer in breadth of knowledge, but in intellectual acuity he was Rabbi Eliezer's superior. The second statement may have been made a few years later than the first. Formerly, Rabbi Eliezer surpassed all the Sages, including Rabbi Elazar ben Arach; later, Rabbi Elazar surpassed them all. *Rabban* Yochanan ben Zakkai here says "all," for in his infinite modesty he included himself.

וֹ אָמַר לָהֶם, צְאוּ וּרְאוּ אֵיזוֹ הִיא דֶרֶךְ טוֹבָה
שֶׁיִּדְבַּק בָּהּ הָאָדָם. רַבִּי אֱלִיעֶזֶר אוֹמֵר
עַיִן טוֹבָה. רַבִּי יְהוֹשֻׁעַ אוֹמֵר חָבֵר טוֹב. רַבִּי יוֹסֵי
אוֹמֵר שָׁכֵן טוֹב. רַבִּי שִׁמְעוֹן אוֹמֵר הָרוֹאֶה אֶת־
הַנּוֹלָד. רַבִּי אֶלְעָזָר אוֹמֵר לֵב טוֹב: אָמַר לָהֶם,
רוֹאֶה אֲנִי אֶת־דִּבְרֵי אֶלְעָזָר בֶּן־עֲרָךְ מִדִּבְרֵיכֶם
שֶׁבִּכְלַל דְּבָרָיו דִּבְרֵיכֶם:

13 [*Rabban* Yochanan ben Zakkai] said to them: Go
forth and see which is the good way that a man should
adhere to. Rabbi Eliezer said: a good eye; Rabbi
Yehoshua said: a good friend; Rabbi Yosei said: a
good neighbor; Rabbi Shimon said: one who considers the consequences; Rabbi Elazar said: a good heart.
Thereupon he [*Rabban* Yochanan] said to them: I
prefer the words of Rabbi Elazar ben Arach to yours
because in his words yours are included.

*   *   *

In some editions דרך טובה reads דרך ישרה. Similarly, we read, "Rabi
said: Which is the right course (דרך ישרה) that a man should
choose?" (*Avoth* 2:1). The difference between these two mishnayoth,
apart from the variant readings, is that Rabi says: שיבור לו האדם,
"that a man should choose," while *Rabban* Yochanan ben Zakkai
uses the expression: שידבק בה האדם, "that a man should adhere
to." As before, there really does not seem to be any justification
for this question since almighty God has marked the path that a
Jew should choose and to which he should adhere, unless, as
some have said, there are two right and good paths which differ
from each other somewhat. Since one path leads to personal
sanctification, to a contemplative state mostly directed toward
God, and the other path leads to the well-being of mankind, Rabi
therefore taught that both of these paths are right and so a third
path should be chosen which combines the two.

Rabban Yochanan ben Zakkai, however, does not speak of choosing a path in life; he asks, "Which path should a Jew adhere to?" The wording implies that the path has already been chosen and the question only refers to persevering on it. This renders our difficulty even greater, for the answers given by the disciples are not self-explanatory, and although the teacher praises all of them, he singles out one as superior. The commentators on Avoth give many complicated explanations to this mishnah. The best one is that of *Rabbenu* Yonah, who says, "Man must endeavor to become ever more perfect and acquire all the good qualities he can, such as humility, modesty, conscientiousness, faithfulness, beneficence, and sincerity. Since it is impossible to reach perfection in all of them, it is advisable to choose one and work on it, and only when you have mastered that one, try to achieve perfection in another. According to this interpretation, *Rabban* Yochanan is asking, "Which is the first quality that a man should strive to perfect?"

RABBI ELIEZER SAID: A GOOD EYE. In the Bible, "the good eye" and the "evil eye" are terms used in the spiritual or moral sense, as in Mishlei, "Whoever has a good eye shall be blessed, for he gives bread to the poor" (22:9); "Eat not the bread of one who has an evil eye, neither desire his dainty meats" (23:6); and "The man who has an evil eye is insatiably greedy for wealth, and he does not know that want shall come upon him" (28:22). We also read, "Take care that your eye is not evil against your needy brother, and that you do not refuse to give to him" (*Devarim* 15:9).

The good eye is a symbol of good intentions and benevolence, while the evil eye indicates malevolence, avarice and greediness. Rabbi Eliezer therefore says: Make beneficence the principle of your life, be kind and friendly not only in your conduct toward your fellowman but also in your judgment of him, and also look kindly on all the precepts of God's Torah, even those that do not mean so much to you. Rabbi Eliezer ben Hurkanos regarded every drop of Divine wisdom as having prime value and therefore retained it just like the well-cemented cistern.

RABBI YEHOSHUA SAID: A GOOD FRIEND. Most commentators explain this by referring to the maxim of Rabbi Yehoshua ben Perachyah, "Acquire a good friend" (*Avoth* 1:16). One of the most valuable possessions a man can acquire in life is a good and faithful friend. Can one really say, though, that a good friend is a path? Is it even within our power to acquire a good and faithful friend? Only God looks into the heart; man must rely on externals. Rabbi Yehoshua ben Perachyah's saying concerns the proper method of study: "Provide yourself with a teacher and get yourself a companion"—a companion to study the Torah with and not necessarily a "good" companion, since that is not in our hands. Such considerations have induced some commentators to apply Rabbi Yehoshua's saying to a man's choice of wife. The same question, however, can be raised about this explanation. Surely a good wife is not something a man is always able to choose for himself, as it says, "A house and riches are an inheritance from fathers, but an understanding wife is from God" (*Mishlei* 19:14).

According to Rabbi Yehudah Lerma's explanation, Rabbi Yehoshua does not mean, "Acquire a good companion," but "Be a good companion." The good path to which man should adhere is that of being helpful and kind to all men. This explanation also conforms to *Rabbenu* Yonah's interpretation. Make kindness the first principle of your life, and once you have developed that virtue to perfection, the other good qualities of mind and character will also be yours. In order to be good to others you will naturally need to develop your own knowledge, to use your intellect and judgment with greater care and to be humble and modest. You will learn to bear insults and take pains to be honest, practice charity and, above all, to love and fear God, all as a natural result of your goodness to others.

RABBI YOSEI SAID: A GOOD NEIGHBOR. This principle is the same as Rabbi Yehoshua's, but with one addition. King David says, הנה מה טוב ומה נעים שבת אחים גם יחד, "Behold, how good and pleasant it is when brethren dwell together in unity" (*Tehillim* 133:1). The word גם (also) is usually not rendered in translation; it seems to be superfluous and therefore is in need of explanation. It is a well-known fact that brothers frequently quarrel with each other when they are together. When they live far apart from each other, one in Paris, the other in Vienna, a third in New York, they write each other the most affectionate letters full of brotherly love and sentiment. If they return to the same town, however, and their interests conflict, then quarrels start afresh. King David therefore says, "Behold how good and pleasant it is when brethren are united, even when they dwell together!"

Be like a brother to your neighbor. Even if your neighbor is a competitor who causes you losses in business, even if he takes honors that you think are due you, or outshines you in learning and good deeds, even if he quarrels with you—in spite of all that, be a good neighbor, help him, give him advice and comfort to the best of your ability. Rabbi Yosei's response is completely in keeping both with the praise of his teacher, who called him a *chasid*, and also with the saying, "One who says to his fellowman, 'What is mine is yours and what is yours is yours' is a *chasid*" (*Avoth* 5:13). If you will always act on this principle, you will always be a good neighbor.

RABBI SHIMON SAID: ONE WHO CONSIDERS THE CONSE-QUENCES. The reply of Rabbi Shimon ben Nethanel is also in keeping with the praise given to him by his teacher. *Rabban Yochanan ben Zakkai* called him sin-fearing. A sin-fearing man will naturally consider whether each of his actions may lead to sin. In choosing his life's vocation, he will select that branch which is least likely to lead to sin. In choosing his life's partner he will seek a pious and virtuous woman and will not be influenced by her dowry, her beauty, or her academic accomplishments. In the matter of education, the attribute of fearing sin is of the utmost importance. Placing high value on material accomplishments is a phenomenon of our time. Our children are encouraged to acquire a knowledge of many languages, academic skills that will assure them lucrative professions and social prestige, at the expense of learning Torah and Jewish ethical values. The unfortunate fruits of such a foolish education are a meaningless existence, unnecessary debts, illness from aggravation for the individual and assimilation and moral corruption for the community.

A parent should wish "that our sons may be as young trees

grown up in their youth" (*Tehillim* 144:12). If the young tree is to grow up straight and strong, it must be planted in good soil and any harmful influence must be kept from it. The wild shoots must be cut and a straight and strong support must be put at its side so that it can lean upon it and grow. Then a strong tree will stand there and bear magnificent fruit in later years. So must we allow our sons to take root in the rich soil of the Torah; they must be saturated with the holy waters of Jewish learning, their wild passions should be contained by Jewish values and sturdy support should be given them through God's holy commandments. Then they will be strengthened and resist all temptations in the storms of life!

If we wish our daughters to be "as the corner-pillars formed after the fashion of a palace" (*Tehillim* 144:12), that is, the pillars which support the sanctuary, let us teach them to value mother-hood, modesty and above all, the genuine fear of God, and to despise fashion and meaningless material acquisitions. Then their houses will become sanctuaries and they will be valuable helpmates to their husbands.

If a man considers the consequences of all that he does, he will always walk calmly and peacefully on the right path and look forward to the next world where infinite joy awaits him.

RABBI ELAZAR SAID: A GOOD HEART. THEREUPON HE [*RABBAN* YOCHANAN] SAID TO THEM: I PREFER THE WORDS OF RABBI ELAZAR BEN ARACH TO YOURS BECAUSE IN HIS WORDS YOURS ARE INCLUDED. The depth and magnitude of Rabbi Elazar ben Arach's statement are difficult to assess, and it is even more difficult to comprehend how his companions' words may be included in his. When someone is said to have a good heart, it means that he is, to a certain degree, benevolent and philanthropic and easily roused to compassion by the suffering of others. Such a person is likely to be kind and a good neighbor, but it is not clear how weighing consequences is connected with a good heart. Let us therefore try to ascertain the true meaning of Rabbi Elazar's words. The physical function of the human heart is to circulate blood through the body. In almost all languages, therefore, it is called the seat of feeling and the source of emotion. In Hebrew, however, intelligence, as well as feeling, are ascribed to the heart. Midrash Koheleth (*parashah* 1, referring to 1:16) lists fifty-eight faculties of the heart, including both mental abilities and perceptual sensations, which can each be traced to a particular passage in the Bible. Rabbi Ya'akov Emden enumerates another sixty-five faculties of the heart in his book, Migdal Oz, also tracing each one to its source in the Bible.

The heart, which lies in the center of the body, is the source of life, corresponding to the Holy of Holies inside the Temple in Yerushalayim, which is the life-center of the world (*Zohar, parashath Shelach*). The Holy of Holies is the dwelling place of the Divine Majesty; the holy Ark, the Tablets of the Law and the *keruvim*, are the center of the spiritual and moral order of the world. The heart warms, stimulates and maintains the whole body, as it is written, "And they shall make Me a Sanctuary and I shall reign in their midst" (*Shemoth* 25:8), that is, God will reign in the hearts of human beings. It does not say, "in its midst (in the Sanctuary)" but "in their midst (among Yisrael)." Scriptural sources closely link the heart with the eye and the brain:

> "Give me your heart my son, and your eyes will keep my paths."
>
> (*Mishlei* 23:26)

> "And you shall not go about after your own heart and your own eyes."
>
> (*Bemidbar* 15:39)

> "The eye sees forbidden things and the heart is desirous of them."
>
> (ibid., Rashi)

> "Create for me, O God, a pure heart and a firm mind renew within me."
>
> (*Tehillim* 51:12)

רוח נכון is translated here as "a firm mind." The Zohar, however, based on the verse: דבר שקרים לא יכון לנגד עיני, "He who speaks lies will not exist before my eyes" (*Tehillim* 101:7), explains נכון as the spirit of truth. To renew the spirit of truth, a pure heart is first needed, for the blemished, troubled, impure and deceitful heart hinders the acquisition of knowledge and prevents the rise of truth. The organ that brings the heart in contact with the outside world is the mouth. He who has a pure heart will let his mouth say only that which his heart thinks. Thus, the pure heart will gain the spirit of truth and a firm character, רוח נכון.

The good heart has yet another merit that perhaps surpasses all its other qualities: it can be broken. In the Holy of Holies, inside the Ark, were not only the Tablets of the Law but also the fragments of the Tablets broken by Moshe when he came down from Sinai and found the people worshiping the golden calf. They would have incurred the death penalty had Moshe not broken the Tablets and gained time for them to repent and do penance. The broken Tablets are a symbol of the broken heart, a symbol of repentance. The evil heart does not repent and the power of sin grows stronger and stronger within it. The good heart is grieved by wrongdoing and the hard crust of sin that always threatens to envelop it is broken and it becomes pure again.

Omniscient God confirms the fact that "the impulse of man's heart is evil from his youth" (*Bereshith* 8:21). To mold a good heart one must consider the consequences of all one's actions— that means fearing sin, for sin is not only evil in itself but it corrupts the heart. In the holy Zohar we are shown specifically how to shape a good heart. The first stage is the לב שומע (the listening heart), like that of the young Shelomo at the beginning of his career (*Melachim* I, 3:9). Listening is learning Torah, and we read וייטב לבו, "and his heart was merry" (*Ruth* 3:7) on which Rashi says, עסק בתורה, "for it had occupied itself with the Torah."

The highest stage of perfection is טוב לב (the good heart). This term is taken from Mishlei 15:15: כל ימי עני רעים וטוב לב משתה תמיד, "All the days of a poor man are evil, but a person with a good heart enjoys a continual feast." The poor man is every man, whatever his material wealth may be. He is born helpless; illness, sorrow and affliction accompany him to the grave. Yet his troubles are self-inflicted due to the folly of his own heart. By cultivating and training his heart, making it responsive to everything good, carefully keeping evil at a distance, man can change its primordially evil character. The wise King Shelomo recommends, "Guard your heart above all things; for out of it come the fruits of life" (*Mishlei* 4:23). One who succeeds in reshaping his heart will be like a מעין המתגבר, an eternal spring, from whose depths flow fountains of happiness.

The master is therefore correct when he insists that Rabbi Elazar ben Arach's answer includes all the words of his colleagues. The man who acquires a good heart will look above and below with a benevolent eye; he will be a good companion to all those who are fortunate enough to associate with him; he will carefully consider the consequences of his deeds because the consequences of man's deeds are often incalculable and cannot be foreseen. A truly good heart is always a safe guide.

יָד אָמַר לָהֶם, צְאוּ וּרְאוּ אֵיזוֹ הִיא דֶרֶךְ
רָעָה שֶׁיִּתְרַחֵק מִמֶּנָה הָאָדָם, רַבִּי
אֱלִיעֶזֶר אוֹמֵר עַיִן רָעָה. רַבִּי יְהוֹשֻׁעַ אוֹמֵר חָבֵר
רָע. רַבִּי יוֹסֵי אוֹמֵר שָׁכֵן רָע, רַבִּי שִׁמְעוֹן אוֹמֵר
הַלֹּוֶה וְאֵינוֹ מְשַׁלֵּם, אֶחָד הַלֹּוֶה מִן־הָאָדָם כְּלוֶֹה
מִן־הַמָּקוֹם, שֶׁנֶּאֱמַר לֹוֶה רָשָׁע וְלֹא יְשַׁלֵּם וְצַדִּיק
חוֹנֵן וְנוֹתֵן. רַבִּי אֶלְעָזָר אוֹמֵר לֵב רָע. אָמַר לָהֶם,
רוֹאֶה אֲנִי אֶת־דִּבְרֵי אֶלְעָזָר בֶּן־עֲרָךְ מִדִּבְרֵיכֶם
שֶׁבִּכְלַל דְּבָרָיו דִּבְרֵיכֶם:

14 He [*Rabban* Yochanan ben Zakkai] said to them
[his disciples]: Go and see which is the evil way which
a man should shun. Rabbi Eliezer said: an evil eye.
Rabbi Yehoshua said: a bad companion. Rabbi Yosei
said: a bad neighbor. Rabbi Shimon said: one who
borrows and does not repay, regardless of whether he
borrows from the Omnipresent, Blessed be He, or
from men, for it is said, "A lawless man borrows and
will not repay his debt but a righteous man is beneficent and gives" (*Tehillim* 37:21). Rabbi Elazar said: an
evil heart. Thereupon he [*Rabban* Yochanan] said to
them: I prefer the words of Rabbi Elazar ben Arach,
for in his words yours are included.

* * *

This is patently the same question that *Rabban* Yochanan ben
Zakkai has just asked, rephrased in the negative. It would be
natural to suppose then that the same answer would apply. That,
however, is not necessarily true.

AN EVIL EYE. Although a "good eye" regards everything that
comes from God as good and shows us that the lessons of the
Torah are wise, even if we do not always understand them, when

someone deviates a bit from the good path he does not necessarily have an "evil eye." Most people cannot be consistently benevolent; as long as things go well, they look up to God with gratitude. But as soon as they encounter problems, they begin to complain about Divine providence. Many of us acknowledge those laws of the Torah which appeal to our intellect, regarding our own intelligence more highly than Divine wisdom; we are indulgent with our friends but will not concede an inch to an opponent. Certainly this is not the good path, but neither is it a completely evil one. An "evil eye" is one which finds fault with God and His rule of the world and knowingly encourages the transgression of the sacred commandments.

A BAD COMPANION. Similarly, a man who is not always a good companion cannot then be regarded as an evil one. When a person is just indifferent to the troubles of his neighbors, he is not necessarily heading down an evil path on this account. It is only when he is intentionally a cruel, unkind and downright inconsiderate neighbor that he treads the evil path.

ONE WHO BORROWS AND DOES NOT REPAY. Only Rabbi Shimon's answer is not precisely the opposite of its companion maxim—"one who considers the consequences of his deeds." Yet most commentators (Bertinoro, for example) believe that reneging on debts does indeed imply a disregard of consequences. The debtor who reneges will lose his credit, acquire a bad reputation and eventually face ruin. That is a matter of experience which cannot be denied and the fact that Rabbi Shimon is moved to furnish proof for it indicates that simple ignorance of consequences is not what he means. Many people in distress are forced to take a loan. They fully intend to repay it but when the time arrives, cannot. Rabbi Shimon does not speak of these people. The real opposite is when someone clearly sees the consequences of his action and does it anyway. The one who does not see the consequences is not on the right path, but not necessarily on the evil path either; only the one who understands that his foolish action will have evil consequences and does not modify his behavior, only he is rushing toward the abyss. There are some who, even on contracting a debt, have no intention of paying it back.

We know that the Sage is referring to them because the verse he cites from Tehillim says ולא ישלם, and not ולא משלם, that is, "the one who will not pay," not "the one who does not pay." One who borrows money with the intention of not repaying it is committing a theft, and the consequences of his crime follow one upon the other. First he will deny the debt, then he will lie to the judges. "You shall not steal, neither shall you deal falsely, nor lie one to another. And you shall not swear by My name falsely..." (*Vayyikra* 19:11-12).

According to Rabbi Wessely, however, the verse from Tehillim refers to the debt of man to his Creator. Countless blessings are bestowed upon man in advance, and for them he owes obedience and thanks to his Creator, and should repay his debt by complying with God's commandments. In the same verse, King David names the two extremes: לוה רשע ולא ישלם, "the wicked man borrows, and pays not," that is, the scoundrel, who wants nothing else but to enjoy himself without paying anything for it, and וצדיק חונן ונותן, "but the righteous man deals graciously, and gives," the just man who not only carefully carries out all his obligations but does even more than his duty by opening his charitable hand.

Our Sages tell us in the Midrash of two men who came to a large inn that served countless visitors and that had thousands of servants to carry out all their wishes. One of the two chose a modest little table, ordered a simple meal and two cups of wine, one cup for the meal and the other for making the blessing after the meal. After he had eaten, he paid the innkeeper and peacefully continued on his way. The second man demanded the nicest seat at the best table. He noisily summoned the waiters, requested all manner of fine dishes and the most expensive drinks. Nothing was good enough for him. At long last he was satiated and tried to sneak out without paying. The servants stopped him and the proprietor saw to his just punishment. In this parable, the large inn is the world, and the visitors are its inhabitants. The pious guest only makes small demands on life and that which he enjoys he tries to pay for by learning Torah, by observing God's sacred commandments and by being kind to his fellowmen. The rogue, however, only wishes to enjoy himself and does not think of paying off his debt to his Father in Heaven. When the time comes to leave this world, the accounts are checked by the proprietor, the Holy One, blessed is He. The pious man who has paid for everything he has enjoyed leaves in peace and enters the World to Come; the malevolent debtor receives his just punishment.

WHETHER HE BORROWS FROM THE OMNIPRESENT, BLESSED IS HE, OR FROM HUMAN BEINGS. The name of God, המקום, is intentionally used here. The literal meaning of the word is "the place." When Ya'akov left his father's house, we are told, ויפגע במקום, "And he encountered the place" (*Bereshith* 28:11). Our Sages explain, "and he prayed to God." In Midrash Bereshith Rabbah 68:9 we find a further elucidation:

"Rav Huna said in the name of Rav Ami,'Why is the Holy One, blessed is He, given the name *Makom* (place)? Because He is the place (location) of the world, yet the whole world is not His place.' This can be proven from what we read in Shemoth 33:21, "And the Lord said, 'Behold, there is a place with Me.' " That is to say, I comprise the whole world, but the universe cannot comprehend Me" (see also Rashi on this verse).

God's name, *Makom*, expresses the philosophical idea of pantheism. God includes everything that He has created, but unlike pantheism, He is not contained in the world. Our Sages therefore oppose the erroneous idea that God is the soul of the world. God is more than that. Man should not suppose that in escaping from this world he can run away from the Omnipresent and avoid paying his moral debts. Man should therefore seek to pay all his debts in this world so that he may find mercy and pardon before the Judge of the universe on the Day of Judgment.

AN EVIL HEART. The Torah says that the constitution (or the inclination) of the human heart is evil from early youth. This does not mean to say that the human heart itself is evil; it says that man can master and subdue the inclination of his heart. If someone fails to train his heart to be responsive only to the good, if he is sometimes overcome by passion and does things that are neither good nor just, he is indeed a fool, perhaps a sinner, but for all that, he does not necessarily have an evil heart. Someone who turns away from God and His holy Torah completely, who gives in to the evil inclinations of his heart at the slightest opportunity, who pursues only the material goods of this earth and strives only for riches and honor, will corrupt his heart more and more until it will no longer be capable of any sincere emotion. That is the evil path which a man should avoid; that is the evil heart. In regard to this, the Wise King says, "The way of the wicked leads them into darkness, so that they do not know any more on what they stumble" (*Mishlei* 4:19).

I PREFER THE WORDS OF RABBI ELAZAR BEN ARACH, FOR IN HIS WORDS YOURS ARE INCLUDED. An evil heart is the worst attribute of all, for one who has an evil heart will also have a malevolent eye, will also be an evil companion and a bad neighbor; he will borrow with the intention of defaulting on his debt, whether he borrows from God or from man. It is by now obvious what a high opinion *Rabban* Yochanan ben Zakkai held of his disciple Rabbi Elazar ben Arach. The *Avoth of Rabbi Nathan* mentions that *Rabban* Yochanan was inconsolable and refused to come out of mourning when one of his sons died. His disciples came to see him in turn, to comfort him. Rabbi Eliezer spoke to him of Adam who had also lost a son and was comforted (*Bereshith* 4:25). "Have I not enough with my own sorrow that you worry me with Adam's grief?" he replied. Rabbi Yehoshua asked him to be like Iyyov and accept consolation, Rabbi Yosei drew his attention to the death of Aharon's two sons, and Rabbi Shimon mentioned the example of King David; they all received similar replies. But when *Rabban* Yochanan saw Rabbi Elazar approaching, he asked his servant to start preparing his bath, "For here is a great man whom I cannot refuse, and I shall have to terminate my mourning."

Rabbi Elazar sat down before his teacher and spoke. "Let me tell you a parable. A king once handed one of his trusted servants a precious treasure to keep for him. The man guarded the treasure day and night, in constant fear of robbery, fire, flood and every other mishap. Finally the longed-for day arrived and he was able to return the treasure to the king unharmed. You, my teacher, were also entrusted with a treasure by the King of kings, the Holy One, blessed is He. You faithfully guarded and kept it; you instructed your son in Torah, in the Prophets and the Holy Writings, taught him the Mishnah, halachoth and aggadoth, and he left this world free from sin. Now do you not want to accept consolation, because you have been allowed to return the precious treasure unharmed?" Then *Rabban* Yochanan said to him, "Rabbi Elazar, my son, you have comforted me as one should be comforted."

טו הֵם אָמְרוּ שְׁלֹשָׁה דְבָרִים. רַבִּי אֱלִיעֶזֶר אוֹמֵר, יְהִי כְבוֹד חֲבֵרְךָ חָבִיב עָלֶיךָ כְּשֶׁלָּךְ וְאַל־תְּהִי נוֹחַ לִכְעוֹס וְשׁוּב יוֹם אֶחָד לִפְנֵי מִיתָתְךָ וֶהֱוֵי מִתְחַמֵּם כְּנֶגֶד אוּרָן שֶׁל חֲכָמִים וֶהֱוֵי זָהִיר בְּגַחַלְתָּן שֶׁלֹּא תִכָּוֶה, שֶׁנְּשִׁיכָתָן נְשִׁיכַת שׁוּעָל וַעֲקִיצָתָן עֲקִיצַת עַקְרָב וּלְחִישָׁתָן לְחִישַׁת שָׂרָף וְכָל־דִּבְרֵיהֶם כְּגַחֲלֵי אֵשׁ:

15 They [the disciples of *Rabban* Yochanan ben Zakkai, each] said three things. Rabbi Eliezer says: Let the honor of your friend be as dear to you as your own, be not easily moved to anger and repent one day before your death; warm yourself by the fire of the Sages but beware of their glowing coals lest you burn yourself, for their bite is like the bite of a fox and their sting is like the sting of a scorpion and their hiss is like the hiss of a serpent, and all their words are like flaming coals.

* * *

How is this mishnah to be divided into three? Rashi counts "Let the honor, etc." and "Be not easily moved, etc." as one statement, "Repent, etc." as the second, and all that follows as the third. Bertinoro and some other commentators accept this. The Rambam, however, thinks that the words, "Warm yourself..." and all that follows must be regarded as a later addition. This view is supported in the Avoth of Rabbi Nathan, the later words being attributed to Rabbi Eliezer as well.

Rabbi Eliezer was excommunicated by the other Sages because he refused to accept their decision in the dispute over the oven of Achnai (*Bava Metzia* 59b). The Sages also speak there of the three forms of excommunication, נידוי, חרם, שמתא, corresponding to the three types of danger mentioned in this mishnah—the fox's bite, the scorpion's sting and the serpent's hiss. The Sages also tell us that Rabbi Eliezer mourned his ex-communication so deeply, and that he so regretted having to stop teaching, that Rabbi Yehoshua and the other Sages withdrew the excommunication shortly before his death (*Sanhedrin* 68a). Thus, the last part of the mishnah may have been added by Rabbi Eliezer when he returned to teaching, warning his disciples that no single authority is great enough to oppose the *Halachah* handed down by the Sages of Yisrael in accordance with the Tradition. The Maharal of Prague teaches us in his commentary that Rabbi Eliezer's maxim summarizes in a few words the whole range of human obligations: duties of man to God ("repent"), of man to man ("the honor of your friend"), and of man to himself ("anger").

LET THE HONOR OF YOUR FRIEND BE AS DEAR TO YOU AS YOUR OWN. In answer to his disciples' question as to what path they should follow to reach eternal bliss, Rabbi Eliezer answered with this maxim and added, "Rabbi Akiva had twenty-four thousand disciples and they all died in early youth because they did not honor each other" (*Yevamoth* 62b), for "One who seeks to honor himself by slighting someone else has no share in the World to Come" (*Yerushalmi, Chagigah* 2:1).

Rabbi Elazar ben Shammua teaches, "Let the honor of your student be as dear to you as your own; let the honor of your friend be as dear to you as the reverence due to your teacher" (*Avoth* 4:15). Some commentators therefore feel that יהי כבוד חברך, "Let the honor of your friend," should read יהי כבוד תלמידך, "Let the honor of your student," since Rabbi Eliezer surely would agree with Rabbi Elazar. Even if we do not change the reading, however, the two maxims do not necessarily conflict with each other. In the study of Torah, the companion with whom we study also becomes our teacher to a certain extent (in the sense of the give-and-take relationship between them); this is the companion to whom Rabbi Elazar is referring. Rabbi Eliezer, however, is speaking of any fellowman, and there it is sufficient to hold his honor as dear as your own.

BE NOT EASILY MOVED TO ANGER. One of our wildest and fiercest passions is anger. In Shabbath 105b, our Sages refer to

Tehillim 81:10, "There shall be no strange god in you." What is the strange god that resides in man? It is the evil inclination. Our Sages therefore teach: One who tears his clothes in anger or throws away his money in anger is to be regarded as an idol-worshiper. He pays homage to the evil inclination in his own heart and permits it to dominate him. When we give in to anger easily we relinquish some of our good sense, "for anger rests in the lap of a fool" (*Koheleth* 7:9). "Fall not into a passion and you will not sin," cautions Eliyyahu the Prophet (*Berachoth* 29b) for not only will anger cause you to make a fool of yourself, but it will certainly induce you to sin. We are even advised to reprove a sage if he becomes angry.

"Rabbi Shimon ben Lakish said, 'When a sage becomes angry, his wisdom leaves him and when a prophet [becomes angry], his ability to prophesy leaves him" (*Pesachim* 66b). Moshe *Rabbenu* became angry with the leaders of the army when Yisrael returned as victors from the war against Midyan. Although his anger was just, it nevertheless caused him to forget, for the moment, the Halachah (*Bemidbar* 31:14-21). And when Elisha the Prophet angrily, though justifiably, refused to give counsel to King Yehoram, he lost his power of prophecy (*Melachim* II, 3:13-14). We know, too, that because Eliav flew into an unjust rage against David, his younger brother, God "rejected him" and chose David instead (*Shemuel* I, 17:28, 16:1-7).

Although we must avoid anger, even when it is just, it is not humanly possible to avoid it entirely. Rabbi Eliezer therefore does not tell us, "Never be angry!" but "Be not easily moved to anger." Indeed, that there are matters over which you should become angry, we learn from two examples: Pinchas, who killed in justified wrath and was rewarded by God, Who was Himself "angered" (*Sifrei* on *Beha'alothecha* 24) and Miryam and Aharon, when "the anger of the Lord was kindled against" them (*Bemidbar* 12:9), but only after they had been warned and had been heard.

Our Sages lay special stress upon controlling your anger in private. Venting your anger against members of your family or your employees, those who are dependent upon you, will force them to be hypocrites and liars, wishing to hide the truth for fear of your anger.

REPENT ONE DAY BEFORE YOUR DEATH. When Rabbi Eliezer said this, his disciples asked, "Can a man know on which day he will die?" Just because he does not know that, the teacher explained, man must repent any evil he has done and return to God every day of his life, for every day might be his last, so that he will always be prepared to stand before the throne of the Judge of the world in purity. *Rabban* Yochanan ben Zakkai explains this idea through a parable: Once a king invited his servants to a banquet without telling them exactly when it would begin. The fools among them said, "Who knows when the king's banquet will ever begin?" and went on with whatever they were doing. The clever ones dressed themselves and stayed alert. When the king summoned them suddenly, the clever men presented themselves in festive attire and were admitted; the fools came unprepared and were turned away. This is the meaning of King Shelomo's words, "Let your garments always be white" (*Shabbath* 153a on *Koheleth* 9:8).

There is another significance in Rabbi Eliezer's words. Repentence is a great gift; however much a man may have departed from the straight path, the return to God is always open to him and will always be accepted, even the day before his death.

WARM YOURSELF BY THE FIRE OF THE SAGES BUT BEWARE OF THEIR GLOWING COALS LEST YOU BURN YOURSELF; FOR THEIR BITE IS LIKE THE BITE OF A FOX, AND THEIR STING IS THE STING OF A SCORPION, AND THEIR HISS, THE HISS OF A SERPENT, AND ALL THEIR WORDS ARE LIKE FLAMING COALS. In his commentary Yain Levanon, Rabbi Wessely explains that a flame brings light and warmth, but can also burn if approached carelessly. The words of the Sages are like a flame that gives light and life, but if they are misused or misunderstood they can be as harmful as the bite of a fox. How so? The teeth of a fox are thin but curved, so that a fox bite causes little pain at first, but when the fox pulls out his teeth, he tears out some flesh as well. The sting of a scorpion is less painful but may result in amputation or death. The hiss of a poisonous serpent heralds certain death.

The Sages' words are the flame of the Torah which has been

preserved intact since God handed it to our great teacher Moshe. Not only to preserve the Tradition, but to maintain it, the Sages instituted certain precautionary measures, called תקנות (regulations), גזרות והרחקות (decrees and prohibitions), and סייגים לתורה (fences around the Torah). The *takanoth* are all too often regarded in our day as minor restrictions, issued by human beings, and therefore not really binding. Small things, like drinking unapproved milk or wine, or not covering one's hair, are like the bite of the fox—hardly noticeable at first, but difficult to escape from. They ease the way to larger transgressions and become firmly entrenched as accepted norms, especially with young people and, like the teeth of the fox, are exceedingly difficult to remove.

Ignoring the more serious *gezeroth*, which affect one's personal moral behavior, is like ignoring the scorpion's sting. Things like modesty and circumspection in our relations with the opposite sex, the laws of chastity and self-control, are standards that can so easily be thrown aside in a permissive society such as ours, but as with a scorpion's sting, ignoring these prohibitions has terrible consequences. By far the most insidious danger is the serpent's hiss of secularization, which, in the guise of science, art, literature and the "modernization" of our liturgy, tears down the remaining fences that protect our Judaism and can only end in complete assimilation.

טז

רַבִּי יְהוֹשֻׁעַ אוֹמֵר, עַיִן הָרָע וְיֵצֶר הָרָע
וְשִׂנְאַת הַבְּרִיּוֹת מוֹצִיאִין אֶת־הָאָדָם מִן־
הָעוֹלָם:

16   Rabbi Yehoshua says: The evil eye, the evil inclination and hatred of his fellow remove a man from
the world.

*   *   *

This saying by the great Rabbi Yehoshua ben Chananya seems
superficially very simple and hardly in need of explanation. Envy
(the evil eye), passion (the evil inclination) and hatred are things
that tend to make a man unhappy in this world, to shorten his life
and to preclude eternal bliss. Yet each of these three evils is
presented separately as if to say that each one alone is especially
significant. If that is the case, why name only these three evils?
There are so many others. Some commentators explain that the
mishnah is meant to correspond with Rabbi Yehoshua's answer to
his teacher, "One who is full of ill will, gives in to passion and
hates his fellowman is not a good companion." Others deduce
that this saying springs from Rabbi Yehoshua's nature, which
induced his teacher to say, "Happy is she who bore him." Still
others are satisfied with an all-inclusive meaning for the three
terms, holding them to be valid whatever the precise interpretation may be.

Among the commentators on this mishnah, the Maharal gives
the most penetrating and adequate explanation. Both in his
Derech Ha-Chayyim, a commentary on Avoth, and in his comprehensive Gur Aryeh, a commentary to Rashi on the Penta-
teuch, he discusses the above problems, basing his explanation on
the history of Yosef found in Bereshith 37:2. The Torah tells us
that Yosef was completely pious; in fact he was known as Yosef
Ha-Tzaddik. But at the age of seventeen he still behaved like a
child, bringing home slanderous reports about his brothers.
Rashi, following the Midrash, says he complained to his father
about three things: that they treated those of their brothers who

were the maidservants' sons contemptuously, that they were not leading a morally pure life and that they ate the flesh of living animals.

The question arises: From where did the Sages of the Midrash derive that Yosef spoke against his brothers on these three points? The Maharal answers that when God created the world, at each point he stated expressly כי טוב, "that it was good." Thus, anything that conforms to the purpose of Creation is טוב (good) and that which runs contrary to it is רע (evil). Only three qualities of man are called evil in the Torah: the evil eye (*Devarim* 15:9), the evil inclination (*Bereshith* 8:21) and the evil heart (in many places). When the Torah says that Yosef brought דבתם רעה (reports of evildoing) to his father, these must have been about what the Torah calls evil. He reported, therefore, that they treated the maidservants' sons contemptuously (an evil eye), they were not leading a morally pure life (an evil inclination) and they ate the flesh of living animals (an evil heart). Similarly, he explains our mishnah: the evil eye, the evil inclination and the evil heart, which produce hatred of God's creatures, run counter to the purpose of the world and therefore remove man from this world.

THE EVIL EYE. The Rambam understands it as greediness, while the other commentators regard it as envy or ill will. Both views can be proved with verses from the Torah. According to another view, Rabbi Yehoshua warns us not to provoke envy and ill will in others. This interpretation has only too often been confirmed in the history of our people in the Diaspora. How much suffering befell Jews because they inspired the envy and ill will of the nations among whom they lived. This envy was often provoked by we Jews ourselves, in ostentatiously flaunting our wealth. It is every man's duty to live his life on earth in humility and modesty and we Jews have particular reason, through force of circumstances, to fulfill this duty.

EVIL INCLINATION. Our Sages teach us that man was born with an evil inclination and that the urge to do good must be gradually awakened through instruction (*Avoth of Rabbi Nathan*). It is our task to ensure that the urge to do good will gain the upper hand, and the best way to achieve that is to study the

Torah, to obey the Divine commandments and to have unwavering trust in God. The evil inclination is as hard as iron, but iron can be forged with fire into useful implements. God's Torah resembles the fire, אש דת, "a fiery law" (*Devarim* 33:2), and when the evil inclination is directed and guided by the Torah, it can be transformed. But if the evil inclination gains the upper hand over man, it can shorten his life and deprive him of eternal bliss.

HATRED OF HIS FELLOW. Opinions also differ with regard to the meaning of שנאת הבריות. Rashi explains it as שנאת חנם (groundless, unfounded hatred), while the Rambam termed it "hatred of mankind." The Avoth of Rabbi Nathan emphasizes the word בריות (God's creatures), and concludes that the lesson here is to love all human beings because they were created by God. Yet we are told, "Truly I shall hate them, O Lord, who hate You...fight those who rise up against You" (*Tehillim* 139:21-22). We must conclude then that the emotion of hate is permissible only when it is directed toward those who scorn God, His Law and the holy Torah. Hatred which is prompted only by jealousy, envy, malice or greed is quite capable of ruining a family, destroying a state and eventually corrupting all of human society. The Sages attribute the fall of the Jewish state and the destruction of the Second Temple to the causeless hatred between the various factions. In modern times, class suppression and race hatred are a sad corroboration of this bitter truth.

וֹ**ז** רַבִּי יוֹסֵי אוֹמֵר, יְהִי מָמוֹן חֲבֵרְךָ חָבִיב
עָלֶיךָ כְּשֶׁלָּךְ וְהַתְקֵן עַצְמְךָ לִלְמוֹד תּוֹרָה
שֶׁאֵינָהּ יְרֻשָּׁה־לָךְ וְכָל־מַעֲשֶׂיךָ יִהְיוּ לְשֵׁם שָׁמָיִם:

17 Rabbi Yosei says: Let the property of your fellowman be as dear to you as your own, and prepare
yourself to study the Torah, for it does not come to
you by inheritance, and let all your deeds be done for
the sake of Heaven.

* * *

The essence of this maxim is that man's chief task on earth is to
improve himself continually, to become ever wiser and more
perfect. Rabbi Yosei was the disciple who replied that the right
path for man is to be a good neighbor; this mishnah is an expan-
sion of his answer. Money is at the center of almost all human
relationships and our attitude toward it, the Sages teach, is one of
the tests by which our worth as people can be recognized (*Eruvin*
65b). Scrupulousness in regard to ownership and property is the
highest accomplishment in social relationships, attained by only a
few people. Rabbi Yosei's warning here does not speak of theft or
fraud or other crimes prohibited by the Torah; it is understood
that Pirkei Avoth deals only with the improvement of permitted
behavior.

Our Sages teach us that if someone has lost an article and
his father has also lost an article, he can try to retrieve his own
loss first; the same applies when it concerns a teacher's loss.
One's own property always has precedence. This is stated in the
mishnah in Bava Metzia 33a. The Sages deduce this from the
verse: אפס כי לא יהיה בך אביון, "Take care that there be no needy
person among you!" (*Devarim* 15:4), to which Rashi comments:
שלך קודם לשל כל אדם, "Your own property precedes that of anybody else." Nevertheless, the Sages add: כל המקיים בעצמו כך סופו
בא לידי כך, "He who strictly observes this, will eventually be
brought to it," which means, "The person who safeguards his
own property first, so as not to become impoverished, and be-

cause of that refrains from giving charity and loving his fellow-man, will eventually become poor himself."

But Rabbi Yosei not only recommends charity in this mishnah. What he teaches is much more far-reaching. The Sages tell us that when you are asked to look after the property of another person, you must guard it just as well as you would your own; that is being a good neighbor. Neither should you look with envy or ill will upon the success and wealth of your friends; that is being a good neighbor! Peace and harmony would govern the earth if all people would take pleasure in their neighbor's good fortune. A German proverb says, "In money matters geniality ceases." We should not make this proverb the yardstick of our lives. Disputes over money, especially in cases of inheritance, often cause such bitter enmity that families are torn apart. We are taught that Yerushalayim was destroyed because its inhabitants insisted on upholding the strict letter of the law without a trace of kindness or mercy, thus exacerbating the hatred and fraternal rivalry which ultimately undermined the State itself. Every man is inclined to think that he is right and that the other fellow is wrong, and if both sides persist in their opinions, discord and hatred result. But Rabbi Yosei teaches: Adopt your opponent's point of view and look at the matter as if you were in his position. Practice לפנים משורת הדין, doing more than what is strictly required of you by the law. You can only gain in the process, even if you might end up losing money.

AND PREPARE YOURSELF TO STUDY THE TORAH, FOR IT DOES NOT COME TO YOU BY INHERITANCE. Even if your father, your grandfather and all your ancestors possessed the greatest treasures of knowledge and infinite wisdom, you have to acquire them again by yourself to profit from them. Torah does not come easily to you, like an inheritance. Prepare yourself, Rabbi Wessely says in his commentary to this mishnah, in the same way as you would prepare for a battle. Indeed, it is a hard war you have to wage when learning Torah, against treacherous enemies and often insurmountable obstacles. This war commences even before you are capable of deciding for yourself; it begins with your parents. "Why should my child learn Hebrew, what use will it be to him later in life? He must acquire knowledge that will enable him to earn a living later," many parents argue, thereby ruining their children's future and robbing them of the greatest treasure of our people.

If the child is fortunate enough to have parents who are eager for him to study Torah, then the struggle begins later. He will see that other children are allowed to play and enjoy themselves, that they devote their leisure hours to music and hobbies, but he must devote all his time to difficult and serious study. Or the child may have to contend with his own lack of ability. Untiring industry and unflinching determination are often needed to overcome insufficient talent, to strenghten and temper the power of the mind.

There once lived here in Mainz two children: the elder was called Loeb and the younger, Nathan. The younger boy was eminently gifted and made splendid progress in his studies, but the elder brother found learning extremely difficult. One day his mother overheard seven-year-old Loeb's prayer: "All-merciful God, please give me the strength and the courage to persevere in my learning, even if I cannot be as smart as Nathan!" From that day she noticed that the older child started to progress rapidly in his studies, too. Both brothers became important and learned men: Rabbi Loeb Ellinger became Chief Rabbi of the County of Mainz, and his brother Rabbi Nathan, the Chief Rabbi of Bingen.

As one grows older it becomes ever more difficult to remain faithful to Torah studies. The struggle to earn a livelihood and support a wife and children, as well as increasing social responsibilities, consume more and more of one's time. But even the person whose vocation permits him to devote the greater part of his time to learning Torah frequently does not do so. A slight indisposition, the short winter days, the heat in summer, any excuse suffices. And even perseverance is not always enough. Just as wine and milk ought to be stored only in clean receptacles so that they do not spoil, so God's Torah needs a pure vessel to contain it. If you wish to preserve the Torah, then take care to keep a pure heart, and be free of sin.

Rabbi Yosei says the knowledge of Torah "does not come to you by inheritance," yet we read in the Torah: תורה צוה לנו משה

מורשה קהלת יעקב, "The Torah commanded to us by Moshe is a heritage of the community of Ya'akov" (*Devarim* 33:4). And so it is; it is a heritage of the community of Ya'akov, but not an inheritance of the individual Jew. The Torah of the community of Ya'akov will never be lost, for there will always be men who will struggle hard to pass it on intact to succeeding generations, but the individual must fight to have it and to hold it.

Rabbi Yosei's words also seem to contradict a passage in the Talmud that refers to the promise in the Torah: ואני זאת בריתי אותם אמר יי רוחי אשר עליך ודברי אשר שמתי בפיך לא ימושו מפיך ומפי זרעך ומפי זרע זרעך אמר יי מעתה ועד עולם , "As for Me, this is My covenant with them, the Lord said, My spirit that rests upon you, and My words that I have placed in your mouth, they will not leave your mouth and the mouth of your seed...from now until eternity" (*Yeshayahu* 59:21). מכאן ואליך התורה מחזרת על אכסניא שלה, "From then onward the Torah always returns to the same inn" (*Bava Metzia* 85a). Once the Torah has been the property of a family for three generations, it will belong to it for all eternity.

Yet today, we see that even though three generations of their ancestors were faithful to the Torah, later generations are not. A parable may help to resolve this contradiction: A man visits a certain town from time to time and always stays at the same hotel. On one such visit, however, the innkeeper tells him regretfully that the house is fully booked and there is no room for him. What should he do? He must look for another inn. The Torah, too, would very much like to sojourn, as it were, in its accustomed place, but its host no longer wants to receive it. The great grandson of the scholar has his house filled with other guests and the Torah cannot stay with him. Make room for the Torah in your house, be prepared always to study it; do not say you have no room (i.e., time) for it.

AND LET ALL YOUR DEEDS BE DONE FOR THE SAKE OF HEAVEN (FOR THE GLORIFICATION OF THE DIVINE NAME). The Rambam made this maxim the basis of the fifth chapter of the שמונה פרקים which he wrote as an introduction to Tractate Avoth. In it he writes that the man who aims at the highest ethical perfection must have one goal, namely that in all his thoughts and feelings, and particularly in his actions, he should seek to draw near to God. The same thought is expressed in a more popular manner by the Rashbatz. All man's deeds can be classified in three groups: 1) the fulfillment of God's commandments, 2) the transgression of those commandments, and 3) the performance of deeds that seem to be neither one nor the other but are regarded by man as unimportant in our relationship to God, such as eating, drinking, sleeping, walking.

The first category, the fulfillment of the commandments, may be further subdivided into those which are performed לשם שמים, purely for the sake of Heaven, those which are grudgingly done as though they were a burdensome obligation, those which are done openly but only for public approval, and those which are done secretly for fear of public ridicule. The man who contributes large sums to a grateful community but refuses to help a poor man whom no one will ever hear about, is not performing the *mitzvah* לשם שמים. The חוקים, the statutes that we must keep although we do not understand them, constitute another good example of a deed done לשם שמים, especially when performed publicly. Other duties we are expected to carry out, the עדות (testimonies), are specifically Jewish in character and are intentionally designed to set us apart from the nations, inevitably evoking opposition. As King David said, "Remove from me shame and contempt because I observe Your testimonies (עדותיך)" (*Tehillim* 119:22).

The second category of the Rashbatz, transgressions of the commandments, may also at times be done לשם שמים, for the glorification of the Divine Name. עת לעשות ליי הפרו תורתך, "There is a time to act for God—they nullify Your Torah" (*Tehillim* 119:126). Rashi comments, "Sometimes it is necessary to transgress the Torah in order to act for God," and cites the example of Eliyyahu the Prophet who built an altar on Mount Carmel, even though it was prohibited to do so anywhere other than in the Temple. God heard his prayer and fire fell from Heaven and consumed the entire sacrifice because it was offered לשם שמים. (See also *Berachoth* 54a.) Another case where the Law was transgressed for the sake of Heaven was when Mordechai the Righteous ordered the community to fast on the Festival of Pesach, and was, of course, blessed with success, to the everlasting glorification of the Divine Name.

The third category is that in which the deeds have no apparent relationship either to the fulfillment or to the transgression of Divine commandments. The man who aims at complete moral perfection must see to it that these deeds, too, contribute to the glorification of the Divine Name. Of course we have to eat and drink, but let us do so with the intention of preserving our lives and our health for the service of God. Let us rest and sleep, as we must, but solely in order to gain more strength to study Torah and to perform the Divine commandments. Let us work hard to earn an honest livelihood and, if God grants us material success, let us use it to do good. Even the very human need to converse with others should be used to bring ourselves nearer to the Torah and not simply to gossip or slander.

According to *Rabbenu* Moshe Alshech, Rabbi Yosei's saying is a further development and confirmation of the saying of the Men of the Great Assembly, which can be regarded as the basis of all Jewish ethics: *Be cautious in judgment.* Rabbi Yosei says: When you must pronounce judgment, regard the property of the losing side as if it were your own and judge it accordingly. *Raise up many disciples.* Rabbi Yosei teaches: Prepare yourself, take pains to learn Torah, for it does not come to you by inheritance, and see to it that the Torah will be preserved for coming generations by instructing others. *Make a fence for the Law.* Rabbi Yosei says: Do everything for the glorification of the Divine Name, for all the precautionary decrees of the Sages have the sole aim of glorifying the Name of the Almighty.

יח רַבִּי שִׁמְעוֹן אוֹמֵר, הֱוֵה זָהִיר בִּקְרִיאַת שְׁמַע וּבִתְפִלָּה וּכְשֶׁאַתָּה מִתְפַּלֵּל אַל־ תַּעַשׂ תְּפִלָּתְךָ קֶבַע אֶלָּא רַחֲמִים וְתַחֲנוּנִים לִפְנֵי הַמָּקוֹם, שֶׁנֶּאֱמַר כִּי־חַנּוּן וְרַחוּם הוּא אֶרֶךְ אַפַּיִם וְרַב־חֶסֶד וְנִחָם עַל־הָרָעָה. וְאַל־תְּהִי רָשָׁע בִּפְנֵי עַצְמֶךָ:

18　Rabbi Shimon [ben Nethanel] says: Be careful in reading the *Shema* and in [the *Amidah*] prayer; and when you pray, do not regard your prayer as a fixed routine but as an appeal for mercy and favor before the Omnipresent, as it is said, "For He is gracious and full of mercy, slow to anger and abundant in lovingkindness, and relenting toward evil" (*Yoel* 2:13); and do not consider yourself wicked.

*　　*　　*

Rabbi Shimon gives us three very important rules to follow: Say your daily prayers very carefully; concentrate your thoughts when you begin to pray; and never lose your self-respect. The connection between the first two rules and the third will soon be explained. The *Shema* and the *Amidah* are the chief constituents of our daily prayers; the first is said twice daily and the latter three times each day, four times on the Shabbath, New Moon and Festivals and five times on the Day of Atonement. It is human nature to treat something so familiar with a certain negligence and to be more careful with something that is said only rarely.

　　The *Shema* consists of three passages from the Torah, two from the Book of Devarim and one from the Book of Bemidbar, all referring to the Ten Commandments, but not repeating them verbatim. Our Sages explain that if the Ten Commandments were listed at the center of our order of prayers, some people would assume that they were the core of Judaism and come to disregard all the other commandments; in our religion one law is just as important as another. The Sages chose three different passages in which the Ten Commandments are referred to in different ways, and from them formed *Keriath Shema*. The word תפילה (prayer) in the mishnah means the *Amidah*, which we generally call שמונה עשרה (eighteen) because this prayer originally consisted of eighteen blessings. A nineteenth was added later. The first three blessings proclaim the glory of the Almighty God; the thirteen middle blessings are a petition to the Almighty for everything that we need and that is good for us; the last three blessings contain the wish that God will receive our prayer graciously, give thanks for everything He has granted us so far, and request peace and perfection.

BE CAREFUL IN READING THE *SHEMA* AND IN [THE *AMIDAH*] PRAYER. We must be aware of several things connected with the prayers: first, the time. The Torah decrees that the hour of lying down to sleep and that of rising up are the times for reading the *Shema*, and both times are strictly limited by the Sages according to the season of the year and other specific conditions. The time of lying down can be any time between nightfall and midnight, but when you pray together with others in a synagogue it is permitted to say the *Ma'ariv* prayer immediately after *Minchah*, towards the end of the day; it is also permitted to say it after midnight, until daybreak, if one has missed saying it before. However, the real *mitzvah* is to say it immediately when night falls. The time for *Keriath Shema* in the morning extends from daybreak until a quarter of the day has passed, so that we must calculate the time correctly, particularly during the long summer days.

You should also be discriminating as to where you pray; the place must be clean and free from bad smells and nothing indecent should be visible there. Your body should also be clean and you should be decently dressed, even when you pray alone. When reading the *Shema*, you must do so each time with the renewed intention of fulfilling God's commandments. We always say קריאת שמע, which emphasizes the reading of the prayer, not merely the saying of it. Each of the words must be said clearly and distinctly, every consonant and every vowel must be pronounced separately, and all the rules of pronunciation must be observed. Do not, for instance, say *"b'cholevavcha,"* but rather, *"b'chol levavcha,"* or *"urithemotho"* instead of *"u-re-i-them o-tho."*

A distracted prayer is also not valid, say the Sages in their interpretation of the verse, "You have not called upon Me, O Ya'akov" (*Yoma* 19b on *Yeshayahu* 43:22). It is extremely difficult to pray with complete devotion and prevent extraneous thoughts from intruding. Devotion in prayer is best achieved by praying in a *minyan* (a quorum of ten) together with other devout people, in the place appointed for prayer, the synagogue. After all, many important prayers can be said only in public. We only have to take particular care not to disturb others and not to allow others to disturb our concentration. "Blessed is the man who listens to Me (i.e., prays devotedly), attentively standing at My gates day after day, to step early over the threshold of the doors of the house of God (i.e., attends synagogue regularly). For whoever finds Me finds life and has obtained favor from God" (*Mishlei* 8:34-35).

AND WHEN YOU PRAY. It is appropriate here to explain the concept of prayer. However simple it may seem, it is not a concept that is easily understood. The need to raise oneself to Almighty God and to submit to Him one's desires and requests is deeply rooted in the human heart. When we praise God's Name in our prayers, we also elevate our own perceptions. We speak of the "arm" of God, the "hand" of God, the "finger" of God, though we know that God is not corporeal, because with our limited faculties that is the only way we can raise ourselves up above our ordinary horizons and draw ourselves closer to Him.

We know that God, in His grace, has promised us that our prayers will be heard and that our petitions will be answered. We know, too, that in answer to the prayers of the pious, in many instances God interrupted the natural course of things and changed the laws of nature. Even so, how can we be so bold as to expect to influence His decisions through our requests or dissuade Him from carrying out that which He has already decided? On our own, we lack the ability to perceive unless He teaches us perception, we perish in sin unless He forgives us, we are overcome in the struggle unless He takes our part, we die from illness unless He heals us. The prescribed prayers are the way offered to us. Although it is our duty to pray, prayer is nevertheless a special grace by which God permits us to influence His decisions and even bring Him to cancel an evil decree, "For he is gracious and full of mercy, slow to anger and abundant in lovingkindness and relenting toward [the already decreed] evil."

DO NOT REGARD YOUR PRAYER AS A FIXED ROUTINE. The word קבע (fixed) may also be understood in another sense. Although God has promised to hear all our prayers, the Sage warns, "Do not expect your prayers to be permanently effective, your requests to be always fulfilled." Even the most deserving supplicant, Moshe *Rabbenu*, prayed to God saying, ואתחנן, "I asked it undeservedly" (*Devarim* 3:23). The word קבע is used by Shammai in Avoth 1:15 (עשה תורתך קבע, "make your study of the Torah a fixed activity"), and Bertinoro explains it in the following way: Make Torah study your fixed and constant employment, your main occupation, while earning a livelihood should appear to you as incidental compared with it. Thus, קבע in this mishnah ought to mean: And do not make prayer your main occupation.

Remember that Rabbi Shimon ben Nethanel lived during the rise of the Essenes. This Jewish sect believed that the highest purpose of life is pious contemplation and continuous prayer. The new Christian sect adopted many ideas from the Essenes and encouraged hermits and monks to seek perfection in a contemplative life dedicated to continuous prayer. Such a view may seem attractive to a pious person, but it is repugnant to the fundamental ideas of Judaism. A Jew must study, learn and understand, but preferably in the company of others. Make Torah learning your main occupation as Shammai teaches, says Rabbi Shimon, for praying all the time will prevent you from learning Torah. Your religious duty is completely discharged when you say the order of prescribed prayers carefully. If you are moved to direct some special prayers to your Creator, then you may do so in the framework of what is called תפילה נדבה, "spontaneous prayer." And even if you pray spontaneously, do not prolong your prayers to such an extent that they become the main occupation of your life.

AND DO NOT CONSIDER YOURSELF WICKED. The prince of commentators, Rashi, interprets the Sage's words in the following manner: Never do anything that you may be ashamed of later; your self-esteem is paramount. Thus a wise man once said to his son, "If you are more concerned with other people's opinion than with your own soul, it is clear that you attach little value to your soul." Similarly, Rabbi Shelomo ben Yitzchak ben Levi, the author of the work Lev Avoth explains: "Avoid evil, not because you are ashamed before others but because you shame yourself; avoid evil even when you are all alone. When passion threatens to overwhelm you, when anger inflames you, when feelings of revenge or hatred master you, then ask yourself if you will not regret the evil deed that you are about to commit. Succeed in mastering your passions and you will honor yourself." This explanation also suits Rabbi Shimon's character. He was called by his teacher ירא חטא (sin-fearing). A person who fears sin considers the effect of his actions on his own soul; one who does not fear sin has a very low opinion of himself.

The Rambam holds a different view. He thinks that Rabbi Shimon is saying: Do not think that you are hopelessly wicked, that you are beyond redemption. Even a great sinner should know that if he returns to God with a sincere heart, all his sins will be pardoned. Our Sages teach, "Even when a person has committed one hundred sins, one greater than the other, if he atones for them, God will have mercy on him; even if he has blasphemed the Name of God in shameless abandon, if he regrets it and atones for it, God will graciously forgive him all his misdeeds" (*Tanna devei Eliyyahu Rabbah* 22). The Rashbatz agrees with Rashi's interpretation and adds another point, connecting the last part of the mishnah with the first two: Do not be wicked by remaining solitary; man was created to live in a community. The fact that most of the prayers are phrased in the plural teaches us that the individual should always be aware of his inescapable involvement with the community.

Bertinoro enlarges on this theme: Do not be wicked by excluding yourself from the good deeds of the community, while Rabbi Shemuel of Ozedah says: Do not believe that you can be wicked without influencing others! כל ישראל ערבים זה בזה, "All

Yisrael are accountable each man for his fellow" (*Sanhedrin* 27b, *Shavuoth* 39a). In another explanation, he also connects these words directly to the preceding words. The first two parts of the mishnah advise us to pray with undivided concentration and sincere devotion; the third part warns us that we may deceive others into thinking that we are praying devotedly even though our minds are actually occupied with other things. Therefore, collect your thoughts before you begin to pray and when you pray, pray sincerely so that you will be able to respect yourself.

From a historical perspective, Rabbi Shimon's third saying may well have been directed at the doctrine of original sin taught by the new and growing Christian sect. This doctrine posits that all human beings are born wicked and would be rejected by God had the founder of that religion not died for them. Judaism does not accept this. We say in our daily prayers: "My God, the soul which you have placed within me is pure. You have created it, You have formed it, You have breathed it into me; You preserve it within me and You will one day take it from me and restore it to me for eternal life" (*Berachoth* 60b). Although the inclination of the human heart is evil, the human soul is pure, unstained by sin, guiltless; it needs no intermediary between itself and the Creator. Every man has the capacity to suppress his evil inclinations and preserve the purity of his soul. Every man may stand directly before the Omnipresent, לפני המקום, (and indeed He is everywhere and the whole world is in Him) without presumption, unburdened by inherent or original sin, and entreat the Almighty to fulfill his wishes. The worst sinner need not despair; at any time he can stand before our infinitely good God to ask for forgiveness and mercy.

יט רַבִּי אֶלְעָזָר אוֹמֵר, הֱוֵה שָׁקוּד לִלְמוֹד
תּוֹרָה וְדַע מַה־שֶּׁתָּשִׁיב לְאֶפִּיקוֹרוֹס וְדַע
לִפְנֵי מִי אַתָּה עָמֵל וּמִי הוּא בַּעַל מְלַאכְתְּךָ שֶׁיְשַׁלֶּם
לְךָ שְׂכַר פְּעֻלָּתֶךָ:

19 Rabbi Elazar [ben Arach] says: Be diligent in the
study of Torah and know what to answer the *epikoros*,
and know too, before whom you labor and that your
employer may be relied upon to pay you the reward
for your work.

*   *   *

The word אפיקורוס (*epikoros*) is related to the word הפקר (ownerless property), according to some commentators, and an *epikoros*
therefore is a person who regards the world as ownerless property, denying the Creation and Divine providence. Others say
that the verb פקר and the noun הפקר are actually derived from
אפיקורוס, a Greek word meaning "a follower of the Epicurean
philosophy." The founder of this philosophy was Epicurus, who
was born in 341 B.C.E. at Gargettos near Athens. At the age of
thirty-six, he opened a school in Athens which attracted many
disciples. He taught that life's highest purpose is mirth, joy and
pleasure and, concomitantly, the avoidance of anything likely to
disturb one's enjoyment. The gods, he thought, live in eternal
rest in the empty spaces between the heavenly bodies, uncon-
cerned about the world, and the world has therefore no need to
be concerned about them. Epicurus himself recommended restraint and moderation, but his later disciples carried their principles to an extreme, indulging in very costly, though beautiful,
banquets. The danger of the Epicurean philosophy, which even
had followers among the Jews, was its rejection of any concept of
Divine influence or moral improvement. The Talmud abounds
with stories of Epicurean Jews who searched for support for their
views. So it was that the word אפיקורס was introduced into the
Hebrew language, to signify an apostate or heretic. From the
proper name, Epicurus, developed the verb פקר, "to pay homage

to Epicurean views, to regard the world as ownerless" (*Sanhedrin* 38b). And from this verb, the noun הפקר, "ownerless property," was formed.

We know that Rabbi Elazar ben Arach was an outstanding man who had a wide-ranging view of the world. His teacher compared him to a steadily increasing spring and gave him precedence over all the Sages of Yisrael, declaring that his sayings were always the most comprehensive. His own saying, too, shows his penetrating understanding of the problems of his time. Yerushalayim had fallen, the Holy Temple was destroyed, the Jewish state was conquered by Rome. Would the Jewish people also be lost to Roman-Epicurean thought? The Epicurean views of the Romans were even more dangerous than Rome's material might, and Jewish youth needed help in resisting such an enticing philosophy. Rabbi Elazar therefore advised his disciples that if they would persevere in their Torah studies they would know how to counter the temptations of the Epicureans. In other words, arm yourself with knowledge before you venture into the treacherous world of ideas.

Rabbi Wessely sees, in the three elements of Rabbi Elazar's saying, a parallel to the three elements of Shimon *Ha-Tzaddik*'s maxim: Torah, Divine service and the practice of lovingkindness.

TORAH / DILIGENCE. The concept of diligent, persevering watchfulness is expressed by the word שקוד, as it is said, נמר שקוד על עריהם, "A leopard watches over their cities" (*Yirmeyahu* 5:6); כי שוקד אני על דברי לעשתו, "For I watch over My word to perform it" (*Yirmeyahu* 1:12); and אשרי אדם שומע לי לשקוד על דלתותי יום יום, "Happy is the man who hears Me, watching daily at My gates" (*Mishlei* 8:34). Only the man who longs for the Torah, expecting to find in it great treasures and sparing no pain in his effort to acquire it, who cannot be deterred by any obstacles but is perseverant in his efforts, will attain it.

LOVINGKINDNESS / KNOW WHAT TO ANSWER THE EPICUREAN. The greatest kindness a man can do for his friend is to help him resist the enticements of the godless. One who knows how to counter the seductive arguments of the unfaithful and prove their views false, is able to save his fellow from sin and vice and eventual ruin. About such a man it is said, "Be wise, My son, and make My heart glad that I may answer him who taunts Me" (*Mishlei* 27:11).

The Rashbatz found it necessary to reassess this mishnah from the viewpoint of contemporary life. In past centuries Jews lived a far more secluded life and always kept apart from non-Jews. Controversy with non-Jewish scholars was rare, and attacks on the Torah less frequent than today. A materialistic view of life threatens to dominate our minds today, very much as the Epicurean philosophy did in Roman times. The Rashbatz sees in this saying a veritable command to study secular knowledge, in addition, of course, to having first studied Torah, so that we will be in a position of דע מה שתשיב לאפיקורוס, "Know what to answer the *epikoros*," in order to protect and preserve our most precious possession from the encroachment of atheism and materialism.

DIVINE SERVICE / KNOW BEFORE WHOM YOU LABOR. The fulfillment of our religious duties often entails hardship and privation. It is to lighten this burden that Rabbi Elazar reminds us that God, the Omnipresent, always observes our efforts with kindness and this awareness on our part will ease every burden, will sweeten every hardship and will turn every privation into enjoyment.

YOUR EMPLOYER MAY BE RELIED UPON TO PAY YOU THE REWARD FOR YOUR WORK. This reminds us of the teaching of Antigenos, "Be not like servants who minister to their master for the sake of receiving a reward" (*Avoth* 1:3). The Sage does not imply that there is no reward for piety and good deeds; he only wants to teach us that we should do good and just things for their own sake and not for the sake of receiving a reward. On the contrary—Rabbi Elazar assures us that the Almighty will reward His pious servants. However, lest we be led astray when we observe that sometimes the wicked prosper and the pious suffer, we must never lose sight of the fact that Almighty God is the One Who has appointed all tasks and that He will not deprive His workers of their well-deserved rewards.

ב

רַבִּי טַרְפוֹן אוֹמֵר, הַיּוֹם קָצֵר וְהַמְּלָאכָה
מְרֻבָּה וְהַפּוֹעֲלִים עֲצֵלִים וְהַשָּׂכָר הַרְבֵּה
וּבַעַל הַבַּיִת דּוֹחֵק:

20 Rabbi Tarfon says: The day is short, the work
load is large, the workmen are sluggish, the reward is
great and the employer is insistent.

*   *   *

Rabbi Tarfon, too, was a disciple of *Rabban* Yochanan ben Zakkai.
He had also been privileged to see the Holy Temple in all its
glory and, being a *Kohen*, to carry out the sacred service in it
(*Kiddushin* 71a). Our Sages tell us that, although he is not counted
among the above-named favorite disciples of the great teacher,
he was all the same one of the great men in Yisrael. In the
Talmud Yerushalmi, Megillah 1, he is called "the teacher of all
Yisrael," and in Yoma 1, "the father of all Yisrael."

THE DAY IS SHORT. Rabbi Chisda's daughters once tried to
persuade their father to sleep a little in the middle of the day. He
answered, "There will come long days (during which man rests in
his grave) so why should we sleep away the short days allotted to
us?" (*Eruvin* 65a). A young boy thinks that his "day" is infinitely
long. Why should he, therefore, sacrifice his youth to continual
study? "Let me first enjoy my youth," he thinks, "for there will be
time enough later for serious things." Not so, for we are but so-
journers on earth, and our "days are like a passing shadow" (*Tehillim*
144:4)—not like the long shadow of a wall that remains in place for
a while, not like the shade of a tree under which we can rest, but like
the shadow of a passing bird (*Midrash Koheleth Rabbah* 6:12).

Thousands of millions of people have dwelt on earth and their
lives have passed without leaving a trace. If man wishes to leave
his mark and assure himself of eternity, let him occupy himself
with what is immortal, the Torah—the tree of life.

THE WORK LOAD IS LARGE. That is what David meant by
the verse: "I have seen an end to every striving but Your com-

mandment is exceedingly broad in scope" (*Tehillim* 119:96). To comprehend completely only one single Divine commandment requires an infinitely wide range of research. Of the Torah itself, Iyyov 11:9 states, "Its measure is longer than the earth and broader than the sea," which does not mean that it is literally longer and broader, of course, but that the earth is the largest yardstick we possess, and it even is not sufficient for measuring the Torah. You cannot measure it at all with an earthly measure; it is infinitely great.

The infinitely great Torah, which comprises all knowledge, was given to us by God to study and comprehend. Rabbi Yishmael says in Midrash Mishlei 24, that the first question God will ask man on the Day of Judgment is whether he has appreciated the gift of the Torah and has studied it. Woe to all who must answer in the negative, woe to all who have only acquainted themselves with the Written Law and have ignored the Oral Law. All the punishments of Hell will befall them. Every Jew is obligated to study the whole of the Talmud—both the *Aggadah* and the *Halachah*—the *halachoth* still in use as well as those which are no longer applicable. With regard to all of them, David said, "How manifold are Your works, O Lord! You have made them all in Your wisdom, the earth is filled with Your possessions" (*Tehillim* 104:24).

THE WORKMEN ARE SLUGGISH. The Sage did not say the men are sluggish, but the workmen. Even those whose vocation it is to study Torah should be reminded to do so, because they, too, can be frequently distracted. Like children, adults will find all kinds of excuses for not learning: either it is too warm or too cold, too bright or too dark; either they are not well or they are in need of rest from "busy idleness;" either they have to pay visits or receive them. The industrious worker, however, overcomes all distractions and tries to study Torah continually and carry out all its holy commandments. When God assigned Moshe forty days and forty nights to learn the Torah, Moshe neither ate, drank nor slept during that time (*Shemoth* 34:28; *Midrash Shemoth Rabbah* 47). We, too, have been offered a great treasure, but unless we exert ourselves to gather it, overcoming fatigue and all other distractions, it will never belong to us. Let us therefore be among the industrious workers and not the sluggish ones.

THE REWARD IS GREAT. Our Sages relate: A pious man once overlooked a sheaf in his field. When he heard about it, he rejoiced and said to his son, "Bring me a bull for a burnt offering and a bull for a thanksgiving offering." The astonished son asked, "Why do you enjoy this *mitzvah* more than the other commandments, Father?" The pious man explained, "You see, my son, we have to obey all the other commandments intentionally, with full understanding; but the commandment to leave the forgotten sheaf for the poor is connected with thoughtlessness on our part, and still we will be blessed because of it (see *Devarim* 24:19). How much more will God reward us for keeping those commandments that we do with full understanding and profound intention" (*Tosefta Pe'ah* 2).

AND THE EMPLOYER IS INSISTENT. The employer of whom Rabbi Tarfon speaks is the Almighty, and this maxim can also explain the enigmatic saying of our Sages: כל מה שיאמר לך בעל הבית עשה חוץ מצא, "Do all that your host tells you to do; but if he tells you to leave, do not listen to him" (*Pesachim* 86b). The great scholar Elisha ben Avuyah, who had become an apostate, was once riding past Rabbi Meir's academy on the Shabbath. The disciples said to Rabbi Meir, "There is your teacher, riding!" Rabbi Meir went out and followed the rider on foot, asking him many questions, which Elisha answered as he rode. Finally Elisha said, "Meir, my son, go back! By the hoofbeat of my horse, I have counted out that we have reached the Shabbath boundary. You must not follow me any further!" Rabbi Meir began to weep, pleading, "Rabbi, turn back with me!" Elisha answered sadly, "I cannot return. On the last Day of Atonement, which fell on the Shabbath, I rode past the ruins of the Holy Temple and heard a Voice call out, "Return, all you erring children, with the exception of Acher (which was Elisha's nickname), who has understood Me and yet has deserted Me" (*Chagigah* 15a).

Yet our Sages teach that Elisha should not have held back, since no sin is great enough to prevent repentance. Therefore we learn: All that the host—that is, the Lord of the universe—tells you to do, do it. Follow all His commandments faithfully and carefully. But do not listen even if God Himself says to you, "Leave Me!" A son, who has caused his father such deep sorrow by sinning that his father refuses to listen to him when he finally does repent, must not obey the father's first angry rebuff. No, and a thousand times no! However coldly his father turns him away, he should continue to beg for forgiveness until his father's heart overflows with love and mercy.

Yisrael was God's favorite people from the beginning, yet no nation has suffered and endured as much as ours. Ya'akov's descendants are now dispersed all over the earth and there is hardly a country that is not stained with the blood of Jewish martyrs. Sometimes it seemed as if the *bnei Yisrael* had found a new homeland, but sooner or later misfortune overtook them. Our Sages explain these events by a parable. Rabbah bar Chana related: We traveled in a ship upon the sea and saw a large fish lying in the midst of the sea; on its back was a deposit of earth and from the earth grew reeds. We did not know that it was a fish and thought it was firm land. We debarked and lit cooking fires on the back of the fish. When the fish felt the heat, it turned and threw us off. Had our ship not been near at hand we should have drowned in the sea (*Bava Bathra* 73b).

We Jews are being tossed about on the sea of life; the ship that affords us protection and salvation is our faith. Within it, we are safe from the raging elements. Yet we would like to live on firm land and quite often we are convinced that we have found a haven in one particular country, until the mammoth fish of anti-Semitism stirs and we are shaken off. Why does the Employer afflict us so, why must we, God's chosen ones, endure so much, why can we not dwell in peace and security like other nations on earth? Our Sages answer this question in Avodah Zarah 4a:

> In olden times, Jewish scholars were exempt from paying taxes. Rabbi Abbahu, who was held in high esteem by the government, commended Rabbi Safra as a great scholar and the latter was exempted from paying taxes. One day government officials put the following question to Rabbi Safra: "It

is written, 'You only have I known from all the families of the earth; therefore I will visit upon you all your iniquities' (*Amos* 3:2). How is it that God loves Yisrael and because of that He punishes them?"

Rabbi Safra could give them no answer, so they wound a scarf around his neck, intending to strangle him. When Rabbi Abbahu saw what was happening, he immediately tried to have him freed. The officials complained that Rabbi Abbahu was to blame that the great scholar that he had praised, whom they had exempted from paying taxes, could not even explain a verse from the Bible. Rabbi Abbahu told them that Rabbi Safra, a Babylonian, was a scholar in Talmud, not a scholar of the Bible, as were the Palestinian scholars. The officials then asked Rabbi Abbahu to explain the verse. Rabbi Abbahu answered with a parable: Two men borrow from a rich man. One is a friend of his, the other is not. From his friend, he will expect to be paid back little by little, whereas from the stranger he will expect payment in one sum.

So does God punish Yisrael. So that the cup of its guilt should not fill to the brim, its punishments are intermittent, permitting it to atone gradually for its sins and so be preserved unto eternity. It is the Almighty's greatest kindness to us that He always admonishes us. Where are the nations that once were the center of the world: the Egyptians, the Assyrians, the Babylonians, the Persians, the Medes, the Greeks and the Romans? Of all the nations of antiquity, only Yisrael has survived, and we owe this to the continual urging of our great Creditor Who does not allow our debt to accumulate and crush us. As it is with the nation, so it is with the individual. God often sends suffering to the righteous to remind us all of what we owe to God. In that sense, suffering may be a blessing in disguise if it causes us to understand and take to heart the admonitions of our Father in Heaven.

כֻּא הוּא הָיָה אוֹמֵר, לֹא עָלֶיךָ הַמְּלָאכָה
לִגְמוֹר וְלֹא־אַתָּה בֶן־חוֹרִין לְהִבָּטֵל
מִמֶּנָּה. אִם לָמַדְתָּ תּוֹרָה הַרְבֵּה נוֹתְנִין לְךָ שָׂכָר
הַרְבֵּה וְנֶאֱמָן הוּא בַּעַל מְלַאכְתְּךָ שֶׁיְּשַׁלֵּם לְךָ שְׂכַר
פְּעֻלָּתֶךָ וְדַע שֶׁמַּתַּן שְׂכָרָן שֶׁל־צַדִּיקִים לֶעָתִיד
לָבוֹא:

21 He would say: It is not incumbent upon you to complete the work, yet you are not free to desist from it. If you have studied much Torah, great reward will be given to you, and your employer will be faithful and pay you the reward for your work; but know that the reward of the righteous will be in the World to Come.

* * *

According to Rabbi Shemuel of Ozedah, Rabbi Tarfon feared that the severity of his previous saying might deter many from occupying themselves with the Torah and from observing God's commandents. If life is too short to complete the work, perhaps it is better not to start it at all. This thought is also found in the Midrash (*Devarim Rabbah* 9):

> A fool comes to the *beith ha-midrash*, inquires about what he will have to learn, and when he is told that the main thing he will have to learn is the Scriptures, but that he will also have to learn the Oral Law, including the six orders of the Mishnah with their sixty tractates, and also all the volumes of the Talmud, including all the *halachoth* and the *aggadoth* contained in them, well then, the fool decides he had better not even begin.

Indeed, it is said, "Wisdom is unattainable for a fool; he therefore prefers not to open his mouth in the *beith ha-midrash*" (*Mishlei* 24:7). He does not understand that wisdom must be acquired gradually.

The words of the Torah are compared to water. Just as the rain flows down from Heaven in drops and collects to form streams and rivers, so man can absorb the words of the Torah, as it were, drop by drop, two *halachoth* today and two tomorrow, until he (his knowledge) becomes like an ever-swelling river.

(Shir Ha-Shirim Rabbah 1)

The explanation of the Tosafoth to Menachoth 99b adds a somewhat deeper dimension to this thought. תנא דבי רבי ישמעאל דברי תורה לא יהיו עליך חובה ואי אתה רשאי לפטור עצמך מהן, "A *tanna* of the school of Rabbi Yishmael taught, 'The words of the Torah should not be like a duty to you, but neither are you at liberty to release yourself from them.'" On the one hand, if you regard the study of the Torah as a duty, you will say, "I have learned a paragraph, so I have done my duty" (See Rashi's explanation). We might also explain: Do not regard the Torah as your only duty, for it is splendid to learn Torah in conjunction with a worldly occupation. Or, in yet a deeper sense, do not think that it is your duty to learn the whole Torah, since it is not within your grasp to complete such a task, but nevertheless you cannot stop learning entirely.

Is it possible that the "teacher of all Yisrael," who previously warned us not to allow any excuse to interfere with our completion of the great task of study before us, now means to tell us that since we can never hope to complete it in any case, we only have to make a minimal effort? Of course not! Rabbi Wessely's explanation closes the gap in our understanding and shows us clearly what Rabbi Tarfon means. No human being, even the most righteous, can perform to utter perfection. Avraham was not successful in everything he did; Yitzchak failed with Esav; King David, and even Moshe, never attained complete success. Yet for all that, they accomplished outstanding deeds, and even though they were enabled to do so only with the help of God, they never hesitated to undertake their tasks. Therefore, although the day is short and the task is great, do not lose heart! Do not worry about completing the work; that will be done by our Father in Heaven Who blesses our efforts and brings us success.

AND YOU ARE NOT FREE TO DESIST FROM IT. One of the most exalted possessions of man is his freedom. What is freedom? A man is usually called free when he can do as he wishes, regardless of the wishes of others. According to that definition, few people are really free. Many nations were founded in freedom and simplicity. But as they grew in power and added to their territory, simplicity of life was replaced with luxury, and individual freedom with class oppression. That is what made their own decline inevitable.

Yisrael's history as a nation has been different. We started out as slaves in Mitzrayim (Egypt) and were freed by God. עבדי הם, "They are My servants," God said (*Vayyikra* 25:55), not the servants of human beings. Our freedom is the Torah, which is often likened to a tree, a simile used to indicate permanence and indestructibility; at times our nation loses its freedom but we always regain it. כי כימי העץ ימי עמי, "For as the days of a tree, are the days of My people" (*Yeshayahu* 65:22). The simile of the tree is also used in literature to indicate a blessing that begins at the foundation of a worldly dynasty and accompanies it throughout its reign. The tree is planted when the ruler is born, and it grows tall and strong as the dynasty flourishes. A thousand years pass and the tree withers as the last ruler of the dynasty, bereft of glory, sinks into the grave.

When our newborn nation came out of Mitzrayim (Egypt), Almighty God planted a tree in our midst, linking our survival to it; but this tree will not wither, for it is not mortal. Thousands of years have passed by and it remains healthy. Our tree is the Torah, called עץ חיים, "the tree of life," למחזיקים בה, "for those who cling to it" (*Mishlei* 3:18). The Torah not only gives us life but also freedom. We are free workers in the service of God; we are never dismissed from his service, not to our last breath. We shall never be able to complete all that is set out for us to do, so we cannot be paid off and told to leave. But with God's help we can become בני חורין, free men. The highest form of freedom is to do that which is good and just, to serve the Almighty with all our heart, with all our soul and with all our might. When we desist from this task we become the slaves of our passions and inclinations, no longer free. Only fools believe that the laws of the Torah were valid only during the early years of our history, that we can do without them today as civilization progresses and science reigns supreme.

IF YOU HAVE STUDIED MUCH TORAH, GREAT REWARD WILL BE GIVEN TO YOU. The Maharal of Prague commented that this mishnah seems to say that the amount of the reward is measured according to the amount of learning, while in different places in the Talmud we learn the opposite. In the first chapter of Berachoth we are told:

> Rabbi Elazar was ill and Rabbi Yochanan came to visit him. He found Rabbi Elazar crying and he asked him, "Why are you weeping? Perhaps because you are afraid that you might die young, without having succeeded in learning much Torah? Have we not learned: It is immaterial whether anyone achieves much or little if only his heart intends honestly to honor the Divine Name!"
>
> (*Berachoth* 5b)

There is therefore no difference between the one who has learned a lot and the one who has learned only a little. The Maharal points out that the solution to this contradiction is found in the last mishnah in Menachoth:

> The burnt offering of cattle, the burnt offering of a bird and the meal offering are each called a fire offering of sweet savor to teach us that whether one offers much or one offers little, it is all the same, if only one directs one's heart toward Heaven.

That does not mean that the sacrifice of cattle and the sacrifice of a bird or of flour are all the same in every sense. If that were so, why would anyone sacrifice a costly bull when flour (used for the meal offering) is far cheaper? It means that the offering of a poor man who deprives himself to purchase flour for his sacrifice is just as acceptable as the offering of a rich man who sacrifices a valuable bull. This teaches us that when a naturally gifted person succeeds in learning in one month more than it takes others a year to learn, he may not necessarily expect a larger reward. The same thing is true when one person can afford to devote all his time to Torah studies, while another person must work hard to earn a living for himself and his family. The measure of our reward, then, is the effort we make, not the amount we accomplish.

To be consistent with this, the Maharal says, the mishnah should read: אם עמלת בתורה הרבה, "If you have worked hard at learning the Torah," rather than אם למדת תורה הרבה, "If you have studied much Torah." Rabbi Tarfon's wording, however, is consistent with the preceding saying. Anyone who hires workmen for a given job is duty-bound to pay them their wages when they complete it; if they do not complete it, they do not receive the wages. But that does not apply to the completion of our task on earth: IT IS NOT INCUMBENT UPON YOU TO COMPLETE THE WORK, YET YOU ARE NOT FREE TO DESIST FROM IT. Furthermore, the obligation to study is not, for instance, like the obligation to wave the *lulav* during the Festival of Sukkoth, to be taken up once a day and then put away again. Rabbi Tarfon says that you must not set aside the Torah after looking into it once every day, but you must devote every free moment to it, for the harder you try, the greater will be your reward.

> Bar He-He asked Hillel, "What is the meaning of the verse, 'Then shall you again discern between the righteous and the wicked, between one who serves God and one who serves Him not' (*Malachi* 3:18)? 'The righteous' is the same as 'one who serves God,' and 'the wicked' is the same as 'one who serves Him not.'" Hillel answered him, " 'One who serves Him' and 'one who serves Him not' both refer to people who are perfectly righteous; but one who studies a chapter one hundred times is not comparable to one who studies it one hundred and one times."
>
> (*Chagigah* 9b)

Hillel's lesson is that the true servant of God is one who endeavors to complete the work he has begun, as far as he possibly can. A pious and God-fearing man who allows himself to be diverted from his path by the difficulties he encounters is not a true servant of God. "I have learned that passage one hundred times," he says, "and still do not know it, but that is sufficient. I have done more than my duty." The true servant of God will go over a passage, however difficult it may be, until he understands and knows it. And if he has not attained his aim on the one-hundredth attempt, he will begin again from the beginning; he will not rest until he is in complete command of the subject.

AND YOUR EMPLOYER WILL BE FAITHFUL AND PAY YOU THE REWARD FOR YOUR WORK. Commentators draw attention to the fact that Rabbi Tarfon says נותנים שכר and מתן שכר in the first and last parts of this mishnah, but here he uses the verb ישלם. השלמה means "payment" and נתינה means "grant," and is a more inclusive term for giving that connotes either paying or donating. In our relationship with God, we cannot really speak of payment since God does not owe us anything; on the contrary, we are God's debtors and however much good we may do, it will not be enough to pay off the debt we owe Him. He is our Creator, our Provider. Whoever we are and whatever we possess we owe Him. We cannot recite the grace after meals unless He has first seen to our provision, we cannot put fringes on our garment unless He has first given us the means to acquire the garment, we cannot affix the *mezuzah* on the doorpost unless He has first granted us shelter, and if He does not give us a son, we cannot perform circumcision. Countless are the kindnesses God bestows upon us in advance. How can we expect additional payment for the comparatively trifling things we do?

The question can be answered with a parable. A rich man takes in a poor orphan boy and brings him up with great care and much love. When the boy grows up, the man employs him in his business. The young man is full of love and gratitude toward his benefactor and applies himself with zeal and devotion. After ten years have gone by, his benefactor hands him a large sum of money as a reward for his work. "My father," says the young man, "how can I accept a reward from you? I owe all that I am to you and it is no more than my duty to return your kindness by helping you." "That is true," says the man. "It is your duty, but you might just as well have shirked your duty, and you did not. After all I did for you, you still might have turned your back on me and left."

Despite our huge debt to God for all we possess, we have the free will to choose to turn away from Him. The gift of free will permits us to decide our path in life, but it also turns our life into a perpetual struggle. Our inclinations, our passions and our weaknesses constantly entice us away from our duty. The temptations facing us on every side are so strong that only ardent love for our Father in Heaven can overcome them. The ample reward we will receive from the Almighty is His mark of recognition for the love and devotion we display in this perpetual struggle of ours.

A Jew brought up in the Jewish faith, used to observing the Divine commandments from early youth and inured to temptation, is conditioned to rest from his work on the Shabbath, observe the dietary laws, the conjugal laws and so forth. And still that is not all he must do to prove that he truly loves God. He must take pains to perform the commandments with a joyous heart, to devote every free minute to the study of Torah, to rejoice that God considers him worthy of enduring privations on His account. It is, simply, our duty to do whatever God has commanded, and to avoid whatever He has forbidden, whether we do so to a greater or lesser degree. The principal thing, however, is to remember that we have already been paid a thousand times over and we have no right to claim a reward for simply doing our duty. The Sages expressed it for us thus: "David said, 'I am not so sure [that I shall] see the goodness of the Lord in the land of the living' (*Tehillim* 27:13), which means, 'Master of the world, I am sure that you will pay a good reward to the righteous in the World to Come, but I do not know whether I shall have a share in it or not'" (*Berachoth* 4a).

BUT KNOW THAT THE REWARD OF THE RIGHTEOUS WILL BE IN THE WORLD TO COME. Elisha ben Avuyah was a great scholar, a disciple of Rabbi Eliezer and Rabbi Yehoshua, a companion of Rabbi Akiva and a teacher of Rabbi Meir. Once he was resting in the shade of a tree, studying, and a man came along the road with his son. The man said, "Do you see, my son, the bird's nest in this tree? Climb up and fetch it for me, but let the mother bird fly away as prescribed in the Law of Moshe." The youth obeyed his father, climbed the tree, let the mother bird fly away and took the nest together with the young birds—but the branch on which he stood broke and he fell to his death. The lamenting father carried his son away. Rabbi Elisha observed this and said, "This boy has fulfilled two of God's commandments, reverence to parents and sending the mother bird away, both of which are said to assure long life. Yet in fulfilling them this young boy's life was cut off!" As a result of this reflection, Elisha became an apostate (*Chullin* 142a).

"If Elisha had known," the Sages comment, "how his own grandson, Rabbi Ya'akov, would later explain the Torah, he would not have become an apostate." It is written: למען יאריכון ימיך ולמען ייטב לך, "in order that you may live long and that it may go well with you" (*Devarim* 5:16). Is there then a long life in this world? And when someone has reached the greatest possible age, does it not seem to him as if he had only lived a short time? Is there in this world any untroubled prosperity? Is not almost every day of human life full of trouble and pain? The promise of the Torah, Rabbi Ya'akov explains, refers to the World to Come: "In order that you may live long"—in everlasting life, "in order that it may go well with you"—in the life of eternal bliss. שכר מצוה בהאי עלמא ליכא, "The reward for keeping any of God's commandments is not given in this world but is reserved for the next" (*Chullin*, ibid.). It is commonly asked why good people are sometimes so unfortunate while sinners are so often successful. There are many answers to this question. One answer is that we cannot judge who is completely good and who is thoroughly bad; only the Omniscient One knows the secrets of the human heart and sees through outward appearances. Another answer lies in the subjective quality of happiness or misery. A person may be poor and sick, yet happy. He derives joy from fulfilling his duty in spite of pain, sorrow and care. On the other hand, there are people who ought to be happy, whose well-being or family or fame is envied by others, but are really so thoroughly miserable and unhappy in private that even the poorest man would not exchange places with them.

Neither answer is complete. If everyone who carefully observes the Shabbath laws were to become rich immediately, and the ones who transgress them were to become instantly poor—if keeping the dietary commandments and preserving conjugal purity would assure us of continued good health, while disobeying these laws would cause us to be punished with illness and death— then there would be no point in having free will. In truth, however, the World to Come is too far removed from most people's thoughts to serve as a motivation for their deeds. It is therefore a true and difficult exercise of free will to believe in the immortality of the soul and to think about the eventual reward or punishment due us for each action that we take, especially when everyone around us doubts and mocks. Rabbi Tarfon's message to us is: Have faith that the righteous will be rewarded in the World to Come, and neither poverty nor pain will induce you to doubt God's great kindness nor to depart from the right path.

Perek Three

עֲקַבְיָא בֶּן־מַהֲלַלְאֵל אוֹמֵר, הִסְתַּכֵּל בִּשְׁלֹשָׁה דְבָרִים וְאֵין אַתָּה בָא לִידֵי עֲבֵרָה, דַּע מֵאַיִן בָּאתָ וּלְאָן אַתָּה הוֹלֵךְ וְלִפְנֵי מִי אַתָּה עָתִיד לִתֵּן דִּין וְחֶשְׁבּוֹן. מֵאַיִן בָּאתָ מִטִּפָּה סְרוּחָה, וּלְאָן אַתָּה הוֹלֵךְ לִמְקוֹם עָפָר רִמָּה וְתוֹלֵעָה, וְלִפְנֵי מִי אַתָּה עָתִיד לִתֵּן דִּין וְחֶשְׁבּוֹן לִפְנֵי מֶלֶךְ מַלְכֵי הַמְּלָכִים הַקָּדוֹשׁ בָּרוּךְ הוּא:

1 Akavya ben Mahalalel says: Consider three things and you will not come into the grip of sin — know from where you came, where you are going and before whom you will have to render an account and reckoning. Where did you come from? A putrid drop. Where are you going? To a place of dust, decay and vermin. Before whom will you have to render an account and reckoning? Before the supreme King of kings, the Holy One, blessed is He.

* * *

Akavya ben Mahalalel lived about 100 years before the destruction of the Holy Temple, and therefore before all the *tannaim* mentioned in the second chapter of Avoth. The first two chapters of Avoth present the chain of succession to the Tradition in chronological order; in the other chapters, the sayings of the *tannaim* are not presented in historical order. Our Sages testify

177

that, among the hundreds of thousands who attended the bringing of the Passover sacrifice in the forecourt of the Holy Temple, no one equaled Akavya in wisdom, humility and fear of sin (*Eduyyoth* 5:6). He was also elected President of the *Sanhedrin*, but turned down the honor (ibid).

Rabi said in Avoth 2:1, "Consider three things and you will not come into the grip of sin — know what is above you: a seeing eye, and a hearing ear, and that all your deeds are recorded [in the book]." This saying is really an elaboration of the third thought mentioned by Akavya, namely the rendering of accounts before the Judge of the universe. Akavya, however, also draws our attention to those ugly qualities that most frequently cause sin: pride, pleasure-seeking and greed. Foolish man, you who proudly disdain your fellow, who exalt yourself in vanity on an imaginary throne, remember your lowly origin. You were formed from a טפה, a [putrid] drop (see Bertinoro on this mishnah). Of what are you so proud? All men have this same beginning, from the mightiest prince to the poorest laborer. Recall your origin, O man, and your pride will disappear and your vanity fade away!

The Sage does not say, "Where you will go," but "Where you are going." From the day of his birth, man is moving toward his death, every day bringing him nearer to it. If the libertine, who staggers from one pleasure to another, or the greedy person, who derives such happiness from heaping treasure upon treasure, were to stop for a moment and think about the inevitably approaching day on which he will have to leave all his treasure behind, and on which his satiated body will become food for maggots and worms, he would think more about the state of his soul than about the accumulation of worldly pleasures. Man is like a cashier in a big bank who sees great sums of money pass through his hands daily. If he did not have to hand in a daily accounting, he might easily be tempted to steal; because he knows that at any time his books may be called in for auditing, he will not give in so easily to temptation. The man who erroneously believes that he will never have to account for his moral commissions and omissions is in a similar position. If he realizes that one day he will have to render account before the Almighty, the Omniscient God, for everything he has done or left undone on earth, he will conscientiously fulfill his duties and try to stay clear of wrongdoing.

The Sage does not say, "You will not sin," but "You will not come into the grip (literally, the hands) of sin." His intention is to teach us that there are two kinds of sinners: those who search after sin and those who are simply not strong enough to resist temptation. If we bear in mind constantly the three things that Akavya mentions, it will prevent us from both actively and passively sinning. Moreover, the meaning of יד is not only "hand" but also "handle" (see also commentary on *Avoth* 2:1). What we think are small, insignificant transgressions ease one into committing ever more serious sins. A tiny "white" lie, a sip or a mere taste of non-kosher food, these are the "handles" of sin by which one is led into immorality, profanation and desecration.

Rabbi Wessely, in his commentary Yain Levanon, derives an even deeper implication from a comparison of Rabbi's mishnah with this one of Akavya. Both Sages say הסתכל (consider), so that you will דע (know), in order to show the significance of man's gift of reason. If man were endowed with superior reason purely for the better enjoyment of earthly pleasures, then surely his body would also have been created superior to the bodies of other creatures. The truth is precisely the opposite: a calf or a lamb needs far less maternal care than a human child; the plant grows from its seed and the tree from its fruit without human intervention. If you *consider* your existence on earth, you will come to *know* that its purpose is not contained in the body but in the potential splendor of the human soul. You will therefore protect your soul by keeping far away from sin and by filling your heart with God's wisdom.

The very humbleness of the human body, says Rabbi Wessely, proves the grandeur of the human soul. "From the mouths of babes and sucklings, You have established strength...When I behold Your heavens...the moon and the stars You have prepared...What is the frail human that You should remember him?...[Yet] You have made him only a little less than the angels..."(*Tehillim* 8:3-6). The commentator asks why the sun is not mentioned in this psalm — surely it is more significant than the moon or the stars? And also, why is the word כוננתה, "You have prepared," used here? Rabbi Wessely explains that just as God prepared the moon and the stars to receive the light of the sun, so man's body was prepared by Him to receive the Divine light of the soul. That is what raises him to the level of the angels and that is why he was given dominion over the earth and its creatures. If we *consider* that man originates in a fetid drop and ends in decay and decomposition, we will *know* that the soul is far more valuable than the body and that we must therefore always nourish it with Torah study and good deeds, and keep it pure by walking in God's ways and avoiding sin.

בֶּ רַבִּי חֲנִינָא סְגַן הַכֹּהֲנִים אוֹמֵר, הֱוֵי
מִתְפַּלֵּל בִּשְׁלוֹמָהּ שֶׁל מַלְכוּת, שֶׁאִלְמָלֵא
מוֹרָאָהּ, אִישׁ אֶת רֵעֵהוּ חַיִּים בְּלָעוֹ:

2 Rabbi Chanina, the deputy High Priest, says: Pray
continually for the welfare of the government — if
not for the fear of it, men would swallow each other
alive.

*   *   *

A deputy High Priest was always appointed to substitute for the
High Priest if, for any reason, the latter became incapacitated
(*Yoma* 39a). Rabbi Chanina was a companion of *Rabban* Yochanan
ben Zakkai and, like the latter, survived the destruction of the
Holy Temple (*Pesachim* 14a; *Eduyyoth* 2:1,2,3; *Yoma* 21b). He died
a martyr's death on the 25th of *Sivan*, the same day on which
Rabbi Shimon ben Gamliel and Rabbi Yishmael met their deaths
(*Orach Chayyim* 580:2), although apparently not in the same year.
With this saying, Rabbi Chanina not only teaches us how to
behave toward the state in which we live, but also explains the
entire concept of statehood. The philosopher Hegel asked,
"Which came first, the individuals forming the state or the state
itself?" This is not a paradox; the point is that if a state is merely
a loose aggregation of individuals, then it is not truly a state. A
true state is an entity whose parts do not exist separately and
which may even exist only conceptually. We may also infer that
the state is a Divinely-inspired institution which provides a social
order enabling men to live together.

    When the Jewish State was destroyed and the Jews were led
into Babylonian captivity, the prophet Yirmeyahu sent them a
letter, saying:

> Thus said the Lord of hosts, the God of Yisrael, to all the
> exiles whom I have caused to be carried away from
> Yerushalayim to Bavel: Build houses and dwell in them, and
> plant gardens and eat the fruit of them, take wives and beget
> sons and daughters, and take wives for your sons and give

your daughters to husbands, that they may bear sons and daughters, that you may multiply there and not be diminished. And seek the peace of the city to which I have caused you to be carried away captive, and pray to the Lord for it; for in it you shall have peace.

(Yirmeyahu 29:4-7)

A pious person needs the protection of the government perhaps more than anyone else. If the state did not protect him from violence, he would be victimized by the treachery, brutality and baseness of its wicked citizens. The Sage therefore says הוי מתפלל, "pray continually," and not merely התפלל, "pray," for the welfare of the government. There are, of course, governments that hardly live up to the ideal—governments that allow arbitrary judgments to take the place of the law, that show preference to some classes of citizens at the expense of others, governments whose executive organs are corrupt. Should the Jew be an obedient citizen to a corrupt government?

Rabbi Chanina lived under such a government. The Roman hegemony was cruel, corrupt and tyrannical, yet he taught his disciples to pray continually for its welfare because even an unfair and despotic government is a thousand times better than anarchy and no government at all. Without some controlling force, "men would swallow each other alive." Lion and tiger kill their prey before they eat it, but man-turned-beast wants to swallow his victims alive! History confirms this; bestial anarchy followed the Peasant Wars and the French Revolution, and in the days of the Paris Commune, which was not an ordered government, terrible and dreadful acts were permitted in the name of the "state." On every Shabbath and Festival, Jews in the Diaspora recite the prayer *Ha-nothen teshuah*, asking the Almighty to further the welfare and peace of the whole country, and particularly of those whom the All-knowing has appointed as rulers over their state.

רַבִּי חֲנַנְיָא בֶּן־תְּרַדְיוֹן אוֹמֵר, שְׁנַיִם
שֶׁיּוֹשְׁבִין וְאֵין בֵּינֵיהֶם דִּבְרֵי תוֹרָה הֲרֵי
זֶה מוֹשַׁב לֵצִים, שֶׁנֶּאֱמַר וּבְמוֹשַׁב לֵצִים לֹא יָשָׁב.
אֲבָל שְׁנַיִם שֶׁיּוֹשְׁבִין וְיֵשׁ בֵּינֵיהֶם דִּבְרֵי תוֹרָה
שְׁכִינָה שְׁרוּיָה בֵּינֵיהֶם, שֶׁנֶּאֱמַר אָז נִדְבְּרוּ יִרְאֵי יְיָ
אִישׁ אֶל־רֵעֵהוּ וַיַּקְשֵׁב יְיָ וַיִּשְׁמָע וַיִּכָּתֵב סֵפֶר זִכָּרוֹן
לְפָנָיו לְיִרְאֵי יְיָ וּלְחֹשְׁבֵי שְׁמוֹ. אֵין לִי אֶלָּא שְׁנַיִם,
מִנַּיִן אֲפִילוּ אֶחָד שֶׁיּוֹשֵׁב וְעוֹסֵק בַּתּוֹרָה שֶׁהַקָּדוֹשׁ
בָּרוּךְ הוּא קוֹבֵעַ לוֹ שָׂכָר, שֶׁנֶּאֱמַר יֵשֵׁב בָּדָד וְיִדֹּם
כִּי נָטַל עָלָיו:

3 Rabbi Chanina ben Teradyon says: If two sit together and words of Torah are not exchanged between them, this is a session of scorners, as it is said,
"And [happy is the man who] never sat in a session of
scorners" (*Tehillim* 1:1). But if two sit together and
exchange words of Torah, the presence of God abides
with them, for it is said, "Then those who fear God
spoke with one another, and God noted and heard,
and a book of remembrance was written before Him
for those who fear God and think about His name"
(*Malachi* 3:16). If this verse refers to two people, how
then do I know that if even one person sits and occupies himself with the Torah, the Holy One, blessed is
He, will determine a reward for him? Because it is
said, "Let him sit alone and keep silent, for He has
laid it (the reward) upon him" (*Eichah* 3:28).

*   *   *

Rabbi Chanina ben Teradyon acted upon this saying all his life,
and indeed, it cost him his life. After destroying Beithar, Hadrian
strictly prohibited the study of Torah, and anyone who disobeyed

this law was liable to the death sentence. The Sage, however, did not stop assembling his disciples around him and teaching them Torah. Rabbi Yosei ben Kisma warned him, but he disregarded the warning. His whole family then suffered for his disobedience: his younger, unmarried daughter was sent to a brothel, his wife was murdered and he himself was tortured to death by the Romans. Wrapped in a *Sefer Torah*, he was dragged to the stake to be consumed by fire, and Hadrian ordered moist wool placed over his heart to prolong the agony. The executioner was compassionate and advised him to remove the wool himself, but Rabbi Chanina refused to hasten death by his own hand. When Rabbi Chanina's eldest son-in-law, the famous Rabbi Meir, risked his life to rescue his sister-in-law from the house of shame, the Romans set savage dogs upon him, but a miracle happened and the dogs did him no harm. When a Jew is attacked by dogs today, he still prays, "Almighty God, Who once saved Meir from the dogs, listen to my prayer!" (*Avodah Zarah* 18a,b).

There are a number of difficulties to be overcome in Rabbi Chanina's saying. The complete verse from Tehillim 1:1 upon which Rabbi Chanina based his saying is, "Happy is the man who has not *walked* in the counsel of the *wicked* nor *stood* in the way of *sinners*, nor *sat* in the session of *scorners*." Commentators of the Bible have pointed out that the order of terms used for transgressors is unexpectedly in diminishing order of strength: the wicked do wrong wantonly and intentionally, sinners do wrong in error or from ignorance, scorners only sin with their mouths. The order of the verbs, however, emphasizes increasing order of strength. Happy is the man who has not "walked" in the counsel of the lawless, who has always carefully avoided having even a passing or temporary connection with people who wantonly and intentionally do evil. "Standing" implies a more lingering contact. You should not "stand" with people who sin in error or from ignorance; a short connection is often unavoidable, but once you have recognized their ways, leave them immediately.

What is meant by "sitting" with scorners? The word "sit" implies settling down for a considerable time, as we read in Bereshith 37:1: וישב יעקב בארץ מגורי אביו, "And Ya'akov settled in the land of his father's sojournings." And so we understand that two who sit down together, not two who meet by chance, are obliged to exchange words of Torah with one another. The Sage does not say that they must literally study the Torah together, for that is not always possible, but that their conversation should reflect the Torah and its teachings. Two who sit down to play cards, for instance, can certainly be called scorners in session. Perhaps they do not mock in the full sense of the word, but they are in effect scorning the holy Torah about which they might be conversing instead of wasting precious time in what is at best a useless game.

This first verse of Tehillim continues, "But his delight is in the Law of the Lord, and in His Law does he meditate day and night" (ibid. 1:2). One who occupies himself with the Torah fulfills God's commandment, "And you shall speak about them (the words of the Torah) when you sit in your house, when you walk by the way, when you lie down and when you rise up" (*Devarim* 6:7). And further, "This Book of the Law shall not depart from your mouth and you shall meditate in it day and night" (*Yehoshua* 1:8). The Torah is an invaluable treasure, a gift, but it only becomes ours if we expend great effort to acquire it (*Avoth* 2:17). The commandment to meditate in the Torah is the most important one of all: ותלמוד תורה כנגד כולם, "But the study of the Torah excels them all" (*Pe'ah* 1:1). The performance of this, above all other commandments, clarifies our thoughts, reveals to us what is wisdom and what is foolishness; it teaches us to look about ourselves with a "spiritual eye," to see the Almighty's miracles and to comprehend the infinite love shown by His great mercy. As we learn to recognize His ways and the ways of the Torah as fair and just, and as we learn to fear God and to love our fellowman, the reflection of the Divine Majesty itself will rest upon each one of us.

THOSE WHO FEAR GOD AND THINK ABOUT HIS NAME. The verse from Malachi is included as confirmation of the maxim, but the verse itself requires explanation. First, "they spoke" is passive: נדברו, instead of ידברו; second, ויקשב יי וישמע, "and God noted and heard," is repetitious; third, what is the difference between ולחשבי שמו, "those who think about His name," and יראי יי, "those who fear God"? To explain these peculiarities, we have to consider the prophet's words in context. Malachi was admonishing the sons and daughters of his people on account of what they had been saying in public. "You have said: It is vain to serve God, and what profit is it that we have kept His ordinance and that we have walked mournfully before the Lord of Hosts. And now we call the proud "happy"; those who are wicked are elevated; those who try God are even delivered [from misfortune]" (*Malachi* 3:14-15).

These ancient phrases have become fashionable again! How often do we hear people of little faith say that only those who swim with the tide will thrive, that the observance of the Shabbath and the dietary laws does not yield any profit, that those who walk in God's ways are often exposed to poverty and sickness? How does all this meaningless talk originate? Solely because they scorn the Torah, because they have removed it from their daily lives.

Furthermore, the prophet says, אז נדברו, which can mean "they persuaded" or "they yielded," as in the expression: כי ידברו את אויבים בשער, "when they speak with (persuade) their enemies at the gate" (*Tehillim* 127:5). Those who truly fear God will yield to one another in their discussions of Torah, each one learning from the other. Those who are working together for a charitable cause will cooperate with each other, eschewing honor and praise. Then, as they yield to others, God will listen to them, and as they honor others, so God will honor them. Although this in itself would be sufficient reward, in yielding to one another, these God-fearing people are showing that they respect God's name. Which is the Name of God? We call Him the Almighty, the Omniscient, the Eternal, all names referring to His individual attributes, yet there is another name that is all-embracing and still more accessible to our comprehension than the four-lettered, unutterable one: the whole Torah is the Name of God. He who studies the Torah wholeheartedly, who tries to penetrate its nature and spirit, who tries to comprehend every turn of phrase and the true meaning of every letter, proves that he truly "thinks about" God's name.

IF THIS VERSE REFERS TO TWO PEOPLE, HOW THEN DO I KNOW THAT IF EVEN ONE PERSON SITS AND OCCUPIES HIM- SELF WITH THE TORAH, THE HOLY ONE, BLESSED IS HE, WILL DETERMINE A REWARD FOR HIM? BECAUSE IT IS SAID, "LET HIM SIT ALONE AND KEEP SILENT, FOR HE HAS LAID IT (THE REWARD) UPON HIM" (*Eichah* 3:28). Literally, ישב בדד וידם כי נטל עליו means, "He will sit alone and keep silent because he has taken it upon him." Who has taken what upon whom? Some commentators interpret this as meaning that God has appointed it (the reward) for the one who has taken the burden of Torah upon himself. Rabbi Ya'avetz the *Chasid* explains that this verse is part of the lament of Yirmeyahu the Prophet, who first describes his awesome distress at the destruction of the Holy Temple (*Eichah* 3:1-20), and then continues: טוב לגבר כי ישא על בנעוריו: ישב בדד וידם כי נטל עליו, "It is good for a man to bear a yoke in his youth. Let one sit in solitude and be submissive, for He has laid it upon him" (ibid. 27-28). Although man may be alone, without a companion to talk to, his early habit of learning Torah will never desert him and he can study by himself; though he may bear a heavy burden in life, he will be confident that God, Who has inflicted "it", the burden, upon him, will also "lay" the reward upon him.

When the Sage asks, therefore, "How do I know that even one individual who sits and occupies himself with the Torah will be rewarded by God?" the answer is צדיק יסוד עולם, "The righteous man is the foundation of the world" (*Mishlei* 10:25). Even if there is only one person who upholds the Covenant with God, as once our father Avraham did, then that one becomes the "foundation pillar" on which the universe rests, that person will "sit alone" and learn by himself "in silence," for he has taken upon himself the task of all Jewry, and he will therefore receive an appropriate reward.

Rashi compares ידם with דמו (to wait) (*Shemuel* I, 14:9) and נטל with נוטל (to decree) (*Shemuel* II, 24:12); thus the verse might mean, "He will sit alone and wait patiently for whatever God has decreed for him." One who studies the Torah alone, with neither the encouragement of a companion nor the approval of others, may feel lonely or forsaken, but he will receive a rich reward from God. Alternatively, *Rabbenu* Menachem Meiri compares ידם

to the Targum Yerushalmi on Vayyikra 10:3, וידם אהרן, "and Aharon praised [the Name]," so that the verse might also mean, "He will sit alone and praise the Name of God, whatever He may have decreed for him." There is no greater praise and glory for the Name of God than when we study His holy Torah.

Another version, also attributed to Rashi, compares נטל with the Aramaic word מטללתא, meaning "roof" or "protection." The verse might thus also be read, "He will sit alone and persevere [in his studies], for God's protection is over him." An illustration of this is seen in the following story.

After the expulsion of the Jews from Spain, a law was enacted under the Emperor, Charles the Fifth, also called Charles the First of Spain, which ordered death by fire to any Jew who set foot upon Spanish soil. Centuries later, a ship with a Jew on board ran aground on the Spanish coast. The law was still in force, so the Jew, who had escaped death from drowning at sea, was now condemned by Spanish law to a fiery death. The king commuted his sentence to life imprisonment. The condemned man happened to have a small Amsterdam edition of Tractate Chagigah with him, which was his salvation, for with it he studied day and night. He completed the tractate many times, pondering over every word, and came to understand all the great wisdom contained in it. Seventeen years passed and the prisoner hardly felt the severity of his imprisonment.

Meanwhile, he grew old and weak and felt death approaching. One night as he stretched out on his wooden bed, he sighed aloud, "I shall die here lonely and forsaken without a loving hand to close my eyes!" That night the dying man had a dream. It suddenly became bright as day in the dark cell and the tall figure of a woman stood at the head of his bed. "I am Tractate Chagigah," she said, "which you studied so well. I have assuaged your loneliness for seventeen years and have come now so that you will not have to die alone; I shall cover your eyes when they close forever. They may do what they like with your lifeless body, but God has assigned you infinite reward in the World to Come." A happy smile transfigured the features of the dying man and his lips murmured the verse: ישב בדד וידם כי נטל עליו, "He will sit alone and persevere [to study the Torah], for God's protection is over him."

ד רַבִּי שִׁמְעוֹן אוֹמֵר, שְׁלֹשָׁה שֶׁאָכְלוּ עַל
שֻׁלְחָן אֶחָד וְלֹא אָמְרוּ עָלָיו דִּבְרֵי תוֹרָה
כְּאִלּוּ אָכְלוּ מִזִּבְחֵי מֵתִים, שֶׁנֶּאֱמַר כִּי כָּל־שֻׁלְחָנוֹת
מָלְאוּ קִיא צוֹאָה בְּלִי מָקוֹם. אֲבָל שְׁלֹשָׁה שֶׁאָכְלוּ
עַל שֻׁלְחָן אֶחָד וְאָמְרוּ עָלָיו דִּבְרֵי תוֹרָה כְּאִלּוּ
אָכְלוּ מִשֻּׁלְחָנוֹ שֶׁל־מָקוֹם, שֶׁנֶּאֱמַר וַיְדַבֵּר אֵלַי זֶה
הַשֻּׁלְחָן אֲשֶׁר לִפְנֵי יְיָ:

4 Rabbi Shimon says: If three ate at the same table and did not utter words of Torah, it is as if they had partaken of an idolatrous meal, as it is said, "For all the tables are filled with excretory things, without space" (*Yeshayahu* 28:8). But three who ate at a table and uttered words of Torah there, it is as if they had eaten at the table of God, as it is said, "And he said to me, 'This is the table which is before the Lord'" (*Yechezkel* 41:22).

* * *

When the Mishnah or the Baraytha mentions Rabbi Shimon, without any other name, it almost always refers to Rabbi Shimon bar Yochai, one of the younger disciples of Rabbi Akiva. Acclaimed both by his contemporaries and by posterity, Rabbi Shimon bar Yochai was one of the most remarkable men that ever lived. In his lifetime people would say, "Happy is the age in which a man like Rabbi Shimon bar Yochai lives," and even today thousands of people pray at his grave every year on the anniversary of his death (the 18th of Iyyar, the 33rd day of the counting of the Omer). His father Yochai sided with the Romans during Hadrian's terrible persecutions of the Jews and that was probably why Rabbi Akiva at first refused to accept young Shimon in his academy (*Pesachim* 112a). Shimon nevertheless became a disciple of Rabbi Akiva and was known as one of the pillars of the Torah, along with Rabbi Yosei, Rabbi Meir, Rabbi Yehudah and Rabbi

Nechemyah. When Rabbi Shimon was sentenced to death by the Romans, he and his son hid in a cave, where they studied Torah continually for thirteen years. After the Emperor Hadrian's death, Rabbi Shimon was sent to Rome. There, because he was able to heal the ailing daughter of Antoninus, the new emperor, Hadrian's decrees against the Jews were abolished.

In addition to achieving greatness in Talmud, Rabbi Shimon also became an expert in the hidden wisdom of Kabbalah and was its principal exponent. That he is called the author of the holy Zohar does not mean that he actually wrote it; the later Sages mentioned in it, his son and his disciples, all received their wisdom from him, so only in that sense can the holy book be called "his."

The questions we seek to answer in order to understand Rabbi Shimon's saying are the following. First, what is the significance of three people eating together? Why not another number? Second, why use the past tense specifying a meal that has already been eaten, when the intention is all such meals, in the present and the future? Third, why does the Sage describe a meal unaccompanied by words of Torah in such strongly opprobrious terms, and the opposite in such exalted ones? After all, everyone must eat. Fourth and fifth, in what way does the verse from Yeshayahu support the maxim, and what do the enigmatic words "without space" signify? Sixth, why does this mishnah not mention a meal in which two, or even one, are at the table? Seventh, how does the verse from Yechezkel, which does not even mention eating, apply to the Sage's words? Eighth, why is the entire meal sanctified retroactively, as it were, and how can these few words of Torah change a meal so radically from an idolatrous sacrifice to a meal shared at God's table?

IF THREE ATE. For some people, eating and drinking are the highest purposes in life. Man consumes more meat than any other flesh-eating creature. The number of oxen, cows, calves, sheep, goats, birds, fish and other creatures consumed by an individual man during his lifetime is colossal. Rabbi Shimon therefore teaches that particularly at mealtimes we have to show that we are worthy of being lords of creation. By speaking words of Torah at mealtimes, we prove that the main purpose of our lives is not physical preservation, feeding our body, but the maintenance of our spirit, which is God-given, and which is God's instrument to assure our dominion over all the other creatures. When three men dine at the same table, they are commanded to recite grace together (זימון) after the meal. Hence, the one who ate, who finished his meal first, will have to wait for the other two, or two will have to wait for the third, to finish. During this interval they should be occupied with words of Torah and not with idle gossip. The Sage does not suggest speaking words of Torah during the meal, since speaking while eating is prohibited in order to prevent choking as a result of food or drink entering the windpipe (*Ta'anith* 5b). The Sage speaks of three men because if there are only two at the table, each one may recite grace by himself and leave as soon as he has finished his meal.

AN IDOLATROUS MEAL. A man does not live on what he eats but on what he digests. Only a small part of the food and drink he enjoys is turned into living matter; most of it passes through his body and is discharged. Food that is superfluous to the body's needs is therefore turned into קיא צואה, "excretory things" (literally: vomit and excreta), and gluttonous feasts are called זבחי מתים, "idolatrous meals" (literally: sacrifices of the dead). In the Torah, idolatrous sacrifices are called sacrifices of the dead because they are forbidden for any use and are therefore considered non-existent. קיא צואה has a use as fertilizer, but זבחי מתים may not even be used for that. The prophet's words בלי מקום (without space) therefore mean "non-existent."

AT THE TABLE OF GOD. When three people have eaten together at the same table and have spoken words of Torah, it is the same as if they had eaten of God's food (i.e., the sacrifices in the Temple), and only the priests were allowed to do that. In fact they were required to consume a part of the sacrifices.

In the verse from Yechezkel cited in the mishnah, the angel speaks of the Lord's table in this way: "The altar of wood...and he said to me: This is the table which is [laid] before the Lord." The altar is apparently called "table," but we are told that the table was for the showbreads while the altar was for the incense offering. By coupling this verse with his saying, Rabbi Shimon reveals its meaning. The showbreads, for which the table was exclusively intended, were consumed by the priests; the incense on the altar was completely consumed by fire, a wholly Divine sacrifice. The angel was therefore telling Yechezkel that, just as the altar is an instrument of Divine service, the priests' consumption of the showbreads for Divine service renders the table a hallowed instrument as well. Thus any table at which we eat and drink and speak words of Torah resembles the table of the showbreads in the Holy Temple. The words of Torah are the "incense" we offer on the "altar" of God which imparts sanctity to the table from which we consume our meal.

If three people who wait to say grace together can thereby achieve such a great thing, it goes without saying that two people who have eaten together — who have no obligation whatever, but wait for each other and speak words of Torah together — dine, as it were, from God's table. The same applies to one person, and no special proof of this is needed. Family meals, when they are properly managed, have the greatest educational value. Children ought to be trained to bless God both before and after meals, and a father should enjoy this often rare opportunity to speak words of Torah to his children and to hear what they have learned. In this way the family table becomes a sacred place, an altar of God.

ה רַבִּי חֲנִינָא בֶּן־חֲכִינַאי אוֹמֵר, הַנֵּעוֹר
בַּלַּיְלָה וְהַמְהַלֵּךְ בַּדֶּרֶךְ יְחִידִי וְהַמְפַנֶּה
לִבּוֹ לְבַטָלָה הֲרֵי זֶה מִתְחַיֵּב בְּנַפְשׁוֹ:

5 Rabbi Chanina ben Chachinai says: One who
stays awake at night and one who goes on his way
alone and one who turns his heart to idleness, sins
against his own soul.

* * *

Rabbi Chanina ben Chachinai was another famous disciple of the
great Rabbi Akiva. His teacher found him worthy of being taught
the hidden secrets of the holy Torah, מעשה המרכבה (*Chagigah*
14b). There are two readings of this saying. In the above reading,
which is found in the oldest manuscripts, the three different
actions which can destroy the soul have parallel syntax. In the
alternate reading, והמפנה, "and one who turns," reads ומפנה, "and
turns," joining the second and third actions to the same subject:
"one who goes on his way alone and turns his heart to idle
things." Rashi and Bertinoro used the second reading and seem
to have accepted it as a necessary correction because the first
reading was not understood. Rabbi Ya'avetz the *Chasid* also wrote
that the first reading was faulty, "since there is no artist who can
explain it." But an artist was found. Rabbi Menachem Meiri
explains the mishnah this way: Man was created with a need for
sleep at night, a need for protection from attack and a need for
occupation. Any man who foolishly goes without sleep, exposes
himself needlessly to danger, or fritters his time away in idleness
is placing his soul at risk, and that is tantamount to committing
suicide.

Rabbi Shemuel of Ozedah also explains the first reading:
Man's life can be compared to a day — childhood is morning,
manhood is midday and old age is evening. The one who awakens only at night, when it is too late to begin a new life, is himself
to blame for the ruin of his soul; the one who spends his mature
years alienating himself from others, without consideration for

even those who depend on him, is also to blame for the ruin of his soul; and the one who is already awake in the morning of his life, who wishes to do good but still turns his heart to unimportant things, forgetting to transmit the love of God to his family — he, too, will ruin his soul. Therefore, young man, awaken early to true life, educate your family, and above all, avoid the lure of your idle whims.

Most interpreters of Avoth, however, use the second reading, ומפנה, "and turns." Rashi, Bertinoro and others explain that Almighty God has bestowed upon us His precious treasure, the holy Torah, not only to teach us the path to perfection in this life and in the World to Come, but to provide actual protection for us against danger. Our Sages relate that Rabbi Yehoshua ben Levi visited and cared for sick people suffering from infectious diseases, without fear of contamination, since the Torah, his continual occupation, protected him. A well-known proverb says: "Night is no one's friend." Dangers threaten at night that do not exist in bright daylight, and a solitary traveler is more likely to encounter danger than one who is not alone. But if a man occupies his mind with Torah on such occasions, he need not fear.

Rabbi Ya'avetz, using the second reading, explains that the warning applies to someone whose principal occupation is the Torah, but fears that so much extra study, as on a journey or in the middle of a sleepless night, will drain his strength. On the contrary, we read in Mishlei 11:24, "that which is spent freely yet increases" is man's strength while he learns Torah; and the words in Mishlei 10:27, "the fear of the Lord prolongs days," are explained by *Rabbenu* Yonah the *Chasid*: "Worries weaken a man's strength and lead to an early death, but the concern to serve God...will not shorten man's days but...prolong them."

According to Rabbi Wessely, the two examples of spare time mentioned in the mishnah must be regarded as just that: examples. If a man does not devote an occasional spare moment to learning during the course of a busy day, it is not such a great offense. However, on any occasion where he might study undisturbed and does not do so, as on a long journey or early in the morning before going to work, he is indeed guilty of a grave sin, עון בטול תורה, "neglect of the study of the Torah," for learning

Torah leads to the fulfillment of all the other commandments. The Wise King says, עד מתי עצל תשכב מתי תקום משנתך, "How long will you lie there, O sluggard? When will you arise from your sleep?" (*Mishlei* 6:9). The commentators ask why Shelomo does not say, "Awake from your sleep." The answer, they say, is that Shelomo is addressing someone who lies in bed awake, indulging his fancy in all kinds of lascivious daydreams. Such a habit is highly dangerous, particularly for a young man, and likely to lead him astray. Anyone who has slept long enough should quickly arise, wash, dress, attend synagogue and then begin his day's work. If you wake up at night and cannot get up to study because it is cold or dark, you should turn your thoughts to serious matters or revise what you have already learned.

TURNS HIS HEART TO IDLENESS. The Wise King says, "Guard your heart above all; it is the source of life" (*Mishlei* 4:23). Many a young man must leave his parents' home in order to study and to prepare for his future vocation. Setting out alone, he will be exposed to all kinds of temptations and passions. A young man must protect himself in this way: first, he should comprehend the seriousness of life; then he should try to find a teacher who will advance his knowledge of Torah; and finally he should acquire a companion with whom to study Torah. If he occupies himself with vain things in his free time, visiting bars and keeping bad company, he will have only himself to blame for the ruin of his soul. Therefore, young man, turn your heart to the Torah and do not worry, for the Lord will protect you on your way.

רַבִּי נְחוּנְיָא בֶּן־הַקָּנָה אוֹמֵר, כָּל־הַמְקַבֵּל
עָלָיו עוֹל תּוֹרָה מַעֲבִירִין מִמֶּנּוּ עוֹל
מַלְכוּת וְעוֹל דֶּרֶךְ אֶרֶץ, וְכָל־הַפּוֹרֵק מִמֶּנּוּ עוֹל
תּוֹרָה נוֹתְנִין עָלָיו עוֹל מַלְכוּת וְעוֹל דֶּרֶךְ אֶרֶץ:

6 Rabbi Nechunya ben Ha-Kanah says: [A man] who takes upon himself the yoke of Torah, from him the yoke of government and the yoke of worldly affairs will be lifted. But [a man] who casts off the yoke of Torah, upon him will be laid the yoke of government and the yoke of worldly affairs.

* * *

Rabbi Nechunya ben Ha-Kanah lived in the time of the Holy Temple and was a contemporary of *Rabban* Yochanan ben Zakkai. In Bava Bathra 10b, it appears that he was one of the latter's disciples, but it is known that *Rabban* Yochanan addressed all his disciples by name except Nechunya, whom he called "Rabbi." Rabbi Nechunya is best known for the prayers he pronounced on entering and leaving the *beith ha-midrash*. On entering he used to say, "May it be Your will, O Lord my God, that no offense may occur through me and that I may not err in a matter of *Halachah*, causing my colleagues to rejoice over me (i.e., over my discomfiture) and so bring sin upon themselves, and that I may not say that unclean is clean, or clean is unclean and that my colleagues may not err in a matter of *Halachah*, causing me to rejoice over them and so bring sin upon myself." On leaving the *beith ha-midrash* he used to say, "I give thanks to You, O Lord my God, that You have set my portion with those who sit in the *beith ha-midrash* and You have not set my portion with those who stand at street corners (or in taverns); for I rise early and they rise early, but I rise early for words of Torah and they rise early for frivolous talk. I labor and they labor; I shall receive my reward for my endeavor one day but they will not receive any reward for their labor. I run and they run; I run to the life of the World to Come but they to the pit of destruction" (*Berachoth* 28b).

His disciples asked him, "Rabbi, by what virtue have you reached such an advanced age?" He replied, "Never in my life have I sought respect through the degradation of my fellow; when someone offended me, I forgave him even before I went to bed. I have been generous with my money, especially by arranging loans for the poor" (*Megillah* 28a). Rabbi Nechunya is also noted for his sagacity and erudition; he is the author of Sefer Ha-Bahir, a work on Kabbalah.

In this maxim he refers to three types of yoke: the yoke of תורה (Torah), the yoke of מלכות (government) and the yoke of דרך ארץ (worldly affairs). Rabbi Wessely says that the Sage here speaks of one who accepts the yoke of Torah despite suffering and affliction. "My life is always at risk, but I never forget Your Torah. The wicked laid a snare for me, but I did not stray from Your precepts" (*Tehillim* 119: 109-110).

Rabbi Shemuel of Ozedah asks why the Sage says "who takes upon himself" and "who casts off" instead of "who takes upon himself" and "who does not take upon himself" the yoke of Torah. A man is inclined to feel overburdened by his worldly problems, but if, because of them, he gives up continual Torah study, we cannot say that he has cast off the yoke of Torah. An ordinary, overburdened Jew cannot be expected to find much time for concentrated study, but if he takes the yoke of Torah upon himself, despite all obstacles, then all the other yokes he bears will be removed from him. Only a man who has the time and means to study and does not do so can be said to cast off the yoke of Torah, and it is he who will be afflicted with other yokes. The Torah enumerates the things he will suffer; he will have to serve his enemies in hunger and thirst, in nakedness and want (*Devarim* 28:48). When a rich man refuses refreshment to a poor man, hostile warriors will come and demand the best wine from his cellar; when a rich man refuses a garment to a poor man, his best clothes will be taken from him (*Eliyyahu Zuta* 16).

The עול מלכות (yoke of government) and the עול דרך ארץ (yoke of worldly affairs) are explained uniquely by Rabbi Shemuel of Ozedah. The world is ruled, he says, both by God's will and by God-given laws of nature. The first is מלכות, "government," which is effectuated by Divine decree, and the second is דרך ארץ, "the way of the earth," that is to say, the natural course of life. One who has truly submitted himself to the yoke of Torah achieves such a degree of piety that he no longer has to be subject to the laws of nature, and sometimes even the will of the Almighty cedes to his. Just think how God's wrath was softened by Moshe *Rabbenu*'s pleas when the Israelites made the golden calf; just remember how Shemuel was granted a thunderstorm in the Holy Land during the dry season, and how Eliyyahu was granted drought for three years in a row to punish the idol-worshiping Jews.

When the Sage says "casts off" instead of "does not take upon himself," it is clear that he must be referring to the same person "who takes upon himself" the yoke of Torah, for one cannot cast off what one has never put on. In this case the "yoke" must be understood to mean perpetual study of the Torah rather than the obligation to observe the commandments. It is recorded that Menachem, Dean of the *Sanhedrin* when Hillel was President, left the Academy and entered the king's service; his example influenced one hundred and sixty others to cast off the yoke of study in exchange for wordly position and wealth (*Chagigah* 16b). They did not cease to be observing Jews, but as it happened, their service became burdensome and oppressive, for they held office under the tyrant Herod. The great Menachem, who might have surpassed Shammai, is today forgotten, while Hillel and Shammai, who refused the worldly pleasures and riches of high office for the sake of bearing the yoke of Torah, escaped the far heavier yokes of government and worldly affairs.

רַבִּי חֲלַפְתָּא בֶּן־דּוֹסָא אִישׁ כְּפַר חֲנַנְיָא
אוֹמֵר, עֲשָׂרָה שֶׁיּוֹשְׁבִין וְעוֹסְקִין בַּתּוֹרָה
שְׁכִינָה שְׁרוּיָה בֵּינֵיהֶם, שֶׁנֶּאֱמַר אֱלֹהִים נִצָּב
בַּעֲדַת־אֵל. וּמִנַּיִן אֲפִילוּ חֲמִשָּׁה, שֶׁנֶּאֱמַר וַאֲגֻדָּתוֹ
עַל־אֶרֶץ יְסָדָהּ. וּמִנַּיִן אֲפִילוּ שְׁלֹשָׁה, שֶׁנֶּאֱמַר
בְּקֶרֶב אֱלֹהִים יִשְׁפֹּט. וּמִנַּיִן אֲפִילוּ שְׁנַיִם, שֶׁנֶּאֱמַר
אָז נִדְבְּרוּ יִרְאֵי יְיָ אִישׁ אֶל־רֵעֵהוּ וַיַּקְשֵׁב יְיָ וַיִּשְׁמָע.
וּמִנַּיִן אֲפִילוּ אֶחָד, שֶׁנֶּאֱמַר בְּכָל־הַמָּקוֹם אֲשֶׁר
אַזְכִּיר אֶת־שְׁמִי אָבֹא אֵלֶיךָ וּבֵרַכְתִּיךָ:

7 Rabbi Chalafta ben Dosa, of the village of
Chananya, says: When ten men sit together and occupy themselves with the Torah, the Divine Presence
dwells among them, for it is said, "God stands in the
congregation of God" (*Tehillim* 82:1). And whence can
it be shown that the same applies also to five? Because
it is said, "And He has established His band upon the
earth" (*Amos* 9:6). And whence can it be shown that
the same applies even to three? Because it is said, "He
judges in the midst of judges" (*Tehillim* 82:1). And
whence can it be shown that it applies even to two?
Because it is said, "Then those who fear God spoke
with one another and God noted and heard" (*Malachi*
3:16). And whence can it be shown that it applies even
to one? Because it is said, "In any place where I shall
cause My name to be remembered, I will come to you
and bless you" (*Shemoth* 20:21).

* * *

TEN MEN. Why does Rabbi Chalafta stress that the Divine Spirit
is actually present among ten men who learn Torah, and why
specifically ten? How does the verse from Tehillim confirm his

statement? Don Yitzchak Abravanel, in his commentary Nachalath Avoth, draws our attention to a parallel idea expressed in Tractate Berachoth 6a: "Ravin bar Rav Adda said in the name of Rabbi Yitzchak: How do you know that the Holy One, blessed is He, is to be found in the synagogue? Because it is said, 'God stands in the congregation of God' (*Tehillim* 82:1). And how do you know that if ten people pray together, the Divine Presence is with them? Because it is said, 'God stands in the congregation of God.'" Whenever ten men assemble for the sanctification of the Holy Name, whether to pray, to judge or to learn Torah, they are called עדת אל, "a congregation of God." (Bertinoro points out that ten men may also form a "bench of judges" under certain conditions.) Of this congregation the Gemara says, "To a gathering of ten the Divine Presence comes first; to three, It comes only after they sit down" (*Berachoth* 6a; *Avoth* 3:3).

The word שכינה, "the reflection of the Divine Majesty," or "the Divine Presence," according to Rabbi Wessely in Yain Levanon, connotes the enlightenment granted to man by the grace of God, as it is said, "The Lord shall cause His countenance to shine upon you and be gracious to you" (*Bemidbar* 6:25). In this mishnah the various numbers — the *edah* (ten), the *agudah* (five), three, two and one — of men who may be worthy of summoning the *Shechinah* can refer to levels of enlightenment as well as to people. The *edah* is considered the highest level. When less than ten men pray, judge or learn together, they must increase their efforts, pray more devotedly, penetrate more deeply the legal issue, or focus their attention more carefully on their studies to merit the activation, as it were, of the Divine Presence. When ten or more sincere, devout men assemble, the atmosphere becomes so sacred that Divine assistance is instantly transmitted. It is as if God were already there, as it were, but the proper atmosphere is required to have His presence felt.

Rabbi Ya'avetz explains this idea with a parable: The king of a great country was accustomed to reside in the large palace he had built in the capital city. Periodically he would sojourn, for weeks at a time, in smaller palaces he had built in the larger cities, and for a few days at a time, in the smaller cities. In the towns he stayed but a day, and in the villages he stopped for a few hours only; this way all his subjects would see him and have access to him. The capital city can be compared to the "permanent residence" of the Almighty wherever ten men assemble to study Torah ("God stands in the congregation of God"); where five people gather for a lofty purpose, there the King of kings sojourns for an extended period ("He has established his band upon the earth"); when three people study Torah together, the King appears in their midst for a short time ("He judges in the midst of judges"); with two, He listens ("and God will listen and hear"), and to one man He only comes ("I will come to you and bless you").

Another illustration of God's immanence and His transmission of spiritual strength in the appropriate circumstances is found in these words: "and Moshe brought forth the people out of the camp to meet with God" (*Shemoth* 19:17). God was, as it were, already there, waiting for the congregation who came to receive the Torah. Our forefathers were so much animated by God's spirit that they understood the lofty teachings given at Sinai without having to study them. "And he announced to you His Covenant" (*Devarim* 4:13) means that the words of God informed the people at once of all the things contained in the Torah so that they instantly became לימודי יי, "scholars of God."

ALSO TO FIVE. A gathering of five is not mentioned in the parallel passage from Berachoth cited above, but the Torah tells us: "And five of you shall chase a hundred [enemies] and a hundred of you shall put ten thousand to rout" (*Vayyikra* 26:8). Rashi asks, "Since one hundred is twenty times five, why does it not say two thousand will be routed by one hundred?" The answer, Rashi says, is אינו דומה מועטין העושין את התורה למרובין העושין את התורה, "The amount of good that can be accomplished when many occupy themselves with the Torah is disproportionately greater than the accomplishments of a few who do so."

Rabbi Chalafta, however, cites part of a verse from Amos to prove his maxim: "and He has established His band upon the earth" (*Amos* 9:6). Both Rashi and the Rambam find the quantity of five implied in the root of the word אגודה, "band," which is אגד, meaning "to bind," since binding is done with the five fingers of the hand. אגודה therefore also means the five fingers. The

Tosafoth in Sukkah 13a prove more clearly that the word אגודה in Amos 9:6 means five, by comparing this verse to another one: "My hand has also established the earth" (*Yeshayahu* 48:13), the hand having five fingers. This deduction is made by a *gezerah shavah*, the comparison of one word with another from an analogous application in the Torah.

Now, how does this verse relate to the dwelling of the Divine Presence? The full verse from Amos is: "Who builds His upper chambers in Heaven and has established His band upon the earth." A parallel verse is: "O Lord, our Master, how mighty is Your name throughout the earth; let Your majesty rule over the Heavens" (*Tehillim* 8:2). The contrast of Heaven to earth in both verses is strikingly similar. The interpretation of the verse from Tehillim by the Sages (*Shabbath* 88b) gives us an insight into the verse from Amos, and so into the mishnah. When the angels protested to God that the perfect Torah should not be given to imperfect human beings, Moshe was allowed to explain to them why God had bestowed the five Books of His Torah on man (earth) rather than on the angels (Heaven). Thus, when a number of men, corresponding to the number of Books of the Torah (His band), assemble to study Torah (on earth), the Presence of God (He has established) will rest upon them.

EVEN TO THREE. Turning once more to the Tractate Berachoth in which Ravin bar Rav Adda demonstrates the several modes of eliciting the Divine Presence, in terms similar to Rabbi Chalafta's, we learn that three who learn Torah are equated with three who sit in judgment. Both groups of three merit the Divine Presence, as evidenced by the verse, "He judges in the midst of judges." The key here is the concept of justice. The Sages explain that justice is administered by a court of three in financial matters; therefore, the Gemara asks, "I might have thought that judges who are only called upon to preserve the peace would not be so much in need of Divine enlightenment." Rabbi Chalafta says that even in matters where a court of only three is necessary, the administration of justice requires Divine enlightenment in order to maintain the high standards of the Torah, and therefore, "justice" also equals "Torah study."

TWO. The significance of the Divine Presence abiding with two who speak words of Torah can be found in the verse: "Those who fear God spoke with one another and God noted and heard" (*Malachi* 3:16), and has been explained above in the third mishnah of this chapter (*Avoth* 3:3). The Gemara notes that if the Presence of God will rest on even one, it will certainly do so if two are worthy. However, the words of two who fear God are "inscribed in the Book" (*Malachi*, ibid.), whereas one person does not merit this privilege.

EVEN TO ONE. The commentators point out that the verb "remember" in the verse cited by Rabbi Chalafta is אזכיר and not תזכיר—"In any place where I will cause My name to be remembered" (*Shemoth* 20:21), not "wherever you will remember Me." The "place" is of course the place of sacrifice, the Sanctuary, which is the only place in which the unutterable Name of God may be pronounced in the form in which it is written. Rabbi Chalafta chooses this verse to teach us that even when a man attempts the difficult task of studying the words of the Torah alone, the Divine Spirit will support him and help him to succeed. Furthermore, lest we think that his merit might be smaller for his having learned alone, utterly dependent upon God's help, that is not so, for the verse continues , "I will come to you and bless you [as though you had accomplished it all by yourself]." Wherever God's Name is remembered, that is, wherever a man devotes himself to the Torah, even alone, there the Divine Spirit will grant enlightenment.

רַבִּי אֶלְעָזָר אִישׁ בַּרְתּוֹתָא אוֹמֵר, תֶּן־לוֹ
מִשֶּׁלּוֹ שָׁאַתָּה וְשֶׁלְּךָ שֶׁלּוֹ, וְכֵן בְּדָוִד הוּא
אוֹמֵר כִּי־מִמְּךָ הַכֹּל וּמִיָּדְךָ נָתַנּוּ לָךְ:

8 Rabbi Elazar of Bartotha says: Give Him from what is His, because you and all that you have are His. Thus we find that David says, "All things come from You, and from Your hand we have given You" (*Divrei Hayyamim* I, 29:14).

*   *   *

Rabbi Elazar (ben Yehudah) was a disciple of Rabbi Yehoshua ben Chananya and the teacher of the *Nasi*, *Rabban* Shimon ben Gamliel the Second, Rabi's father. He was known for his great scholarship and unbounded generosity. Whenever a collection for charity was made, the collectors carefully avoided him since they knew he would give more than he could afford (*Ta'anith* 24a). His maxim seems very simple: It is clear and evident that we ourselves and all that we possess belong to the Almighty, our Creator, our Supporter and the Guide of our destinies, and so whatever good we have must originate from His hand. The Sages relate that our father Avraham was noted for the hospitality which he practiced and through which he led people to a knowledge of God. Avraham refused to accept thanks from the strangers to whom he graciously offered refreshment in his tent. He would tell them, "You should not thank me. I am only the administrator of this property which has been entrusted to me by a great and noble Master. He has ordered me to share it." The strangers would then ask, "Who is that high lord?" And Avraham would say, "He is the Almighty, the Creator of Heaven and earth." The strangers would then cry out fervently, "Praise to the God of Avraham!"

We learn from this that our property is only an entrusted possession. Why, then, did Rabbi Elazar say תֶּן לוֹ מִשֶּׁלּוֹ, "give Him from what is His," rather than הַחֲזִיר לוֹ מִשֶּׁלּוֹ, "give Him back what is His"? The word תֶּן (give) indicates quite intentionally that the kind God in His mercy regards the alms we give to the poor as a present given to Him. Similarly, a father who receives a birthday present from his young son does not say, "Foolish boy, why buy a present for me with money that I have given you? I could buy it myself." No, the father is pleased with his son for not spending all his pocket money on himself, and for wishing to use some of it to give his father joy. He accepts it as a gift, not as repayment. Rabbi Elazar cites the verse from Divrei Hayyamim to prove his point.

Our Sages enlarge upon this concept in several places. "Honor God with your wealth" (*Mishlei* 3:9, cited in the *Pesikta* to *Devarim* 14:22). Similarly, "Who has given Me anything before, that I should repay him?" (*Iyyov* 41:3). The Holy One, blessed is He, says, as it were: Honor Me with what I have given you. Could you carry out the commandment of circumcision on your child if I had not given you a son? Could you affix a *mezuzah* to your doorpost or build a parapet on your roof if I had not given you a house? Could you offer the filings of your herds if I had not caused them to be born? Could you consecrate the tenth of your corn to Me if I had not caused it to grow?

"He gives bread to all living creatures, for His kindness lasts forever" (*Tehillim* 136:25). But God chooses good people and appoints them His messengers, both to implement His will and to give them merit. "Riches profit not on the day of wrath, but righteousness delivers from death" (*Mishlei* 11:4). God guided the hand of Rabbi Akiva's daughter to kill the poisonous serpent that was about to bite her on her wedding day. It was obvious that her life was spared because of the unbounded charity she showed a poor man at the wedding feast (*Shabbath* 156b).

Rabbi Yitzchak said: What is the meaning of the verse רדף צדקה וחסד ימצא חיים צדקה וכבוד, "He who strives for righteousness and kindness shall find life, righteousness and honor" (*Mishlei* 21:21)? Does that mean: He who strives for *tzedakah* will find *tzedakah*? If a man is kind to his fellowman, the Holy One, blessed is He, provides him with the means to do good deeds. He will find life, for charity saves from death.

(*Bava Bathra* 9b)

The fortune of such a man will not be reduced by the valuable gifts he donates to the poor; on the contrary — God will bless him to such an extent that he will be able to donate more and more, and be honored as a benefactor of the poor, a man chosen by God as His messenger.

ט רַבִּי יַעֲקֹב אוֹמֵר, הַמְהַלֵּךְ בַּדֶּרֶךְ וְשׁוֹנֶה
וּמַפְסִיק מִמִּשְׁנָתוֹ וְאוֹמֵר מַה־נָּאֶה אִילָן
זֶה מַה־נָּאֶה נִיר זֶה, מַעֲלֶה עָלָיו הַכָּתוּב כְּאִלּוּ
מִתְחַיֵּב בְּנַפְשׁוֹ:

9 Rabbi Ya'akov says: He who walks by the way
studying and breaks off his study to exclaim, "How
beautiful is this tree! How fine is that field!" the
Torah regards him as if he had sinned against his own
soul.

* * *

Rabbi Ya'akov was the father of Rabbi Eliezer, whose faithful
rendering of the Mishnah was greatly praised. He lived at the
time of *Rabban* Yochanan ben Zakkai, that is, the time of the
destruction of the Holy Temple. According to most interpreters,
this mishnah speaks of the duty of devoting every free moment to
Torah study. Even though admiration of the tree and the field is
a form of praise to the Holy One, blessed is He, Who has created
all that is beautiful, yet Torah study is more important. It can
hardly be assumed that Rabbi Ya'akov sees anything wrong in the
observation of nature and in the admiration of the Creator's
works. After all, Sefer Tehillim contains splendid descriptions of
nature, especially in Psalm 104 (ברכי נפשי), "Bless [the Lord] O
my soul," and the prophets often remind man to look at God's
beautiful world and consider the splendor and greatness of the
Creator. The Sages, too, prescribe blessings to be said in appreciation of nature.

There is some difference of opinion among the commentators
about which verse Rabbi Ya'akov is referring to, for it is inconsistent that he cites none in particular. Perhaps this means that
Rabbi Ya'akov feels that not just one verse, but the entire Torah,
confirms his maxim. Rabbi Shemuel Galante explains that the
key word is המהלך: man is "one who walks," who progresses, who
can develop from small beginnings to high perfection, as compared to an angel העומד, "who stands," who remains as he was
created (*Benayoth Beramah*). "Thus says the Lord of Hosts: If you

will walk in My ways and if you will keep My charge...I will give you places to walk, among those that stand by" (*Zecharyah* 3:7). Those who walk in the way of God strive to perfect themselves and their lives.

The word נאה not only means "attractive" but also "pleasing," pleasing enough to distract the serious student from his studies; the אילן (tree) can be considered the tree of knowledge, which entices him to taste the attractive fruit of philosophy and other disciplines without the support of Torah; and a ניר is not an ordinary field, but one that has just been cultivated, like a man who has learned only a few of the teachings of Judaism and is easily persuaded, by the supposedly "new ideas" of his time, to relinquish God's Torah. Since he has studied some Torah and should know how to appreciate it, then not only one verse but the whole Torah will bear witness against him. All the greatest philosophical systems have ultimately been disavowed or disproven, or have contradicted one another in the course of time, but the Torah contains only eternal truth. Just as God is eternal, so is His Torah.

רַבִּי דּוֹסְתָּאִי בַּר יַנַּאי מִשּׁוּם רַבִּי מֵאִיר
אוֹמֵר, כָּל־הַשּׁוֹכֵחַ דָּבָר אֶחָד מִמִּשְׁנָתוֹ
מַעֲלֶה עָלָיו הַכָּתוּב כְּאִלּוּ מִתְחַיֵּב בְּנַפְשׁוֹ, שֶׁנֶּאֱמַר
רַק הִשָּׁמֶר לְךָ וּשְׁמֹר נַפְשְׁךָ מְאֹד פֶּן־תִּשְׁכַּח אֶת־
הַדְּבָרִים אֲשֶׁר־רָאוּ עֵינֶיךָ. יָכוֹל אֲפִילוּ תָּקְפָה עָלָיו
מִשְׁנָתוֹ, תַּלְמוּד לוֹמַר וּפֶן־יָסוּרוּ מִלְּבָבְךָ כֹּל יְמֵי
חַיֶּיךָ, הָא אֵינוֹ מִתְחַיֵּב בְּנַפְשׁוֹ עַד שֶׁיֵּשֵׁב וִיסִירֵם
מִלִּבּוֹ:

10 Rabbi Dosta'i Bar Yannai says in the name of Rabbi Meir: Whoever forgets even one word of his study, is regarded by the Torah as if he had sinned against his soul, for it is said, "Only take heed of yourself and guard your soul diligently, that you may not forget the things which your eyes have seen" (*Devarim* 4:9). Now you might suppose that the same would apply if what he had studied were too difficult for him. However, the Torah adds, "and lest they be removed from your heart all the days of your life." Thus he is guilty of sinning against his soul only if he sits down [idly] and removes [thereby] the words of the Torah from his heart.

* * *

When Shalmanezer, king of Assyria, destroyed the kingdom of Yisrael and banished the ten tribes, he settled heathen people in the Holy Land. Lions attacked and killed many of them, so they asked the king to send them a teacher to teach them the Torah of Yisrael to protect them. The king sent them a Jewish sage who instructed them in the service of the One and only God, but they also retained their former idol worship. These were the Cutheans or Samaritans, who observed only some of the Torah's commandments, but not all. Some of their descendants still form a small community in Shechem (Nablus). That sage's name was Rabbi Dosta'i bar Yannai, but he was not the sage who authored this mishnah (*Yalkut Shimoni, Melachim* II, 17). The use of the title "Rabbi" in the Midrash is probably a mistake, since this title was not yet in use, and as we see from the text, the sage of this mishnah was a disciple of Rabbi Meir and therefore lived in the second half of the second century of the common era.

Rabbi Meir, the son-in-law of Rabbi Chananya ben Teradyon, was one of the most outstanding disciples of the great Rabbi Akiva. The name Meir, which means "shining light," was given him by his contemporaries on account of his great scholarship and his wonderful teaching methods. This name was so generally accepted that in the course of time his original name was forgotten. Following the example of his great teacher, Rabbi Akiva, Rabbi Meir compiled a collection of mishnayoth which the saintly Rabbi Yehudah used as the foundation of the mishnayoth we still learn today. Every mishnah, therefore, in which no name is cited, is attributed to Rabbi Meir or to the Tradition received from him, as it is said: סתם משנה רבי מאיר.

WHOEVER FORGETS EVEN ONE WORD. Rabbi Meir reminds us that the severest punishment awaits one who forgets "even one word" of Torah, once he has learned it, but the commentary makes it clear that he is speaking only of one who deliberately forgets, through lack of constant study and review, by sitting idly. Whatever Torah you may have acquired יסורו מלבבך, "will be removed from your heart"; it will depart even though you do not cast it away intentionally. You will forget it and it will be your own fault, because you occupy yourself with vain things, even if you do not actually prefer these vain occupations to reviewing what you have learned. "Rabbi Yehoshua ben Korcha said, 'Whoever studies the Torah and does not review it is likened to one who sows without reaping.' Rabbi Yehoshua said, 'He who studies the Torah and then forgets it is like a woman who bears children and neglects them so much that they die and are buried'" (*Sanhedrin* 99a). "The more you learn," Rabbi Zera says, "the more you will be able to comprehend with your mind, as it is said: אם שמוע תשמע לקול יי אלהיך, 'The more you hearken to the voice of the Lord your God,' the more receptive you will become to it" (*Shemoth* 15:26, cited in *Sukkah* 46b).

The words of the Torah are only too easily forgotten, says Rabbi Meir, basing his interpretation on the verse: לא יערכנה זהב וזכוכית ותמורתה כלי פז, "[the words of the Torah] are as hard to acquire as golden vessels and precious jewelry and as easily broken as vessels of glass" (*Iyyov* 28:17). An excuse can be made for the man who has lost his knowledge as the result of weakness. Rabbi Yehoshua ben Levi used to say to his children, "Honor the old man who has forgotten his learning due to weakness, for he resembles the broken tablets—they, too, were given a place in the Sanctuary" (*Berachoth* 8b). In order to prove his love and reverence for the Torah, the healthy man must devote his time, as far as possible, not only to Torah study but also to the review of what he has already learned.

יא **רַבִּי חֲנִינָא בֶּן־דּוֹסָא אוֹמֵר, כֹּל שֶׁיִּרְאַת חֶטְאוֹ קוֹדֶמֶת לְחָכְמָתוֹ חָכְמָתוֹ מִתְקַיֶּמֶת, וְכֹל שֶׁחָכְמָתוֹ קוֹדֶמֶת לְיִרְאַת חֶטְאוֹ אֵין חָכְמָתוֹ מִתְקַיֶּמֶת:**

11 Rabbi Chanina ben Dosa says: He in whom the fear of sin takes precedence over his wisdom, his wisdom will endure; but he in whom wisdom takes precedence over the fear of sin, his wisdom will not endure.

* * *

The preceding mishnayoth extol the sanctity and importance of learning Torah; Rabbi Chanina's saying teaches us that no matter how much wisdom you acquire, if you do not support it with a true fear of sin, you will not hold on to it. This saying and the two following it reflect Rabbi Chanina's own most outstanding qualities. The power of Rabbi Chanina ben Dosa's prayer is said to have been wonderful; whatever he requested of God was granted. Although he was an extremely poor man, he would never request riches for himself. Only once did he give in to his wife's urging and ask for wealth, but she herself made him withdraw the request, for she had seen in a dream that the pleasures of this world would harm him in the World to Come (*Ta'anith* 25a).

The commentators find a number of difficulties in this mishnah. To begin with, it seems to contradict Hillel's saying, "An ignorant person cannot fear sin" (*Avoth* 2:6). If knowledge is a prerequisite for fear of sin, how can Rabbi Chanina say that fear of sin goes before wisdom? We cannot assume that Rabbi Chanina holds a different opinion than Hillel, since his maxim is a generally accepted moral prinicple. Rabbi Shemuel of Ozedah asks further, "If wisdom endures only when the fear of sin goes before it, what will occur when fear of sin and wisdom are simultaneous or equal?" Rabbi Wessely has found the answer. He says that this is not a question of precedence in time, but in values. The fear of sin comprises far more than the mere dread of shame or punishment. The heart of a pious man must be filled with love of God to such an extent that he fears violating a commandment like a loving son who fears to do anything that might cause his father grief. He must fear sin even more than he desires wisdom, though he has been taught over and over that learning is the supreme virtue.

The apparent contradictions in this mishnah fall away when we examine what the Sages have said on the subject. Rabbi Shimon ben Nethanel, as we have seen (*Avoth* 2:11), was called a ירא חטא, "a sin-fearing man," and his lesson is to consider first and always in life whether or not our deeds will lead to sin; our own knowledge is imperfect and cannot be relied on. *Rabbenu* Yonah teaches that the endeavor to acquire wisdom grows through the effort to utilize it in practice, but wisdom acquired only for its own sake will in the end be an encumbrance. Rabbi Ya'avetz cites verse 17:16 in Mishlei: "What good are the means to purchase wisdom in the hands of a fool, seeing that he has no heart in it?" One who does not have the determination to live in accordance with the principles of wisdom will not benefit from what he has learned; indeed, he will do himself and others harm.

Rabbi bar Rav Huna said, "Every man who possesses knowledge without the fear of Heaven is like a treasurer who is entrusted with the inner keys but not the outer ones. How is he to enter?" (*Shabbath* 31a-b). Rava used to say to his disciples, "I beseech you, do not inherit a double *Gehinnom*" (*Yoma* 72b). That is to say, anyone who denies himself the pleasures of life on earth in order to devote himself to Torah study, but does not follow that which he has learned, turns his life into Hell on earth and ends in eternal ruin. The Royal Singer also teaches: ראשית חכמה יראת יי, "The fear of the Lord is the beginning of wisdom" (*Tehillim* 111:10). The Torah itself tells us that the fear of God must precede everything else, as it is said, "And now,Yisrael, what does the Lord your God demand of you? Nothing but to fear the Lord your God, to walk in all His ways and to love Him and to serve the Lord your God with all your heart and with all your soul, to keep the commandments of the Lord and His statutes which I command you this day for your own good" (*Devarim* 10:12-13).

Our Sages infer from these verses that the fear of God is not decreed; man is to fear God of his own volition, his own free will.

This thought is deduced from the words, "What does the Lord demand *from you*?" (מעמך)— from that which is solely dependent upon you. Possessing inborn character traits, being strong or weak, encountering a favorable or unfavorable environment, does not depend upon our own will; but to fear God, to love Him and to walk in His ways depends entirely on our own decision. When this decision is taken, the foundation of our happiness in this world and in the World to Come is firmly established. Thus, as we will see, Rabbi Chanina ben Dosa's three maxims give consoling assurance to the boy, the youth and the man: Always have the fear of God in your heart and even if you lack the outstanding abilities of a scholar, the wisdom of the Almighty will support you and help you to attain and preserve wisdom! To the talented and learned he says: The final aim of all knowledge is the fear of committing a sin; the wisdom you have attained will only endure when it serves to strengthen your conscientiousness. Wisdom becomes foolishness in a man who does not fear sin.

יב הוּא הָיָה אוֹמֵר, כֹּל שֶׁמַּעֲשָׂיו מְרֻבִּים
מֵחָכְמָתוֹ חָכְמָתוֹ מִתְקַיֶּמֶת, וְכֹל
שֶׁחָכְמָתוֹ מְרֻבָּה מִמַּעֲשָׂיו אֵין חָכְמָתוֹ מִתְקַיֶּמֶת:

12 He [Rabbi Chanina ben Dosa] would say: A person whose deeds exceed his wisdom shall have enduring wisdom, but one whose wisdom exceeds his deeds shall not have enduring wisdom.

*   *   *

Bertinoro teaches that the previous mishnah refers to the Divine prohibitions, while the present mishnah relates to God's positive commandments. This observation, although correct in itself, does not suffice to explain the mishnah. The commentators find a number of obscure points that have to be explained. To begin with, how can we compare quantity of deeds with quantity of wisdom? Assuming that the Sage is referring to someone who carries out more Divine commandments than he has learned about, we must ask, "How can anyone obey the commandments if he has not learned them?" Rabbi Shemuel of Ozedah points to the additional paradox that arises when one's deeds and wisdom are equal: Does wisdom endure in that case? And what of the lessons we learned elsewhere: "Learning is not the main thing, but doing" (*Avoth* 1:17), and "Learning is greater than doing, for learning leads to doing" (*Kiddushin* 40b).

Rabbi Chanina ben Dosa cannot possibly be teaching that someone who gives preference to Torah study over all the other commandments will not retain his wisdom. It is a well-established principle that כל העוסק במצוה פטור מן המצוה, "He who is occupied with a *mitzvah* need not interrupt it to do another *mitzvah* except when the second *mitzvah* is one that cannot be postponed." For example, גמילת חסדים עם המתים, "the kindness shown to the deceased" by attending to the burial preparations, is an extremely meritorious act. Still, when there are others available to do this sacred duty, the one who devotes his time to learning or teaching Torah earns equal, if not more, merit. *Rabbenu* Yonah holds that the intention is the decisive factor here. If you sincerely intend to practice everything that you learn, God will credit your intentions as though they were deeds; your deeds will therefore outweigh your wisdom and your wisdom will therefore endure. If you learn purely for the sake of increasing your knowledge, never applying it in practice, your deeds will never measure up to your learning and you will not retain it. This explanation, however, gives almost the same meaning to this mishnah as that of the preceding one and Rabbi Chanina would hardly be repeating himself.

The key to this mishnah is contained in chapter 22 of the Avoth of Rabbi Nathan. It is deduced from the words our ancestors spoke to our teacher Moshe at Mount Sinai: נעשה ונשמע, "All that the Lord has said, we will do and we will hear" (*Shemoth* 24:7). That is to say, even if we do not yet understand it, we will not make the fulfillment of the Divine commandments dependent on our comprehension. This great principle has remained a byword for our people since that time. There are Divine commandments that we understand at once: Honor your father and your mother, do not murder, do not steal. Others we only comprehend through careful study, such as the blowing of the *shofar* on Rosh Hashanah, or the taking of the four species on Sukkoth. There are also commandments which we cannot understand at all, such as the precepts regarding the red heifer and the prohibition against wearing clothes of wool mixed with linen. We must do good deeds whether we understand the reason for them or not. In this way our deeds will have greater merit and will reinforce whatever we learn; thus our wisdom will endure. A man can hardly accomplish anything good if he must first prove that all his knowledge is valid. ראשית חכמה יראת יי שכל טוב לכל עשיהם, "The fear of the Lord is the beginning of all wisdom, good understanding to all those who carry out God's commandments" (*Tehillim* 111:10)—without exception!

יג הוּא הָיָה אוֹמֵר, כָּל שֶׁרוּחַ הַבְּרִיּוֹת נוֹחָה
הֵימֶנּוּ רוּחַ הַמָּקוֹם נוֹחָה הֵימֶנּוּ, וְכֹל
שֶׁאֵין רוּחַ הַבְּרִיּוֹת נוֹחָה הֵימֶנּוּ אֵין רוּחַ הַמָּקוֹם
נוֹחָה הֵימֶנּוּ:

13 He [Rabbi Chanina ben Dosa] would say: One who is pleasing to his fellowmen is pleasing also to God; and one who is not pleasing to men is also displeasing to God.

*   *   *

Our Sages teach in Yoma 86a that the deeper meaning of the verse, "And you shall love the Lord your God..." (*Devarim* 6:5) is that the Name of Heaven will be beloved because of you. Learning Torah, Mishnah and Talmud is a Jew's primary task, but at the same time he should speak pleasantly to people and be honest in business so that people will say of him, "Happy is the man who learns Torah, happy is the father who has taught him Torah and woe unto the man who has not studied Torah!" Of him God says, "You are my servant, Yisrael, in whom I will be glorified" (*Yeshayahu* 49:3). If someone who studies Torah is discourteous to others and dishonest in business, what do people say? "This man has studied Torah and see how corrupt he is, how ugly are his ways!" Of him it is said "...and they desecrated My holy Name when it was said of them, 'These are *Hashem*'s people but they departed from His land' (*Yechezkel* 36:20)."

This does not mean that one should do just anything to earn praise and favor. A rabbi or community leader who is highly esteemed because he permits the people great laxity in religious matters is not really respected for his integrity. Outstanding people are frequently surrounded by flatterers who praise them, but this is only praise from the mouth, not praise from the heart, and cannot be a true measure of their worth.

ומצא חן ושכל טוב בעיני אלהים ואדם, "So shall you find grace and good understanding in the sight of God and man" (*Mishlei* 3:4). You will only gain God's good favor by acquiring the true esteem of men. You must not, however, expect to find favor with all men; that is not possible. Envy always exists among men. Even Mordechai the Sage "was agreeable to the majority of his brethren" (*Esther* 10:3). There must therefore have been a minority who did not approve of his actions (*Megillah* 16b). We now see how Rabbi Chanina's three maxims follow verse 111:10 in Tehillim: "The fear of the Lord," one whose fear of sin precedes his wisdom, has attained "the beginning of wisdom"; for one whose deeds are more than his wisdom, "good understanding" will be granted "to all who carry out" the commandments; and one who gains his fellowman's true esteem, "his praise will abide" at God's throne "to all eternity."

יַד רַבִּי דּוֹסָא בֶּן הָרְכִּינַס אוֹמֵר, שֵׁנָה שֶׁל־
שַׁחֲרִית וְיַיִן שֶׁל־צָהֳרַיִם וְשִׂיחַת הַיְלָדִים
וִישִׁיבַת בָּתֵּי כְנֵסִיּוֹת שֶׁל־עַמֵּי הָאָרֶץ מוֹצִיאִין אֶת־
הָאָדָם מִן־הָעוֹלָם:

14　Rabbi Dosa ben Harkinas says: Morning sleep
and midday wine, children's talk and sitting in the
assembly houses of the ignorant remove a man from
the world.

*　　*　　*

Rabbi Dosa was probably a disciple of Hillel. The Gemara in
Yevamoth 16a relates that he lived to an old age and that his
younger brother, Yonathan, was a disciple of Shammai.

MORNING SLEEP. A German proverb says, "The morning
hour has gold in its mouth," and the ancient Romans used to say,
"The dawn is a friend of the muses." In the early morning a man
has his full strength, he is rested from the strains of the previous
day and not yet pressed with the rush of the new day. It is a good
time to collect his thoughts and absorb the treasures of knowledge. But if he lingers idly in his bed, he not only wastes the
valuable morning hours but also will remain idle for the rest of
the day. It is a physiological fact that an excess of sleep renders a
person weak and indolent. We have been commanded by almighty God to read the *Shema* early in the morning; by seven
o'clock in midsummer, that time has already passed. When you
sleep past seven o'clock, therefore, you miss the opportunity to
fulfill this commandment. The *Shulchan Aruch* begins with the
words: "Be like a lion, rise early from bed for the service of the
Creator." Let us hurry to synagogue to say the morning prayers.
Ah, but morning sleep is so sweet and pleasant, one rests so well in a
half-awakened state! Nevertheless we must gather all our will power
and pull ourselves out of bed, rouse ourselves to serve the Creator.

MIDDAY WINE. The poets of all nations sing the praise of
wine. The Torah calls it "sacred for praising the Lord" (*Vayyikra*

19:24). The Psalmist says that it "gladdens the heart of man," (*Tehillim* 104:15) and the Wise King Shelomo recommends it for rejoicing the heart. When wine is drunk in excess or at the wrong time, however, it may do serious harm:

> Who has woe and who has suffering? Who has strife, who [has] complaints and who [has] needless injuries? Who has reddened eyes? Those who tarry long at the wine, those who come to try out new drinks! Do not look upon wine, how red it is, how it lends color to the glass, how smoothly it flows. For in the end it will wound like a snake and sting like a viper. Your eyes shall see strange things and your heart will think nonsense, and you will be as one shaken about in the midst of the sea or who lies on top of a mast. They strike me and I feel nothing; they push me and I do not feel anything; when I awaken I will continue and seek wine anew!
>
> (*Mishlei* 23:29-35)

One or two glasses of wine taken during a meal will ordinarily do no harm, but excess drinking heats the blood and causes erratic, often disgraceful, behavior. Thus our Sages teach: Why does the Portion about the Nazarite (who abstains from drinking) follow immediately that of the unfaithful wife (*Bemidbar* 6 and 5)? To teach us that excessive and untimely indulgence in wine leads to immorality (*Berachoth* 63a).

CHILDREN'S TALK. The Sage probably means "playing games," which is a waste of time even for children, and certainly so for adults. Games can undoubtedly lead to unseemly behavior because the senses become overexcited and men and women mingle. Although it is good, indeed necessary, for a father to attend to his young children, he ought to guard against spending too much time on play and not enough on developing their minds.

SITTING IN THE ASSEMBLY HOUSES OF THE IGNORANT. The Jews have been chosen by God to be a holy nation, a kingdom of priests. It is therefore not fitting for a Jew to indulge in gossip in taverns or to perform other unseemly acts. His spare time should be devoted to the study of Torah and the performance of good deeds. As we were reminded in the commentary on the third mishnah of this chapter:

> Happy is the man who did not walk in the counsel of the wicked, who did not stand in the way of sinners, who did not sit in the session of scorners; but his delight is in the Law of the Lord; and in His Law does he meditate day and night. He will be like a tree planted by the streams of water, that will bring forth its fruit in season; whose foliage shall not wither and whatever he does shall prosper.
>
> *(Tehillim* 1:1-3)

The Almighty will make him happy in this world as well as in the World to Come.

טו רַבִּי אֶלְעָזָר הַמּוֹדָעִי אוֹמֵר, הַמְחַלֵּל אֶת־
הַקָּדָשִׁים וְהַמְבַזֶּה אֶת־הַמּוֹעֲדוֹת
וְהַמַּלְבִּין פְּנֵי חֲבֵרוֹ בָרַבִּים וְהַמֵּפֵר בְּרִיתוֹ שֶׁל־
אַבְרָהָם אָבִינוּ וְהַמְגַלֶּה פָנִים בַּתּוֹרָה שֶׁלֹּא
כַהֲלָכָה, אַף עַל פִּי שֶׁיֵּשׁ בְּיָדוֹ תּוֹרָה וּמַעֲשִׂים
טוֹבִים, אֵין לוֹ חֵלֶק לָעוֹלָם הַבָּא:

15 Rabbi Elazar of Modi'in says: Someone who profanes sacred things and who neglects the festivals and who humiliates his fellowman in public and who violates the covenant of Avraham our father, and who interprets the Torah in a manner contradictory to the *Halachah*—though he may have the knowledge of Torah and [do] good deeds—he has no share in the World to Come.

* * *

Rabbi Elazar of Modi'in was a disciple of the great *Rabban* Yochanan ben Zakkai and was one of the outstanding scholars who led the people after his master's death. Like his renowned companion, Rabbi Akiva, he took an active part in Bar Kochva's uprising. One of the Cutheans accused him of wanting to surrender the Beithar fortress to the Romans, and in a fit of rage, Bar Kochva killed this great teacher of Israel. From that moment, the fate of Beithar was sealed and the last flare-up of resistance against the Romans was stifled. Since then, the Jewish people have never risen *en masse* against their oppressors.

This mishnah implies that there are two kinds of sinners: those who are so overcome by their passions that they knowingly transgress God's holy commandments, and those who have been misled, and transgress the holy commandments believing that they do no wrong. There is a big difference between them. Those who give in to their passions and sin knowingly will receive their punishment, whether it is light or serious, and once punished, their sin will be forgiven. Even if their crime is punishable by death at the hand of man, they will have a share in the World to Come. But those who do not regard the laws of the Torah as binding and for this reason transgress, will have no share in the World to Come!

This principle is taught in the Torah: והנפש אשר תעשה ביד רמה מן האזרח ומן הגר את יי הוא מגדף ונכרתה הנפש ההוא מקרב עמה. כי דבר יי בזה ואת מצותו הפר הכרת תכרת הנפש ההוא עונה בה, "But the one who [sins] with a high hand, whether native-born or a stranger, blasphemes the Lord; that soul shall be uprooted out of the midst of his people. Because he scorns the word of the Lord and has broken His commandments, that person shall surely be uprooted; his sin cleaves to him" (*Bemidbar* 15:30-31). The Torah distinguishes between great and small sins, and when someone sins in error, or despite good intentions, his punishment will suit his sin. But one who sins "with a high hand," as Ibn Ezra explains, "to show to all the world that he is not afraid of God," no matter what his sin is, desecrates the Name of God. Sins of thoughtlessness and passion are rooted in the body, but sins of misguided religious opinions spring from the soul, and for such sinners there will be no life in the World to Come.

There are five types of people who deviate from traditional Judaism. The worst are those deviants who deny God's existence, like the materialists, the atomists and the pessimists. The second type believe in the existence of a Deity, but do not believe that He created the world. They regard both the world and the Deity as eternal, as did Aristotle and his school. The third type do indeed believe that there is a God and that He has created the world, but deny that man was created in His image, that is, that he has a Divine soul. These are like the monists who maintain that body and soul are one and the soul is merely the product of the functioning of the body's organs. The fourth type are those who recognize the transcendence of the human soul but deny that Yisrael are the Chosen People, a kingdom of priests and a holy nation destined to bear God's Name on earth, and they do not credit revelation and prophecy. The fifth group comprises all those who do believe in God, the Creator of the universe, acknowledge the godliness of the human soul and the preference given to Yisrael among the nations, but who attack the Torah, doubt its integrity and regard some of its commandments either as no longer binding, or as requiring reinterpretation by themselves. These five types of deviants, then, are the sinners who Rabbi Elazar says have no share in the World to Come, even if they have learned Torah and have accomplished good deeds.

WHO PROFANES SACRED THINGS. This phrase refers to the sacrificial animals in the Holy Temple. The ox destined for the burnt offering was an ox like any other: it could have been used for work, it could have been slaughtered anywhere, its flesh could have been cooked or roasted as one liked, it could have been eaten wherever and whenever one liked. Once the required three words were spoken: הרי זה עולה, "This is for a burnt offering," the quality of the ox changed. It was now קדוש ליי, "holy to the Lord." Sacrificial animals had to be slaughtered in the Holy Temple, offered there and consumed there by fire on the altar. Any deviation from these rules, any other use of the sacrifice after it was sanctified, or any other place of slaughter, was a desecration. Even the mere intention to consume the offering at a time or place different from the prescribed one was considered a desecration and invalidated the sacrifice (פיגול). To call the sacred things חולין, "not holy," on principle, is a denial of the Almighty, a disavowal of the existence of the only God from whom sanctification comes. "A lawless man, in the pride of his countenance, says, 'He will not avenge!' All his thoughts are, 'There is no God'" (*Tehillim* 10:4).

AND WHO NEGLECTS THE FESTIVALS. Our kind God has appointed the Shabbaths and Festivals as a sign that He is the Creator and Ruler of the universe. "[The Shabbath]...is a sign between Me and the *bnei Yisrael* forever that in six days the Lord made heaven and earth and on the seventh day He ceased work, and rested" (*Shemoth* 31:17). The Festivals commemorate the miracles He worked. Nature follows eternal, unchangeable laws, but miracles do happen. The Almighty has at times intervened in the laws of nature and caused actions which are contrary to nature, showing that He alone is the Ruler of the universe which He governs in accordance with His own will. Someone who scoffs at the Shabbath on principle disavows God as the Creator of the universe, and someone who scorns the Festivals disavows God's management of the world.

AND WHO HUMILIATES HIS FELLOWMAN IN PUBLIC. We are supposed to respect the image of God in every human being. Humiliating someone publicly, not in the heat of anger or passion, but simply because you disregard his feelings, shows that you do not believe in the concept of man being in God's image, that you are denying the sublimity of the human soul.

AND WHO VIOLATES THE COVENANT OF AVRAHAM OUR FATHER. The Sage does not mean a Jew who does not wish to enter Avraham's covenant, or even one who has neither been circumcised nor has had his son circumcised. The Sage is speaking of one who, on principle, disavows the significance of the covenant which the Lord seals in our flesh, one who rejects the special character of the people chosen by the Almighty from among all the nations of the world. That soul will be denied immortality.

AND WHO INTERPRETS THE TORAH IN A MANNER CONTRADICTORY TO THE *HALACHAH*. Belief in the Divine origin of the Torah, both the Written and the Oral Law, both the parts we may come to understand and the parts we will never understand, admits no exceptions. Someone who does not believe in the revealed Torah, and treats it like a literary work, will conclude that he may alter it to suit his own interpretation. The Sages relate that when Menashe, king of Yehudah, asked why Moshe had to accept all of the Torah, even the seemingly unimportant things (like the name of Elifaz's concubine) a Heavenly voice answered him, "If you had [only] sat down to speak against your brother, to slander your own mother's son, I would have kept quiet. But you thought that I was like you and [for that] I shall punish you and [then] show you My omnipotence (*Tehillim* 50:20-21, cited in *Sanhedrin* 99b). Thus, Menashe was one day captured by the king of Bavel and condemned to be burned alive. He prayed to all the gods, in vain; but finally, when his heart turned to the one God, the Almighty had mercy on him and saved him.

A contemporary example might be someone who uses any festive flowers on the Festival of Sukkoth, instead of the Four Species, or someone who teaches that the *sukkah* has only a symbolic meaning in our day and that therefore there is no need to dwell in it as long as we remember what it stands for — or whatever other pretty homilies the modern Reform rabbis may teach. Know, therefore, that someone who regards the Written and the Oral Law as man's work, subject to his own arbitrary interpretations, will have no share in the World to Come, even if he knows the Law and does good deeds besides. You may ask how anyone whose opinions are so remote from the Torah could acquire Torah knowledge and do good deeds. This was a common occurrence during the period preceding ours. Jews were brought up by pious parents to study the Torah and even to love their studies during their formative years, but they became acquainted with philosophy, the sciences and the so-called "spirit of the age" in their later years, and were then persuaded to oppose the teachings of Judaism. From habit, they now and again did a good deed, but for the most part, they exerted a most detrimental influence upon other Jews.

The worst of them, so-called Mendelsohnians like David Friedlander, at first used their knowledge of the Torah to fight, then to distort, and finally to ridicule traditional Judaism. Some even used their good deeds to make the world believe that they, the apostates, were better people than the faithful believers. They did immeasurable harm to Judaism, and the *epikorsuth* that flowed from Berlin like a torrential river flooded the Jewish world and destroyed everything in its path; it almost seemed as though Judaism itself would founder, God forbid. Disintegration and decay reached the most remote villages. Rabbis and teachers with "modern" training vied with each other in misleading young and old alike to betray the God of our Fathers. Newspapers, journals, pamphlets and books carried the deadly poison abroad. This pernicious movement began a hundred years ago [from the time of writing in the 1870s]; within fifty years it had already acquired such great influence that everyone assumed that no trace of genuine Judaism would be left at the end of the next fifty years.

The dreaded fifty years have now passed and Judaism exists, indeed blossoms. With the help of God it will continue to exist and blossom eternally, even though many dried-up leaves will fall off and be scattered by the wind. It would be wrong, however, to maintain that these sad circumstances were the fault of only the fifth type of sinner in Yisrael, that is, the Reform rabbis. All five types of deviating Jews have done their share to cause the decay. Every Jew who attends a public school and a university himself or sends his children there must know how much hostility to Judaism is taught there. Boys and young men are taught that the world is composed only of atoms, that power and substance are set in motion by precise and unchangeable natural laws. The almighty will of the Creator and Ruler of the universe has no place in these systems. The concept of a transcendent human soul is ridiculed as "blind faith," freedom of will is disputed or attributed to the instinctual drives of the human body. Judaism's teaching of virtue and vice, of the free will of the individual, is ridiculed and science seeks a physiological cause for all good and evil.

These ideas alienate our youth. As parents, however, you should not rebuke your children by overwhelming them with reproof. Rather, draw their attention to the fact that scientists, in their attempt to explain what is supernatural, change their opinions from decade to decade; many things once regarded as scientific truth are now considered errors, and many more will undoubtedly have the same fate in decades to come. The sublime truth of Judaism is forever irrefutable. Time has no power over it, it cannot be disproved by any science or so-called science. King David complained about atheists in his time, too. Centuries ago, philosophers denied that God created and continues to direct the world and that the human soul is immortal. All the ancient civilizations sooner or later began to ridicule and persecute the Chosen People; and even the Jewish king Menashe, as early as 2500 years ago, tried to impute false meaning to the Torah.

Now as always, Judaism must depend upon the faithful believers in Yisrael who have always walked in God's ways, like Avraham and Moshe, like Eliyyahu and Yeshayahu, Hillel and

Rabbi Akiva, Rashi and the Rif (Rabbi Yitzchak Alfasi), Rabbis Yechezkel Landau and Moshe Sofer, and we must try to do as they did. The greater the dangers that threaten us and our generation, the more we must resist, the more energetic we must be in extolling the heritage of our people. Yisrael has overcome grave and powerful threats in its long struggle for survival; with the Almighty's assistance, we shall overcome this one as well.

טז רַבִּי יִשְׁמָעֵאל אוֹמֵר, הֱוֵי קַל לְרֹאשׁ
וְנוֹחַ לְתִשְׁחֹרֶת וֶהֱוֵי מְקַבֵּל אֶת כָּל־
הָאָדָם בְּשִׂמְחָה:

16   Rabbi Yishmael says:

(One reading:) Be particularly courteous to a venerable old man, and also be obliging to those whose hair is still black, and receive every man with joy.

(A second reading:) Rise easily [to serve your Creator] at the beginning of your life, in your youth, and when you have grown old you will not find it too hard to serve God, and be courteous and friendly to every man.

(A third reading:) Be courteous to a prince, obliging to his officials and receive every man with joy.

(A fourth reading:) Rise up easily to the height of knowledge [and] practice always, then you will find it easy to serve the Most Gracious, and receive every man with kindness.

*   *   *

This mishnah is so obscure, and has been explained in so many different ways, that it requires a different translation for each interpretation. Although only his first name is mentioned, we know that this Sage is Rabbi Yishmael ben Elisha, scion of an outstanding priestly family and the companion who most often opposed Rabbi Akiva in halachic discussion. As a child, Rabbi Yishmael was taken as a hostage to Rome; when Rabbi Yeshoshua ben Chananya arrived in Rome and heard that a lovely Jewish child was in prison, he went and stood outside the prison and called out, "Who gave Ya'akov for a spoil, and Yisrael to the robbers?" (*Yeshayahu* 42:24). The child called out the concluding verses from inside the prison, "Indeed it is the Lord, against whom we have sinned. For they would not walk in His ways, neither were they obedient to His Law." When Rabbi Yehoshua heard that, he said, "This boy will one day be a great teacher in Israel; I will not rest until I have freed him." And so he did. The boy went home with him and in just a few years Rabbi Yishmael ben Elisha became one of the greatest teachers in Yisrael (*Gittin* 58a). He was only thirteen years old when Rabbi Nechunya ben Ha-Kanah (see *Avoth* 3:6) accepted him as a pupil.

Rabbi Yishmael compiled the thirteen basic rules we recite in our daily prayers: רבי ישמעאל אומר בשלוש עשרה מדות התורה נדרשת בהן (beginning of *Midrash Sifra*). Rabbi Akiva and he are called "the fathers of the world" (*Yerushalmi, Rosh Hashanah* 1:1). Both were well-versed in pharmaceutics and they occasionally traveled together through the country, healing the sick. Rabbi Yishmael's generosity was particularly praised. He provided the daughters of the poor with clothing and jewelry to enhance their marriage prospects, and when he died, all the daughters of Yisrael wept for him. He provided food for women whose husbands had to go to war, and whenever he saw needy Talmud scholars, he saw to all their needs. His mother revered him so much that she wanted to drink the water in which he had washed, but he would not allow it. His wisdom even surpassed his pulchritude.

The first reading of Rabbi Yishmael's maxim is that of the Rambam. הוי קל לראש—When you meet a venerable aged man, then regard yourself as small and insignificant compared with him; serve him and obey him, ונוח לתשחרת, but do not therefore assume that you may be discourteous to a young man whose hair is still black. Rather, treat everyone, great or unimportant, old or young, with friendly courtesy.

The second reading accords with Rashi's explanation. In it, ראש has the sense of "beginning" (similar to ראשית). "Arise easily to serve your Creator, at the beginning of your life, in your youth." The word תשחרת is understood to mean "age," as it is said, הילדות והשחרות הבל, "Youth and old age are in vain" (*Koheleth* 11:10). Bertinoro's commentary on this mishnah explains that the word תשחרת may be derived from שחור, "black," implying either the hair of the head, that is, a young man, or it may imply the darkness of the face in old age. Similarly, he explains that the word ראש may mean "beginning", implying youth, or "head" as in ראש ישיבה, "the head of the college" who was usually an older man.

The third reading given above accords with a different explanation of Rashi's, in which ראש is taken to mean "head" or "prince," and תשחרת is connected with the talmudic word שחוור, "official" (*Sifrei, Devarim* 6). Rabbi Yishmael is apparently giving us a practical rule: When you are courteous to the prince or to his official and friendly to all human beings, you can only benefit from it. Rashi adds a few puzzling words to his commentary, however, to show us that this cannot be the Sage's true meaning: למה רחל מבכה על בניה, "Why [so]? Rachel [is] weeping for her children." It is not known whether Rashi had this reading of the mishnah or whether he added these words himself. In either case, these words lead to a deeper explanation of the text which Rashi himself calls דרך נסתר (hidden): "Why is Rachel weeping for her children?" The Midrash relates that all the Patriarchs and the Matriarchs tried to placate the Holy One, blessed is He, Who was angry because Menashe had erected an idol in the Sanctuary. But God would not allow His anger to be assuaged. Then our mother Rachel stepped forward and said, "Lord of the universe, whose mercy is greater, Yours or that of human beings? Surely Yours. Behold, when the time of my marriage arrived, they took my sister under the canopy and not only did I keep silent, but I even helped my sister to guard her secret, and so I introduced my rival into my own house. Now if I, flesh and blood, was not jealous of my competitor, how can you, the Merciful One, be jealous of idols who have no real substance? Kind Father, forgive my children that they have prayed to another god apart from You." And the Lord said to Rachel: "You have defended your children well; there will be a reward for your action" (see Rashi on *Yirmeyahu* 31:15).

Let us recall the time during which Rabbi Yishmael lived. It was one of the most painful periods in Jewish history; every individual Roman was an enemy of the Jews, and Hadrian offered a reward for every murdered Jew. What would have been more natural than for such a tortured people to deeply hate their torturers? But the Jewish people never hated their enemies. We Jews always regarded our sufferings as a just punishment for our sins, and regarded our oppressors as the messengers of Divine providence. This is the secret of our endurance. To keep silent in suffering as Rachel did, to exert great self-control, is a virtue that receives the highest acknowledgement at God's thone.

So Rashi explains היו קל לראש: Whatever evil a prince may decree, make light of it, however hard it may be; ונוח לתשחרת: However much the ruler's officials may torture you, be nevertheless always courteous and obliging to them; והיו מקבל את כל האדם בשמחה: And receive everyone, even those who hate and harass you, with joy — not only בסבר פנים יפות, "with a friendly countenance," as Shammai said, but בשמחה, "with true joy." Why? As Rachel wept for her children and her tears were successful at God's throne, so our suffering, too, will be rewarded if we but endure it in the proper spirit. You might still wonder why Rabbi Yishmael clothed his advice in such obscure terms. The Talmud says that the Sages, for political reasons, frequently disguised their teachings in mysterious words so that not everybody would understand them, in order to avoid further torture and harassment from their oppressors.

יז רַבִּי עֲקִיבָא אוֹמֵר, שְׂחוֹק וְקַלּוּת רֹאשׁ
מַרְגִּילִין אֶת־הָאָדָם לְעֶרְוָה. מַסֹּרֶת סְיָג
לַתּוֹרָה, מַעְשְׂרוֹת סְיָג לָעֹשֶׁר, נְדָרִים סְיָג
לַפְּרִישׁוּת, סְיָג לַחָכְמָה שְׁתִיקָה:

17 Rabbi Akiva says: Jesting and levity accustom a
man to lewdness. The *Mesorah* (Tradition) is a fence
around the Torah, the tithes are a fence for riches,
vows are a fence for abstinence, a fence for wisdom is
silence.

*   *   *

Rabbi Akiva's influence on Jewish history is prominent. He was
the first to try to arrange the vast material of the Oral Law
systematically; he wrote down for the first time the mishnayoth,
the Tosefta, the Sifra, Sifrei and the Seder Olam Rabbah on
Biblical and Talmudic history. He was as great a teacher as he
was a scholar, and he also contributed greatly to the general
welfare of his community. He was pious, feared sin, loved God,
and his submission to the Divine will was evident in everything he
did. His life story is amazing. His father was a convert to Judaism,
and Rabbi Akiva grew up in complete ignorance, earning his
bread as a shepherd, until the daughter of a rich nobleman
interested him in studying the Torah. She left her father's house
to marry him and they lived in severe poverty for many years.
Probably no one has ever suffered as much as Rabbi Akiva did in
order to acquire knowledge.

For sixteen years, he sat at his teachers' feet without saying a
word, just listening. When at last he raised his voice, he defeated
his own teacher in discussion. Eventually as many as twenty-four
thousand men and youths gathered around him in open fields to
hear him teach. Still later he saw his disciples die before his eyes,
watched a tyrannous regime overcome the man whom he had
regarded as the promised redeemer, Bar Kochva, and lived
through Yisrael's most ignominious defeat. Though everything
seemed to be lost, Rabbi Akiva never lost his trust in God. This

trust gave him the courage to begin teaching again in his old age. He trained a whole new generation of scholars, men who became the "pillars of Judaism." His activities provoked the Romans to anger, however, and he was imprisoned and, finally, gave his life for the sanctification of the Divine Name. As he was being tortured, he affirmed the unity of God and praised Him for having been allowed to show his infinite love for his Creator with his death.

This mishnah is the first in a series of sayings which afford us an insight into the deep thoughts of this great man. When the Men of the Great Assembly founded a new Jewish state after the Babylonian exile, they warned: "Draw a fence around the Torah!" The Torah resembles a lovely garden in which grow precious trees, useful plants and the most beautiful flowers. The garden would soon be destroyed if it were not surrounded by a fence. Rabbi Akiva, finding his nation in a similar position of retrenchment after defeat, refers to that saying of the Men of the Great Assembly, but he himself recommends five special kinds of fences.

JESTING AND LEVITY ACCUSTOM A MAN TO LEWDNESS. According to *Rabbenu* Yonah, this part of the saying also refers to a kind of fence, although the word itself is not used. The opposite of jesting and levity, which is serious and dignified behavior, is actually the fence in this case, but Rabbi Akiva expresses his idea in a roundabout manner for greater emphasis. The word שחוק, "jesting," is similar in meaning to צחוק, "laughter." קלות ראש is a concept found only in Rabbinic literature and means "light-headedness" or "levity" in contrast to כובד ראש, "heaviness of head" or "seriousness." The commentators believe that this is a warning not to indulge excessively in jesting and social amusements. The Sages explain that the term קלות ראש refers especially to excessive levity between the sexes, as it occurred during the celebration of שמחת בית השואבה, "The rejoicing at the place of the water-drawing," during the Sukkoth Festival in the days of the Temple (*Sukkah* 51b). At that time and for that reason the Sages established the rule of separate seating for men and women in the synagogue. If such a warning was necessary in such a place, how much more ought we to beware of the mingling of the sexes that takes place in our modern places of amusement.

THE *MESORAH* (TRADITION) IS A FENCE AROUND THE TORAH. Shimon *Ha-Tzaddik* mentioned the Torah first when he spoke of the foundations of the world (see *Avoth* 1:2). The Torah is the oldest document in the world and yet it has remained intact, unabridged, unadulterated and unchanged from the day when Moshe received it on Sinai until the present day. The early Sages counted and fixed the phrases, words and letters of the Torah. Although its written style sometimes varies in that the letters *vav*, *alef*, and *yud* are sometimes written and sometimes omitted, it is by no means an arbitrary occurrence. The correct text has been determined by the מסורה, the Tradition, established by the Sages. Any error or copying mistake is thus excluded or easily corrected, for a *Sefer Torah* containing mistakes is not permitted to be read before the congregation.

The Talmud records a difference of opinion among the Sages on the question of whether to determine *Halachah* according to the way a word of Torah is written or the way it is read: יש אם למסורה או יש אם למקרא. Rabbi Akiva's opinion is that the read form, the מקרא, is decisive. He therefore stresses the need for the *Mesorah* as a protective fence. This protective fence is even mentioned in Scriptures. When our ancestors returned from Bavel, the leaders renewed the custom of Moshe *Rabbenu* to read out passages to the assembled community: "And they read in the Book, in the Law of God, explicitly so that they would understand the reading" (*Nechemyah* 8:8). According to the Gemara (*Nedarim* 37b), one opinion holds that the words, "so that they would understand the reading," means the *Mesorah*.

The *sofrim* (Mesorites) learned the Law by organizing it into groups of similar *halachoth*, numbering the groups, and then memorizing them according to numbers; they called this the *Mesorah*. Rabbi Akiva also collected the *halachoth* systematically, according to general principles, to aid the memory. According to another opinion, the *Mesorah* means purely the Oral Law. You might conclude in the latter case that a solely oral tradition would lend itself to human error and forgetfulness. That is precisely why Rabbi Akiva emphasized that the function of the Tradition, the *Mesorah*, the Oral Law, is to preserve for all time the correct interpretation of the written word.

THE TITHES ARE A FENCE FOR RICHES. From all the different types of tithes which our ancestors once had to give to the *kohanim, levi'im*, and to the poor, we now, outside of the Holy Land, have only to give a tenth of our income and property for charitable purposes; income includes earnings, inheritance or dowry. Rabbi Yochanan teaches עשר תעשר עשר בשביל שתתעשר, "If you give the tenth part away, you will become rich" (*Ta'anith* 9a).

The Sages tell us that we should tithe once from property and regularly from income, based on the verse: וכל אשר תתן לי עשר אעשרנו לך, "And whatever You will give me, I shall repeatedly tithe to You" (*Bereshith* 28:22). The double use of the word עשר in the Biblical verse is meant to teach us: 1) to repeatedly tithe and 2) to give a double tithe, that is, a fifth of our property and income, so that even a wealthy person should not give more than this and impoverish himself. No one will become poor by helping the needy, and even a rich man needs Divine assistance in order to preserve his wealth.

The story of Binyamin *Ha-Tzaddik* in the Gemara clearly illustrates this point (*Bava Bathra* 11a). Binyamin was in charge of the charity fund in a year of great scarcity. When the public funds ran out, he helped the destitute mother of seven children from his own pocket. Some time later he became ill and when he was on the point of death, the angels assembled before the Heavenly throne and pleaded for him: "You have said that one who preserves even one soul in Yisrael is considered as one who has preserved the whole world." And God commuted Binyamin's death sentence and added twenty-two more years to his life.

VOWS ARE A FENCE FOR ABSTINENCE. The Sages use the strongest terms of disapproval when speaking about taking vows; they compare it to building an altar outside the Holy Temple (*Nedarim* 22a). It is thus not surprising that the commentators question Rabbi Akiva's recommendation of vows in this mishnah. They conclude that he is referring to a particular type of vow, a vow that is meant to curb one's passions and strengthen one's fear of sin. Great *tzaddikim* have taken such vows: the Patriarch Avraham refused the offer of a rich reward from the king of Sodom saying, "I have raised my hand (made a vow) to *Hashem*, God most high, Maker of heaven and earth, that I will not take so much as a thread or a shoestring; nor shall I take anything of yours!" (*Bereshith* 14:22-23). Boaz also vowed, saying, "as *Hashem* lives" (*Ruth* 3:13) and some Sages say that he was thus exorcising his evil inclination so that Ruth could lie at his feet until morning without his touching her. When David was pursued by Shaul and on several occasions had the opportunity to kill him, and was sorely tempted to, he swore the oath, "as *Hashem* lives" to help him overcome the temptation (*Shemuel* I, 26:10). These Biblical oaths were taken for the sole purpose of upholding the commandments, of impressing them more deeply "upon the heart," for the Sages tell us that this is really the meaning of the words על לבבך, "upon your heart," in the verse "And these words which I command you this day shall be upon your heart" (*Sifrei* on *Devarim* 6:5).

A FENCE FOR WISDOM IS SILENCE. The subtle reversal of word order in this phrase alerts us to its importance. The Oral Law is a fence around the Written Law, tithes are a fence for a wealthy man, vows are a fence for unbridled passion, but the fence for wisdom is named only at the very end of the sentence: silence. Rabbi Akiva is telling us that all the other fences are important, but silence is imperative! Knowledge does not necessarily mean wisdom. Wisdom is attained through cultivation of high morals ("avoid levity for it leads to immorality"), through respect for the Tradition ("learn according to the *Mesorah*"), through sensible use of property and income ("take tithes for the poor") and through vigilance in keeping the commandments ("vow to abstain from sin"). That is how to attain wisdom; but how can we preserve it? Through silence. Rabbi Akiva listened in silence for sixteen years to the teachings of wise men. The Wise King Shelomo also said: חושך אמריו יודע דעת, "He who is cautious with his words is knowledgeable" (*Mishlei* 17:27).

יח הוּא הָיָה אוֹמֵר, חָבִיב אָדָם שֶׁנִּבְרָא
בְּצֶלֶם, חִבָּה יְתֵרָה נוֹדַעַת לוֹ שֶׁנִּבְרָא
בְצֶלֶם, שֶׁנֶּאֱמַר כִּי בְּצֶלֶם אֱלֹהִים עָשָׂה אֶת־הָאָדָם.
חֲבִיבִין יִשְׂרָאֵל שֶׁנִּקְרְאוּ בָנִים לַמָּקוֹם, חִבָּה יְתֵרָה
נוֹדַעַת לָהֶם שֶׁנִּקְרְאוּ בָנִים לַמָּקוֹם, שֶׁנֶּאֱמַר בָּנִים
אַתֶּם לַיָי אֱלֹהֵיכֶם. חֲבִיבִין יִשְׂרָאֵל שֶׁנִּתַּן לָהֶם כְּלִי
חֶמְדָּה, חִבָּה יְתֵרָה נוֹדַעַת לָהֶם שֶׁנִּתַּן לָהֶם כְּלִי
חֶמְדָּה שֶׁבּוֹ נִבְרָא הָעוֹלָם שֶׁנֶּאֱמַר כִּי לֶקַח טוֹב
נָתַתִּי לָכֶם תּוֹרָתִי אַל־תַּעֲזֹבוּ:

18 He [Rabbi Akiva] would say: Privileged is man to have been created in God's image. But it was a special favor that it was made known to him that he was created in God's image, as it is said, "For in the image of God did He create man" (*Bereshith* 9:6). Privileged are Yisrael to be called children of God. But it was a special favor that it was made known to them that they are called children of God, as it is said, "You are children to the Lord your God" (*Devarim* 14:1). Privileged are Yisrael because a precious instrument was given them, but it was a special favor that it was made known to them that a precious instrument was given them, through which the world was created, as it is said, "For I have given you a good teaching: Do not forsake my Torah" (*Mishlei* 4:2).

* * *

This mishnah reveals several very deep and exalted concepts about the character of mankind as a whole, and about the special nature and potential of the Jewish people in particular. When Rabbi Akiva said, seventeen hundred years ago, that man is privileged, he clearly meant that all men are privileged, not only

Jews. This was a remarkable declaration in an age when the idea
of equal rights was still unknown. Rabbi Akiva was proclaiming a
basic tenet of Judaism, that man is created in the likeness of God,
and this had been stated long before in the Torah. Our Sages
teach the following about this idea: The words ברכי נפשי את יי,
"My soul, praise the Lord," appear five times in the Psalms, each
time to describe one of the five ways in which the human soul
may be likened to the Holy One, blessed is He (*Berachoth* 10a). As
God permeates the whole world, so the soul permeates the whole
body; as God sees but cannot be seen, so does the human soul; as
God nourishes the world, so the soul nourishes the whole body;
as God is pure, so is the soul pure; as God reigns in secret, so
reigns the human soul. My soul shall praise its Creator for every
one of these likenesses to Him. All human beings, without exception, bear within them the image of God and this quality is
ineluctable as well as imperishable. God commanded that the
body of an executed criminal be buried with dignity, not left
hanging like carrion, because even a person who has committed a
capital crime does not lose his likeness to God. The Divine spark
in man cannot be extinguished; the soul breathed into being by
God does not die. The worst sinner can begin life anew with
remorse and repentance, and work his way up to the highest
degree of perfection possible.

The commentators ask why Rabbi Akiva cites a verse from the
Torah mentioned after the flood, which occurred sixteen hundred and fifty-six years after the Creation, whereas the concept of
the Divine image is introduced soon after the account of Creation
(*Bereshith* 1:26-27, 5:1). The cited verse is taken from a later
portion that emphasizes the difference between man and all the
other creatures of God's universe. The Rambam begins his great
philosophical work, Guide of the Perplexed, with an investigation of this concept. He proves linguistically that צלם (image) and
דמות (likeness) refer exclusively to a spiritual, rather than a bodily, likeness and that this spiritual attribute is vastly different
from even the extrasensory or psychic qualities of animals. We
can praise the lion's courage, the dog's faithfulness, the cat's
modesty, the dove's conjugal loyalty, and man's as well, but only
man can be courageous *and* faithful, modest *and* loyal, and only

man can override his natural instincts and choose virtue over vice. Only man can clothe his thoughts in words and impart them to his fellow. All this shows us that the superior qualities of the human soul originate solely in its likeness to God.

Man, however, has one quality which is unknown in the animal kingdom: insatiability. When he uses this quality for the attainment of wisdom and self-perfection, he will know joy and bliss. "You make me know the path of life; in Your presence the fullness of joy, in Your right hand bliss forevermore" (*Tehillim* 16:11). When he is insatiable in his desire to acquire the material things of this earth, he will fall into the clutches of sin and vice and unhappiness. Rabbi Akiva's words remind us, too, of Akavya's warning (*Avoth* 3:1) to remember our lowly origin so that we do not fall into the grip of sin. But Rabbi Akiva tells us to remember our origin in that we are created in the image of God, and therefore, we must be worthy of such a privilege.

A SPECIAL FAVOR THAT IT WAS MADE KNOWN TO HIM. When someone possesses a great treasure but does not know it, it is as if he does not possess it; when a child shows great talent or special gifts but does not appreciate and develop them, they will be wasted. Man was notified of his privileged status when Noach and his family left the ark after the flood: "And God blessed Noach and his sons and He said to them'...Everything that moves, that lives, it shall be yours for food... However I shall demand your lifeblood; at the hand of every animal will I require it; and at the hand of man, even at the hand of every man's brother, will I require the life of man. Whoever sheds man's blood, by man shall his blood be shed, for in the image of God did He create man' " (*Bereshith* 9:1-6).

God has raised man high above all the other creatures and appointed him the ruler; he has permitted him to kill and consume them for food. On the other hand, God has strictly prohibited the killing of a human being, and anyone who does so risks the severest punishment. Why? Surely the wild animal that has no intellect cannot be held responsible for its actions. Man, however, created in the image of God, has control over his actions and by his actions (obedience to God) can perfect his immortal soul. Therefore, anyone who kills another person not only commits a physical sin but also a spiritual one: he prevents the soul of his victim from serving God and he prevents his own soul from achieving perfection. Rabbi Wessely says that this verse from Bereshith, which Rabbi Akiva cites, implies the immortality of the human soul. There are, he says, five names for the human soul: *nefesh, ruach, neshamah, chayyah* and *yechidah. Chayyah* is the word for animal used in this verse; since the word literally means "living," it is also applied to the human soul because of its immortality. According to our Tradition, the words "I shall demand your lifeblood" refer to a case of suicide. But since a suicide eludes punishment for his crime by dying, the Torah adds by way of explanation, "at the hand of every *chayyah*" — meaning, "I shall demand retribution for the blood shed by the suicide by punishing his immortal soul."

PRIVILEGED ARE YISRAEL...AS IT IS SAID, "YOU ARE CHILDREN TO THE LORD YOUR GOD." Again Rabbi Akiva recalls a verse from the Torah to support his thesis, again he skips over earlier references to it, and again cites only part of the verse: "You are children to the Lord your God, you shall not cut yourselves, nor make any baldness between your eyes, for the dead. For you are a holy people unto the Lord your God and the Lord has chosen you to be a treasured people to Himself above all the nations that are on earth" (*Devarim* 14:1-2). Other verses in the Torah which refer to Yisrael's special status always mention the condition that Yisrael must continue to walk in God's ways in order to maintain their privileges as a holy people and as a kingdom of priests, and if they depart from God's ways, they will lose that status.

The word "children" is used in this verse and not in the others. A son remains a son, whether he is a source of joy or of worry for his father, and that is the relationship of Yisrael to their God. When the people of Yisrael slip back into sin, they are no longer a kingdom of priests or a holy nation, but they remain God's children; in spite of their depravity, they are recognized as such. "I have raised and brought up children, and they have rebelled against Me... Ah, sinful nation, a people laden with iniquity, a seed of evildoers, children that are corrupters"

(*Yeshayahu* 1:2,4). Although God is "angry" with the sinful people of Yisrael, He still calls them His children and He will never exchange them for another nation. Just as God will always remain our Father, we must always perform our filial duties. Even if we Jews want to give up our privileges, if we decide not to be the Chosen People, if we want to shake off the Heavenly yoke completely and mix with the other nations, we can never do that. "And that which comes into your mind shall not be at all, that you say, 'We will be like the nations, as the families of the countries, to serve wood and stone.' As I live, says the Lord, surely with a mighty hand and with an outstretched arm and with fury poured out will I rule over you" (*Yechezkel* 20:32-33). God does not want to part from us and we cannot part from Him.

Since, therefore, "You are children to the Lord your God," you must not indulge in excessive mourning rites like other nations; do not disfigure yourselves by cuts or shaving or any other means. The death of a beloved one signifies that he has been called by your own mutual Father in Heaven, and one day, you too will be called. Where Akavya ben Mahalalel starkly admonishes man (*Avoth* 3:1), reminding him of the dust and decay awaiting him at the end of his life, Rabbi Akiva gives a more comforting sort of admonition, reminding us of the sublime elevation of the human soul at the conclusion of life on earth — but only if that life has been lived in a manner worthy of being received by its Father in Heaven at the appointed time.

PRIVILEGED ARE YISRAEL, BECAUSE...IT WAS MADE KNOWN TO THEM THAT A PRECIOUS INSTRUMENT WAS GIVEN..."A GOOD TEACHING...MY TORAH." Man is privileged over all other creatures since he was created in the image of God. Yisrael are privileged above all other human beings in that they are called God's children, but their greatest privilege is that God gave them the precious instrument through which He created the world. In his explanantion of this saying, Rabbi Wessely turns to several verses in Mishlei which precede the verse cited by Rabbi Akiva:

> My son, despise not the chastening of the Lord, neither be weary of His correction. For, whom the Lord loves, He corrects; even as a father [corrects] the son in whom he

delights. Happy is the man who has found wisdom and the man who has gained understanding from it. For the merchandise of it is better than the merchandise of silver and its gain [better] than fine gold. It is more precious than rubies, and all your treasures are not to be compared to it. Length of days is in its right hand, in its left hand riches and honor. Its ways are ways of pleasantness and all its paths are peace. It is a tree of life to them that lay hold of it, and happy is everyone who leans on it.

(Mishlei 3:11-18)

In Mishlei the Torah is always called חכמה, בינה, דעת, "wisdom," "understanding" and "knowledge." The Wise King Shelomo continues by explaining why the Torah is so great and splendid, saying:

The Lord with *wisdom* (the Torah) founded the earth, with *understanding* (the Torah) He established the heavens, with His *knowledge* (the Torah) the depths were broken up and the clouds drop down the dew.

(Mishlei 3:19-20)

Further confirmation of this point is found in verse 4:6 of Devarim: כי הוא חכמתכם ובינתכם לעיני העמים, "For this (the Torah) is your wisdom and your understanding in the eyes of the nations." Rabbi Akiva calls the Torah כלי חמדה, "a precious instrument," which is analogous to the expression in Hoshea 13:15, אוצר כל כלי חמדה, "A treasure containing all the precious instruments." Taking this idea a step further, the Torah is not only a precious treasure, but it is the very instrument itself through which God created the world. There are different opinions on this subject among the interpreters. Bertinoro takes the matter figuratively, explaining that the whole of Creation only came into existence on account of the Torah. But this interpretation does not agree with the wording of the mishnah.

Rashi takes the matter literally: the Torah says, as it were, I have been the tool of the Creator of the world. בראשית ברא אלהים אלהים, "With *reshith* God created the world, and the Torah is called *reshith*, as it says of itself, 'The Lord has acquired me as the beginning *(reshith)* of His way' *(Mishlei* 8:22)." Rashi elucidates his interpretation with a midrash: "When an architect wants to build a palace, he first designs building plans, according to which the floors are to be constructed, the corridors are to run, the rooms and the halls are to be shaped. In the same way, the Torah is to be regarded as a building plan of the world." Judaism teaches that, if God had so desired, He could have arranged the earth's rotation to take one thousand days, or only one hundred, instead of three hundred and sixty-five. He could have shaped the dry land and the seas differently, or formed the people, the animals and the plants in another fashion entirely. God shaped the world as it is in His wisdom; His wisdom is revealed to us in the Torah; the Torah teaches man the principle of free choice, which is in turn built on the concepts of virtue and vice, of right and wrong, of truth and falsehood, of chastity and immorality, and these are the principles by which the whole world functions. Celestial bodies, geographical and geological formations, and all forms of life are arranged to suit man, and man is formed in such a way that he is able to live in accordance with the precepts of the Torah.

In this sense the Torah is the blueprint of the world's Architect. What a great privilege it is for Yisrael to have this wonderful Torah as a present! Yisrael is and will remain first among the nations — even in a state of humiliation — as long as it preserves the Torah.

To a certain extent, Rabbi Akiva's saying is analogous to that of Akavya ben Mahalalel *(Avoth* 3:1); Akavya reminds us of the insignificance of human origin — Rabbi Akiva points out its sublimity; Akavya reminds us of where the human body will be buried — Rabbi Akiva tells us that all God's children return to their Father in Heaven; Akavya says that one day we will have to render accounts before the All-just, incorruptible Judge — but Rabbi Akiva says we are blessed with the gift of God's most precious jewel, the Torah, which is our guide in life, our protection in death and the means by which we shall one day find grace before His sacred countenance.

יט הַכֹּל צָפוּי, וְהָרְשׁוּת נְתוּנָה, וּבְטוֹב
הָעוֹלָם נָדוֹן, וְהַכֹּל לְפִי רֹב הַמַּעֲשֶׂה:

19 Everything is foreseen, yet freedom of choice is given, and the world is judged with kindness, and everything is according to the nature of the majority of the deeds [that have been done].

* * *

An important commentary on this very difficult mishnah is the Introduction to Avoth by the Rambam, a work which elicited either wholehearted approval or severe criticism from the other great commentators. He speaks of the apparent contradiction in Rabbi Akiva's saying; that is, if everything is foreseen (and we are taught that God surely does foresee everything, for all His attributes are infinite and all-embracing), then how can man have been given freedom to choose his own actions (for we are also taught that man has indeed been given this ability)? His explanation can be summed up in the words of the prophet, "For My thoughts are not your thoughts" (*Yeshayahu* 55:8). Human perception of God's attributes is so restricted by the limits of man's understanding, that we cannot even speak of a contradiction in this case. The two truths coexist, he says, but on two different levels, as it were, a human and a Divine. Some, like Rabbi Avraham ben David, criticized the Rambam for "awakening doubts in pious minds" but others, like Don Yitzchak Abravanel, praised him for "admitting that human knowledge does not suffice to resolve the question," and thus publicly sanctifying God's Name in a widely-read philosophical work.

Somewhere along the line, the contributions of the great Jewish philosophers to science and literature were overlooked by the world at large. For centuries, the words of the secular philosophers dominated educated thought throughout the Western world, so that by the nineteenth century of the common era (the beginning of the so-called Modern Age) "enlightened" man assumed that everything was discoverable and explorable. The past and the future of the whole universe could be postulated, he thought, by human reason; therefore he could deduce true information about God, about his own soul and about immortality.

Most commentators, however, prefer Rashi's interpretation of the mishnah: Everything that man does or thinks, even in secret, is seen and revealed before the Holy One, blessed is He, and yet man is allowed to choose between good and evil.

The Rashbatz tries to solve the contradiction between God's omniscience and the freedom of human will by suggesting certain limits with regard to both. He bases his opinion on the passage in Tractate Sanhedrin (107a) where the Sages say that Bathsheva was David's appointed wife, but that David did not wait for the appointed time. Had David been able to control his passion and waited, God would have arranged for their marriage by some means. From this we learn that man is given a chance to shape whatever talents are given him and he may employ them either in the service of virtue and fear of God or to the contrary. It is therefore highly desirable for us to observe children and encourage their natural talents to develop in the right direction, rather than to enforce a vocation upon them that will not harmonize with their nature.

AND THE WORLD IS JUDGED WITH KINDNESS. Crimes are sometimes committed for noble motives, while good deeds can be performed just as well for ignoble reasons. When someone makes a large, public donation, motivated by ambition or vanity, then the deed itself is good, but the motives are not. Embezzling money, even if it is to help a desperate friend, is still a crime albeit motivated by a good heart. Rabbi Akiva tells us that God judges all deeds favorably, for He sees everything and knows the most secret thoughts of man, whereas a human judge may allow pure motives to secure pardon for evil deeds and evil motives to lessen the value of good deeds.

AND EVERYTHING IS ACCORDING TO THE NATURE OF THE MAJORITY OF THE DEEDS. Rabbi Akiva uses the singular form מעשה (deed) and although most interpreters assume that the plural form is meant to follow the expression לפי רוב, "according to the majority," it is incumbent upon us to investigate what the singular form implies. Rabbi Wessely has a different view than the other commentators. He thinks that מעשה refers to the act of Creation and not to the deeds of man, and supports his thesis with many verses from Tehillim in which the word מעשה specifically means both the works of God in nature and the wonders that God has wrought in opposition to the natural laws.

Alternatively, we can even explain the use of the word מעשה in the singular form as referring to the deeds of the righteous. We read (*Tehillim* 37:32-33), "The wicked one [the evil inclination] lies in wait for the righteous and seeks to slay him. The Lord will not leave him in his hand, nor condemn him when he is judged." The greater a man is, the more he has to fight his evil inclination. Hardly a day goes by on which the evil inclination does not strive to throw the pious man down and to kill him morally. In this constantly-recurring fight, man would succumb were not God to assist him. He supports him and only thus does the pious man succeed in persevering on the right path. When man appears, then, before the throne of the All-just to receive reward or punishment for what he accomplished on earth, one might think that he will not be credited for what he accomplished only with God's assistance. The All-kind God, however, credits him for his good deeds as if he had done them without any assistance and "will not condemn him when he is judged." Thus we can explain הכל לפי רוב המעשה as "Everything is assessed according to most of the deed." Even though some of the deeds of the righteous are only accomplished with God's assistance and therefore only most of the deed is done by the pious man himself, nevertheless God will credit the righteous man's deeds as if he had achieved everything by himself.

There is an alternative reading for this phrase: אבל לא (but not) instead of הכל (everything), which Rashi says does not, in any case, change the meaning of the text. Whether we say "Everything is [judged] according to the nature of the majority of the deeds," or "but not in accordance with the number of deeds," Rabbi Akiva is saying, "God does not destroy the world for the sinful deeds of man, but keeps an account of all his deeds for the Day of Judgment." The Divine scales weigh quality, not quantity. The Rambam asserts, however, that it is not the magnitude of the deeds, but their number that is decisive. In other words, it is better to give one coin to a thousand needy people than to give a thousand coins all at once to one charitable cause, because this is how man trains his character. Don Yitzchak Abravanel does not accept this explanation, saying that it does not fit the text. Rabbi Akiva is reflecting upon cosmic ideas in these three sayings: the governance of the world, the opposing forces of predetermination and free will, and final judgment. Why then would he suddenly refer to personal character-building? Rabbi Akiva's saying must mean, therefore, that God knows the course of events in advance and still has bestowed free will upon man; God judges the world with kindness, but nevertheless it can happen that a righteous person will suffer in life and a wicked one prosper; the reason for this is that Divine justice will be meted out only in the World to Come, according to the majority of deeds performed in this world. Thus, for the minority of bad deeds which the righteous do, they are punished in this world so that they can have the full reward for their majority of good deeds in the World to Come, and conversely with the wicked.

Rabbi Shemuel of Ozedah explains that Rabbi Akiva told us in the previous mishnah that Yisrael is privileged, above all other nations, to have received the precious Torah, and now he wants to say that when the Day of Judgment arrives, no Jew will be able to claim that he could not find the right path, for הכל צפוי, "Everything is clearly foreseen," and man has only to obey the Torah. We must understand that it is man's mission that is foreseen—what he should do, not necessarily what he will do. Not all men choose to walk on the right path. But even if we stray, we shall always remain His dearly beloved children and know that all "the world is judged with kindness," including the wicked, and the world will be saved from destruction by the רוב המעשה, "the majority of deeds," done by the righteous. This mishnah follows naturally after the previous one. The Torah is called לקח טוב, "a good teaching," for according to its principles the world was created, according to its principles the world is governed, and according to its principles the deeds of men are judged mercifully.

כ הוּא הָיָה אוֹמֵר, הַכֹּל נָתוּן בְּעֵרָבוֹן,
וּמְצוּדָה פְּרוּסָה עַל־כָּל־הַחַיִּים, הֶחָנוּת
פְּתוּחָה וְהַחֶנְוָנִי מַקִּיף, וְהַפִּנְקֶס פָּתוּחַ וְהַיָּד כּוֹתֶבֶת,
וְכָל הָרוֹצֶה לִלְווֹת יָבֹא וְיִלְוֶה, וְהַגַּבָּאִין מַחֲזִירִין
תָּדִיר בְּכָל־יוֹם וְנִפְרָעִין מִן־הָאָדָם מִדַּעְתּוֹ וְשֶׁלֹּא
מִדַּעְתּוֹ, וְיֵשׁ לָהֶם עַל מַה שֶּׁיִּסְמְכוּ, וְהַדִּין דִּין אֱמֶת,
וְהַכֹּל מְתֻקָּן לַסְּעוּדָה:

20 He [Rabbi Akiva] would say: Everything is given on pledge and a net is spread out over all the living. The shop is open, and the merchant extends credit, the ledger is open and the hand records, and whoever wishes to borrow—let him come and borrow. The collectors make their appointed rounds each day and take payment from man, with or without his consent. And they have that on which they can rely, and the judgment is a true judgment. And everything is ready for the festive meal.

* * *

This mishnah introduces several graphic metaphors which Rabbi Akiva uses to enlighten us about the management of the world; it is a continuation of, and a conclusion to, all his previous sayings. He has just described all the privileges bestowed upon Yisrael and called them gifts of infinite value. Now he explains that everything is really only a loan which we must pay back by living a worthy life filled with good deeds. In addition to this loan of everything we possess, God extends his protection, like a net which is spread over all men. The world itself is like a vast shop filled with beautiful and valuable items of all kinds, and it is always open. Anyone can enter the shop and take as many items as he wishes and not pay a penny for them, for the storekeeper extends credit to all. But absolutely all the debts are recorded in His ledger, and each man, whether king or beggar, is responsible for his own debts. Sooner or later each person will have to pay in some form, knowingly or unknowingly. One person may have good fortune, another hard luck, but nothing happens by chance. We do not know why or how judgment is meted out; we only know that the judgment is always just, that sooner or later all debts will be paid, and that everyone will be ready for the final, eternal banquet in the World to Come.

EVERYTHING IS GIVEN ON PLEDGE. The word ערבון means "pledge" or "surety" for a debt (*Bereshith* 38:18,20). The commentators are in some doubt as to precisely what sort of pledge Rabbi Akiva means here. Rashi mentions two possibilities. It may mean that every man must be the surety for his fellow, be responsible for his behavior, whether good or bad. Consequently every man must do his utmost to keep the next man from doing evil. Alternatively, it may be man's soul which is God's surety for the deeds he does on earth. If man succeeds in overcoming his evil inclination, his soul will rise to God after death; if not, his soul will have to atone for his behavior in the World to Come. Bertinoro defines the "pledge" as a restraint imposed on man which prevents him from escaping Divine judgment wherever and whenever he is called to it. In the same vein, he explains the protective "net" of God as the "evil net" of the fisherman (*Koheleth* 9:12) which traps the fish unexpectedly whenever the fisherman decides to pull it in. Man should therefore be prepared at all times with a "balanced account" of his life.

THE MERCHANT EXTENDS CREDIT. The idea of "credit" being extended indefinitely, which most commentators accept, must be objected to in the light of what has already been said about sin and punishment and free will. Rabbi Akiva seems to be saying that it is an added privilege for us to have unlimited time to pay for our evil deeds, and the liberty of deferring payment is an extension of our free will. Yet we have learned from the Sages elsewhere (*Avodah Zarah* 4a) that it is God's special mercy to man that He punishes quickly, not waiting until the measure of his sin is so full that the sinner has to be annihilated. The interpretation of this is further complicated if we recall the commentary in Kiddushin 40a which teaches that no "credit" whatever is granted when the Divine Name has been profaned. This sin evokes immediate and severe punishment. According to *Rabbenu* Nathan, the author of the Aruch, this is to be taken as the exception that proves the rule. The profanation of God's Name does not permit deferred punishment. Other sins may be accumulated, as it were, to allow the sinner to repent and/or to "pay off his debt" with good deeds. In the event that the sinner is completely unrepentant, then God will not wait to exact punishment until his sins are so many that he deserves annihilation, but will begin to exact gradual retribution. One thing, however, is certain: "The hand records" all bad actions as debts requiring payment.

AND WHOEVER WISHES TO BORROW — LET HIM COME AND BORROW. Although it is reproachable to accumulate debts carelessly, borrowing in itself is not. After all, everything we are and possess is from God and only one thing rests with us: the serious desire to serve Him and to pay off our debt as much as possible through noble deeds and being God-fearing, as David said, "Everything is from You and we can repay You only that which we have received from Your hand" (*Divrei Hayyamim* I, 29:14). In certain cases, we are even called upon to make debts. Although it is better to make do with little, even on the Shabbath, than to have to take charity from others, it is a higher degree of piety to borrow for the purpose of celebrating the Shabbath and the Festivals properly, even though we have to rely on God's help to repay the loans (see *Beitzah* 15b on *Nechemyah* 8:10).

AND THE COLLECTORS MAKE THEIR APPOINTED ROUNDS EACH DAY. Who are the collectors? According to most commentators, they are the natural forces. The rain that waters and makes fertile one man's field and brings him prosperity, floods another's, bringing misfortune; the storm that purifies the air also damages buildings and sinks ships at sea; the hot rays of the sun that enrich the corn and sweeten the fruit, also spread disease. God thus sends His admonishers, as it were, to remind man that his days on earth are transitory and that he should repent if he has departed from the right path. Although man only harvests that which he has sown, he often overlooks his own errors and forgets the sins he has committed, believing that his sufferings are merely happenstance and that there is no good reason for his misfortunes. All the forces working in nature, whether they have a beneficial or a harmful effect on man, are God's messengers sent by Him to reward or to punish in accordance with His holy wish. There is no such thing as chance, and if we think there is, it is because we are unable to comprehend the subtle interrelationship of events.

THE JUDGMENT IS A TRUE JUDGMENT. Why does Rabbi Akiva repeat the word "judgment"? The Divine court does not merely make a just decision, but the entire process of judgment is true and just. All the circumstances are weighed and the true motives are understood; strict justice is tempered by mercy and compassion. As Moshe said, Almighty God is like the rock in the sea, unshaken by the surging waves, His action is complete, perfect; He does not judge men according to His perfection, but considers their weaknesses. Although "all his paths are justice," and He will in no way diminish the reward of the righteous, He will approve of any possible leniency toward the greatest sinners in order to avoid the slightest injustice, "for He is just and right" (*Devarim* 32:4-5).

AND EVERYTHING IS READY FOR THE FESTIVE MEAL. These words form the conclusion, and at the same time the summary, of Rabbi Akiva's sayings. All that the Holy One, blessed is He, has created in His world is only a preparation for one great purpose. You should not imagine that the good things you do in this world are perfect; you should not think that the bad things in this world are the worst that will ever happen. This world is only a preparation for the World to Come. It is sometimes necessary for the righteous to be tested and to suffer; it is sometimes necessary for punishment to be deferred to allow time for repentance; it is sometimes necessary to reward the wicked in this world for the little good they have done on earth and so to exclude them from the great banquet of eternal bliss. Nothing is forgotten and no influence can sway the court from a judgment of truth, but man will only become aware of this truth on the day of the feast. Only if the Almighty's actions could be understood in their entirety would we realize that all His ways are completely in keeping with justice. Man is like a fly that has a lifespan of one day, born in a tiny corner of a large, magnificent building. No matter how far it travels from its corner before the end of its short life, how much will it have seen of the large and magnificent building? How much of this large, magnificent world can we explore and understand during our short life? And how can we presume to judge God's management of the world with our limited comprehension? However, as we learn from the words of the prophet (*Malachi* 3:13 ff.), all the complaints of men against Divine providence will cease on the day of final reckoning; then everyone will recognize that all the events of this life have not been a final objective, but only a preparation for the World to Come.

כא רַבִּי אֶלְעָזָר בֶּן־עֲזַרְיָה אוֹמֵר. אִם אֵין תּוֹרָה אֵין דֶּרֶךְ אֶרֶץ, אִם אֵין דֶּרֶךְ אֶרֶץ אֵין תּוֹרָה. אִם אֵין חָכְמָה אֵין יִרְאָה, אִם אֵין יִרְאָה אֵין חָכְמָה. אִם אֵין דַּעַת אֵין בִּינָה, אִם אֵין בִּינָה אֵין דַּעַת. אִם אֵין קֶמַח אֵין תּוֹרָה, אִם אֵין תּוֹרָה אֵין קֶמַח:

21 Rabbi Elazar ben Azaryah says: Where there is no Torah, there are no ethics; where there are no ethics, there is no Torah. Where there is no wisdom, there is no fear of God; where there is no fear of God, there is no wisdom. Where there is no knowledge, there is no understanding; where there is no understanding, there is no knowledge. Where there is no flour (sustenance), there is no Torah; where there is no Torah, there is no flour.

* * *

Rabbi Elazar ben Azaryah was a member of the distinguished family of priests who descended from Ezra. When *Rabban* Gamliel the Second was removed from office, Rabbi Elazar was elected President (*Nasi*) and head of the academy at Yavneh although he was only eighteen years old at the time. When *Rabban* Gamliel was later reinstated, Rabbi Elazar continued in office, alternating with *Rabban* Gamliel as *Nasi*. (*Rabban* Gamliel would preside for two weeks, and then Rabbi Elazar for one week.) Rabbi Elazar's great concern for his people led him to Rome in the company of *Rabban* Gamliel, Rabbi Yehoshua ben Chananya and Rabbi Akiva in order to try to counteract Emperor Domitian's plans to annihilate the Jews. Because of his great learning, Rabbi Elazar's contemporaries called him "the spice box" (*Gittin* 67a). He was also renowned for his temperate nature, in contrast to *Rabban* Gamliel's severe one. *Rabban* Gamliel closed the portals of learning to those whose purity of character he was not firmly convinced of, while Rabbi Elazar had the gates of the academy opened wide, allowing everybody to enter and to strengthen their character by a closer acquaintance with the Torah. Rabbi Elazar lived long and was always active in the public welfare. Rabbi Yehoshua ben Chananya once said, "An era during which a man like Rabbi Elazar ben Azaryah lives cannot be called bleak."

WHERE THERE IS NO TORAH, THERE ARE NO ETHICS; WHERE THERE ARE NO ETHICS, THERE IS NO TORAH. The term "Torah" sometimes refers simply to the learning of Torah and at other times it includes the observance of all the teachings revealed by God. When Shimon *Ha-Tzaddik* calls the Torah one of the three pillars of the world (*Avoth* 1:2), he must mean Torah study, for otherwise *avodah* and *gemiluth chasadim* would be included in the concept and only one pillar would support the world: Torah. Rabbi Elazar ben Azaryah refers here to both the study and the practice of the whole Torah.

Derech eretz is a most complex concept. It is sometimes translated as "ethics" or "good manners," but this is only part of its meaning and it is difficult to find one expression which translates the concept adequately. The literal translation, "the way of the land," is meaningless. *Derech eretz* is usually understood to mean courtesy and modesty in human relationships but this, too, is incomplete. Our Sages employ the term *derech eretz* to mean all those good and beautiful things which are not directly commanded by the Torah, but are in keeping with its spirit, and conversely, the avoidance of all those things which are not directly prohibited by the Torah, but yet do not accord with its spirit. This concept encompasses the realms of good manners and higher morality. For example, a Jew is duty-bound by the commandments to help someone in pain or trouble. If he forms a committee to assist the whole community, solicits funds from wealthy donors and distributes them conscientiously to the needy, then he is more than fulfilling the commandment, yet only doing that which is in keeping with the spirit of the Torah. Conversely, although God has commanded us to assist our needy brethren by granting them interest-free loans, to do so because we hope to acquire the pledged property by foreclosure is totally against the spirit, if not the law, of the Torah. The highest human morality is implicit in the Torah and taught in all the sacred writings; more than that, it is unimaginable without the Torah.

The interdependence of the two concepts, Torah and *derech eretz,* has yet another dimension. We have seen that Torah includes both the primary stage of study and learning as well as the more complex task of practicing the teachings and commandments in a way (*derech*) that will lead us to a higher moral level. Rabbi Elazar therefore says: If we Jews have not reached the higher morality, then we have either studied incorrectly or not practiced the teachings of the Torah well enough. Proper observance of the Torah must lead to the highest and purest morality.

WHERE THERE IS NO WISDOM, THERE IS NO FEAR OF GOD. First we should ask: What is חכמה (wisdom)? Rabbi Yitzchak Luria, called "the holy one," is said to have been transported in a dream to the academy of Rabbi Akiva. When he told his disciples his dream, they asked him to relate what he had learned there. "My children," the Sage said, "seventy years would not suffice to teach you what I learned in those moments." In a similar way, one could say, a generation would not suffice to explain what has been taught about the concept of חכמה in the Written and the Oral Law and in the books of the later Sages of our people. The following remarks are "like a drop from the sea," and touch only upon that which is necessary for the understanding of our mishnah. חכמה is described to us in Iyyov 28:

> But where shall wisdom be found, and where is the place of understanding? Man does not know its value and it is not found in the land of the living. The abyss says: It is not in me, and the sea says: It is not with me... Gold and crystal cannot equal it and it cannot be exchanged for fine gold. Corals and pearls do not compare with it, for the price of wisdom is above rubies...Whence then does wisdom come and where is the place of understanding? It is hidden from the eyes of all living, kept secret from the birds of the air. Destruction and death say: We heard its fame with our ears. God understands its ways and knows its place.

Is Rabbi Elazar's teaching an impossible hope? If we cannot learn to fear God without first acquiring wisdom, and if wisdom is a secret known only to God, how are we to understand this maxim? Furthermore, we have learned that a man's ability to acquire wisdom is predetermined by God, but he has freedom to decide by himself whether he will fear God as he should (see discussion above, *Avoth* 3:11). This implies that fear of God is independent of wisdom. To our further confusion, the Wise King Shelomo teaches that wisdom is all about us, "in the streets...at the gates...in the city" (*Mishlei* 1:20-21), and it need not be searched for!

The apparent contradiction between the description of wisdom in Iyyov and that in Mishlei is explained by Rabbi Shimon in Parashath Toledoth of the Zohar. Rabbi Shimon says that the verse in Mishlei חכמות בחוץ תרנה ברחבת תתן קולה, uses the word חכמות in the plural form, and therefore denotes Divine wisdom, which comprises a greater and lesser one. Divine wisdom, חכמה העליונה, is mostly hidden from us in this world, as described in Iyyov, and encompasses the understanding of concepts like God's unity, the immortality of the soul, the management of the universe and all supernatural phenomena. We call this wisdom metaphysics. It is only partly revealed, תתן קולה, "it speaks to us," in the form of nature. This is the second type, the lesser wisdom, חכמתא זעירא, the wisdom of the physical world. Rabbi Shimon teaches us, however, that the two are ultimately one, the lesser wisdom is included in the supreme wisdom and that is why Shelomo says הכן בחוץ מלאכתך ועתדה בשדה לך אחר ובנית ביתך (*Mishlei* 24:27), that is to say, strive to understand the wisdom revealed in nature (בחוץ), so that one day you will be able to enter the field (בשדה), the blessed fields of paradise, and know the Divine wisdom. Afterwards, אחר, it is explained, when you know the secret wisdom, you will build your house, ובנית ביתך, that is, you will cause your soul to become perfect and whole.

While contemporary philosophy endeavors to draw metaphysics into the sphere of human knowledge, Judaism teaches that all these sublime teachings are beyond human understanding and that we owe our awareness of them only to Divine revelation. Great thinkers have evolved countless "proofs" for these metaphysical concepts, but all these proofs lack mathematical evidence and each new philosophical school is soon replaced by another. For us, the teachings of supreme wisdom are not in the sphere of knowledge, but in that of faith. It is a sad fact that man will acknowledge only that which can be proven and which suits his own desires. If he is asked to accept the highest wisdom from the Torah and its teachers, to master his passions and suppress his evil inclinations, to give up some pleasures and do without material acquisitions, he resists with all his might.

When Rabbi Elazar says, "Where there is no wisdom, there is no fear of God," he means the supreme wisdom, the faith in God and in His Torah, which both scholars and unlearned men can attain. Faith is the foundation of that highest of moral achievements, fear of God; and the lesser wisdom, which we can study in this world, is one of the paths leading toward it. All wisdom, however, is valueless without action. "Behold," says Rabbi Ya'avetz in his commentary, "a simple, ignorant woman who surrenders her life for the sanctification of the Divine Name, possesses supreme wisdom; the learned man who disavows God in order to save his own life, is devoid of supreme wisdom despite all his knowledge."

As for the second half of Rabbi Elazar's statement, "Where there is no fear of God, there is no wisdom," let us examine the meaning of the term "fear." יראה is not fear of punishment but actually a profound feeling of reverence resulting from the observation of God's overwhelming power, omniscience, goodness and, above all, the miracles He performs. This concept of יראה is closely linked to that of אהבה (selfless love). Since supreme wisdom cannot be irrefutably demonstrated and its teachings do not always agree with our inclinations and desires, the human heart tends to reject it, and it is only through יראה—reverence and love of God—that the human heart can accept it. This is also taught by our Sages in the holy Zohar (*Parashath Bereshith*): "It says in Psalms, 'The beginning of wisdom is the fear of the Lord' (*Tehillim* 111:10). It should really say, 'The final purpose of all wisdom is the fear of the Lord,' for it is the fear of God that opens the only gate through which man can attain the level of supreme wisdom. That is the gate mentioned in the verse, 'Open for me the gates of righteousness, I will enter them and thank the Lord. This is the gateway to *Hashem*; the righteous shall enter through it' " (*Tehillim* 118:19-20).

WHERE THERE IS NO KNOWLEDGE, THERE IS NO UNDER-STANDING; WHERE THERE IS NO UNDERSTANDING, THERE IS NO KNOWLEDGE. The concepts of דעת (knowledge), and בינה (understanding), are extremely difficult to define. The opinion of most commentators follows that of the Rambam: *da'ath* denotes inborn intellectual ability, while *binah* refers to the independent development of the mind. This is borne out by the first of the middle blessings in our daily prayer: אתה חונן לאדם דעת ומלמד לאנוש בינה. We are graced with *da'ath* (perception) and taught *binah* (insight). The mind is inherently capable of comprehension (sensory perception), memory (recall of previous perceptions), definition (of individual concepts), differentiation (among concepts), comparison (of qualities) and reasoning (forming judgments about abstract ideas, inferring one thing from another). These qualities are all encompassed in *da'ath*, while *binah* works on them and develops them.

The sense of the maxim is therefore: If we have low intellectual capability, we cannot develop knowledge to any high degree. And if we are gifted, but do not attempt to develop our gifts, then all our potential is wasted. The Sayings of the Fathers, however, are precepts of moral and religious behavior and do not relate to logic or intellect; therefore we infer that Rabbi Elazar must mean something else as well.

The greatest danger to our faith is misguided thinking. When one deviates from the truth in one's thoughts, accepting illusion and falsehood as truth, it is difficult indeed to return to the right path. One who believes blindly without understanding is the easiest of all to be led astray. What is expected of us, then, is to understand God by refining our natural senses, by observing nature carefully and studying what has happened in the past (*da'ath*), and better still, to absorb the teachings of the Torah to the best of our ability (*binah*) so that we may aspire to that part of the Divine wisdom which was revealed to man (*chochmah*). Without applying our natural mental talents (*da'ath*), the supreme revealed wisdom will remain unknown to us; we cannot penetrate it with our understanding (*binah*). But if we were not to employ our mental talents, bestowed by God, for comprehension (*binah*) of the revealed wisdom, then even the knowledge that we absorb by observation of nature and history (*da'ath*) will remain closed to us. This is the meaning of what the Sages taught: גדולה דעת שנתנה בין שתי אותיות שנאמר כי אל דעות יי, "Great is the knowledge that has its starting point in God and finds its ultimate goal in God" (*Berachoth* 33a).

WHERE THERE IS NO FLOUR, THERE IS NO TORAH. Most commentators explain that "flour" means physical sustenance; if man is unable to satisfy his basic physical needs, he will be unable to occupy himself with Torah. Furthermore, our Sages teach that oppressive poverty blunts the senses, which are necessary for acquiring the knowledge needed to understand God, as we have just learned (*Eruvin* 41b). Similarly, Ulla teaches, "Anxiety about livelihood adversely affects Torah learning, as it is written, '[A life full of anxiety] disturbs the thoughts of the skilled (i.e., scholars) so that they cannot progress in their studies' " (*Sanhedrin* 26b on *Iyyov* 5:12). Note that Rabbi Elazar says "flour" and not "bread." The difference between flour and bread is that flour keeps for a long time and can be made into different things, while bread stays fresh for a very short time. Thus Rabbi Elazar tells us that the sustenance we seek should not be just a precarious day-to-day existence, but should be at least enough to provide for the immediate future.

WHERE THERE IS NO TORAH, THERE IS NO FLOUR. Bertinoro, *Rabbenu* Yonah and many others explain that there is no purpose in having food if one does not have Torah. The Rashbatz, however, says that this is a forced explanation. He proposes a different reading: אם אין תורה אין קמח יש תורה יש קמח, "Where there is no Torah, there is no sustenance, but where there is Torah there is sustenance as well." He who devotes himself to Torah study need not be concerned about his bodily needs, for God will provide for him, as it is written, "I was young and now have grown old but I have never seen a righteous man forsaken and his offspring forced to beg for bread" (*Tehillim*

37:25). This idea is mentioned in many other verses in the Torah as well (*Devarim* 29:8; *Yehoshua* 1:8; *Tehillim* 1:1-8; *Yeshayahu* 40:31 cited in *Kiddushin* 82b).

Without changing the original version of the text, however, we can find a more satisfactory explanation. Rabbi Elazar suggests here a method for learning Torah. Just as flour is the product of processing, so a Torah student should not swallow his studies without "processing" them. He should mentally grind and crush the seeds of knowledge, cracking the outer shells first to release the inner kernels, and winnow out the worthless chaff. At the outset of his studies, however, the student does not have enough discernment to undertake this refining process. He must first fill up his mental storehouse with knowledge, and only afterwards will he be able to refine it — to find contradictions between one tractate and another, to compare different passages from the Talmud and thus discern the truth. Rabbi Shemuel of Ozedah supports this explanation with the verse: החכם ,יענה דעת רוח וימלא קדים בטנו: הוכח בדבר לא יסכון ומלים לא יועיל בם "The wise man who answers every question with acute discernment has previously filled himself with knowledge, carefully separating every item that is useless for his education" (*Iyyov* 15:2-3). He also adds another explanation: There are two kinds of food, one for the body and the other for the soul, one for this world and the other for the World to Come. When there is no food for the body, one cannot devote oneself to Torah studies; but when there is no Torah, then there is no food for the soul.

כב הוּא הָיָה אוֹמֵר, כֹּל שֶׁחָכְמָתוֹ מְרֻבָּה מִמַּעֲשָׂיו לְמָה הוּא דוֹמֶה, לְאִילָן שֶׁעֲנָפָיו מְרֻבִּין וְשָׁרָשָׁיו מֻעָטִין וְהָרוּחַ בָּאָה וְעוֹקַרְתּוֹ וְהוֹפַכְתּוֹ עַל פָּנָיו, שֶׁנֶּאֱמַר וְהָיָה כְּעַרְעָר בָּעֲרָבָה וְלֹא יִרְאֶה כִּי־יָבוֹא טוֹב וְשָׁכַן חֲרֵרִים בַּמִּדְבָּר אֶרֶץ מְלֵחָה וְלֹא תֵשֵׁב. אֲבָל כֹּל שֶׁמַּעֲשָׂיו מְרֻבִּים מֵחָכְמָתוֹ לְמָה הוּא דוֹמֶה, לְאִילָן שֶׁעֲנָפָיו מֻעָטִין וְשָׁרָשָׁיו מְרֻבִּין, שֶׁאֲפִילוּ כָּל־הָרוּחוֹת שֶׁבָּעוֹלָם בָּאוֹת וְנוֹשְׁבוֹת בּוֹ אֵין מְזִיזִין אוֹתוֹ מִמְּקוֹמוֹ, שֶׁנֶּאֱמַר וְהָיָה כְּעֵץ שָׁתוּל עַל־מַיִם וְעַל־יוּבַל יְשַׁלַּח שָׁרָשָׁיו וְלֹא יִרְאֶה כִּי־יָבֹא חֹם וְהָיָה עָלֵהוּ רַעֲנָן וּבִשְׁנַת בַּצֹּרֶת לֹא יִדְאָג וְלֹא יָמִישׁ מֵעֲשׂוֹת פֶּרִי:

22 He [Rabbi Elazar ben Azaryah] would say: Any man whose wisdom exceeds his deeds, to what can he be compared? To a tree whose branches are many but whose roots are few. The wind comes and uproots it and overturns it upon its face. Of such a man it is said, "And he shall be like a lonely tree in the wasteland and shall not see when good comes, he shall dwell upon the parched soil in the wilderness, a salt-saturated land which is uninhabitable" (*Yirmeyahu* 17:6). But any man whose deeds exceed his wisdom, to what can he be compared? To a tree whose branches are few but whose roots are many. Even if all the winds of the world come and blow upon it, they cannot move it from its place. Of such a man it is said, "And he shall be like a tree planted by the waters which spreads out its roots to the water, it need not be afraid when the heat comes, and its leaf shall remain fresh. It will not be troubled in the year of drought, neither will it cease to bear fruit" (*Yirmeyahu* 17:8).

*   *   *

Neither the Rambam nor Bertinoro explain this mishnah in their respective commentaries on Avoth; in fact, the former states that he has already discussed an identical saying by Rabbi Chanina ben Dosa (*Avoth* 3:12). This is astonishing in view of the difference between the two sayings and the difficulty in harmonizing Rabbi Elazar's simile about the tree with Yirmeyahu's. Rabbi Elazar's "tree" is rooted in good deeds, while the prophet's "tree" is rooted in faith (*Yirmeyahu* 17:7). Rashi explains the omission in the commentaries by observing that the words of Yirmeyahu did not appear in many old manuscripts of Tractate Avoth. Another point that requires explication is the comparison of deeds to roots, and of wisdom to branches. Since Rabbi Akiva and the Elders held that study is greater than practice (*Kiddushin* 40b), wisdom ought to be compared to roots. Rashi justifies the comparison with the words of Rabbi Shimon ben *Rabban* Gamliel: ולא המדרש הוא העיקר אלא המעשה, "Study is not the main thing but practice" (*Avoth* 1:17).

Rabbi Chayyim ben Betzalel points out that Yirmeyahu is not speaking specifically about a man of faith but about any righteous man, and conversely, when he speaks of one who lacks faith in God, he means any unworthy person. In the שער ההכנעה (Chapter on Humility) of the Chovoth Ha-Levavoth, *Rabbenu* Bachyei tells us firmly that the only measure of a wise man is how many good deeds and how few transgressions he does during his stay on earth. These commentaries help us to understand that knowledge is only of real value when it causes us to do good and prevents us from doing evil. Rabbi Elazar is really telling us that someone who concentrates more on doing good deeds than on accumulating knowledge will be far stronger morally than someone who has vast knowledge but does not utilize it to perform good deeds; the latter lacks the moral support of his actions.

The question remains: Why does Rabbi Elazar compare deeds to the roots of a tree? Surely deeds arise from learning, as our

Sages say, "Great is learning for it leads to action" (*Kiddushin* 40b). The Wise King Shelomo says, "Dedicate your actions to God and your thoughts will be the right ones" (*Mishlei* 16:3). Surely it seems that the opposite should be true, that good thoughts should produce good actions. A careful observation of human nature, however, reveals that establishing good habits is an important factor in shaping good character. Good habits, behavioral as well as mental and spiritual, if practiced in youth, remain throughout life. A wise person once said, "What is man? Man is the sum of his actions." The Torah was granted to our fathers at Sinai because they said, "We will do" before they said, "We will listen." Actions strengthen thoughts; therefore, deeds are the roots through which the tree acquires strength to stand up in the face of all the storms of life.

כג רַבִּי אֶלְעָזָר בֶּן חִסְמָא אוֹמֵר, קִנִּין
וּפִתְחֵי נִדָּה הֵן הֵן גּוּפֵי הֲלָכוֹת. תְּקוּפוֹת
וְגֵמַטְרִיָאוֹת פַּרְפְּרָאוֹת לַחָכְמָה:

23 Rabbi Elazar ben Chisma says: The laws on the sacrifice of birds and family purity, they, *they* are the principal laws; astronomy and geometry are only added condiments to wisdom.

* * *

A tale is told in the Talmud that *Rabban* Gamliel and Rabbi Yehoshua once traveled together on board a ship (*Horayoth* 10a). The latter had provided himself with enough provisions to last the journey and even to help out the *Nasi, Rabban* Gamliel, whose own provisions were insufficient. "How did you know that our voyage would take so long?" asked *Rabban* Gamliel. Rabbi Yehoshua answered, "A certain star rises once in seventy years and leads sailors astray. My calculations indicated to me that this star would appear just now and it did." When the *Nasi* praised the astronomical knowledge of his friend and companion, the other replied, "At home there are two scholars, Rabbi Elazar ben Chisma and Rabbi Yochanan Gudgada, who possess amazing knowledge in all the sciences, but they have neither bread to eat nor raiment to wear." When *Rabban* Gamliel returned home he decided to offer generous assistance to both scholars, but they modestly refused to accept it.

From this tale, we learn that Rabbi Elazar ben Chisma was one of the outstanding men of science of his time, yet from his saying we clearly see that he held the secular sciences to be less important than revealed Torah. Rabbi Elazar ben Chisma singles out the disciplines of astronomy and mathematics because they are different from all the other sciences. (In ancient times, all of mathematics was called geometry.) Mathematics has a great advantage over all the other sciences because it is absolutely exact. The truths taught by mathematics are irrefutable: Twice two is four, $(a+b)(a+b) = a^2+2ab+b^2$, the sum of the three angles of a triangle is equal to two right angles. These and all the other truths of mathematics cannot and will not be denied by any sensible person. Other sciences are based on hypotheses that are daily disproved and replaced by new ones. The science of physics embraces a great number of hypotheses which were regarded as irrefutable truths for centuries, but were completely rejected later. The teaching that nature abhors a vacuum, for example, was once a basic tenet of physics while today it is regarded as a fallacy. In medicine, a surplus of blood was considered for many years to be the cause of most illnesses, and generations of people had their lives shortened by needless bloodletting. A firm principle in law was that no one could be convicted unless he first admitted his guilt, a principle that led to the use of torture to secure confessions.

Mathematics is the foundation of most other disciplines — without it civilization and culture, trade and industry, art and science would not function, and neither agriculture nor music could exist. Astronomy is closely linked to mathematics, though many of its most important ideas are based on hypotheses. Astronomy is the oldest science, yet the study of it still inspires amazement and admiration. Astronomical forecast is one of the greatest triumphs of the human mind. Since Rabbi Elazar ben Chisma was both a skilled mathematician and an astronomer, it is understandable that his maxim draws a comparison between these particular sciences and the teachings of the revealed Divine wisdom.

Tractate Kinnin deals with the laws of the sacrifice of birds. The word *kinnin*, literally, means "nests" and, figuratively, means "a pair of doves" which constituted one of the sacrificial offerings required in certain cases of recovery or purification after illness or childbirth. Pairs of doves were also offered for vows and as voluntary gifts. The Sages wrote a whole tractate on the problems and questions involved in the offering of this sacrifice, and it is one of the most difficult texts in the Talmud to understand. The laws of family purity are the precepts relating to menstruation. Opinions differ as to which complicated section of these laws is referred to here. Some say that the mishnah refers to the determination of the correct time for immersion in a *mikveh*, while others say it refers to the determination of which type of blood renders a woman a *niddah*. How trivial it may seem to compare mathematics and astronomy, on which rests the whole edifice of worldly knowledge, with the precepts on which doves are acceptable for sacrifice, and with the detailed regulations concerning menstruation! Bearing in mind, however, the wisdom of the Sage who suggests this comparison, we understand that he chose these two topics intentionally, and he stresses this by repeating the word "they."

Rabbi Wessely calls this mishnah the keystone of the entire third chapter of Avoth, whose principal emphasis is the transcendence of the Torah and our duty to study it. This chapter also mentions wisdom frequently, and this final mishnah reminds us that whatever wisdom we learn by ouselves is insignificant compared with the wisdom laid down in the Torah and revealed by God. Rabbi Wessely notes the placement of the words הלכות (laws) and חכמה (wisdom) in the saying. The Divine, revealed wisdom, called *Halachah* by our Sages, is derived from the Hebrew root meaning "walk." In revealed wisdom, there are always several paths to choose from, only one of which is the one that God intends as the right one, as it is said, "And make known to them the way in which they are to walk" (*Shemoth* 18:20). Mathematics is a science which man has derived purely from theory, that is to say, its reality is only in his mind; astronomy is a science that man has learned strictly from his observation of nature. In both sciences, there is only one path of truth and wisdom: a condition or circumstance is either true or false — error is not possible. In the wisdom revealed by God, however, there exist both purity and impurity, morality and immorality, work and rest, pride and humility, mercy and cruelty; there are many possible degrees between two extremes. When man is puzzled as to which path to choose, the answer is always: Walk the way prescribed by the Almighty, for that is the way of wisdom; the path defined as wise in the Torah is the correct one.

THEY, *THEY* ARE THE PRINCIPAL LAWS. The laws of קינין and פתחי נדה are the גופי הלכות, the "bodies of the laws" or "the embodiment of all the laws," the main path to wisdom. Rabbi Yosef Karo (*Kesef Mishneh, Hilchoth Yesodei Ha-Torah*, ch. 4) explains that the Sage contrasts these seemingly mundane subjects to the original and far-reaching theories of mathematics and astronomy, for the purpose of teaching us the true value of the precepts of the Torah. Such splendid sciences are merely condiments to the main course, which is the unpretentious but vital body of laws given to us by our Creator. Condiments, although not essential, are nevertheless a valuable addition to a meal. Rabbi Elazar ben Chisma's choice of this metaphor is worthy of our attention. The Sages tell us to learn the sciences in order to earn the esteem of other nations, as it is said, כי הוא חכמתכם ובינתכם לעיני העמים, "For this is your wisdom and your understanding in the eyes of the nations," (*Devarim* 4:6 cited in *Shabbath* 75a). Furthermore, a knowledge of mathematics and astronomy is necessary for a full understanding of *Halachah* (to fix the calendar, for example).

Most of the 613 commandments have a physical, visible element which focuses one's mind on the spiritual process it represents. The *matzah* and bitter herbs of the Pesach Festival remind us of the travails and eventual liberation of our ancestors; the counting of the *omer* before the Festival of Shavuoth actualizes for us our longing for spiritual freedom; the *shofar* carries us in spirit before the Throne of Judgment; the *sukkah* teaches us to trust absolutely in God. Each commandment is the "body" which houses the spirit of the Divine intention it is meant to convey. Thus, קינין and פתחי נדה are called, literally, "bodies of the laws." Although they may seem insignificant in the "eyes of the nations," especially when compared to the honorable sciences of astronomy and mathematics, they are not only an integral part of supreme wisdom — they are "bodies" which possess a superior spiritual essence. In addition, they are both directly concerned with that most mysterious and miraculous phenomenon, procreation, which we are commanded to sanctify in all respects.

When Rabbi Elazar ben Chisma exalted these precepts in his saying, it was no longer possible to observe all of them fully, for the Temple no longer existed and sacrifices could not be offered. If we must guard the sanctity of commandments which cannot be carried out at all today, like קינין, how much more careful ought we to be with commandments like הלכות נדה, most of which we can carry out today but, sadly, many do not. The purity and the sanctification of the Jewish people depend upon the performance of these *mitzvoth*. מקוה ישראל יי מה מקוה מטהר טמאים כך הקב"ה מטהר את ישראל, "God is the *mikveh* of Yisrael, for just as a *mikveh* purifies the impure, so the Holy One, blessed is He, purifies Yisrael" (*Yoma* 8:9).

Perek Four

בֶּן־זוֹמָא אוֹמֵר, אֵיזֶהוּ חָכָם, הַלּוֹמֵד
מִכָּל־אָדָם, שֶׁנֶּאֱמַר מִכָּל מְלַמְּדַי
הִשְׂכַּלְתִּי כִּי עֵדְוֹתֶיךָ שִׂיחָה לִי. אֵיזֶהוּ גִבּוֹר,
הַכּוֹבֵשׁ אֶת־יִצְרוֹ, שֶׁנֶּאֱמַר טוֹב אֶרֶךְ אַפַּיִם מִגִּבּוֹר
וּמֹשֵׁל בְּרוּחוֹ מִלֹּכֵד עִיר. אֵיזֶהוּ עָשִׁיר, הַשָּׂמֵחַ
בְּחֶלְקוֹ, שֶׁנֶּאֱמַר יְגִיעַ כַּפֶּיךָ כִּי תֹאכֵל אַשְׁרֶיךָ וְטוֹב
לָךְ. אַשְׁרֶיךָ בָּעוֹלָם הַזֶּה וְטוֹב לָךְ לָעוֹלָם הַבָּא.
אֵיזֶהוּ מְכֻבָּד, הַמְכַבֵּד אֶת הַבְּרִיּוֹת, שֶׁנֶּאֱמַר כִּי
מְכַבְּדַי אֲכַבֵּד וּבֹזַי יֵקָלּוּ:

1 Ben Zoma says: Who is wise? He who learns from
all men, as it is said, "From all those who have taught
me I have learned understanding, for your testimonies are my conversation" (*Tehillim* 119:99). Who is
mighty? He who subdues his passions, as it is said,
"He who is slow to anger is better than a mighty
person and he who controls his emotions is better
than the conqueror of a city" (*Mishlei* 16:32). Who is
rich? He who rejoices in his portion, as it is said,
"When you enjoy the work of your hands, then you
will be happy and it will be well with you" (*Tehillim*
128:2); "You will be happy"—in this world, "and it
will be well with you"—in the World to Come. Who is

honored? He who honors others, as it is said, "For those who honor Me, I will honor, and those who despise Me shall be held in contempt" (*Shemuel* I, 2:30).

* * *

Shimon ben Zoma was one of four great scholars who engaged in deep metaphysical research; only one of them, Rabbi Akiva, did not suffer for having immersed himself in these studies. Shimon ben Azzai died young; Elisha ben Avuyah became an apostate; and Shimon ben Zoma, himself, eventually suffered mental illness and also died young. In his prime, however, Shimon ben Zoma was regarded as one of the greatest scholars in Yisrael, a symbol of wisdom and an eminent דרשן (expositor) (*Berachoth* 57b, *Sotah* 49b). Our Sages tell us that he once stood on the Temple Mount, looking down on the multitude of Israelites streaming toward it and said, "Blessed be the One Who knows the secret thoughts of every individual, Who has created all these people to ease my life. The first man had to work so hard to enjoy a slice of bread! He had to plough and sow, to thresh and winnow, to grind and sift, knead and bake. But I have all these tasks done for me, my bread is ready because all these people work for me! So many workers must combine their efforts to satisfy the needs of one individual. A good guest will say, 'My host has gone to much expense and effort to serve me meat and wine and bread.' An ungrateful guest, however, will complain, 'What have I had? A small slice of bread, a small piece of meat, one cup of wine! My host would have gone to the same expense and effort for himself and his family in any case!' " (*Berachoth* 58a). A good man is grateful for the little he enjoys on earth; an evil man is dissatisfied in spite of rich gifts and blessings. Thus we begin to appreciate what makes up the character of a wise man.

The first question that arises from this mishnah is: Why does the Sage single out only the four qualities of wisdom, might, wealth and honor? Rabbi Yochanan singled out the same four qualities, saying that they are prerequisites for attaining the gift of prophecy (*Nedarim* 38a). Both Sages reflect the words of

Yirmeyahu: "Thus said the Lord: Let not the wise man glory in his wisdom, neither let the mighty man glory in his might, let not the rich man glory in his riches, but let him that glories, glory in this, that he understands and knows Me; that I am the Lord who administers mercy, justice and righteousness on earth, for in these things I delight, says the Lord" (9:22-23). The first three qualities named in Yirmeyahu correspond to this mishnah; the fourth is also in harmony since one who is just and righteous honors others and will therefore be honored by them. An individual is personified by his soul/mind and the particular body in which it dwells. His possessions may be considered an extension of his person. As we see, Shimon ben Zoma points out that human beings must live with and for each other, and so mind, body and possessions are joined by a fourth partner: the relationship with others. Thus the four qualities, wisdom (development of the mind), might (development of the body), wealth (possessions) and respect (good relationship with others), comprise the whole of man. Wisdom, valor, wealth, respect—what sublime concepts! Who can attain them? Few people are privileged to achieve even one of them. Yet, Shimon ben Zoma teaches us how we all can acquire them for ourselves.

WHO IS WISE? HE WHO LEARNS FROM ALL MEN. Rabbi Wessely tells us that although the word חכם is given wide and varied use in the Torah, it never connotes a person who has merely accumulated knowledge, even knowledge of the Torah. It refers to one who tries to acquire the teachings of the Torah with the full intention of putting them into practice and living his life in accordance with them. Thus, a חכם has to be humble and modest as well as learned, and, above all, must not depend solely on his own erudition. For example, Hillel and Shammai, the greatest scholars of their time, immediately deferred their own judgment when two weavers who lived near the Dung Gate, the poorest neighborhood in Yerushalayim, told them about the judgment they had heard from Shemayah and Avtalyon. Both Sages immediately settled the *halachah* according to the opinion of the masters (*Eduyyoth* 1:3). The true חכם subordinates his own wisdom to Tradition and endeavors to learn from all men.

The illustrative verse in this mishnah reads: מכל מלמדי השכלתי,
"From all those who have taught me I have learned understanding" (*Tehillim* 119:99). Rashi explains that the verse means "I
have learned something from each one." Most interpreters, however, prefer the interpretation, "I have learned more understanding than all my teachers," מכל meaning "more than all" rather
than "from all," and derive their interpretation from the setting of the verse in the context of the whole stanza in Tehillim:
מה אהבתי תורתך כל היום היא שיחתי: מאיבי תחכמני מצותך כי לעולם
היא לי: מכל מלמדי השכלתי כי עדותיך שיחה לי. "Oh, how I love Your
Torah! All day long it is my conversation. Your commandments
make me wiser than my enemies, for they are always with me. I
have learned more understanding than all my teachers, for Your
testimonies are my conversation." King David's love of Torah was
paramount in his life. His enemies, though also scholars and even
more well-versed in Torah than he, had not made Torah their
guiding principle and did not live according to its precepts. They
used the Torah only to achieve fame and honor; wisdom was
transitory in their case. David, however, wished to do nothing
more than to live his whole life according to the Torah, and thus
he became even wiser than those who had taught him.

According to this interpretation, we can still explain how the
verse proves the saying by comparing the way the word שיחה is
used in verse 99 with the way it is used earlier, in verse 97. In
כל היום היא שיחתי, the word שיחתי means "my conversation,"
whereas in כי עדותיך שיחה לי, the words שיחה לי mean "I have a
conversation." When something is dear and beloved to a person,
he not only wishes to speak about it himself, but also wishes to
hear what others have to say about it. King David not only spoke
about the Torah to others constantly, he also wished to hear their
opinions in the course of his conversations with them. The one
"who learns from all men," therefore, is clearly expressed in the
words שיחה לי; David grew wiser than all of his teachers because
he wished to hear the opinions of all men and learn from them.

It is noteworthy that Ben Zoma asks, "Who is wise?" using the
word חכם, while his answer uses a word whose root is שכל. חכמה
(wisdom) is usually attained by someone who has been blessed
with natural intellectual ability, and this ability is innate (see

above, *Avoth* 3:21). Ben Zoma wishes to teach us, however, that even a person who is not naturally gifted can become a *chacham* if he applies himself to Torah study with zeal. His mental faculties will actually improve through perseverance, and even more so if he holds to the principle of learning from all men. By quoting the verse from Tehillim, Ben Zoma teaches us that one who learns from all men will not only be granted חכמה, great wisdom, which is ordinarily acquired only through intellectual effort, but also שכל, divinely-inspired wisdom, which cannot be obtained by the human intellect alone.

WHO IS MIGHTY? HE WHO SUBDUES HIS PASSIONS. A mighty person is considered a hero when he performs brave deeds and vanquishes his enemies. But a real hero's strength must be tempered by wisdom; a true hero does not let himself be carried away by anger nor by a desire for vengeance, not even by pride in his own strength. He is "slow to anger" and "controls his emotions."

WHO IS RICH? True wealth is not the possession of material riches, but satisfaction with what God has granted. Ben Zoma proves the truth of this idea by citing the verse, "When you enjoy the work of your hands..." Real enjoyment, even of material possessions, can be experienced only when you are satisfied with what you have. One who constantly strives for more wealth never stops to enjoy the wealth he already has. When we look at this verse in context, we see that there is more to be learned: אשרי כל ירֵאי יי ההולך בדרכיו, "Happy is everyone who fears God, who walks in His ways" (*Tehillim* 128:1). When you realize that all your worldly possessions come from God, and when you truly revere and love your Provider, you will naturally feel obligated to work hard to sustain yourself and your family and to serve God better. In so doing, you will truly enjoy the fruits of your labor, whatever the total amount may be, knowing that God has provided enough for your needs.

WHO IS HONORED? Honor has two meanings. In one sense, it refers to the external recognition we bestow upon others. A scholarly, rich or powerful man may be honored for his knowledge, wealth or power regardless of whether he deserves honor for his inner qualities. Honor, in the other sense, is attained only by someone who is honest and worthy of respect in every way and for everything that he does, regardless of whether men honor him outwardly or not. Ben Zoma is concerned with what we have to do to achieve the latter, true honor. "All that the Holy One, Blessed is He, has created, He has created for His honor" (*Yeshayahu* 43:7). The celebration and pronouncement of God's honor can only be performed by man. How? By conducting himself in the world as God has commanded him to. Some commandments are easy to understand, such as honoring parents and loving our fellowman and being honest in business, but they are neither more nor less important than those commandments which are difficult or impossible to understand, such as those which deal with impurity and forbidden foods.

We are to be kind to animals, yet we may slaughter some for food; we may use and enjoy plant life, but we may not mix certain species. Man will only be honored truly when he truly honors all of God's creatures, for that is the way to honor God. Ben Zoma quotes the verse in Shemuel to remind us that the Lord rebuked Eli's sons for dishonoring His Name only when they were negligent in offering the sacrifice. This sin may at first seem to us only a slight infringement compared to their other immoral deeds, but it signifies a lack of regard for God's commandments which are so transcendent that an ordinary bull can be transformed into a sanctified offering by a simple pronouncement. A relatively simple action becomes a serious matter when God decrees it to be so, and out of respect and honor for God, we must regard it as such. Nevertheless, the principal commentators on this mishnah have looked for meanings behind the simple, clear wording of the text. Rabbi Shemuel Galante connects this saying with Rabbi Moshe Isserlis' explanation of the following mysterious verses in Bereshith:

> And a river went out of Eden to water the garden, and from there it split and became four headwaters. The name of the first is Pishon...which encompasses the whole land of Chavilah, where there is gold. And the gold of that land is

good; there is bedellium and the onyx stone. And the name of the second river is Gichon...that encompasses the whole land of Cush. And the name of the third river is Chiddekel (Tigris)...that flows toward the east of Ashur (Assyria). And the fourth river is the Perath (Euphrates).

(Bereshith 2:10-14)

Rabbi Isserlis says that Eden represents the Divine Spirit and the trees planted there are the Israelites, while the river that issues from it is the Torah. The first thing man strives for is gold (i.e., material possessions). This may be "good gold" if it is used in the furtherance of Torah and human kindness, and so will reflect Divine light like the precious bedellium and onyx stones, and be honorable in the sight of God and of man. The second thing man strives for is honor, which easily turns to crude ambition when a man surrounds himself with slaves (i.e., the slaves that came from Cush) and ignores his spiritual development. The third hint of what leads man astray is contained in the name of the third river, חדקל (Chiddekel). The first two letters, ח and ד, together spell חד, "sharp," as when one is said to have a "sharp eye." Man is easily deceived into relying on the sharpness of his eye (his perceptions), and thus, acquiring knowledge of the sciences may easily be substituted for the more profound thinking and higher faith needed to acquire Torah knowledge. The name of the fourth river, פרת, gives us the letters פ and ר, which suggest the human sexual urge פרו ורבו, "be fruitful and multiply," which is often the cause of man's downfall. Misused wealth, immoderate ambition, wisdom gone astray, and unbridled passion—these are the four rivers that draw man away from Eden, from the Divine Spirit. Ben Zoma teaches us how to use these four qualities as a blessing instead of a curse: learn wisdom from all men, control your mind and your passions, avoid envy, greed and idleness, and respect all of God's creatures.

Rabbi Yosef Ya'avetz bases his explanation of the mishnah on the very profound and central Jewish concept of man's duty to God. If the four qualities Ben Zoma finds in all men are molded in the service of God, they will assure man of everlasting life, even after his physical death, but if they are not perfected and their possessor turns away from God, these same qualities will cause him to "die" long before his physical death. We often see the valuable gifts of wisdom, might, wealth and honor causing great unhappiness to those who possess them, resulting in bitterness, anger, greed, dissatisfaction and even tyranny. Don Yitzchak Abravanel points out that Ben Zoma's saying accords with the three basic professions: teaching, military service and business. The main goal of teaching is the transmission of wisdom ("Who is wise?"); the main requirement for military service is heroism ("Who is mighty?"); the object of business is the acquisition of wealth ("Who is rich?"). In all three professions, however, honor is sought in the end ("Who is honored?").

The Talmud tells us that Alexander the Great asked similar questions of the Sages of the south (i.e.,Yisrael), hoping to challenge their wisdom and authority. "Who is wise?" he asked them, expecting to be answered, "You, O king, who conquered the greatest nations on earth." The Sages answered him, however, הרואה את הנולד, "One who foresees his actions," that is, that Alexander's conquests were senseless and would end in defeat and anarchy. Alexander then asked, "Who is mighty?" expecting to be hailed as the greatest hero of all time. The Sages answered him, "That hero is greatest who conquers his own passions." And indeed, Alexander's uncurbed passions brought about his early death and the destruction of his empire. And who could be wealthier than the conqueror of most of the world's treasures? Yet the Sages told Alexander that he was not wealthy, with all his plunder, for he had become greedy and would never be satisfied with what he possessed. Finally, Alexander asked a fourth question: "What should one do to be acceptable to one's fellowmen?" (This corresponds to Ben Zoma's fourth question, "Who is honored?") The Sages replied, "Hate the government and the head of state. If a person is prepared to speak up against the tyranny of the government, he will be endeared to his countrymen." Alexander is said to have replied that a better answer would have been, "Love your king and be good to your fellowman," an altered version of Ben Zoma's concluding words (*Tamid* 32a).

בֶּן־עַזַאי אוֹמֵר, הֱוֵה רָץ לְמִצְוָה קַלָּה
וּבוֹרֵחַ מִן־הָעֲבֵרָה, שֶׁמִּצְוָה גוֹרֶרֶת
מִצְוָה וַעֲבֵרָה גוֹרֶרֶת עֲבֵרָה, שֶׁשְּׂכַר מִצְוָה מִצְוָה
וּשְׂכַר עֲבֵרָה עֲבֵרָה:

2 Ben Azzai says: Hasten to do even a light commandment and flee from [all] sin; for one commandment leads to another commandment and one sin leads to another sin, since the recompense for a commandment is [inherent in] the commandment and the recompense for a sin is [in] the sin.

*　　*　　*

Shimon ben Azzai died young, but he is regarded as the most ingenious of all the great scholars in Yisrael. He combined great mental acuity with diligence, so that the Sages said: "Persistence in study ceased with Ben Azzai's death" (*Sotah* 49b). He is said to have refused to marry in order to study Torah undisturbed, although he taught the importance of marriage (*Yevamoth* 63b), and in another place it is said that he was married for a short time to a daughter of Rabbi Akiva. Ben Zoma is called the symbol of wisdom and Ben Azzai is called the symbol of piety (*Berachoth* 57b). He was one of the four great scholars who penetrated deeply the secrets of esoteric philosophy, and one of the three who suffered for it. In his early youth Shimon ben Azzai was a disciple of Rabbi Akiva but he soon outgrew his teacher's instruction and became his companion. His knowledge was so extensive that he could say of himself without presumption that he surpassed all the Sages of Yisrael with the exception of Rabbi Akiva. The compilation of the Mechilta is ascribed to him. It is most likely that Ben Azzai's saying follows Ben Zoma's because they were contemporaries, but the commentators give an additional reason for it. As we shall see, Ben Azzai's words teach us that Ben Zoma's strictures are not so hard to comply with if only we know how.

HASTEN TO DO EVEN A LIGHT COMMANDMENT AND FLEE FROM [ALL] SIN. Just as the hero hurries with joy to battle, so you should run to fulfill a commandment, even if it seems an unimportant one to you. Do not wait until a commandment comes looking for you, as it were; seek opportunities, like a brave man who does not wait to be called to do great deeds. Do likewise with sin; flee from it before temptation steps up and traps you. *Rabbenu* Alshech (in his commentary to *Parashath Emor*) points out that Ben Azzai says הוי רץ...ובורח rather than simply רץ...ובורח. This means, "Always be hastening" and "Always be fleeing from." When you become accustomed to doing good deeds you will find it much easier to control your passions and even to ignore the words of evil companions (i.e., friends who laugh at your observance). *Rabbenu* Alshech adds that this mishnah is meant to warn us about the danger of self-satisfaction. Do not think that since you have already done so many good deeds, you can afford to pass up another good deed, however insignificant it may seem, or that you can afford to indulge in what seems to be only a minor sin; a minor sin leads to major ones and failing to grasp the opportunity to do one *mitzvah* leads to forfeiting the opportunity to do other *mitzvoth*. The definite article ה is used with the word "sin" to impute to it a meaning like "the one and only sin." This suggests that we must flee from a light sin as though it were all sins.

FOR ONE COMMANDMENT LEADS TO ANOTHER COMMANDMENT AND ONE SIN LEADS TO ANOTHER SIN. All education is based on the formation of good habits. Moreover, good habits ennoble the human heart just as bad habits exert a destructive influence. "Rabbi Yishmael teaches: Sin dulls the heart of man, as it is said, '...neither shall you make yourselves unclean with them that you should be defiled thereby,' meaning that one impurity engenders another" (*Yoma* 39a on *Vayyikra* 11:43). The All-kind God has arranged this world in such a way that a person who wants to fulfill his obligations will succeed. The Sages say, "And now, if you commence to obey, you will also succeed in continuing to be obedient to My voice, for only the beginning is hard" (*Mechilta* on *Parashath Yithro*). Likewise, it is said that if a man is anxious to be righteous and to help others, the Holy One, blessed is He, provides him with the means to do so (*Bava Bathra* 9b). All of God's commandments are closely linked, so that a person who consciously transgresses "only one" is perforce denying all, and what can he be, other than an apostate! Remember that the number of positive commandments (248) corresponds to the number of a man's limbs, and that the number of prohibitions (365) corresponds to the sinews of the body; all together they form the organism, and not one part can be dispensed with. Man is a microcosm of all the worlds, for he was created in God's image, and one commandment is a microcosm of the whole Torah. That is why Yisrael was told ולעשות התורה והמצוה, "to practice the Torah and the commandment" (*Divrei Hayyamim* II, 14:3). He who understands and performs even one commandment completely is assured of understanding and the opportunity to perform them all, whereas even the slightest evil deed will remove him from God's presence and lead him to other sins.

THE RECOMPENSE FOR A COMMANDMENT IS [INHERENT IN] THE COMMANDMENT. Rabbi Ya'avetz explains this part of the mishnah with the verse: "Sanctify yourselves and be holy" (*Vayyikra* 20:7). Here, God has promised that He will assist us to become sanctified: הבא לטהר מסייעין אותו, "Anyone who wishes to live in purity will receive Divine assistance" (*Yoma* 38b, 39a). Every *mitzvah* we fulfill brings us nearer to God. Can there be a better recompense than being able to draw closer to the Holy One, King of kings? What better reward can there be for doing a *mitzvah* than fulfilling another *mitzvah* and coming even closer to God?

THE RECOMPENSE FOR A SIN IS [IN] THE SIN. Rabbi Ya'avetz, however, does not mention the final words, שכר עברה עברה, in his explanation. Is it possible that they were missing from his Mishnah text? Both the Rambam and Rashi fail to elucidate the meaning of these words but do say that they were added erroneously by a later copyist. Since earlier commentators like the Rashbatz and Abravanel also discussed these words, we know they considered them part of the original text. These two scholars treat the term שכר as גמול, "return," which can imply either "reward" or "punishment" and so evades the problem, too.

Bertinoro explains that the recompense for doing a commandment is the satisfaction we feel when we do as God has commanded us; this explanation is not valid for the recompense of sin, however, because any pleasure we might derive from committing a sin is not in itself a transgression. This, therefore, does not completely explain the mishnah either. The author of ענת אלי, Rabbi Eliyyahu ben Yitzchak Sarahsohn, the Rabbi of Michailischak, provides us with a remarkable explanation of this mishnah: The true recompense for a *mitzvah* will be given us for doing it solely because we understand that God has commanded us to do it; the true recompense for avoiding a transgression will be given us because we recognize that it is a transgression of the Divine will. This is true whether or not we understand the intrinsic good or evil in a particular deed, as we do in the commandment to honor parents or not to commit murder. We will receive our just due even if we do not understand the inner nature of a commandment like *kashruth*, or of a prohibition like *sha'atnez*, and we know, in either case, the actual reward or punishment will not be completed in this world. We shall accordingly have to explain that שכר מצוה מצוה means, "The recompense for the observance of a Divine commandment is especially granted because we performed the deed through recognition that it was commanded by God," and that שכר עברה עברה means, "The recompense for the avoidance of a transgression is granted because we regard the evil deed as a transgression of the Divine will."

Rabbi Scheuer of Mainz, in his commentary Turei Zahav, edited by his grandson, Rabbi Samuel Bondi, follows Bertinoro's view; he attempts to explain why Ben Azzai did not say עונש (punishment) for a sin instead of שכר. The שכר (reward) for doing a *mitzvah*, whatever it will be, provides us with a second *mitzvah* in that the receipt of the reward is considered another *mitzvah*, and that provides us in turn with the opportunity to receive another reward, and so on. With a sin, however, this relationship does not exist; there is just one punishment for each sin. To receive punishment for a committed sin is not another sin and so the Sage does not say עונש עברה עברה, "The punishment for sin is sin." No! The recompense given for a sin concludes the personal consequences of that sin. We must conclude then, that the recompense for a *mitzvah* is God's blessing, which brings ever-renewed blessing, while the recompense for transgression is the "curse" on the sinner that his sins will sooner or later, inevitably, inexorably, bring to him. Therefore, hasten to fulfill even the easiest commandment, or you will lose the opportunity to perform all the others which would have followed it; flee from even the smallest sin so that you do not have to suffer from all those which will follow it. Whatever sacrifice you may be called upon to make in the observance of the Divine commandments, make it knowing that you will ultimately profit from it. Let us inscribe Ben Azzai's rule of life in our hearts in letters of fire: it is the key to eternal life.

הוּא הָיָה אוֹמֵר, אַל־תְּהִי בָז לְכָל־אָדָם
וְאַל־תְּהִי מַפְלִיג לְכָל־דָּבָר, שֶׁאֵין לְךָ
אָדָם שֶׁאֵין לוֹ שָׁעָה וְאֵין לְךָ דָּבָר שֶׁאֵין לוֹ מָקוֹם:

3 He [Ben Azzai] would say: Do not despise any man and do not deem anything unworthy, for there is no man who does not have his hour and no thing that has not its place.

* * *

According to the commentary of Bertinoro, the Sage tells us here not to base our judgment of other people, or even of dumb creatures, on the amount of good or harm they can do us. Rabbi Wessely rightly objects to this interpretation, arguing that to interpret this mishnah as a simple piece of prudent advice would run counter to the underlying consistency of the entire tractate. The advice of the Sages is clearly meant to help us improve our behavior for the glorification and sanctification of God, not for our own personal benefit. Rabbi Wessely explains that Ben Azzai's saying is a continuation of Ben Zoma's counsel in the first mishnah of this chapter. The only way to earn esteem and respect for yourself is to esteem and respect other people, for in that way you are showing respect to your Creator. All men were created in the image of God, not just the obviously pious and righteous people you know. Ben Azzai implies that a man who is a criminal or a fool is a human being just like you, and if you cannot find anything to say in his praise, then rather say nothing, but you have no right to despise him. As it is said, "One who depsises his neighbor is a heartless person, but an understanding man keeps silent" (*Mishlei* 11:12).

The Sages tell us: יש קונה עולמו בשעה אחת, "There are people who acquire eternal life in a single hour" (*Avodah Zarah* 17a), that is, the worst sinner may suddenly repent. In that "hour," by returning to the right path, he is capable of achieving a higher degree of sanctification than someone who has never sinned. Ben Azzai concludes the mishnah with the reminder that not only all men, or all living creatures, but all of God's creation exists for a purpose, even though we do not know what that purpose is. Even King David, when he was a young man, questioned the value of such things as spiders and madness. When he was older a spider actually saved his life by spinning its web across the entrance to the cave he was hiding in, and on another occasion he saved himself from death by feigning madness at the court of King Achish (see *Shemuel* I, 21:11-16). The Sages also tell us of Rabbi Meir who once wanted to pray for the death of his persecutors, but his good wife Beruryah cited a verse from Tehillim to him. "How can you pray for their death?" she asked. "For it is said, יתמו חטאים מן הארץ ורשעים עוד אינם; the verse does not say, חוטאים (sinners), but חטאים (sins). 'When sin ceases,' that is, when the sinners repent, 'then the wicked will be no more.' " And Rabbi Meir prayed for them and they repented (*Tehillim* 104:35, cited in *Berachoth* 10a).

רַבִּי לְוִיטַס אִישׁ יַבְנֶה אוֹמֵר, מְאֹד מְאֹד
הֱוֵי שְׁפַל רוּחַ שֶׁתִּקְוַת אֱנוֹשׁ רִמָּה:

4 Rabbi Levitas of Yavneh says: Be exceedingly humble in spirit, for mortal man's hope is the worm.

* * *

Rabbi Levitas is not known to have written anything other than this saying, but the great Rambam establishes its importance. According to the Rambam, the path of virtue is always in the middle between two extremes. Cowardice and foolhardiness are two reprehensible extremes, and courage is the virtue which is the middle path; avarice and extravagance are two extremes which should be balanced into a combination of thrift and generosity. שפל רוח is the opposite of pride and means the complete abnegation of the self. The Sages tell us, says the Rambam, that humility is greater than wisdom and even greater than fear of God. And yet humility (ענוה) is a more moderate version of שפל רוח. The moderate middle path is what the Rambam usually recommends, and humility is the middle path between pride and complete self-disregard. Pride, however, is so reprehensible that it is not sufficient to practice just humility in this case; therefore, the Rambam says that in order to avoid pride, we must go to the opposite extreme, to שפל רוח. Most commentators agree with this interpretation. Let us say then, that שפל רוח means excessive humility, since literally, the word שפל means low, in the sense of debasement. The word רוח is much more difficult to translate, however. It is usually said to mean the spirit, as it is used in the Torah for one of the five parts of the human intellect: נפש (person), רוח (spirit), נשמה (soul), חיה (the living being), יחידה (the individual being). Each of the five represents a profound concept, far beyond the simple translation of the word. We find the word רוח used in *Koheleth*: והרוח תשוב אל האלהים אשר נתנה, "And the spirit shall return to God Who gave it" (12:7).

But the Torah also tells us, ורוח אלהים מרחפת על פני המים, "And the Spirit of God moved upon the face of the waters" (*Bereshith* 1:2). What does that mean? Has God a body that we may speak also of

His spirit? Rabbi Samson Rafael Hirsch says we must understand
it as "the Breath of God which hovered over the waters." In
Daniyyel 8:8 we find the expression: לארבע רוחות השמים, "toward
the four regions of heaven," or the four directions toward which
the wind, the airstreams, the moving forces in the world extend
and beyond whose reach there can be nothing. And again in
Yonah 1:4 we find the expression רוח גדולה, "a great storm." In all
these expressions, the underlying sense of the word רוח is movement. Non-living forms on earth are always at rest, except for the
air, and as we have seen, the moving force in the air is also called
רוח. Intellect is also a type of movement. Man is capable of
controlling his own movement or spirit, but does not always do
so; the intellect should always be moving, but not always in the
same way. In this sense the Torah speaks of a spirit or state of
mind, that may be long (ארך רוח) or short (קצר רוח), high (גבה רוח)
or low (שפל רוח). The "high" mentality can overshoot its mark, as
when jealousy takes possession of a person and incites him to
regrettable behavior. The "low" spirit is one that is consciously
controlled at all times so that a sudden storm of emotion will not
sweep away all restraint. The "short" mentality is one that can be
swept away quickly, as when anger consumes a person and goads
him into stupid or harmful behavior. וקצר רוח מרים אולת, "One
who is impatient acquires folly as his portion" (*Mishlei* 14:29; see
Rashi on this verse). The "long" view, of course, gives a man time
to consider his response, master his passion and control his
"movement." This control over the mind, which in turn holds the
emotions in check, is a precious quality, to be nurtured and
guarded like a jewel. It will help you to attain the higher wisdom
and, through this, fear of God.

MORTAL MAN'S HOPE IS THE WORM. The word תקוה is
usually understood as "hope." Rabbi Moshe Almosnino and other
commentators protest that no one is likely to hope to become
food for worms. Therefore, Rabbi Lippman Heller seeks a different explanation for this word; in his Tosafoth Yom Tov he says
that the root of the word תקוה in this mishnah is probably not קוה
(hope), but קו (line), as in the verse תקות חוט השני, "this line of
scarlet thread" (*Yehoshua* 2:18). Thus, the reading would be:

"Be exceedingly humble in spirit because the line (or measure) for all men is, in the end, their mutual fate as food for worms." Both Rabbi Ya'avetz and Rabbi Shemuel of Ozeda accept the translation of תקוה as "hope," but their reading seems to have been: מאד מאד הוה שפל רוח בפני כל אדם, "Be exceedingly humble in spirit before every man," implying that the meaning of the mishnah is, "Remain humble even with evil people for their hope is the worm."

"Hope" is not a completely accurate translation of the word תקוה, however, as we can see from these verses: וכשכיר יקוה פעלו, "And as a hireling hopes for (expects) the reward of his work" (*Iyyov* 7:2) and תאות צדיקים אך טוב, תקות רשעים עברה, "The desire of the righteous is only good"—that is, to acquire wisdom, knowledge of and nearness to God—"but the expectation of the wicked is wrath" (*Mishlei* 11:23). Both attain what they desire; but for the self-indulgent, proud man, death will be the end, while for the humble man death is only the beginning of his reward. Similarly, Ya'akov said: לישועתך קויתי השם, "I expect Your salvation, my Lord" (*Bereshith* 49:18). Thus, a more precise translation is "expectation."

Rabbi Levitas uses the word אנוש for "man." There are four words in Hebrew which can only be translated in English as "man": אדם, אנוש, גבר, איש. The word אדם is derived from אדמה and means "son of the earth"; אנוש is from אנש, "to be weak," and means "weak mortal man." גבר is "strong man," and איש, the perfect man, as it is said, אשרי האיש,"happy is the man" and איש האל, "man of God." Thus we can understand that Rabbi Levitas is telling us that man is weak, and unless he uses his intellect to master his emotions he can only expect to be recompensed for his actions on earth, and that death will be the end of his expectations. All worldly goods, all worldly feelings cease with death, as it is said: במות אדם רשע תאבד תקוה, "When a wicked man dies his expectations will perish" (*Mishlei* 11:7).

Rabbi Lehmann did not live to complete his commentary. He died on Nissan 23, 5650 and the concluding chapters were written by Rabbi Eliezer Liepman Philip Prins. Rabbi Prins preceded his commentary with the following introduction:

I have been entrusted with the task of completing this commentary on Pirkei Avoth, which Dr. Lehmann ל"ז has presented to his readers in such an inspiring way. Although the extent of my knowledge, as well as my· ability to address myself to such a discerning readership, have been overestimated, I will nevertheless attempt to undertake this task. I especially consider it a privilege to take part in such an important work that has, so far, achieved impressive and beneficial results. Moreover, there seems to me no better way to perpetuate the memory of the author than by completing the commentary in his style and spirit.

May I be allowed, however, to start with a short introduction.

According to our Sages, the curse mentioned in *Parashath Ki Thavo*: גם כל חולי...אשר לא כתוב, "Also every sickness...which is not written" (*Devarim* 28:61) includes, among other misfortunes, the death of the righteous. One of our great scholars was once asked to explain how the Sages derived this meaning. His answer was: The continuous process of civilization, the ever-alert human mind and the never-ceasing activities of man constantly cause new questions to arise. An encompassing, deep knowledge, profound wisdom and understanding are needed to be able to derive the answers to such questions (יערות דבש).

As I myself witnessed, Dr. Lehmann ל"ז, as *Rav* of Mainz, was plied with questions as a result of every new discovery which had an impact on daily life. I heard him patiently explain the reasons for the prohibition of traveling by train on the Shabbath; after the establishment of a telephone network throughout Germany, he received hundreds of questions about whether speaking on the telephone on Shabbath was permissible. It was a wonder to see how securely he navigated across the boundless sea of Torah by means of comparing and assessing the methods and systems by which the Torah is explained, in order to arrive at the correct *halachic* decision. The death of the righteous—in this case, of our righteous and learned teacher, Dr. Lehmann ל"ז—is indeed a blow "which is not written," for it is a great loss that so much of Dr. Lehmann's inspiring erudition remained unwritten.

Thus, it was not granted him to complete his commentary to Pirkei Avoth, a work so essential in our time, when it is necessary to demonstrate how Jewish ethics, though they date back thousands of years, remain enduring and relevant in the face of today's society and creeds. Shall I be able to succeed, then, in continuing to convey this to our readership?

The answer to this, too, can be drawn from the inexhaustible wellspring of our sacred writings. The Talmud relates that Rabbi Abba, upon meeting with other Sages, prayed that his words would find a willing ear among his colleagues. However, when he did pronounce a *halachic* decision, the other Sages ridiculed him. "Why are you laughing at me?" he asked. "Did I take your coats [and make myself look ridiculous by putting on clothes that do not fit me]?" Rabbi Asia answered him: "The Sages were correct in laughing at you [for it is not your clothing, but your prayer that is being laughed at]" (*Beitzah* 38a,b). In other words, whoever intends to search for truth, and wishes to communicate it to others, has to pray for guidance in arriving at the truth. Even Heaven cannot grant his prayer to find a willing ear, if what he teaches is incorrect!

Thus whoever wishes to pray before beginning his lecture or his studies should rather pray as Rabbi Nechunya ben Ha-Kanah did: ולא אכשל בדבר הלכה, "that I should not err in deciding *Halachah*" (*Berachoth* 28b). Rabbi Nechunya also added: "in order that my colleagues should not rejoice." The meaning of this addition is not very clear. Is it conceivable that the colleagues of a personality of the stature of Rabbi Nechunya ben Ha-Kanah would gloat over his failure to teach the correct *halachah*?

This problem is clarified by an incident related in *Bava Bathra* 133b. As Rav Ilish was about to pronounce a *halachic* decision which was not in line with the opinion of earlier authorities, Rav made him aware that he was mistaken. Thus, Rav prevented him from handing down a wrong decision and this caused Rav to rejoice. We can, therefore, understand the meaning of Rabbi

Nechunya's prayer in this sense: I do not want to give my colleagues occasion to rejoice that they prevented the teaching of mistaken decisions, but rather that the Almighty enable me to arrive at the correct *halachah* from the start.

May it be the will of the Almighty to guide this writer in successfully bringing these commentaries to the understanding of worthy readers in the spirit of our holy Torah.

רַבִּי יוֹחָנָן בֶּן־בְּרוֹקָה אוֹמֵר, כָּל־הַמְחַלֵּל
שֵׁם שָׁמַיִם בְּסֵתֶר נִפְרָעִין מִמֶּנּוּ בְּגָלוּי,
אֶחָד שׁוֹגֵג וְאֶחָד מֵזִיד בְּחִלּוּל הַשֵּׁם:

5 Rabbi Yochanan ben Beroka says: One who profanes the Name of God in secret will suffer the penalty
of being unmasked in public; this is true whether the
desecration of the Name is done in error or intentionally.

*   *   *

The name of this Sage appears frequently in our sacred literature. He was a friend of Rabbi Elazar ben Chisma and lived at the
time when *Rabban* Gamliel and Rabbi Elazar ben Azaryah headed
the academy at Yavneh. We are told that he served publicly only
once, on Rosh Hashanah, as a reader in the synagogue at Usha.
According to some commentators, his saying should be considered an extension of the previous one by Rabbi Levitas about
humility. Superficially, there is no connection between the sayings. We have been taught, however, that overweening pride is
tantamount to desecrating God's Name secretly; Korach's punishment for his presumption in trying to oust Moshe from the
leadership was the same as that of blatant desecrators of the
Name. Therefore, beware! When you become too proud of your
own accomplishments, are you not really denying the fact that
without God's assistance you would not have accomplished anything?

Pride is an emotion that leads inevitably to jealousy, ambition
and ultimately, to greed—passions that can tear society apart,
causing "cracks in the earth" like that which swallowed up
Korach and his band (*Bava Bathra* 74a). The punishment for
desecrating God's Name is always carried out in public, as in the
case of Korach and of the Israelites who made the golden calf.
Aharon *Ha-Kohen* realized that the people were secretly becoming unfaithful to God; he therefore agreed to their making the
golden calf in order to expose the sinners publicly before Moshe,

as it is said, כי פרע הוא כי פרעה אהרן, "that the people were unruly, for Aharon had let them loose" (*Shemoth* 32:25). Rashi explains that פרע in this case means "uncovered, exposed." The Torah tells us, "If your own brother...should secretly tempt you, saying, 'Let us go and serve other gods'...do not listen...do not pity him...but your hand should be the first to...stone him and afterward all the people... And all Yisrael will hear and fear and sin no more" (*Devarim* 13:7-12). This perhaps explains why Rabbi Yochanan says נפרעין instead of נפרע, using the plural instead of the singular. We might expect that a sin committed in private should be paid for privately, in accordance with the principle מדה כנגד מדה, "measure for measure." This mishnah teaches us that the desecrator of God's Name, even in secret, must and will be unmasked in public so that society will recognize the gravity of the sin and realize its potential danger for the entire nation.

Rabbi Yochanan might also have said just כל המחלל את השם, "One who profanes the Name," instead of כל המחלל שם שמים, "One who profanes the Name of God," or, at the end, just אחד שוגג ואחד מזיד, "whether...in error or intentionally," without repeating בחלול השם, "the desecration of the Name." The commandment of קדוש השם, "sanctification of the Holy Name," and the prohibition of חלול השם, "desecration of the Holy Name," have many ramifications and it is important to understand how they are applied. You are obliged to preserve your life and health at all costs: וחי בהם, "and live [but not die] by them [God's statutes]" (*Vayyikra* 18:5); yet on the other hand, you should show your love for God ובכל נפשך, "even with your own life" (*Devarim* 6:5). The Talmud tells us, however, that you should go to the extreme of sacrificing your life only if otherwise you will be forced to worship idols (forced conversion), to commit incest or to murder. Other commandments and prohibitions may be overlooked in certain, special cases, and even then, only when one is absolutely sure what the Law is in each particular case.

We may consider, for example, the case of military service. We read, "Do not forget to respect God and the king" (*Mishlei* 24:21). It may be a sanctification of God's Name to help preserve the security of your country and the peace; on the other hand, military service often requires you to transgress many laws. How often do we hear young people using patriotism as an excuse to overlook the holiness of the Shabbath, the bother of obtaining permitted foods, the embarrassment of saying the prescribed prayers! There are indeed some times when we can best serve the Lord by violating His Law, but Rabbi Nathan says, if we do so, God will know whether it was really necessary for the sanctification of His Name (Rambam, commentary on *Berachoth* 9:5). Rabbi Yochanan's saying helps us to understand that we do not have to be ashamed if we break God's Law in order to save a life or to obey the law of the land, but only if we do so within the prescribed limits and truly for the sake of the Divine Name. How careful we are to guard our own good name; how much more carefully ought we to guard the Name of God!

רַבִּי יִשְׁמָעֵאל בְּנוֹ (שֶׁל רַבִּי יוֹחָנָן בֶּן
בְּרוֹקָא) אוֹמֵר, הַלּוֹמֵד עַל־מְנָת לְלַמֵּד
מַסְפִּיקִין בְּיָדוֹ לִלְמוֹד וּלְלַמֵּד, וְהַלּוֹמֵד עַל־מְנָת
לַעֲשׂוֹת מַסְפִּיקִין בְּיָדוֹ לִלְמוֹד וּלְלַמֵּד לִשְׁמוֹר
וְלַעֲשׂוֹת:

6 Rabbi Yishmael, son of Rabbi Yochanan ben Beroka, says: One who learns in order to teach will be enabled to learn and to teach; but one who learns in order to practice will be enabled to learn and to teach, to preserve and to practice.

* * *

The *bnei Yisrael* were encamped in the plains of Moav, at the end of their wanderings, and also close to the death of their unique leader and prophet Moshe. Once again Moshe assembled his flock around him, old and young, men, women and children, those born to the faith and those converted to belief in the One God. After bidding them farewell in the incomparable verses of *Ha'azinu*, recounting to Yisrael once more their mission on earth and reviewing their past, present and future, he said to them: שִׂימוּ לְבַבְכֶם לְכָל הַדְּבָרִים אֲשֶׁר אָנֹכִי מֵעִיד בָּכֶם הַיּוֹם אֲשֶׁר תְּצַוֻּם אֶת בְּנֵיכֶם לִשְׁמֹר לַעֲשׂוֹת אֶת כָּל דִּבְרֵי הַתּוֹרָה הַזֹּאת, "Set your hearts unto all the words which I testify to you this day, that you command your children to preserve all the words of this Torah, by observing them [for all time]" (*Devarim* 32:46).

The word אֲשֶׁר (that) indicates that Moshe is thanking the people in advance for their compliance with his request, i.e., that they will continue to preserve the Torah and pass it down through all the generations to come (*Sifrei* on this verse). Moshe says specifically לִשְׁמֹר לַעֲשׂוֹת, "preserve by observing," for the Torah can only be passed on by active performance of its precepts. Keeping the scrolls of the Law behind lock and key and not studying them will assure their disappearance in less than a generation. Yisrael's surest enemies were always those who tried to entice them away from the Torah, not those who tried to destroy them with the sword. As long as Yisrael maintained and preserved God's Law, even though they were dispersed throughout the world, they existed as a nation; but those who denied the sanctity of the Torah perished without leaving a trace behind. Rabbi Yishmael is concerned only with those who do preserve the Torah. They are both those "who learn in order to teach" and those "who learn in order to practice."

ONE WHO LEARNS IN ORDER TO TEACH. Teaching is a noble profession and Rabbi Yishmael welcomes future teachers of Torah who will spread Jewish knowledge and open eyes that have been closed to it. However, this reading of the mishnah: הלומד על מנת ללמד is not accepted by all the commentators. Many feel that the Torah student should have no other purpose than to want to learn Torah only for its own sake. Rashi believes that there is another reading: "One who learns in order to teach will not be enabled to learn and teach." Rashi does not believe that Rabbi Yishmael would encourage his disciples to believe or hope that they might achieve a particular goal by learning, for such egotists will not even succeed in learning, much less teaching.

Others have said that the reading must be: הלומד על מנת ללמוד, "One who learns in order to learn..." for the most important task we have is learning Torah, and sooner or later learning will lead to doing. This reading may be substantiated by Rabbi Yochanan's explanation of the beautiful verse, "For the priest's lips should keep knowledge, and they should seek the Law at his mouth, for he is an angel of God" (*Malachi* 2:7). Angels are each given only one mission to accomplish for God. Only when a teacher resembles an angel, that is to say, when he is totally absorbed in learning, is one permitted to hear Torah from him (*Mo'ed Katan* 17a). One who learns with no other thought in mind will eventually be able to teach competently and only such a person will become successful as a teacher.

There is one other reading of this saying: הלומד על מנת ללמד מספיקין בידו ללמוד, "One who learns in order to teach will be enabled to learn." This brings to mind the common sight of a synagogue or a *beith ha-midrash* only half-filled, with a few elderly gentlemen at prayer or reading over a few verses from the Mishnah. Young people are nowhere to be seen. We may feel a certain amount of respect for these few elderly gentlemen who firmly carry out certain commandments, but we should really pity them because they are unable to understand what they are saying and certainly cannot explain their actions successfully to their children. It is your duty, Jewish fathers, to give your children an education which will fill them with the sublime spirit of our holy Torah!

Rabbi Eliyyahu of Vilna explains this mishnah very clearly. He first recalls that the Sages said, "From the Torah, the Prophets and the later Writings, it may be shown that one is allowed to follow the road one wishes to pursue" (*Makkoth* 10b). Freedom of will, the Creator's most precious gift—which gives virtue its value and vice its unworthiness, which distinguishes man from animals—allows man to fashion his own fate even if he is born in chains. We read in Yeshayahu 48:17, "I am the Lord, your God, Who teaches you for your profit, Who leads you by the way that you will go." He gives us the means to distinguish between true and false, between right and wrong, between good and evil, but it is up to us to choose. Mishlei 3:34 states, "He who sides with scorners will become a scorner." God would not allow Bilam to curse the Jewish people when the mighty king Balak repeatedly asked him to, but Bilam's words show that he would very much have liked to ally himself with Balak. In spite of all the Divine warnings, he persevered in his evil intentions and so God took him along his chosen path. "Go [then] with these men," if you are resolved to go, the angel told him—for your lot is with them, and in the end you will perish (Rashi on *Bemidbar* 22:35). Rabbi Eliyyahu of Vilna therefore concludes that if your reason for learning Torah is pure, you will achieve your goal.

TO PRESERVE AND TO PRACTICE. Rabbi Yishmael extends this mishnah to include the principle לשמר ולעשות. This is an unusual juxtaposition of words. The word לשמר points to the proper understanding of לעשות, which can mean either to initiate an action or to continue an action already begun. As we recalled earlier, Moshe used the same words to instruct our ancestors to preserve the Law after he died. We find similar wording in many places in the Torah: אשר ברא אלהים לעשות, "which God created to continue creating" (*Bereshith* 2:3), and ושמרו בני ישראל את השבת לעשות את השבת, "The *bnei Yisrael* shall [continue to] preserve the observance of the Shabbath" (*Shemoth* 31:16). When we learn Torah in order to לעשות, "to practice," we are learning לשמר ולעשות, "to preserve and to practice." The Sage does not speak of learning for the sake of examining or judging the Torah; that type of learning (as the Reform Jews do) is certain to lead one completely off the path. It is understood that this mishnah refers only to one who is learning in order to fulfill the commandment. When we learn Torah, we must "do it"; we must live in its spirit and according to its precepts. Only then will we attain our goal, whether that goal is learning for its own sake or learning in order to teach.

רַבִּי צָדוֹק אוֹמֵר, אַל־תִּפְרוֹשׁ מִן־הַצִּבּוּר
וְאַל־תַּעַשׂ עַצְמְךָ כְּעוֹרְכֵי הַדַּיָּנִין וְאַל־
תַּעֲשֶׂהָ עֲטָרָה לְהִתְגַּדֶּל־בָּהּ וְלֹא קַרְדּוֹם לַחְפָּר־
בָּהּ, וְכַךְ הָיָה הִלֵּל אוֹמֵר וּדְאִשְׁתַּמֵּשׁ בְּתָגָא חֲלָף,
הָא לָמַדְתָּ כָּל־הַנֶּהֱנֶה מִדִּבְרֵי תוֹרָה נוֹטֵל חַיָּיו מִן־
הָעוֹלָם:

7　Rabbi Tzadok says: Do not set yourself apart from the community, and do not act the counsel in the office of judge. Do not make it [the Torah] a crown with which to aggrandize yourself, nor a spade with which to dig. Thus Hillel would say: One who makes use of the crown [of the Torah] will pass away. Thence you may learn that anyone who derives personal gain from the words of the Torah takes his own life out of this world.

*　　*　　*

This is the text that was accepted for our prayer books. Rabbi Shelomo ben Yitzchak *Ha-Levi* the Elder also has it in his commentary Lev Avoth. In our mishnayoth, however, the first two sayings are left out, apparently because they are ascribed to others: to Hillel (*Avoth* 2:5) and to Rabbi Yehudah ben Tabbai (ibid. 1:8). Most commentators of the Mishnah believe that Rabbi Tzadok's saying is directed to community officials: rabbis, teachers, synagogue officers. Such positions are truly honorable although they are a great burden to those who take them seriously—those who suppress their own interests and work only to further the community's welfare. Happy is the community whose leaders regard congregational office as a worthy vocation and carry out their duties devotedly, regardless of whether the congregation shows its appreciation. They emulate Moshe *Rabbenu*, who said, "The Lord commanded me to teach you at that time" (*Devarim* 4:14). The Sages explain his words thus: "The

Almighty has taught me without claiming recompense; I therefore do not ask remuneration from you [for teaching]" (*Nedarim* 37a).

The Torah bestows three treasures upon one who occupies himself with it: long life, wealth and honor—"long life to its right and to its left wealth and honor" (*Mishlei* 3:16). The community of Yisrael enjoys long life because it clings to the commandments. It has been statistically proven that those Jews who keep the dietary and ceremonial laws have a longer life span and are less susceptible to some diseases than other people. The Gemara (*Shabbath* 63a) gives this explanation of the verse in Mishlei: Those who grasp the Torah with their right hand (that is, with all their strength) will have not only length of days but also riches and honor (without making a special effort to attain them); but those who grasp with the left hand will find riches and honor, but not length of days since vanity dims their senses, greed controls them and sensual pleasure is their true goal. They will not pause to consider Yisrael's mission nor Yeshurun's immortality.

Although most commentators have a different opinion, it is most likely that Rabbi Tzadok's sayings do not refer to the vocations of rabbi and teacher, since the traditional reading, beginning with אל תפרוש מן הצבור, "Do not set yourself apart from the community," would not logically apply to those already working for and serving the community. We know that Rabbi Tzadok lived through the terrible years of civil strife that preceded the destruction of the Second Temple and the Jewish state. We know, too, that Rabbi Tzadok meant to warn the people against the Essenian practice of observing only one or two commandments and transgressing others. We may therefore understand that he uses the word צבור to refer not just to the community but also to the totality of the commandments (as in *Melachim* II, 10:8).

DO NOT ACT THE COUNSEL IN THE OFFICE OF JUDGE. Hillel and Yehudah ben Tabbai have also taught this rule, but Rabbi Tzadok gives it a slightly different emphasis: Who among men can presume to pronounce judgment on the importance of a commandment or the magnitude of a transgression? Who can ascertain what harm is done to our souls when we disregard a commandment because we think it is not so important?

NOT...A CROWN WITH WHICH TO AGGRANDIZE YOUR-
SELF, NOR A SPADE WITH WHICH TO DIG. We do not need to
use our performance of the commandments to show off our
virtues; a modest man does not flaunt his modesty. Purity of
mind and heart will result from our words and actions and we do
not have to announce our principles to the world.

ONE WHO MAKES USE OF THE CROWN WILL PASS AWAY.
The word חלף can mean both "pass away" and "he is mistaken, he
is on the wrong path." By mixing up cause and effect, means and
purpose, one can err so much that one will pass away not only to
death but to total insignificance, and efface every last trace of
oneself from this world.

ANYONE WHO DERIVES PERSONAL GAIN FROM THE
WORDS OF THE TORAH TAKES HIS OWN LIFE OUT OF THIS
WORLD. Do not, says Rabbi Tzadok, use Torah study as an
excuse to withdraw from the world. The continuance of mankind
depends on marriage, and the future of mankind on the purity
and sanctity within family life. Your children, who inherit from
you the crown of Torah, must be prepared to take up the
challenges of life by possessing a thorough knowledge of our
faith so that both we and they will be assured of a portion in
the World to Come.

רַבִּי יוֹסֵי אוֹמֵר, כָּל־הַמְכַבֵּד אֶת־הַתּוֹרָה
גּוּפוֹ מְכֻבָּד עַל הַבְּרִיּוֹת, וְכָל הַמְחַלֵּל
אֶת־הַתּוֹרָה גּוּפוֹ מְחֻלָּל עַל־הַבְּרִיּוֹת:

8 Rabbi Yosei says: One who honors the Torah will himself be honored by mankind, but one who disdains the Torah will be disdained by mankind.

* * *

The supreme value we attach to every word of our Sages induces us to study this saying more thoroughly, and not to be satisfied with a literal reading of the text. Why, we ask ouselves, does Rabbi Yosei say גוף מכבד and גוף מחלל, which mean to us "personal honor" and "personal disdain"? Why would Rabbi Yosei be concerned with how we can earn honor or compromise our honor when the Sages have told us הרחק מן הכבוד, "Keep away from honor." Let us consider the life and times of Rabbi Yosei in order to help us understand his saying correctly. This period in Jewish history is called alternatively the "Time of Danger," the "Time of Judgment" and the "Time of Apostasy." The Roman Emperor, Hadrian, was not satisfied with the destruction of the Jewish state; he sought to stamp out all vestiges of the Jewish religion as well. His edicts forbade reciting the *Shema*, performing circumcision, laying *tefillin*, observing the Shabbath and teaching the Torah. Ordination of rabbis was stopped and not only were Yisrael's future leaders and their teachers condemned to death, but the entire town where any ordination took place was liable to be destroyed. Furthermore, the rise and spread of the missionizing Christian sect began just at that time and in that area of the Galil (Galilee) where Rabbi Yosei was head of the *beith din*.

Marcus Aurelius Antoninus, one of the emperors who followed Hadrian, was a philosopher who held to the tenets of stoicism and reason. Thus the Jewish community dared hope that Hadrian's cruel laws might be revoked if a sufficiently worthy delegation were sent to Antoninus in Rome. Rabbi Shimon ben Yochai and Rabbi Yosei's son, Rabbi Eliezer, were chosen. When

the mission met with success and Hadrian's edicts were repealed
by Antoninus, the whole community rejoiced—all except Rabbi
Yosei. The difficulties that his delegation had encountered in
Rome, particularly their confrontation with enthusiastic propo-
nents of the new religion (see *Me'ilah* 17a,b), lead us to believe
that this wise and far-seeing teacher understood the dangers
awaiting his people. It is true that Antoninus' daughter had
interceded for the delegation because her new religion preached
love of one's fellows, but at the same time it sought to invalidate
the practice of the Divine laws, the commandments of the Torah.
Rabbi Yosei understood that the new belief could do more harm
than all the coercive measures of the Roman government. He
knew that his neighbors, the men of the Galil, "were more concerned with their honor than with their fate" (*Yerushalmi,
Kethubboth* 4:14). He knew, too, that "the inhabitants of Tsippori
(Sephoris, his own city) are hard-hearted and although they hear
words of Torah, they do not practice them" (*Ta'anith* 3:4). With
all this in mind, we begin to understand why the maxim held
such significance for Rabbi Yosei in his time.

Historical significance, however, is the least of the values to be
found in Pirkei Avoth. They were written down because of their
value to us in all times and in all places. The fire with which
Nimrod meant to eradicate Avraham, for his belief in the One
God, was kept burning and has threatened the Jewish people in
every period of our history. Likewise, the sugar-coated treachery
of Lavan toward Ya'akov has been repeated throughout the ages
by our enemies. In the perennial attempts to destroy the Jewish
people, apparent honor and esteem often concealed hatred. The
Sages tell how Pharaoh sent his carriages to bring Yosef's family
to Egypt in state—and hid idols in them (*Midrash Rabbah* on
Bereshith 94:3). The Sages hold that Achashverosh, who appeared
to honor the Jews by inviting them to eat and drink at his table,
and who may even have served them kosher wine, was more of
a threat to their long-term survival as a people than was
Haman, who admittedly wanted to destroy, kill and annihilate
every Jew.

Rabbi Yosei's saying is clearly applicable to the dangers that
lurk in our day as well. The political freedom and social privi-

leges we enjoy today lay temptations in our path: the attainment
of social status with its spurious honors, the relaxation of moral
restrictions and its attendant immodesty. Each is a step toward
our final rejection of the Law. Rabbi Samson Rafael Hirsch once
said, "Faith turns a man into a man; the Law turns him into a
Jew." Immoderate ambition leads to social permissiveness, which
leads in turn to the temple of lust and therein stands the altar of
apostasy. Do not believe that it is easy to help overly ambitious
people to return to the right path. They may be likened to the
scoffers who, having an answer to everything, were told by the
prophet, "Because you said, 'We have made a covenant with
death, and with Hell we are in agreement; and when the scouring
scourge shall pass through, it shall not come to us,' you shall
yourselves be trodden down by that scourge" (*Yeshayahu* 28:15-18).
The scoffers jeer at warnings about the danger they are in, but
know fully that they are placing themselves outside of Judaism.
This may well have happened in Tsippori; Rabbi Yosei's advice is
meant to correct the main flaw in the nature of his fellow towns-
men. If they had used their great ambition in the service of the
Torah, they would have received the highest honors.

Reverence for the Torah involves both the mind and the
emotions and is, in truth, an expression of the purest selflessness.
Your feeling for the sanctity of the Torah should inspire you to
carry the Scrolls always in the right hand, never to place a sacred
book on the seat of a chair, and always to show honor and respect
to Torah students and scholars. Your intellect will impel you to
respect every letter and line of the Torah, to seek an explanation
if you see a word out of order or an extra or omitted letter, for
every dot is holy and significant.

Rabbi Yosei does not mind whether this reverence is a matter of
feeling or of intellect, whether it is a result of selflessness or scientific investigation, as long as it causes true respect to be shown for
the Torah. This respect will, in turn, lead to more careful observance of the commandments, even by less committed Jews. Why
does Rabbi Yosei speak of dishonor to the Torah as well? It is
most likely that the second part of his saying is intended to prod
those who call themselves less observant, who learn and know
and yet still sully the honor of the Torah by not respecting

persons more humble than themselves. Why do some wealthy men scorn the daughters of poor rabbis or scholars as suitable daughters-in-law, seeking only young women with ample dowries for their sons? How can it be that a pious woman was overheard telling her maid, "You need not set out a clean napkin for the young *yeshivah* student who eats with us on Tuesdays!" This is dishonor to the Torah.

ט רַבִּי יִשְׁמָעֵאל בְּנוֹ אוֹמֵר, הַחוֹשֵׂךְ עַצְמוֹ
מִן־הַדִּין פּוֹרֵק מִמֶּנּוּ אֵיבָה וְגָזֵל וּשְׁבוּעַת
שָׁוְא, וְהַגַּס לִבּוֹ בְּהוֹרָאָה שׁוֹטֶה רָשָׁע וְגַס רוּחַ:

9 Rabbi Yishmael, son of Rabbi Yosei, says: He who
shuns the office of judge rids himself of hatred, robbery and perjury. But he who presumptuously makes
decisions in law is foolish, lawless and arrogant.

י הוּא הָיָה אוֹמֵר, אַל־תְּהִי דָן יְחִידִי שֶׁאֵין
דָּן יְחִידִי אֶלָּא אֶחָד, וְאַל־תֹּאמַר קַבְּלוּ
דַעְתִּי שֶׁהֵם רַשָּׁאִים וְלֹא אָתָּה:

10 He would say: Do not judge alone, for there is
only One who can judge alone. And do not say, "Accept
my view," for they and not you have that authority.

*   *   *

The simplicity of the first part of this saying evokes the obvious question: "In that case, what will become of the administration of justice?" You might expect that the great rabbi, in
phrasing his advice, would want to encourage judges to assume
the responsibility of making legal decisions, to pass just sentences
and to settle disputes, rather than discourage them. We therefore
must conclude that this saying was not intended to advise qualified men against accepting a judgeship, as it may appear.

HE WHO SHUNS THE OFFICE OF JUDGE. Who is entitled to
be a judge in Yisrael? Yithro, nobleman of Midyan, father-in-law
of Moshe Rabbenu and one of Pharaoh's three political counsel-
ors (*Sanhedrin* 106a), set the parameters of qualification for
Moshe. He advised him to appoint judges for the people who are
"independent, able men, that fear God, men of truth, hating
unjust gain" (*Shemoth* 18:21). Rabbi Hirsch explains in his commentary that judges in Yisrael must be men of both material and

spiritual wealth, who know that their ability is a gift of God and
have such strong faith that they do not waver in their judgment
nor fear the enmity of the accused; they must be men who do
not seek personal gain and will forego their own rights if
necessary. Jewish justice must be pronounced in God's name:
אלהים נצב בעדת אל בקרב אלהים ישפוט "God stands in the congregation of God, in the midst of the judges He judges" (*Tehillim* 82:1);
therefore a Jewish judge is a representative of God. His knowledge must be sweeping and comprehensive, since he has to weigh
all manner of claims, large and small, property damage and
personal injury, robbery and slander, as outlined for us by Rabbi
Yehudah *Ha-Nasi* in the Mishnah. He himself must hear and
understand without intermediaries, documents or interpreters.
He must not only be qualified, but must be accepted and ap-
proved by society as a man of integrity. His wrong judgment is
considered like taking another man's life (*Bava Kama* 119a); his
responsibility is enormous. He must be ever vigilant to avoid the
pronouncement of unnecessary oaths or perjury by the litigants.
Rabbi Yishmael's words must therefore be understood as a reminder of the onerous burden that a judge in Yisrael must bear,
rather than as simple advice for avoiding judicial responsibility.

HE WHO PRESUMPTUOUSLY MAKES DECISIONS. The expression הגס לבו seems to imply a judge who has become so
familiar with the type of cases which come before him that he
indifferently and automatically passes judgment without making
full use of his acumen, training and objectivity. The word הוראה
means "instruction." The rabbi, מורה הוראה, who instructs his
congregants in questions of *Halachah*, must make decisions very
much like a judge. When an ordinary Jew eats a slice of bread, for
example, he is involved in the performance of at least ten commandments! Even before the wheat is planted, a Jew must observe
the prohibitions against combining the kinds of animals pulling his
plow. Then he must beware of mixing the kinds of seeds he sows,
and when he harvests and threshes the wheat there are other laws to
be observed; finally, it must all be tithed. Even after the flour is
milled and the bread is baked, *challah* must be separated.

It is not surprising that a Jew needs instruction from an

expert to be sure that he, or those who have performed these duties for him, have fulfilled all the commandments. Until the time of Rabbi Yehudah *Ha-Nasi*, this instruction (the Oral Law) was passed on from generation to generation by word of mouth. Rabbi Yehuda *Ha-Nasi*, known as Rabi, codified it all and wrote it down in the six orders of the Mishnah, and the Sages amplified it further in the Talmud. How comprehensive must the expert's knowledge be, therefore, who wishes to instruct others in observance. There are, furthermore, often two ways of understanding a particular law: the stricter and the more lenient interpretation. The Talmud tells us: "One who preaches the lenient decisions of Shammai and the lenient decisions of Hillel is a lawless person, and one who preaches the more stringent decisions of both, of him it is said, 'The fool walks in darkness'(*Koheleth* 2:14)" (*Eruvin* 6b). Rabbi Yishmael is speaking to those whose learning is insufficient and therefore make ill-advised decisions like these; such people are lawless, foolish, indeed arrogant.

DO NOT JUDGE ALONE, FOR THERE IS ONLY ONE WHO CAN JUDGE ALONE. As a rule, the application of the Law in civil affairs is entrusted to three judges (first mishnah in *Sanhedrin*). According to the wording of the *baraytha* in Sanhedrin 5a, however, an authority who is acknowledged as extremely capable may act as a judge alone, and his judgments are completely valid. In either case, the conscientious judge should try to influence the litigants with all the means at his disposal to settle the matter. The best-known commentators on this saying are Rashi and Rabbi Yonah Girondi, and they differ in their interpretations. Rashi believes that only God, Who thoroughly knows men's thoughts and actions, can be a sole judge; a human being should not dare to sit in judgment alone between two parties. He finds proof in the Talmud Yerushalmi, Sanhedrin 1:1, in which Rabbi Yehudah ben Pazi says this about the mishnah: "Even the Holy One, blessed is He, does not judge alone; for it says, 'The hosts of Heaven stand on His right and on His left' (*Divrei Hayyamim* II, 18:18)."

Rabbi Yonah Girondi says that when you are clearly the most capable judge present and you are acknowledged so by everyone, you may function as a judge on your own. His explanation seems to be derived from the Talmud Bavli, and it fits in with what we know of Rabbi Yishmael's background. "Once," Rabbi Yishmael himself relates, "my ancestors were well-to-do people living in the Galil. They lost a great part of their fortune because, among other reasons, they acted as sole judges in monetary matters" (*Bava Kama* 80a). How did this occur? In Shemuel II, 8:15, we read: "And David executed judgment and kindness unto all his people." The Midrash explains: When he had executed judgment, in other words, helped one man to win his case and passed sentence on the other, King David took money from his own pocket to compensate the one who had been fined, particularly when the loser was poor. This explanation enables us to understand better the wording of David's prayer: "I have done what is just and right; leave me not to my exploiters" (*Tehillim* 119:121). In other words, it would sometimes happen that the litigants would swear a false claim before the tribunal and so rob him of part of his wealth.

Rabbi Yishmael's father, likewise, so much feared giving a mistaken sentence that he often compensated the sentenced person with his own money and in this way impoverished himself. "Do you want to judge alone?" asks Rabbi Yishmael. "Then you need more than a princely fortune. There is only one man in our generation who would be able to do that and that is Rabi." The Sages tell us, "From Moshe to Rabi there was no one else who combined knowledge of the Torah, public esteem and wealth to such a degree as they" (*Gittin* 59a).

AND DO NOT SAY, "ACCEPT MY VIEW," FOR THEY AND NOT YOU HAVE THAT AUTHORITY. This part of the saying is surely independent of the previous one, because otherwise it would be redundant. If you are not to judge cases on your own, it is obvious that you should not force your opinion on the other authorities. Rabbi Yishmael is still addressing those whose arrogance permits them to apply for a judgeship even though their knowledge of Torah is insufficient (see *Sanhedrin* 7b). He is warning those wealthy and privileged members of the community that even though they should, of course, practice justice and righteousness, unless they are thoroughly qualified they should not consider themselves competent to make judicial decisions.

יא רַבִּי יוֹנָתָן אוֹמֵר, כָּל־הַמְקַיֵּם אֶת־
הַתּוֹרָה מֵעֹנִי סוֹפוֹ לְקַיְּמָהּ מֵעֹשֶׁר, וְכָל־
הַמְבַטֵּל אֶת־הַתּוֹרָה מֵעֹשֶׁר סוֹפוֹ לְבַטְּלָהּ מֵעֹנִי:

11 Rabbi Yonathan says: He who fulfills the Torah out of poverty shall also fulfill it out of wealth; he who neglects the Torah out of wealth shall also neglect it out of poverty.

* * *

Our daily experience would lead us to believe that the simple meaning of this saying is not true. Many people fulfill the Torah under the most difficult conditions and never reach the ideal of fulfilling it in material comfort as well. They live in poverty and die in poverty. Rabbi Yonathan does not say בעני (in poverty), however, but מעני (out of poverty), so we must ask ourselves what, precisely, he means. Rabi, the wealthy Rabbi Yehudah *Ha-Nasi*, once opened his storehouse to the poor in a year of great scarcity, saying, "Let those enter who have studied Torah, *Halachah* or the commentaries." Rabbi Yonathan ben Amram entered and asked for food. When Rabi asked if he knew Torah, *Halachah*, or the commentaries, Rabbi Yonathan said, "No." "Then how can I give you food?" asked Rabi. "Feed me as the dog and the raven," answered Rabbi Yonathan, and Rabi gave him food. Afterwards, when Rabi began to regret having given food to a man without learning, his son, Rabbi Shimon, said, "Perhaps that man was Yonathan ben Amram, your disciple who has always held to the principle of not using the Torah for his own material benefit." When this proved to be true, Rabi said, "All may now enter" (*Bava Bathra* 8a).

This story is a fitting background to Rabbi Yonathan's mishnah. Starvation borne for the sake of not dishonoring the Torah is indeed קיום תורה, "fulfillment, affirmation of the Torah." How pleased must the Sage have been to reap the benefit of Rabi's kindness without having had to use his knowledge of the Torah to earn food. The Sages tell us, "Who is rich? He who rejoices in his portion" (*Avoth* 4:1). The Sages also say, "No man dies with even half of his desires fulfilled; if he has one hundred, he wishes for two hundred" (*Koheleth Rabbah* 1:13, 3:10). A man who values earthly possessions never reaches his ideal; the more he acquires, the more he thinks he needs; he will never be content with what he has. Thus, being truly rich means being content. Our inferior, human understanding defines poverty and wealth in relation to the amount of money and possessions we have. Even worse, we equate material wealth with general superiority. If someone steals ten coins, we regard him as a thief, but if he steals a million coins, he is respected as a millionaire!

The Wise King prayed that he be spared both wealth and poverty: שתים שאלתי מאתך אל תמנע ממני בטרם אמות: שוא ודבר כזב הרחק ממני ראש ועשר אל תתן לי הטריפני לחם חקי, "Two things have I asked of You; deny me them not before I die: Remove far from me falsehood and lies; give me neither poverty nor riches; feed me with my allotted bread" (*Mishlei* 30:7-8). The temptations of wealth may drive a man to sin just as surely as the hardships of poverty. Both a poor man and a rich man find it difficult to take time out to nourish their souls with the wealth of Torah; the poor man works long hours and feels that God has neglected him, while the rich man is diverted by so many earthly considerations and responsibilities that he thinks he is beyond the need for Divine assistance. The poor man's faith is tried by external obstacles which may in fact be easier to overcome than the inner trials that test the wealthy man's faith. We say of a man, "He is poor but honest," when it would be more complimentary in a spiritual sense to say, "He is rich but honest." King Shelomo's prayer implies that wealth is the greater of the two evils; poverty may lead to the sin of theft, but wealth may lead to atheism.

Still, we must search even more deeply to fully understand what Rabbi Yonathan is trying to tell us. If you can survive the outward, physical trials of a materially difficult life and emerge with your spirit strong and your faith true, you will be better prepared to withstand the test of a materially comfortable life. The entire history of our nation shows just such testing—testing through suffering which requires unbounded trust in God, for the sake of subsequent periods of wealth and abundancy. God led us through the desert for forty years to teach us to uphold the Torah sincerely, מעני (out of poverty), without any material means of support; He did this in order to test us, to make us spiritually strong enough to care properly for the Land of milk and honey He would give us. But in time we forgot His Law and did not uphold the honor of the Torah and the commandments, and so we were turned out of the Land. We have been tested over and over again, and time after time we have failed the test. Rabbi Yonathan urges us to remember! If we fulfill the precepts of the Torah, we need fear neither poverty nor wealth.

י**בּ** רַבִּי מֵאִיר אוֹמֵר, הֱוֵי מְמַעֵט בְּעֵסֶק
וַעֲסֹק בַּתּוֹרָה וֶהֱוֵי שְׁפַל־רוּחַ בִּפְנֵי כָל־
אָדָם וְאִם־בָּטַלְתָּ מִן־הַתּוֹרָה יֶשׁ־לְךָ בְּטֵלִים הַרְבֵּה
כְּנֶגְדֶּךָ וְאִם־עָמַלְתָּ בַּתּוֹרָה יֶשׁ־לוֹ שָׂכָר הַרְבֵּה לִתֵּן
לָךְ:

12 Rabbi Meir says: Limit your business activities
and occupy yourself with the Torah instead, and be of
humble spirit before all men. If you neglect the Torah
you will have many causes for neglecting it, but if you
toil in the Torah, God has abundant reward to give
you.

*   *   *

To guard successfully against the dangers of both wealth and
poverty, Rabbi Meir recommends neither neglect of your business nor complete absorption in it. Limit your business activities
and use the time gained for Torah studies. This admonition is in
complete contrast to our modern habits. Children are so conditioned to the priority of earning money that when they leave
school and enter the "school" of life, they devote themselves so
completely to their worldly occupations that they have hardly
any time left for intellectual pursuits, and certainly not for the
study of Torah. Today we refer to the way we earn our living as
a "calling," signifying that we are "called" to it, and we attach to
it a sacred importance which overrides every other aspect of
living, including observance of the Shabbath, the dietary laws
and many other commandments. What we say is a "calling" is an
occupation we choose ourselves; a real calling is that which God
summons us to do for His transcendent purpose. The real calling for which the Father of mankind has created every Jewish
soul is summed up in the three things that we say at a *brith milah*:
לתורה לחופה ולמעשים טובים, "for Torah, for marriage and for good
deeds." This is our real calling; our daily occupation is only the
means by which we may attain these three things.

There was never a Sage that considered an honest trade too lowly to be a respectable means of support for himself and his family. Rabbi Meir was distinguished among his contemporaries by his outstanding sagacity and his great learning. It would have been easy for him to obtain ample remuneration because of his extraordinary talents, but he earned his living as a clerk. Rabbi Meir was an excellent clerk, earning three *sela'im* per week. He used one for food and drink, one for clothing and with one he supported needy scholars. His disciples asked him, "Master, with what will you help your children?" He answered them, "If they are righteous they will fare well, as King David said, 'I have never seen a righteous man forsaken, whose progeny was forced to beg for bread' (*Tehillim* 37:25). But if they are not righteous, why should I bequeathe my belongings to God's enemies?" (*Midrash Koheleth Rabbah* 2:17). Yet Rabbi Meir was indeed concerned with the education of his children. "Rabbi Meir teaches: One should always teach his son a clean and easy craft, and earnestly pray to Him to Whom all wealth and poverty belong, for neither poverty nor wealth comes from one's trade but from Him, as it is said, 'The silver is mine and the gold is mine, says the Lord of Hosts' (*Chaggai* 2:8). Rabbi Nehorai (that is, Rabbi Meir) also said: I disregard all trades in the world and teach my son only Torah, for every other trade helps a man only in his youth, but in his old age he is exposed to hunger. The Torah stands by him in his youth and gives him a future and hope in his old age" (*Kiddushin* 82b).

This was the view of all the Sages. Rabbi Chiyya added these words to his daily prayer: "May it be Your will, O Lord our God, that your Torah may be our occupation and that our heart may not be sick nor our eyes darkened!" (*Berachoth* 16b). Even in the days of the great academies, the idea of making Torah, rather than business, one's profession, was spoken of in connection with prior generations. "Rabbah bar bar Chanah said in the name of Rabbi Yochanan, reporting Rabbi Yehudah ben Ilai: See what a difference there is between the earlier and the later generations. The earlier generations made the study of Torah their main concern and made their daily work subordinate to it, and both concerns prospered. The later generations made their work their main concern and study of the Torah subordinate, and neither prospered" (*Berachoth* 35b).

The history of the Jewish people confirms that money and possessions are not the most important things in life. The rulers under whom we lived prevented us from earning a living like our contemporaries did, and thus we were forced to become merchants. Despite this restriction on the most elementary of human rights, we taught our children Torah and awakened in them a sense of morality and spirituality which has preserved our people through the centuries. But if we nowadays tell a Jew, "Limit your business activities and occupy yourself with the Torah," he objects most strenuously and claims that he does not have sufficient time. He will add that his grandparents had an easier life, both simpler and less expensive, but that today it is impossible for him to exist without working all the time at his profession or business. A dispassionate examination of the facts will show that there has probably not been any period during which the fulfillment of the Torah did not meet with difficulties, that the supposed demands of contemporary life only exist in our imagination and we might do better to resist them rather than to try to satisfy them.

AND BE OF HUMBLE SPIRIT BEFORE ALL MEN. The words שפל רוח cannot satisfactorily be understood in their literal sense. This term is also used in mishnah 4:4 and its meaning was explained there, but the addition of the words "before all men" here seems to convey the idea that a humble spirit does not in itself suffice. You may be convinced that modesty and simplicity are desirable traits but have not the courage or strength to say so or act accordingly in front of other people, especially when it is not fashionable. Being "of humble spirit" is not enough then; acting so, "before all men," is necessary.

IF YOU NEGLECT THE TORAH YOU WILL HAVE MANY CAUSES FOR NEGLECTING IT. Granted that earning a living makes great demands on your time—but ask yourself how many hours you find to spend in restaurants and cafes, on hobbies and other forms of recreation, or just simply doing nothing. Surely you could find some more time for learning and observing the Torah even without limiting your business activities. "When returning home from the field in the evening, a man should go to synagogue. If he is used to reading the Torah, let him learn the Torah, and if he is used to learning Mishnah, let him learn Mishnah, and then let him recite the *Shema* and say the prayers..." (*Berachoth* 4b). The fact that Jews have a better social position today should be the strongest incentive to devote more time to the Torah, and not less. You need only the courage of your convictions to do what you know is right; let others follow the fashion.

> His brother's name was Yaktan ("the small one"). Rabbi Acha asks: Why does he bear the name of Yaktan? Because he only carried on his business in a small way. What did he gain by doing that? His reward was that he became the ancestor of thirteen great families. If this applies to the small man who limits his business activities, it must apply so much more to the big businessman who restricts his hours of business.
>
> (*Midrash Bereshith Rabbah* 37:7)

Every day new obstacles appear in our path, new pretexts for neglecting our Torah. By overcoming all the obstacles and all the difficulties, we will enjoy the finest and richest reward of Heaven.

יג רַבִּי אֱלִיעֶזֶר בֶּן־יַעֲקֹב אוֹמֵר, הָעוֹשֶׂה
מִצְוָה אַחַת קוֹנֶה לוֹ פְּרַקְלִיט אֶחָד
וְהָעוֹבֵר עֲבֵרָה אַחַת קוֹנֶה לוֹ קַטֵּגוֹר אֶחָד, תְּשׁוּבָה
וּמַעֲשִׂים טוֹבִים כִּתְרִיס בִּפְנֵי הַפֻּרְעָנוּת:

13 Rabbi Eliezer ben Ya'akov says: He who fulfills
one commandment gains for himself one advocate
and he who commits one sin acquires for himself one
accuser; repentance and good deeds are a shield
against punishment.

*   *   *

Both the previous mishnah and this one refer to the positive
value of Torah study. This mishnah, however, points out what
can be achieved when Torah study is translated into deeds. Man's
soul will not be improved by simply hearing lectures and
speeches, but rather by the deeds he performs. In the Avoth of
Rabbi Nathan (end of ch. 22), we read, "Wisdom is not achieved
with words, and eloquence does not indicate wisdom — only
deeds; for talking too much leads to sin, as it is said, 'Sin is hidden
in a multitude of words' (*Mishlei* 10:19) and 'Even a fool is
counted wise when he keeps quiet' (ibid. 17:28)." Our ancestors
placed the deed above all else at Sinai: נעשה ונשמע, "We will do
and we will hear." In this spirit we still are inspired by men who
do good deeds. Unfortunately, when we look around us today we
see a great gap between what we do and what we ought to do.
Our attitude toward the sincere performance of our religious
obligations needs strengthening and improvement; we need to
renew our commitment to a moral and observant life.

Our generation is immersed in activities which are influenced
by empty words and meaningless slogans, and which leave no
time for good deeds and human kindness. Let us not be fooled,
either, into thinking that the moral ills of our day can be cured by
lectures, social clubs or even sermons. Only the full return to a
complete commitment to Torah and the commandments will do
it. Only true repentance will be able to check the religious decline

of our generation. The spiritual wealth left to us by our most
learned Sages has been replaced today with the banner of "the
Science of Judaism," מדעי היהדות. The lives and works of our great
philosophers and writers are written about in journals, but what
is the good of such intellectual exercise? Many library shelves are
filled with "Judaica" to be sure, just as they are filled with other
kinds of research and folklore, but what is accomplished with all
this? The ranks of our righteous and God-fearing men are not
increased by it; not one more person follows the path of our great
forebears in living a pure Jewish life of morality and commitment
to God.

The denigrators and persecutors of the Jewish people call us
crass, materialistic and money-grabbing. What would they say if
every one of us kept the Shabbath as it should be kept, with all his
heart, closed his business with no exceptions or reservations and
publicly refused all gain or profit one day a week? What a sanctification of God's Name that would be in the eyes of the world!
The observance of just this one commandment would be a powerful advocate for us, as it is said, "He who fulfills one commandment gains for himself one advocate."

The commentators agree, of course, that Rabbi Eliezer does
not refer to human advocacy or human accusation. Fulfillment of
all the commandments and prohibitions remains our duty, irrespective of human approval or disapproval. Our cases will be
brought before the Judge Who is everywhere at all times, Who
knows all our deeds, good and bad, sees what we do or fail to do.
That is why even one good deed may serve as a valid advocate for
us and one deviation from our duty may be an eloquent accuser.
Rabbi Shemuel, son of Nachmani, taught, in the name of Rabbi
Yonathan: When you perform one commandment in this world,
it will precede you in the World to Come; when you commit one
sin in this world, it will cling to you and precede you on the day
of judgment" (*Sotah* 3b).

Why do we need an advocate at all, you may well ask, since
God is omniscient? Perhaps the answer lies in the effect of the
deed upon ourselves. How many of our fellow Jews have removed themselves almost completely from the community of
Yisrael, have embraced the current idols and have forsaken God?

Yet still they perform one good deed which maintains a fragile thread of connection: they bring their eight-day-old sons into the covenant of Avraham. Who can doubt that this single action can balance out many serious omissions? "And when his soul draws near to the grave...if there is an angel with it, a single advocate, one among a thousand to vouch for a man's uprightness, then He is gracious to him, saying: Save him from going down into the pit, I have found a ransom" (*Iyyov* 33:22-24). Similarly, only one transgression can cast a shadow over all our good deeds. "For there is not a just man on earth who does good and does not sin" (*Koheleth* 7:20). The only remedy for both a weak advocate and a strong accuser is the sincere resolve to return to God's ways. The power of repentance and forgiveness is probably the greatest of God's miracles, repeated again and again with every human being who is sincerely moved to *teshuvah*.

יד רַבִּי יוֹחָנָן הַסַּנְדְּלָר אוֹמֵר, כָּל־כְּנֵסְיָה
שֶׁהִיא לְשֵׁם שָׁמַיִם סוֹפָהּ לְהִתְקַיֵּם
וְשֶׁאֵינָהּ לְשֵׁם שָׁמַיִם אֵין סוֹפָהּ לְהִתְקַיֵּם:

14 Rabbi Yochanan *Ha-Sandlar* says: Any assembly
which is in the name of Heaven will be lasting, but
one which is not in the name of Heaven will not be
lasting.

*   *   *

When the term לשם שמים is used here, it means "for the sake of
Heaven," indicating the selfless, pure motivation of an action
that a Jew does for God alone. God is, of course, not only the God
of Heaven but also the God of earth. Why, then, "for the sake of
Heaven" and not "for the sake of Heaven and earth"? We read in
Tehillim, "The heavens are the heavens of God, but the earth he
has given to mankind" (115:16). Heaven remains solely God's
while the earth was given to men as well. Thus we say, "for the
sake of Heaven" to denote something done purely for God alone.

ANY ASSEMBLY. The source of Rabbi Yochanan's terminology is explained in the Avoth of Rabbi Nathan (ch. 40): "An
example of an assembly for the sake of Heaven is that of the
Great Assembly, although another reading compares it to the
assembly of Yisrael at the foot of Mount Sinai; an example of an
assembly that does not gather for the sake of Heaven is that of the
gathering of the people when the languages were confused (see
Bereshith 11:1-9)." It is not difference of opinion among people
that renders a gathering unworthy of the name כנסיה לשם שמים,
but rather their impure motives. "Every controversy which is in
the name of Heaven will in the end achieve a lasting result, and
every controversy which is not in the name of Heaven will have in
the end ephemeral results" (see below, *Avoth* 5:21).

The spokesmen of apostasy today try to legitimize their devia-
tions from the Law by saying that differences of opinion and
varied interpretations have always existed among our people.
The differences of today, however, are of another sort entirely.

When Hillel and Shammai, or Abbaye and Rava had differing interpretations of the scope of a law, there was never the slightest doubt in anyone's mind as to the binding power of the law itself. The only example in our history that the apostates might point out as a difference that was not for the sake of Heaven, is that of the Karaites who flatly denied the legitimacy of the Oral Law. But the Karaites removed themselves from the mainstream of authentic Judaism because of their deviation, and consequently suffered the fate of near-extinction, proving the rule of this mishnah. We learn that the Great Assembly was called "great" because the Men of the Great Assembly restored the crown of God's Law to its previous splendor (*Yoma* 69b). The Sages of the Great Assembly taught us that God's eternal truth and God's Chosen People are preserved only through Divine might, not mortal human power. In recent history, men calling themselves rabbis have formed synods and congresses in order to destroy that Law which the Great Assembly preserved and which has sustained Yisrael to this very day. All those gatherings have experienced the fate of "any assembly which is not in the name of Heaven."

טו רַבִּי אֶלְעָזָר בֶּן שַׁמּוּעַ אוֹמֵר, יְהִי כְבוֹד
תַּלְמִידְךָ חָבִיב עָלֶיךָ כְּשֶׁלָּךְ וּכְבוֹד חֲבֵרְךָ
כְּמוֹרָא רַבָּךְ וּמוֹרָא רַבָּךְ כְּמוֹרָא שָׁמָיִם:

15 Rabbi Elazar ben Shammua says: Let the honor of your student be as dear to you as your own; let the honor of your colleague be as dear to you as the reverence due to your teacher; and let the reverence due to your teacher be as dear to you as the reverence due to Heaven.

* * *

This saying deals with three types of honor (your own, your student's and your colleague's) and two kinds of reverence (to your teacher and to God). No one needs to be reminded to guard his own honor, for everyone wants other people to think well of him. Our desire for a good name is even admirable, as long as it does not degenerate into immoderate ambition. We understand, therefore, that Rabbi Elazar begins with the reminder that students are worthy of a great deal of respect. Although the sharp distinction between כבוד (honor) and מורא (fear or reverence) indicates clearly that we must distinguish between the respect we give to our students and the great reverence we feel for God, we must nevertheless be very considerate of our students' honor, guarding their feelings as well as their good name just as carefully as we guard our own. Jews are usually sensitive about this (indeed, some call us supersensitive) for we have learned from experience that we are often held individually responsible for the honor of the entire community, whether we observe our religion or not. The Talmud, moreover, is filled with admonitions to guard one's honor. For instance, if you cannot afford to wear special clothes on the Shabbath, wear your weekday clothes rather than ask for charity; earn your living humbly, if you must, rather than depend on charity. We pray to God every day to provide us with the means to earn a living honorably, בכבוד.

Rabbi Elazar ben Shammua was a disciple of Rabbi Akiva, the

companion of Rabbi Meir, the teacher of Rabbi Yehudah *Ha-Nasi*, and a barrel-maker by trade. His advice concerns the relationship of teachers to their students. The Avoth of Rabbi Nathan (ch. 27) gives us the classic example of this: When Moshe *Rabbenu* asked his disciple Yehoshua to "Choose for us men and go out..." (*Shemoth* 17:9), his words "for us" accorded Yehoshua equal status with himself. By treating a student with honor, Rabbi Elazar implies, you will also increase his eagerness to learn. "Rabbi Nachman ben Yitzchak said: Why are the words of the Torah likened to a tree? It is stated, 'It is a tree of life to them that grasp it' (*Mishlei* 3:18). This teaches us that as a larger tree may catch fire from a smaller tree, so an older scholar may learn from a younger one. Similarly, Rabbi Chanina said: I have learned much from my teachers, and from my companions more than that, but from my students most of all" (*Ta'anith* 7a). The cordiality and mutual respect between teacher and student in the Torah world has no equal in terms of other human relationships.

LET THE HONOR OF YOUR COLLEAGUE BE AS DEAR TO YOU AS THE REVERENCE DUE TO YOUR TEACHER. Ben Zoma teaches us that to earn respect and honor you have to respect your fellowman, no matter who he is (*Avoth* 4:1). When Rabbi Elazar says חברך he means "your colleague" in learning only. Certainly we must honor all men, for all men are colleagues and brothers. But when we and those around us are dedicated to a life of Torah and observance of the commandments, then our colleagues become our teachers. King David learned only two things from Achithofel and yet called him "Master" (see comments after *Avoth* 6:3). Honor granted for material reasons is always imperfect. The rich man is contemptuous of the poor man, the latter is envious of someone else, brothers and friends become bitter rivals in business, and even the stimulus of intellectual competition is usually marred by petty jealousies in secular scholarly circles. Companions in learning Torah, however, should remain good friends even during the sharpest intellectual arguments. The truth for which they contend belongs to all of them together; it does not lose anything by the fact that many share it. On the contrary, it only gains.

Rabbi Chama ben Chanina said: What is the meaning of the words, "Iron sharpens iron and a man sharpens his companion" (*Mishlei* 27:17)? Thus do two scholars sharpen each other's minds in studying the Law. Rabbah bar bar Chana said: Why are the words of the Torah likened to fire, as it is said, "Is not My word like fire, says the Lord" (*Yirmeyahu* 23:29)? This is to teach that just as fire does not ignite by itself, so too the words of the Torah do not endure with him who studies by himself; this is in agreement with what Rabbi Yosei ben Chanina said: What is the meaning of the words, "a sword is upon the lonely and they shall become fools" (*Yirmeyahu* 50:36)? This means that destruction comes upon scholars who confine themselves to private study, and they become guilty of error and sin.

(*Ta'anith* 7a)

The words of the Sages throughout the Talmud reveal many moving examples of the great honor and respect they accorded each other:

When Rabbi Eliezer fell ill, his disciples went in to visit him...[and asked for instruction]. He said to them: Guard the honor of your colleagues. (*Berachoth* 28b)

Rabbi Yosei said: I have never disregarded the words of my colleagues; I know that I am not a priest, yet if my colleagues were to tell me to ascend to the dais, I would ascend. (*Shabbath* 118b)

Mar bar Rav Ashei said: I am unfit to judge in a lawsuit between scholars. Why? A scholar is as dear to me as myself and a man cannot see anything to his own disadvantage. (ibid. 119a)

But the honor you show to a colleague must be intensified to reverence in your relation to a teacher who has introduced you to the Torah. "You are obliged to give a higher degree of reverence to your teacher than to your father..." and the Law is specific on this point, listing precisely how to do this (*Shulchan Aruch, Yoreh De'ah*, 242). Still, we might question how Rabbi Elazar can insist that our reverence toward our teacher ought to equal the reverence we show to God Himself.

There is a *baraytha* in Pesachim 22b that tells about Shimon Ha-Amsuni who interpreted the accusative preposition את, used throughout the Torah, as a part of speech which extends the meaning of its object. Thus, he explained, in the verse: בראשית ברא אלהים את השמים ואת הארץ, "In the beginning God created the heaven and the earth" we must understand that "the heaven and the earth" includes all the heavenly bodies and all the elements which make up the earth. Similarly, in the verse כבד את אביך ואת אמך, "Honor your father and your mother," father and mother include stepfather and stepmother, grandfather and grandmother. But when he came to the verse את יי אלהיך תירא, "You shall fear the Lord your God," he desisted from his explanation, holding it impossible to extend the fear of God to another. His disciples then asked, "What about all the instances which you have already interpreted?" He answered, "Just as I was rewarded for interpreting them, so will I be rewarded for refraining here." However, Rabbi Akiva came and subsequently taught that, "You shall fear the Lord your God" includes scholars of the Torah.

As it is said, "The words of our teachers stand next to the words of the Torah, not as rivals but as friends, and they are even dearer to Yisrael than the words of the Torah" (*Yerushalmi, Berachoth* 1:4). We learn from this that true reverence for God necessitates the highest degree of honor toward our Sages.

טז

רַבִּי יְהוּדָה אוֹמֵר, הֱוֵה זָהִיר בְּתַלְמוּד
שֶׁשִּׁגְגַת תַּלְמוּד עוֹלָה זָדוֹן:

16 Rabbi Yehudah says: Be cautious in study, for an error in study amounts to intentional sin.

*   *   *

There are three different readings, from various manuscripts, for this mishnah: תַלְמוּד, תַּלְמִיד, לִמוּד. The reading we have chosen, תַלְמוּד, draws attention to one's method of learning Torah, for it means specifically "learning Torah." The reading לִמוּד extends the meaning to any kind of studies, while the reading תַלְמִיד refers to teaching the Torah. No other type of study demands more careful attention than study of Torah. In the scale of perfection, described by Rabbi Pinchas ben Ya'ir, which progresses up to the ultimate possession of רוח הקדש (Divine inspiration), "Torah" and "precision" are the two lowest degrees (*Avodah Zarah* 20b); Torah is placed lower than precision. Admittedly someone who has not learned anything cannot have acquired the precision and conscientiousness necessary to lead a dutiful life; yet it is equally certain that someone who does not approach the study of God's Torah with precision and care will never derive any benefit from it. Our Torah scrolls are written without vowels, without punctuation, and without sentence division. Just to read them requires our full attention. Your method of study therefore, is as important as what you study: Torah and precision together are the first steps.

As for the contents of God's word, the immensity and the depth of the material demand the most devoted interest and continual effort. At the same time, you must learn how to apply the law to the complicated demands of daily life. Finally, to ensure that once you have learned it, it will remain your inalienable spiritual property, you are in need of special Divine assistance. Our Sages, the great masters of the Torah, speak emphatically of the great devotion required to ensure that we benefit from our Torah studies.

Rabbi Yitzchak said: If a man says to you, "I have labored and not found," do not believe him. If he says, "I have not labored but still have found," do not believe him. If he says, "I have labored and found," you may believe him. This is true in regard to words of Torah, but in business, all depends on the assistance of Heaven. And even for the words of Torah this is true in regard to penetrating the meaning, but as for remembering what one has learned, all depends on the assistance of Heaven. (*Megillah* 6b)

It says, "Man is born to trouble as the sparks fly upward" (*Iyyov* 5:7) and that refers to the words of the Torah, as it says, "When you let your eyes flutter from it, it is no more" (*Mishlei* 23:5). (*Berachoth* 5a)

The words of the Torah are forgotten only through inattention. (*Ta'anith* 7b)

The words of the Torah are hard to acquire, like vessels of fine gold, and are easily destroyed, like vessels of glass. (*Chagigah* 15a)

One can learn Torah for twenty years and forget it again in two years. (*Avoth of Rabbi Nathan* 24:6)

What a world of experience, knowledge and information of all kinds is contained in the Torah! Let us single out some examples: The first commandment Yisrael received was to sanctify the beginnings of the months and to count months and years according to the course of the moon. For the fulfillment of this duty, a precise knowledge of astronomy is required. The laws concerning which animals may be eaten led Jews to study medicine, anatomy and physiology. The Levites became musicians and mastered the skills and theory of song and instrumental music. Dividing the Holy Land into territories and regulating boundaries (ערובין) led to a knowledge of geometry, surveying and other mathematical skills. The prohibition of work on the Shabbath entails a comprehensive study of thirty-nine different categories of human activity and manual skill, and our Sages had to be expert in every one of them!

Torah studies, therefore, do not divert a Jew's attention from the world, its discoveries, inventions and new achievements. On the contrary—an observant Jew is eager to examine everything and learn how God's Law may be applied to it. Thus, we see that since there is really no progress, no invention of the human mind, which does not affect a Jew's life directly or indirectly, all these things require an evaluation in accordance with the guidelines of the Torah. What would happen if an engineer built a bridge or a house and made an error in construction? There is no question about his responsibility for the entire amount of damage caused by his error. His intention was certainly not destructive, but he was negligent. Some errors can be excused and forgiven, but an error of knowledge arising from neglect or imprecision in any area of Torah study, just as in engineering, cannot be forgiven. Rabbi Yehudah himself explains this in another place: " 'Tell My people of its crime and the house of Ya'akov of its error' (*Yeshayahu* 58:1). 'My people'—those are the Torah scholars; their errors are counted like intentional sins. 'The house of Ya'akov'— those are the ignorant people; their intentional wrong is looked upon as an error" (*Bava Metzia* 33b). Rabbi Yehudah's lesson is: The standards in Torah learning are extremely high; an error in learning is considered an intentional sin.

יז רַבִּי שִׁמְעוֹן אוֹמֵר, שְׁלֹשָׁה כְתָרִים הֵן,
כֶּתֶר תּוֹרָה וְכֶתֶר כְּהֻנָּה וְכֶתֶר מַלְכוּת,
וְכֶתֶר שֵׁם טוֹב עוֹלֶה עַל גַּבֵּיהֶן:

17 Rabbi Shimon says: There are three crowns—
the crown of the Torah, the crown of priesthood and
the crown of kingship; but the crown of a good name
surpasses them all.

*   *   *

Rabbi Shimon speaks of three crowns but actually names four.
This is to teach us that any of the three crowns may be worn only
by someone who also bears a good name. The expression
"crown" indicates power and influence, and we learn here that a
person can hold a position of power as a Torah sage, as a priest or
as a political ruler. Why is it, then, that without the crown of a
good name, the other three crowns are worthless?

As we shall see, the fourth crown is the only one whose
acquisition lies entirely in our own hands. In all three cases, it is
only when the office is held by a sincere, conscientious person
who is devoted to his job and does it properly, that a good name
is accorded to him. Thus, a good name is the active proof of a
man's right to any of the other three crowns he possesses. And,
just as each of the three crowns includes the crown of a good
name in this way, strictly speaking, we may say that the crown of
Torah actually includes that of royalty and priesthood. For at one
and the same time Yisrael received the Torah and was designated
"a kingdom of priests" (*Shemoth* 19:6). Yisrael was to have kings who
were also priests; the state was to be God's as was the Temple and all
were to serve God in harmonious unity. Although the ideal was
never fully realized, we see how the three crowns could be united in
the person of David, king of Yisrael, whose every thought, word and
deed was in the service of God and in adherence to the Torah and
who, thus, earned for himself the title of priest, as it says, "The Lord
has sworn it and will not alter His counsel: you are a priest forever,
according to My word..." (*Tehillim* 110:4).

Yisrael's first and only mission is the faithful observance of God's word, the Torah. For this purpose, Yisrael has her scholars, priests and kings, the whole organism that directs her national life along the paths prescribed by the Torah. In other states the bearers of the royal crown and the bearers of the priestly crown were always in conflict; in the Jewish state, God's people were to be spared this antagonism by means of the harmonious compatibility of a kingdom of priests. From the highest in rank to the lowest, every person in Yisrael was dependent on the masters of the Torah and obeyed their rulings. This unreserved surrender to the demands of the Torah found its symbolic expression in the sacrifices in the Sanctuary which were under the dominion of the priests. Overseeing the smooth functioning of all, sat the king on his throne, but as the verse says, "and he shall read in [this book, the Torah] all the days of his life that he may learn to fear the Lord his God...[and] that his heart will not be raised above his brethren and that he may not turn aside from the commandment to the right nor to the left" (*Devarim* 17:19-20). Sage, priest and king—the prestige of each is totally dependent on the way each one honors the Torah, and only when the bearer of each crown honors the Torah will his name be honored by posterity.

BUT THE CROWN OF A GOOD NAME SURPASSES THEM ALL. The priest's crown and the king's crown, and even the crown of the Torah sage, are all gifts from God. They are conferred with Divine sanction on competent mortals. The crown of a good name, however, is ours to earn; עולה, it "rises up" from the depths to the heights, from earth to Heaven, and therein lies its superiority over all the other crowns.

רַבִּי נְהוֹרַאי אוֹמֵר, הֱוֵי גוֹלֶה לִמְקוֹם
תוֹרָה וְאַל־תֹּאמַר שֶׁהִיא תָבוֹא אַחֲרֶיךָ
שֶׁחֲבֵרֶיךָ יְקַיְמוּהָ בְיָדֶיךָ וְאֶל־בִּינָתְךָ אַל־תִּשָּׁעֵן:

18 Rabbi Nehorai says: Exile yourself to a place of Torah, and do not say that it will follow you, for your associates are the ones who keep it in your hand, "and do not rely upon your own understanding" (*Mishlei* 3:5).

*   *   *

This saying is connected with an event in the life of Rabbi Elazar ben Arach who, according to one opinion, is identical with Rabbi Nehorai. The Talmud states:

> Rabbi Chelbo taught: The wine of Perugaytha and the warm baths of Diomseth cut off the ten tribes from Yisrael. Rabbi Elazar ben Arach also visited there and was so attracted by it that his learning vanished. Upon his return, he had forgotten so much that instead of reading החדש הזה לכם in the scroll (*Shemoth* 12:2), he read החרש היה לבם. The scholars prayed for him and he regained his knowledge. And it is thus that we learn, said Rabbi Nehorai: Exile yourself to a place of Torah.
>
> (*Shabbath* 147b)

A *baraytha* on that passage states that his name was not Nehorai but Nechemyah; others state that his name was Rabbi Elazar ben Arach but he was called Nehorai because he enlightened (נהיר) the eyes of the Sages in *Halachah*. His saying, however, goes far beyond this one experience and contains a lesson for everyone. The expression הוי גולה, "Exile yourself," at once engages our interest. Ordinarily we would say: הלוך למקום תורה, "Go to a Torah environment," or even: הוי דר במקום תורה, "Live in a Torah environment." The word גולה, "exile," is usually used for one who has accidentally killed someone and escapes to a place of refuge where he must remain for his own safety. The expression conveys the same idea that we find in Makkoth 10a: Rabbi

Yochanan said that the words of the Torah are a refuge for one who has committed unintentional murder. The linkage of the words of the Torah with ערי מקלט, "cities of refuge," imports great significance to the Sage's admonition. We are to understand that knowledge—or ignorance—is a matter of life and death! It is the fulfillment or non-fulfillment of God's will. You may never excuse your lapses on the grounds that you are ignorant of your obligations. In secular law too, ignorance of a law does not shield the guilty from the consequences of their crimes. Therefore, let us heed the golden hint expressed in the words, "Exile yourself to a place of Torah," and understand that the Torah can be a refuge and can provide expiation.

"If you search for it as for silver and hidden treasures, then you will understand what fear of the Lord is and will find knowledge of God" (*Mishlei* 2:4-5). Rabbi Shimon ben Lakish explains this verse in the Midrash: "We must search for the words of the Torah for they will not seek us out. This resembles someone's trade; if he does not pursue his customers, the customers will certainly not pursue him." If we were fully convinced of the truth that man cannot live on bread alone, that he lives on the word of God, we would not regard it as unreasonable to leave our own home and search for a true Torah environment. Anyone will leave home to go in search of his bread; we ought to feel the same about our spiritual food.

FOR YOUR ASSOCIATES ARE THE ONES WHO KEEP IT IN YOUR HAND. No one, not even the most capable and experienced businessman, can do business in solitude. The salesman must have buyers; the buyers must have suppliers. Some reciprocal process is implicit in the acquisition of goods—both material and spiritual. True, you might store up spiritual treasures in your head, collecting them in solitude, remote from the world. To ensure that they do not remain in your head, however, like unproductive hoarded capital, to translate your splendid thoughts into deeds, you must associate with like-minded companions. The knowledge that you have acquired with the good influence and help of your friends will only come to fruition, however, if, as the Wise King says and Rabbi Nehorai repeats, you "do not rely upon your own understanding" (*Mishlei* 3:5).

יט　רַבִּי יַנַּאי אוֹמֵר, אֵין בְּיָדֵינוּ לֹא מִשַּׁלְוַת
הָרְשָׁעִים וְאַף לֹא מִיִּסּוּרֵי הַצַּדִּיקִים:

19 Rabbi Yannai says: It is not in our hands to explain the well-being of the wicked nor the afflictions of the righteous.

*   *   *

Pure reason has never answered the question of why the wicked so often prosper and the righteous suffer. Many distinguished and enlightened thinkers have occupied themselves with this puzzle, without solving it. Rabbi Yannai tells us that we will never solve it because it is beyond our comprehension, because it presupposes a knowledge of the correlation between cause and effect which is beyond the reach of human erudition; it simply is not in our power to comprehend it. We see before us a drop of water containing countless living cells, a blade of grass, whole and perfect, and we cannot explain it. The poor man at times envies the rich man's abundant happiness, his gold, his pleasures and his honors. Does not the rich man, though, occasionally envy the poor man's robust health, his physical strength, his peace of mind in bearing his burdens? Who is the fortunate one? Why does the Psalmist tell us, "When you eat from the labor of your hands, then you will be happy and it will be well with you" (*Tehillim* 128:2)? *Sefer* Tehillim is especially rich in reflections on this question:

> Do not compete with evil men, nor be envious of those who do evil. For they shall soon be cut down like grass and fade away like the green herb. Trust in the Lord and do good; dwell in the Land and cherish faith. Seek delight in the Lord and He will give you the desires of your heart. The humble shall inherit the earth and delight in the abundance of peace. Better a few with the righteous than a multitude of many wicked. For the arms of the wicked will be broken, but the Lord upholds the righteous. The

Lord knows the days of men of moral integrity and their inheritance shall be for all eternity.

(Tehillim 37:1-4, 11, 16-18)

The wicked are compared to grass and herbs which are not only easily cut down, but can rot from within because of their shallow roots. When you trust completely in God, however, you will be solidly rooted in his eternal protection. The answer to the question seems to be that we cannot judge men by their appearance. True happiness and true achievement are often not as they seem to us. It takes very few possessions to make a righteous person happy, for he knows that good or bad fortune on earth is not always what it seems. We cannot know if our happiness is recompense or testing; nor do we know what our reward or punishment will be. We must listen to the words of Rabbi Yannai and believe with complete faith that we will be rewarded at last by the just and true Judge.

בֶּן רַבִּי מַתְיָא בֶּן־חָרָשׁ אוֹמֵר, הֱוֵה מַקְדִּים
בִּשְׁלוֹם כָּל־אָדָם וֶהֱוֵה זָנָב לָאֲרָיוֹת וְאַל־
תְּהִי רֹאשׁ לַשּׁוּעָלִים:

20 Rabbi Mathya ben Charash says: Be the first to greet every man; be rather a tail to lions than a head of foxes.

*   *   *

Not only Rabbi Mathya, but all our great Sages, taught that a mark of good character is courtesy to others. The greatest teachers would receive the humblest beggars with a kind word. The Talmud states:

> A favorite saying of Abbaye was: A man should always be subtle in the fear of Heaven because a "soft answer turns away wrath" (*Mishlei* 15:1). One should be on good terms not only with one's brethren and kindred but with every man, down to the heathen in the marketplace, so that one will be beloved above and well-liked below... It was related about Rabbi Yochanan ben Zakkai that no man ever greeted him first, not even the heathen in the marketplace.
>
> (*Berachoth* 17a)

When we show respect to all men without distinction, the fear of God is also expressed, for every human being embodies the image of the Creator.

The simple courtesy of greeting another person first is evidently of more than simple merit, for we find it mentioned in several places in the Talmud. "Rabbi Chelbo said in the name of Rav Huna: If you know that your friend is in the habit of greeting you, greet him first. For it is said, 'Seek peace and pursue it' (*Tehillim* 34:15). And if your friend greets you and you do not return the greeting, you may be called a robber" (*Berachoth* 6b). The question is asked in Tractate Kallah: Are we duty-bound to greet idolaters? The answer is that we are expressly told to greet them, even on their holidays. If that is so, why has the question been asked? The question, it is explained, refers to whether we should greet an idolater first, and the answer is also affirmative. When the question is asked about murderers, adulterers and those liable to the death penalty, however, the ruling is that we must answer their greeting, but we may not greet them first. We learn from this that all men have a right to be treated courteously, but we must never overlook their true characters: a fox's head is an intrinsic part of a fox and a lion's tail remains very much part of a lion.

The Talmud Yerushalmi (*Sanhedrin* 4:8) points out that this mishnah challenges the popular refrain, "It is better to be the head of foxes than the tail of a lion." Julius Caesar also preferred being the first in a small city to being second in Rome. We see the obvious contrast between Caesar's vain ambition and Jewish worldly wisdom. Rabbi Mathya ben Charash teaches us that it is better to affiliate ourselves with humble, God-fearing people than with important men of questionable morals. And Rabbi Yosei teaches, "Not the place honors the man, but the man honors his place" (*Ta'anith* 21b).

כ**א** רַבִּי יַעֲקֹב אוֹמֵר, הָעוֹלָם הַזֶּה דוֹמֶה לִפְרוֹזְדוֹר בִּפְנֵי הָעוֹלָם הַבָּא; הַתְקֵן עַצְמְךָ בִּפְרוֹזְדוֹר כְּדֵי שֶׁתִּכָּנֵס לַטְּרַקְלִין:

21 Rabbi Ya'akov says: This world is like the vestibule before the World to Come; prepare yourself in the vestibule so that you may enter the palace.

*   *   *

What happens after the seventy or eighty years we are allotted on earth? We do not know; we cannot even guess. It does not seem reasonable that our existence ceases at the end of such a short span of time. Indeed, this Sage is telling us that our world is too narrow and small to encompass the full recompense due us for the good or evil we manage to accomplish during our life in it. The Talmud explains, "Rabbi Yehoshua ben Levi said: What is the implication of the verse, 'My commandments which I command you this day to do them' (*Devarim* 7:11)? 'This day' you must do them, not tomorrow; 'this day' you can do them, but you will not receive the reward today for doing them" (*Eruvin* 22a). It is also said, "When you take the trouble to prepare [food] on the eve of Shabbath, you can eat on Shabbath, but if you have not made preprarations on the eve of Shabbath, what will you eat on Shabbath?" (*Avodah Zarah* 3a). Rabbi Ya'akov himself is cited in Chullin:

> There is no precept in the Torah that is mentioned together with its reward and from which we cannot infer that there will be a resurrection of the dead. That is to say, the promise of a reward presupposes some state of existence after this temporal state. Thus, you are commanded to honor your parents, "that it may be well with you and that you may prolong your days" (*Devarim* 5:16); and you are commanded to let the mother bird go and take her young, so "that it may be well with you and that you may prolong your days" (*Devarim* 22:7). It is also written that a father said to his son: Go up to the top of the building and bring me down some

young doves. The son went up to the roof, let the dam go and took the young ones, but on the way down he fell and was killed. Where is this man's length of days and where is his happiness? The meaning of the verse can only be that "prolonged days" refers to the World that is infinitely long, and "that it may be well with you" refers to the World that is perfectly good.

(*Chullin* 142a)

We must therefore prepare ourselves in this world so that we will be allowed to enter the World to Come—the Palace where we can behold God's glory for ourselves.

כב הוּא הָיָה אוֹמֵר, יָפָה שָׁעָה אַחַת
בִּתְשׁוּבָה וּמַעֲשִׂים טוֹבִים בָּעוֹלָם הַזֶּה
מִכֹּל חַיֵּי הָעוֹלָם הַבָּא, וְיָפָה שָׁעָה אַחַת שֶׁל־קוֹרַת
רוּחַ בָּעוֹלָם הַבָּא מִכֹּל־חַיֵּי הָעוֹלָם הַזֶּה:

22 He would say: One hour of repentance and good deeds in this world is worth more than the whole life of the World to Come; and one hour of spiritual bliss in the World to Come is worth more than the whole life of this world.

*   *   *

Good deeds and repentance are two things that we are specifically urged to do without delay. "Repent one day before your death," says Rabbi Eliezer (*Avoth* 2:15), and since we do not know when that day will be, tomorrow may be too late. The Wise King says, "Man has no power over the spirit to contain it; neither has he power over the day of death" (*Koheleth* 8:8). The Sages explain, "Nobody can say, 'Wait until I have finished my accounts,' or 'until I have set my house in order, and afterward I will come'" (*Midrash Devarim Rabbah* 9:3). In our holy language the same word, מדות, can mean "attributes" and also "garments." Attributes clothe the soul just as garments envelop the body. If more time is granted to us in the vestibule to eternity, we may employ it to discard the unworthy traits that disfigure our better selves. For what is repentance if not סור מרע, "removing yourself from evil," by discarding bad habits and inclinations! The sincere determination to stop transgressing is the surest way to gain entrance to the Palace, and it does not take very long since even the intention is considered sufficient. That is the meaning of Rabi's words, "One may acquire eternal life in one hour" (*Avodah Zarah* 17a).

Rabbi Eliyyahu of Vilna, of blessed memory, is said to have shed bitter tears in his hour of death. Asked about this, he answered, "I am crying because the farewell from this beautiful, splendid world causes me pain, because I know that life in the World to Come, in the event that it is granted to me, does not possess any of the riches of this world. As long as I am here, I can still perfect my soul by fulfilling God's laws. In the World to Come, all the treasures of the earth will not buy me the chance to perform even one more commandment; how should I not weep?"

We know as little of the splendor and bliss of the life after death as one born blind knows of the difference between colors. A favorite saying of Rav was, "The next world is not like this world. In the next world there is no eating or drinking nor propagation nor business nor jealousy nor hatred nor competition, but the righteous sit with their crowns on their heads, feasting on the brightness of the Divine Presence" (*Berachoth* 17a). Rabbi Chiyya bar Abba said in Rabbi Yochanan's name, "All the prophets prophesied only about the Messianic era; but as for the World to Come, 'no eye has seen except the Lord's what He has prepared for one that waits for Him' (*Yeshayahu* 64:3, cited in *Sanhedrin* 99a). We must conclude, therefore, that we are simply incapable of imagining the immeasurable bliss which we will enjoy in the World to Come. All the happiness of all the hours of this life with its fighting and struggling, with its victories and defeats, does not measure up to one hour of life in the World to Come.

רַבִּי שִׁמְעוֹן בֶּן־אֶלְעָזָר אוֹמֵר, אַל־תְּרַצֶּה **כג**
אֶת־חֲבֵרְךָ בִּשְׁעַת כַּעֲסוֹ וְאַל־תְּנַחֲמֵהוּ
בְּשָׁעָה שֶׁמֵּתוֹ מֻטָּל לְפָנָיו וְאַל־תִּשְׁאַל לוֹ בִּשְׁעַת
נִדְרוֹ וְאַל־תִּשְׁתַּדֵּל לִרְאוֹתוֹ בִּשְׁעַת קַלְקָלָתוֹ:

23 Rabbi Shimon ben Elazar says: Do not seek to appease your companion at the time of his anger nor comfort him while his departed one lies before him, nor question him while he is making a vow, and try not to see him at the time of his humiliation.

* * *

This mishnah teaches us that the right deed must be done at the right time if it is to be effective. These examples are not specifically Jewish cases, but are general human situations which show that an intention, praiseworthy in itself, carried out at the wrong time can have unprofitable and even dangerous results. We see this truth more clearly when we consider the commandments. If, for example, someone wanted to acclaim God by observing the Shabbath rest, but not at the prescribed time appointed by God, he would not be celebrating God's Shabbath and, in addition, he would be unlawfully canceling necessary working hours. The same applies to all the commandments that have to be observed at a fixed time. The four examples cited by Rabbi Shimon, however, may be timed according to one's own judgment, and they teach us that good intentions alone are not enough. An angry person may be restrained from attacking someone else but in the heat of his anger he is not capable of listening to words of reason. The time for a mitigating word will come when his burning anger has subsided and he is once again in control of himself. Similarly, comforting a mourner on the loss of a beloved relative is a praiseworthy act, but not while his departed one still lies before him. As long as the remains of his beloved relative are not yet buried in the earth, the mourner is distraught and not capable of being comforted. Untimely comfort is ineffective and even hurtful; comfort offered during the prescribed days of mourning is helpful and healing.

In the case of someone taking a vow, we must realize that a man takes a vow upon himself only in a particularly serious moment of his life, for normally it is not permitted. "Are you not satisfied with what the Torah has prohibited, that you impose voluntary renunciation upon yourself?" ask our Sages in such a case. "One who takes a vow resembles one who builds an altar for idols, and one who fulfills it is regarded as if he had brought a sacrifice on it" (*Nedarim* 22a). Yet at certain times, when temptations or inner passions threaten to overwhelm us, it may be meritorious to strengthen our resolve with the aid of a vow. Even then, the Law provides for the annulment of the vow when factors arise that were not foreseen when the vow was taken. Asking questions to instill doubt in one who is seriously taking upon himself a permissible vow is therefore out of order and embarrassing.

The last warning in this mishnah teaches us that tact and delicacy are an essential part of compassion. When men of wealth and high position fall low they will be particularly sensitive about their honor and dignity. Do not intrude upon them when they want to be alone and unobserved, for they have not yet become reconciled to their new condition. This sensitivity is human nature; when the first human beings sinned, the Merciful One was considerate of their feelings. The Torah says specifically that God did not appear to Adam and Chavah at the moment that they sinned and felt shame. It was only after they had covered their nakedness that they heard the voice of the Lord God (*Midrash Yalkut Bereshith*, 27).

כד שְׁמוּאֵל הַקָּטָן אוֹמֵר, בִּנְפֹל אוֹיִבְךָ אַל־
תִּשְׂמָח וּבִכָּשְׁלוֹ אַל־יָגֵל לִבֶּךָ, פֶּן־יִרְאֶה
יְיָ וְרַע בְּעֵינָיו וְהֵשִׁיב מֵעָלָיו אַפּוֹ:

24 Shemuel *Ha-Katan* says: Rejoice not when your
enemy falls and let not your heart exult when he
stumbles, lest the Lord see it and be displeased and he
turn his wrath from him (*Mishlei* 24:17-18).

*   *   *

Many commentators draw attention to the fact that this saying is
taken entirely from King Shelomo's Mishlei. First, we must understand that there was never any discrepancy between the teachings of our Sages and the lives they lived. Whenever they
pronounced a saying that originated elsewhere, it was to emphasize the meaning and correctness of the thought itself. What is
most unusual in this case is that Shemuel, known as *Ha-Katan*
because he made himself "small," or humble, before others
(*Yerushalmi*, *Sotah* 9:13), is the Sage quoted in the Talmud as
saying something which seems to contradict this mishnah. In
Berachoth 28b, when Shimon *Ha-Pekuli* arranged the eighteen
benedictions of the *Amidah* prayer for *Rabban* Gamliel in Yavneh,
Rabban Gamliel then asked the Sages, "Can anyone among you
frame a benediction relating to the *Minim* (Sadducees)?" Shemuel
Ha-Katan arose and composed this benediction: "And for the
slanderers let there be no hope, and let all wickedness perish in a
moment and let all Your enemies be speedily cut off." If we were
to conclude from this, however, that the fall of Yisrael's enemies
would give satisfaction to Shemuel, we would be mistaken. This
Sage had a character of such unusual piety, modesty and self-
effacement that he was able to attain the degree of prophecy. His
mentality could not endure a base emotion such as malicious joy.
It is related that once the Sages who were gathered at Yavneh heard
a voice from Heaven saying, "There is one person here upon whom
the Divine Presence would shine but for the unworthiness of his
generation." All eyes turned to Shemuel (*Sanhedrin* 11a).

And so we see that it was only because he had such noble qualities that he was trusted to compose a prayer of negative intent against the slanderers of his time, that would be valid for all time. Anyone else might have permitted personal feelings to affect his response. Very few people are capable of repressing personal feelings completely. We understand, therefore, that his prayer is directed at an enemy that seriously endangers the congregation of God. When we study his saying in *Pirkei Avoth*, understanding the nature of the Sage makes us realize what a difficult request it is. It is not human to be without enemies; indeed, the more we adhere to the path of truth and morality, the more we are likely to have opponents who do not share our view of life. This opposition can turn into open, embittered hostility against which we are powerless, but our love of mankind must be stronger than the hatred facing us. It takes two to maintain hostility, and we can neutralize hatred only by banishing hostile feelings from our hearts. We conclude our daily prayer with the request: אלהי נצור לשוני מרע ושפתי מדבר מרמה ולמקללי נפשי תדם ונפשי כעפר לכל תהיה, "My God, guard my tongue from evil and my lips from speaking falsehood. Let my soul be silent to those who curse me, and let my soul be as the dust to all things" (*Berachoth* 17a). While it may be human nature to seek revenge and to retaliate when attacked, taking pleasure in an enemy's downfall is an undesirable trait that can neither be justified nor even excused. "Do not hate your brother in your heart...do not take revenge nor bear a grudge against the sons of your people" (*Vayyikra* 19:17-18). Even more difficult is the duty to repay, as it were, evil with good. "If your enemy is hungry, give him bread to eat, and if he is thirsty, give him water to drink, for you will heap coals of fire on his head and God will reward you" (*Mishlei* 25:21-22).

כה אֱלִישָׁע בֶּן אֲבוּיָה אוֹמֵר, הַלּוֹמֵד יֶלֶד לְמָה הוּא דוֹמֶה לִדְיוֹ כְתוּבָה עַל־נְיָר חָדָשׁ, וְהַלּוֹמֵד זָקֵן לְמָה הוּא דוֹמֶה לִדְיוֹ כְתוּבָה עַל־נְיָר מָחוּק:

25 Elisha ben Avuyah says: When one teaches a child, to what can it be compared? To ink written on clean paper. When one teaches an old man, to what can that be compared? To ink written on blotted paper.

*   *   *

Elisha ben Avuyah proved the truth of his saying in his own life. He was the only one among the thousands of great Sages in Yisrael who became an apostate and set himself apart from his people. His companions then called him Acher ("different"). Among the reasons usually given for this extraordinary occurrence are the foreign influences brought to bear upon him at an early age in his father's house. Apart from the great men of Yerushalayim, many famous Romans visited the house. Elisha soon adopted Greek culture and mores, absorbing both good habits and bad.

Whenever, throughout the Torah, the expression of God's will is introduced with the word לאמר (saying), we understand that we must take particular care to pass the request on and to keep it alive for all time. Furthermore, Avraham became the ancestor of God's people solely because he impressed the words of God's Law upon his children and his household (*Bereshith* 18:19). Moshe *Rabbenu*, in his parting words to his flock, bade them to teach God's words diligently to their children (*Devarim* 6:7). Our ancestors were always preoccupied with the education of young impressionable minds and took great care that their first and principal lessons would be Torah.

As soon as a child is able to speak, his father must teach him Torah and the reading of the *Shema*. What is meant by

Torah? "Moshe commanded us the Torah, a heritage of the congregation of Ya'akov" (*Devarim* 33:4). What is meant by the *Shema*? "Hear O Yisrael, the Lord is our God, the Lord is One" (ibid. 6:4).

(Sukkah 42a)

A child must be taught in early youth, when his heart is still pure and not filled with other thoughts, that which should remain his inalienable possession throughout life. Acher sought to destroy the spiritual seed that he had sown himself, as Elisha ben Avuyah, and ultimately tried to drive students away from their studies in Torah academies. "What are you doing here?" he would say to the students. "You are a mason by trade, you a carpenter, you a painter and you a tailor. Why are you wasting your time with the Torah?" (*Yerushalmi, Chagigah* 2:1). Unfortunately, even today some people regard worldly life and its material demands as the first and only aim of education. They seriously believe that our sacred heritage—the words of the Torah, the prophets and King David, the historical record of our people, the Law and purpose of our life as explained in the Talmud—is only meant for people who are to become rabbis one day. When we withhold Torah from our children, when it is not the first thing we teach them, when it is not the ultimate goal and purpose of acquiring all other knowledge, we rob them of their most precious heritage. The Avoth of Rabbi Nathan (ch. 24) relates the maxim in this way: "He [Elisha ben Avuyah] would say that one who learns Torah in his youth will acquire its words as his own and they will flow smoothly from his mouth. That is the meaning of the proverb, 'If you have not desired them in your youth, how will you acquire them in your old age?'"

The Sifrei on *Parashath Ekev* (ch. 34) tells us: "Rabbi Shimon ben Yochai taught: 'The sated soul has no taste for the sweetest honey'(*Mishlei* 27:7), that is, a sated soul is a person who did not study in his youth, 'but to the hungry soul every bitter thing tastes sweet' (ibid.), that is, a hungry soul is a person who has studied since childhood." The image of the ink and the paper shows us that what matters in teaching is not the method used to teach, but the content of the message taught and the personal way in which the message is delivered. Just as a beautiful letter can be written with bad ink and an ugly letter with fine ink, similarly, the best pedagogic rules cannot achieve any success when applied by an incompetent teacher; a capable teacher, however, can succeed without clever devices or fancy methods. This truth we learn from God's commandment, "And you shall teach them diligently to your children" (*Devarim* 6:7), which turns all fathers into teachers with or without benefit of a teaching diploma. The chief lesson of this saying is: It is never too early to initiate the education and instruction of our children in the precepts of the Torah; anything omitted in the formative years will be difficult to make up for later.

כו

רַבִּי יוֹסֵי בַּר יְהוּדָה אִישׁ כְּפַר הַבַּבְלִי
אוֹמֵר, הַלּוֹמֵד מִן־הַקְּטַנִּים לְמָה הוּא
דּוֹמֶה לְאוֹכֵל עֲנָבִים קֵהוֹת וְשׁוֹתֶה יַיִן מִגִּתּוֹ,
וְהַלּוֹמֵד מִן־הַזְּקֵנִים לְמָה הוּא דוֹמֶה לְאוֹכֵל עֲנָבִים
בְּשׁוּלוֹת וְשׁוֹתֶה יַיִן יָשָׁן:

26 Rabbi Yosei bar Yehudah, from Kefar Ha-Bavli, says: He who learns from young men is like one who eats unripe grapes and drinks wine from the wine press; he who learns from old men is like one who eats ripe grapes and drinks old wine.

*   *   *

Just as youth is the most suitable time for learning, so maturity is the fitting time for teaching. This is especially true of Torah study. You might think that the age of a teacher is not so important, since the Torah is whole and complete and needs only to be passed on from father to son and from teacher to pupil. There is however, an essential difference between the instruction of a mature, experienced teacher and that of a young, inexperienced one. The unripe grape, though already a grape, is not only sour but unhealthy to eat; unfermented wine may be sweet but it, too, is not so healthy. What is lacking in the unripe grape and the unfermented wine? The grape needs the sun in order to ripen and the wine needs to have its impurities removed. Experience in life is the sun that ripens one's knowledge and the strainer that clarifies the mind.

The Sifrei on *Parashath Ekev* explains this idea with two verses: "Your love is better than wine" (*Shir Ha-Shirim* 1:2), and "With aged men there is wisdom, and in length of days understanding" (*Iyyov* 12:12). Love of Torah is like wine; it has the taste of wine even when it is new, but improves as it ages. Yet, as the Talmud reminds us in Shabbath 152a, "Rabbi Yishmael, son of Rabbi Yosei, said: 'With aged men there is wisdom...' (ibid.)—wise men grow wiser with the increasing wisdom they acquire, but ignorant men become more foolish as they grow older, as it is said, 'He removes the speech of trusted men and takes away the understanding of the elders' (*Iyyov* 12:20)." Do not think, therefore, that age in itself always qualifies a teacher. Old age without useful experience, a mind that has not benefited from thought and study, from the events of a lifetime, cannot guard against folly. In such a case, it is better to be taught by a worthy youth who understands the purpose of life at an early age than by a foolish old man.

כז רַבִּי מֵאִיר אוֹמֵר, אַל־תִּסְתַּכֵּל בַּקַּנְקַן אֶלָּא בְּמָה שֶׁיֶּשׁ־בּוֹ, יֵשׁ קַנְקַן חָדָשׁ מָלֵא יָשָׁן וְיָשָׁן שֶׁאֲפִילוּ חָדָשׁ אֵין בּוֹ:

27 Rabbi Meir says: Look not at the vessel but at its contents. A new vessel may be full of old wine and an old vessel may not contain even new wine.

*   *   *

This maxim is a logical corollary to the two previous sayings, and all three point to fairly obvious truths which recent generations have found easy to ignore or misunderstand. The so-called Reform Movement despises the lessons of the past, drawing inspiration only from modern ideas. They do not consider the essence of a thought but reject it outright because of its form. Our fathers taught: בנין ילדים סתירה וסתירת זקנים בנין, "The building by youth is destruction, whilst even the destruction by the old is building" (*Nedarim* 40a). Pure wine is derived from the grape only after pressing, treading and further refining. We today require a comparable process of purification in order to see the realization of our ancient ideals, to see our grandchildren inspired by the spirit of our great ancestors. "Happy is our youth that has not disgraced our old age" (*Sukkah* 53a).

כ‍ח

רַבִּי אֶלְעָזָר הַקַּפָּר אוֹמֵר, הַקִּנְאָה
וְהַתַּאֲוָה וְהַכָּבוֹד מוֹצִיאִים אֶת הָאָדָם מִן
הָעוֹלָם:

28 Rabbi Elazar Ha-Kappar says: Envy, lust and thirst for honor drive a man from this world.

*   *   *

Envy combines several vices into one: it piles insatiable greed onto inordinate pride and tops them with misanthropy. It not only seeks to destroy the happiness of others, but it also erodes the tranquillity of the person in whose heart it has settled. It breeds maliciousness, injustice, hypocrisy and hatred; what it cannot possess it will ruin. Jealousy, lust and immoderate ambition will surely cause a man great sorrow, but can it drive him from this world? How are we to understand Rabbi Elazar's words? The first sins mentioned in the Torah were precisely these. The first murder in this world arose from envy, and was indeed punished with expulsion from God's world. The greedy craving for ever-more worldly pleasures brought man so low that human life was almost extinguished on earth by the flood. And thirst for honor turned homogeneous mankind into a multilingual multitude that never again knew peace or tranquillity on this earth. And what happened to Kayin (Cain) also happened to Korach, Bilam, Do'eg, Achithofel, Geichazi, Avshalom, Adoniyyah, Uzziyyahu and Haman: "One who sets his eyes on things to which he has no right will not obtain what he seeks, and what he already possesses will be taken from him" (*Sotah* 9a).

The Sayings of the Fathers have listed a series of things which "drive a man from this world." Idleness and morning sleep, wine at noon, pride, anger and hatred are all such vices (*Avoth* 2:16, 3:14), but Rabbi Elazar indicates that envy, greed and thirst for honor comprise all the other vices. For one thing, the other vices tend to dominate man only at certain times; but none of these three can ever be shaken free once it takes control. "Envy rots the bones" (*Mishlei* 14:30), and "slays the fool" (*Iyyov* 5:2). "Deferred hope makes the heart sick but a wish which has come true is a tree of life" (*Mishlei* 13:12). If a fulfilled wish resembles a life-giving tree, then ungratified desire is a tree of poison, consuming you and shortening your life. These three passions are thirsts that can never be quenched, obsessions that involve even the most trivial matters and never let you rest. Some other passions may be temporarily satisfied. The victims of these three, however, cannot be redeemed.

כט הוּא הָיָה אוֹמֵר, הַיְלוֹדִים לָמוּת וְהַמֵּתִים לְהֵחָיוֹת וְהַחַיִּים לִדּוֹן, לֵידַע וּלְהוֹדִיעַ וּלְהִוָּדַע, שֶׁהוּא אֵל הוּא הַיּוֹצֵר הוּא הַבּוֹרֵא הוּא הַמֵּבִין הוּא הַדַּיָּן הוּא הָעֵד הוּא בַּעַל דִּין הוּא עָתִיד לָדוֹן. בָּרוּךְ הוּא, שֶׁאֵין לְפָנָיו לֹא עַוְלָה וְלֹא שִׁכְחָה וְלֹא מַשּׂוֹא פָנִים וְלֹא מִקַּח שֹׁחַד, שֶׁהַכֹּל שֶׁלּוֹ. וְדַע שֶׁהַכֹּל לְפִי הַחֶשְׁבּוֹן, וְאַל־יַבְטִיחֲךָ יִצְרְךָ שֶׁהַשְּׁאוֹל בֵּית מָנוֹס לָךְ, שֶׁעַל כָּרְחֲךָ אַתָּה נוֹצָר וְעַל כָּרְחֲךָ אַתָּה נוֹלָד וְעַל כָּרְחֲךָ אַתָּה חַי וְעַל כָּרְחֲךָ אַתָּה מֵת וְעַל כָּרְחֲךָ אַתָּה עָתִיד לִתֵּן דִּין וְחֶשְׁבּוֹן לִפְנֵי מֶלֶךְ מַלְכֵי הַמְּלָכִים הַקָּדוֹשׁ בָּרוּךְ הוּא:

29 He would say: Those who are born are destined to die, the dead to rise again and the living to be judged; in order to know, to teach, and to make it known that there is a God, that He is the maker, He is the creator, He is the discerner, He is the judge, He is the witness, He is the plaintiff, He will judge in the future. Blessed is He, for in His presence there is no wrongdoing, no forgetting, no favoritism, no bribe-taking, for all is His. Know also that everything will happen according to the reckoning. And do not let your desire persuade you that the grave will be a refuge for you, for against your will you were formed, against your will you were born, against your will you live and against your will you shall die, and against your will you shall have to give acount and reckoning before the supreme King, the Holy One, blessed is He.

* * *

THAT THERE IS A GOD is the chief point of this saying. The highlights of human existence—birth, death, resurrection and final judgment—are merely signposts along the way of man to one end and purpose: the acknowledgment of the existence of God. Each signpost marks off stages in man's existence, both his temporal and his eternal existence, and each of them is a wondrous puzzle for human intelligence to grapple with. We can perceive the temporal state, between birth and death, although we cannot explain it; the state after death is beyond our knowledge or comprehension. The more that science teaches us about the temporal state, the more it convinces us that the mechanism of the cosmic system is incomprehensible to us. Yet our own inextinguishable thirst for knowledge is splendid confirmation of the higher nature that is within ourselves, and that must somehow be related to the Highest Being. All the insoluble mysteries of life that astonish us with their perfection are a manifestation of the One Who provided them for us and a reminder of the One Who alone can solve them. Even our evil inclinations are part of this mysterious harmony in that they can be turned to good by our own efforts and self-control.

THOSE WHO ARE BORN ARE DESTINED TO DIE. Rabbi Elazar Ha-Kappar might easily have said, "Those who live are destined to die," or, more logically, "Man is destined to die." The significance of his choice of words, הילודים, "infants—those who are born of humans," carries a deeper meaning. Every living creature must die, yes; but man alone has a mortal frame which clothes an immortal soul, the Divine spirit breathed into him by his Creator. "And the Lord God formed man from the dust of the ground, and breathed into his nostrils the breath of life; thus man became a living being" (*Bereshith* 2:7). Man is composed of two elements: a material body and a spiritual soul. Death can only claim the material part, the dust which returns to the earth; his immortal soul returns to God. How do we know that body and soul will arise again and be united and judged in eternal existence? The resurrection and reunion of these elements in another state of existence is not stated explicitly in the Torah, but the Sages have deduced it from many references and hold the opinion that it is so clearly true and logical that it is taken for granted.

How foolish it is to go about our daily business and forget that we continuously draw nearer to the hour of our judgment. Yet most people do not like to be scolded; man cannot bear rebuke. "Abba Kohen Bardela said: Woe betide the day of judgment, woe betide the day of reproof. Bilam, the wise man of the Gentiles, was unable to withstand the rebuke of his donkey...Yosef's brothers, all older than he, could not bear his rebuke...how much more so will we suffer when we are called to account by God?" (*Midrash Rabbah, Bereshith* 93:10). We also read, "If they were wise, they would understand this, they would consider their own last days" (*Devarim* 32:29). The thought of death by itself, however, will not move a man to reflect on his behavior during his temporal existence. If death were truly the end, it would be the haven and refuge of wicked men. Most people act as if they think that they will never leave this world, and they give no thought whatsoever to their death, even though there are intimations of their eventual demise all around them, in every facial wrinkle and every gray hair and in every internal impulse of their better selves to rebel against the material temptations which surround them. Why is this so? Because they regard the present moment as complete. Would they but listen to the words of the Wise King:

> Rejoice, young man, in your childhood, let your heart cheer you in the days of your youth;
>
> Follow the path of your heart and the sight of your eyes—but be aware that for all these things God will call you to account.
>
> Rather banish anger from your heart and remove evil from your flesh—for childhood and youth are futile.
>
> So remember your Creator in the days of your youth...
>
> Before the silver cord snaps and the golden bowl is shattered, and the pitcher is broken at the fountain, and the wheel is smashed at the cistern.
>
> Then the dust will return to the earth as it was, and the spirit will return to God Who bestowed it.
>
> Vanity of vanities, said Koheleth; all is vanity.
>
> (*Koheleth* 11:9-12:7)

IN ORDER TO KNOW, TO TEACH AND TO MAKE IT KNOWN. All that happens to man in his temporal existence and all that will happen to him after he leaves it, occurs for the primary, transcendental purpose of acknowledging God's existence: to learn about it, to teach it to our children and to make it known by our own behavior, so that the knowledge will spread in ever-widening circles until all mankind will know and acknowledge this fact. You may have learned it in your youth as theoretical knowledge, but it did not fill your heart and arouse you to act upon it. "Beware that you do not forget the Lord, your God, by not keeping His commandments..." (*Devarim* 8:11). The holy bond (*kiddushin*) that binds husband and wife in a Jewish marriage is very similar to the holy bond that exists between God and every soul who faithfully tries to fulfill His commandments. In every blessing that we utter, the words: אשר קדשנו במצותיו, "Who has sanctified us with His commandments," remind us that both the *mitzvoth* and *kiddushin* link us directly to God. Neglect of the commandments leads to forgetting God, Who is the very reason and purpose of our existence; observance of the commandments is our link to God, a link that extends beyond the grave.

THAT HE IS THE MAKER, HE IS THE CREATOR. The commentators differ on the interpretation of the words יוצר, "the Maker" or "Former," and בורא, "the Creator," as they are used in this mishnah. Rabbi Elazar Ha-Kappar says "the Maker" first and then "the Creator." According to one view, God has formed objects in the world in a way that reveals their intrinsic created character. The marble in a slab was created by God, but it is worked by the artisan into a form which is subject to and limited by the inherent characteristics of the stone. Human logic tells us, therefore, that creation preceded formation; therefore, we must ask why the order of the words is reversed in this mishnah. We can grasp the idea that God's influence on the spiritual side of man accords with the spiritual nature of the Divinity, and we can also perceive that His Presence is manifested to us in the forms and shapes of terrestrial existence. However, the whole subject of how Divine design is manifested materially presents an insoluble mystery for us. God's influence on the spiritual side of man is clearer to us because it is more in accordance with His purely spiritual character. The Sage therefore transmits the lesson in an ascending order: God is not only "the Maker," a fact which we can see in His miraculous works, but also "the Creator," a fact which is inscrutable to us, but which we can rely on as a fundamental truth, as it is said, "In the beginning, God created the Heaven and the earth" (*Bereshith* 1:1).

HE IS THE DISCERNER. God is not only the Creator and the Maker of the universe—of the whole and of every part—but He is also aware of everything that transpires in it. As it is said, "He Who implants the ear, shall He not hear? He Who forms the eye, shall He not see? He Who teaches man knowledge, shall He not know?" (*Tehillim* 94:9-10); and, "The Lord looks down from Heaven...upon all the inhabitants of the earth. He fashions their hearts together; He discerns all their deeds" (ibid. 33:13-15). The Talmud helps us to understand the last verse. "Rabbi Levi said: From the fact that God fashioned all men's hearts alike, we can deduce that God not only knows human deeds, but He even knows them beforehand, when they are still in men's hearts" (*Yerushalmi, Rosh Hashanah* 1:3). Similarly, Rabbi Elazar said: Master of the universe! What is easier for a potter, to make a hundred jugs or to inspect them? Probably to inspect them. Rabbi Abbin said: He Who alone in His world has created all hearts, therefore also has a knowledge of their deeds long before they perform them" (ibid.). Thus we see that, just as Rabbi Levi concludes from the fact that God is "the Maker," so is he "the Discerner," similarly, Rabbi Elazar and Rabbi Abbin conclude this from the fact that He is "the Creator," and Rabbi Elazar Ha-Kappar affirms this from the fact that He is both "the Maker" and "the Creator."

HE IS THE JUDGE...THE WITNESS...[AND] THE PLAINTIFF, HE WILL JUDGE IN THE FUTURE. When God's judgment acquits us, then no power on earth can find anything against us, and when the Judge of truth finds us guilty, then neither king nor good connections can protect us from Divine justice. Likewise, only the Divine Witness can attest to thoughts, intentions and feelings as well as the deed itself; His evidence is irrefutable and stands firm against "the sorcerers...the adulterers...the false swearers and those who oppress the hireling...the widow and the orphan, and who turn aside the stranger from his right, not fearing Me, says the Lord of Hosts" (*Malachi* 3:5). For the wrongs we do to our fellowmen, they will one day act as plaintiffs against us; but for the wrongs we do to God—our moral transgressions— God will Himself be the Plaintiff. Furthermore, even if our case may be postponed for some time, it will definitely be judged one day in the future. Complete understanding of this concept is movingly described in the Talmud:

> When *Rabban* Yochanan was ailing, his disciples found him weeping...[He explained to them the reason:] If I were being taken today before a human king who is here today and tomorrow in the grave, whose anger does not last forever, who cannot imprison me forever and who cannot sentence me to everlasting death, who can be persuaded with words and bribed with money, even then would I weep.
>
> Now that I am being taken before the supreme King, the Holy One, blessed is He, Who lives and endures forever, Whose anger is everlasting, Who can imprison me forever or sentence me to death everlasting, and Who cannot be persuaded with words nor bribed with money—nay, more!— when there are two ways before me, one leading to the Garden of Eden and the other to *Gehinnom*, and I do not know by which I shall be taken, shall I now not weep?
>
> (*Berachoth* 28b).

As certain as we are that God will one day judge everyone and everything, final judgment is veiled in deep, insoluble mysteries for us, mysteries which may be alluded to in the reverse order of this mishnah. That is, in a worldly court, the plaintiff offers evidence first, then the witness corroborates it, and finally the judge passes sentence. The reversed order of these words in this saying tells us something important: There is no comparison between earthly justice and Divine justice. The transcendence of God's future judgment is the mightiest incentive for devoting ourselves ardently to our moral duty, serving Him.

IN HIS PRESENCE THERE IS NO WRONGDOING, NO FOR-
GETTING, NO FAVORITISM, NO BRIBE-TAKING. At God's tribunal, right, justice and integrity are intrinsic; why then even
mention wrongdoing? God knows all; why mention forgetting?
And since there is no way to suborn God, for He is perfect and
lacks nothing, how can the Sage speak of bribes? The Rambam
comments that Rabbi Elazar must be referring to שוחד מצוות,
"bribery through obeying the commandments." Do not imagine
that a righteous person who piles up a large number of good
deeds to his credit will escape punishment for the one or two small
sins he may have committed. The Sages all teach that this is not true,
for that would indeed be bribery. As it is said, וסביביו נשערה מאד,
"... round about Him it storms most severely" (*Tehillim* 50:3), and
the Sages explain: הקב"ה מדקדק עם סביביו אפילו כחוט השערה, that God
is very precise with those who stand round about Him [that is, the
righteous] and does not leave unpunished even the smallest sins
committed by them (*Yevamoth* 121b). Also, the verse, "A God of
faithfulness and without iniquity" (*Devarim* 32:4) indicates to us
that punishment will be exacted of the wicked in the World to
Come, even for the slightest transgression; it will be exacted of
the righteous, too, but for them, in this world (*Ta'anith* 11a). The
Rambam's explanation of bribery as "bribery through obeying
the commandments" needs further elucidation. With every *mitzvah* that we obey, we further our own welfare and that of society
as a whole. With every transgression that we commit, we spread
harm and corruption in the world. That is why the individual
good deed cannot cancel the sinful deed, and cannot be used as a
bribe to affect our destiny. Divine judgment takes into account
both the deed and its effect in the overall scheme of things, "for
all is His."

KNOW ALSO THAT EVERYTHING WILL HAPPEN ACCORD-
ING TO THE RECKONING. This mishnah gathers together an
extraordinary number of concepts basic to Jewish thought. It
encompasses, as we have seen, the span of man's existence from
before his birth until his eternal destiny, and tells us clearly that
the sole purpose of his entire existence is to proclaim the existence of God. It tells us that life itself attests to the existence of

God, and this idea emphasizes that, even though we cannot fully comprehend how, everything in creation is one continuous, harmonious whole, lasting from the beginning to the end of days. Every atom, every action is calculated and foreseen and has its place in the totality of God's reckoning.

AND DO NOT LET YOUR DESIRE PERSUADE YOU THAT THE GRAVE WILL BE A REFUGE FOR YOU. Rabbi Elazar returns to his starting point: All men are destined to die, but do not hope that the grave will be an escape for you. If, during your lifetime, you have forgotten all that Rabbi Elazar speaks about in this saying, you may well ask yourself why you should worry about your behavior since death is inevitable in any case. The Talmud tells us:

> Rabbi Yehudah ben Rabbi Nachmani explained the meaning of the verse, "Trust not in a friend; do not rely on the Master" (*Michah* 7:5). The friend is the evil inclination; if he says to you, "Sin and the Holy One will pardon," do not believe him. The Master is the Holy One, blessed is He. If you will ask, "Who testifies against me?" the stones of the house and the beams thereof where your sin was committed will testify against you. Rabbi Zerika said, "The two angels that always accompany you will testify against you"; and others say, "Your limbs will testify against you."
>
> (*Chagigah* 16a)

Know that you have no control whatever over your creation, your birth, or your death, and that you cannot escape giving an accounting for all your deeds. "The Rabbis said: When a man departs to his eternal abode, all his deeds are recounted to him in detail and he replies, 'Yes, that is so.' He is then requested to sign for them and he signs. What is more, he then acknowledges the justice of the verdict and says, 'You have judged me well' " (*Ta'anith* 11a). Rabbi Acha remarks: "It is said, 'A lamp of God is man's soul, probing all inner chambers' (*Mishlei* 20:27). Just as worldly kings have informants who report every single matter to them, so the Holy One, blessed is He, has his informants reporting to him everything that man does in secret...that is, man's

soul...[men] are astonished when God calls to account every individual...That is similar to one who has married the king's daughter and cannot imagine how the king knows all that he does
wrong in his home" (*Pesikta Rabbathi*).

FOR AGAINST YOUR WILL YOU WERE FORMED. Since you
were placed in the world against your will, perhaps you will
suppose that you cannot therefore be held responsible for your
deeds. If you had a choice, you may claim, you might have chosen
to forego all the pleasures of this world in order to be sure of your
place in the World to Come. That is not possible either, as we
learn from this parable of Rabbi Ya'akov, the Dubnow *maggid*:

> Once there was a happily married couple. The husband was
> ugly and deaf and the wife was blind and quarrelsome.
> Because of her blindness, she had no idea how ugly her
> husband was and because of his deafness, he was not dis-
> turbed by her nagging. One day they heard of the miracle
> cures of a famous doctor and they decided to ask him to heal
> their infirmities. The doctor demanded a high fee which
> they gladly agreed to pay.
>
> The cure was successful. The husband regained his hearing
> and the wife regained her sight. But that ended their matrimo-
> nial peace; the husband now heard his wife's scolding and the
> wife was disgusted by her husband's ugliness. When the doctor
> presented his bill for payment, they not only refused to pay,
> but even demanded compensation from him.
>
> The doctor finally agreed to their demands but made the
> following stipulation: Since he had caused their unhappiness
> with his cure, he insisted upon restoring their happiness by
> returning to them their infirmities. They did not agree to
> this either. "By not agreeing to my stipulation," the doctor
> told them, "you prove that you are now happier than you
> were before, so you must pay me."

This is man's dilemma. It is true that we came into this world
without volition and must live our lives and die against our will;
nevertheless, we are responsible for what we do with our lives
while they are ours to live, and God will hold us to account for it.

Perek Five

בַּעֲשָׂרָה מַאֲמָרוֹת נִבְרָא הָעוֹלָם. וּמַה **א**
תַּלְמוּד לוֹמַר, וַהֲלֹא בְּמַאֲמָר אֶחָד יָכוֹל
לְהִבָּרְאוֹת, אֶלָּא לְהִפָּרַע מִן־הָרְשָׁעִים שֶׁמְּאַבְּדִים
אֶת־הָעוֹלָם שֶׁנִּבְרָא בַּעֲשָׂרָה מַאֲמָרוֹת וְלִתֵּן שָׂכָר
טוֹב לַצַּדִּיקִים שֶׁמְּקַיְּמִין אֶת־הָעוֹלָם שֶׁנִּבְרָא
בַּעֲשָׂרָה מַאֲמָרוֹת:

1 By ten utterances the world was created. What does that teach us? Could it not have been created by one utterance? It is only to call to account the lawless who destroy the world that was created by ten utterances, and to give good reward to the righteous who preserve the world that was created by ten utterances.

* * *

It is generally accepted by Torah authorities in the Talmud, Midrash and Pirkei de Rabbi Eliezer that these ten utterances were those stated in the first chapter of Bereshith: "God said, Let there be light...; Let there be a firmament...; Let the waters gather together...; Let the earth sprout...; Let there be lights...; Let the waters swarm...; Let the earth bring forth the living creatures...; Let us make man...; Be fruitful and multiply." These are nine. The tenth was the beginning of Creation itself: בראשית ברא אלהים את השמים ואת הארץ, "For a beginning God created the Heaven and the earth." This point is stressed in Tehillim: "By the word of God the heavens were made and by the breath of His mouth all their

363

host" (33:6). The expression ויאמר אלהים, "God said," is to be understood in a figurative sense; God's pronouncements are described in the form of utterances in order to facilitate human understanding of the Divine will. Nine utterances were directed to objects: to the water—to gather together, to the earth—to grow plants, and so on. The first utterance was not addressed to any object because there were none; heaven and earth themselves were called into being out of nothing (*ex nihilo*), thereby invalidating any theory of the eternity of space.

Considering that the world was not created all at once, as it just as well might have been, but in ten stages beginning with heaven and earth and culminating in the creation of man and in the pronouncement of man's custodianship of the world, we must realize that man is the final aim, the crown of the whole creation. Each stage served as a foundation for the one following it, until ultimately, the heavens above and the whole earth with all its vegetable, mineral and animal potential was laid at man's feet to serve him in his purpose. This fact is reflected on every page of the Torah and throughout recorded history. All the nations retell the legend of a great flood which depleted the earth of its inhabitants. The Torah, however, relates the whole incident in detail, and explains that the flood was caused by man's iniquity. Because of man's depravity the whole world was destroyed; such is the power of wicked men. Yet the Torah also tells of men who contributed to the preservation of the world. Yitzchak increased the world's food supply; Ya'akov warded off the devastation of a vast famine; Aharon stopped a plague that threatened to decimate the human race. Such is the power of the righteous. This is the obvious meaning of the mishnah, but this would apply if the world had been called into being through one single utterance of God as well. Our imagination can hardly encompass one such act of creation, much less a tenfold one, and so we must pause to wonder what it means.

Let us select the utterance, "Let there be light." We have observed that light works according to certain laws, and the regularity with which this has been happening for centuries induces us to say of these and similar laws of nature that they are eternal, inviolable laws. Any deviation from these laws would seem to be supernatural. If a sudden cessation of light on earth were to occur, if the sun and the moon suddenly stopped in their courses, we would hardly believe it, even if we saw it for ourselves. Very few of us realize that the continuous, unbroken regularity of any law of nature is perhaps a greater miracle than its interruption. What appears miraculous to us is actually the discredit of our assumption that the laws of nature are eternal. When we learn from God's Word that the light ceased shining in Egypt for three days to punish the tyrannical Pharaoh, or that at Yehoshua's request the earth's revolution was stopped and the sun "stood still," then we understand that neither the light nor the laws of light are absolutely inviolable. Light was created in the original state of darkness through one of God's ten special pronouncements. When, in the course of time, the light was withdrawn, it was in order to educate mankind, "to call to account the lawless who destroy the world that was created by ten utterances."

The utterance, "Let the waters gather together" teaches us that the waters were originally spread over the entire earth. Therefore, a flood that covered the whole world and restored it to its original condition is not as miraculous, so to speak, as the remarkable world system of waterways that was created. Each of the ten parts of Creation seems to be a potential force that was called into being and which would eventually provide retribution to the wicked and reward to the righteous. The gradual unfolding of Creation teaches us that God is Lord and Master over all of nature as well as King over the world of man. Thus, Rabbi Yochanan connects the ten verses of homage due to our King (which we say on Rosh Hashanah in the *Musaf* prayer when we are standing before God, the King of kings) with these ten utterances of Creation (*Rosh Hashanah* 32a).

עֲשָׂרָה דוֹרוֹת מֵאָדָם וְעַד נֹחַ, לְהוֹדִיעַ
כַּמָּה אֶרֶךְ אַפַּיִם לְפָנָיו, שֶׁכָּל הַדּוֹרוֹת הָיוּ
מַכְעִיסִים לְפָנָיו עַד שֶׁהֵבִיא עֲלֵיהֶם אֶת־מֵי הַמַּבּוּל:

2 There were ten generations from Adam to Noach,
to show how long-suffering He is, seeing that all these
generations acted contrary to His will, until He
brought upon them the waters of the Flood.

עֲשָׂרָה דוֹרוֹת מִנֹּחַ וְעַד אַבְרָהָם, לְהוֹדִיעַ
כַּמָּה אֶרֶךְ אַפַּיִם לְפָנָיו, שֶׁכָּל־הַדּוֹרוֹת
הָיוּ מַכְעִיסִים לְפָנָיו עַד שֶׁבָּא אַבְרָהָם אָבִינוּ וְקִבֵּל
שָׂכָר כֻּלָּם:

3 There were ten generations from Noach to
Avraham, to show how long-suffering He is, seeing
that all these generations acted contrary to His will,
until our father Avraham came and earned for himself the merit of them all.

*   *   *

The ten generations from Adam to Noach encompassed one
thousand, six hundred and fifty-six years, from the Creation to
the Flood. The ten generations from Noach to Avraham lasted
three hundred and forty-eight years. The two thousand years of
these twenty generations represent the אלפיים תוהו, the time of
historical chaos, during which mankind apparently evinced no
trace of intellectual or spiritual development. This being so, the
mishnah addresses the question of why each of these generations
is listed by name in the Torah. The fact that God brought about
the extinction of all mankind because of its moral corruption, and
that only Noach and his family were saved, does not logically
require us to know the names of all those whose offspring perished. The mishnah explains to us that the ten generations are
mentioned by name in the Torah to emphasize to us that God did

not punish man each time he sinned greatly. Rather, He held His anger, waited patiently, as it were, for a long time before letting loose His retribution in the devastating Flood. Difficult as it may be, we should all learn from this to be patient when things do not turn out as we would like them to. If we were able to plan our destinies, our human short-sightedness would probably arrange for everything that man does in this world to be acknowledged and recompensed immediately, good for good and bad for bad. If you stop to think about it for a moment, you will realize that this would immediately cancel the very freedom of will which raises us above the other creatures.

The nightingale sings beautifully, the dog scents a track, the hyena mangles its prey, the snake envenoms other creatures— none of these deserve praise or reprimand, reward or punishment for their actions. They cannot change their behavior; only man is capable of doing good and evil. He alone, therefore, deserves either reward or punishment for his actions. If this reward or punishment were administered immediately, however, he would soon adapt his behavior accordingly and his choice would not really be free. If our fathers' good deeds had been recompensed completely and at once, we, their children and grandchildren, would not benefit from their merit at all. Imagine our despair if we had only the little good we do ourselves to rely on! But נוצר חסד לאלפים, God "repays goodness to thousands of generations." When Moshe *Rabbenu* asked God for an insight into His unfathomable rule of the universe, he was told that forbearance is one of the Divine methods of government. We will never be able to comprehend what this means. We know that the Omniscient God did not wait, so to speak, for ten generations, expecting moral improvement in the people. The Omniscient was fully "aware" that such a return would not take place. Even after a cataclysmic flood, ten more generations continued to rebel against God's Law. These ten generations surely deserved harsher treatment than the first ten, yet God sent Avraham שקיבל שכר כלם, "who earned for himself the merit of them all" — whose greatness was able to atone for all the generations of wrongdoing. We cannot comprehend such forbearance, but we must not forget it.

זְעֲשָׂרָה נִסְיוֹנוֹת נִתְנַסָּה אַבְרָהָם אָבִינוּ
וְעָמַד בְּכֻלָּם, לְהוֹדִיעַ כַּמָּה חִבָּתוֹ שֶׁל־
אַבְרָהָם אָבִינוּ:

4 Our father Avraham was tested with ten trials and he stood firm through them all, to show how great the love of our father Avraham was for God.

*   *   *

The ten tests of Avraham were:

1) when Nimrod threw him into a furnace to see if his faith would waver;

2) when he was commanded to leave home and family, never to settle in any place permanently;

3) when a severe famine forced him to go down to Egypt;

4) when his wife Sarah was seized, first by Pharaoh and later by Avimelech;

5) when he had to fight against five mighty kings in order to save his nephew Lot;

6) when he was allowed to foresee that his descendants would be slaves and strangers in far-off lands and have great difficulty in perpetuating his teachings;

7) when he had to send Hagar away;

8) when the banishing of Yishmael, his firstborn son, prevented him from supervising his education;

9) when he was commanded to circumcise himself;

10) when he was commanded to sacrifice his son Yitzchak.

The obvious question about this mishnah is: Why did God have to test Avraham when He knew in advance how Avraham would respond? The answer, of course, lies in the second half of the mishnah, but it is not necessarily self-explanatory.

TO SHOW HOW GREAT THE LOVE OF OUR FATHER AVRAHAM WAS FOR GOD. Avraham's understanding and knowledge of God was unique in his time. It was apparently the Divine intention that this knowledge be disseminated in the world through Avraham and his descendants. Ordinary teaching from father to son would not have accomplished this on a large enough scale. Avraham's trials became public knowledge. Through them, his select status with the One God, and all his actions and behavior, were widely publicized. The unique covenant that God made with Avraham and his descendants was not made in order to show favoritism to a chosen few; it was made to set an example for mankind through Avraham's unparalleled devotion to the will of God and his pure, selfless love for God. All of humanity was supposed to learn from Avraham's example. That is why God sent these trials to Avraham and is still sending trials to us. Testing wicked people will not provide the desired results; it is the best people who are tested. God's trials are to show mankind how a pious, moral person is capable of rising to great heights. "My son, despise not the chastening of the Lord, neither be weary of His correction; for whom the Lord loves, He corrects, even as a father corrects a son in whom he delights" (*Mishlei* 3:11-12).

Our Sages explain the verse צדיק יבחן יי, "The Lord tests the righteous" (*Tehillim* 11:5) in the same vein: "When the potter wants to test his wares he strikes the pots, but not the flawed ones which would fall to pieces; he strikes the strong ones that will stand up to the blow" (*Bereshith Rabbah* 55:2). The prophets, too, mention Avraham's special status: "Look unto the rock from which you are hewn, and to the hole of the pit out of which you are dug. Look unto Avraham, your father, and unto Sarah who bore you; for I called him alone and blessed him and made him many" (*Yeshayahu* 51:1-2). And truly, Yisrael as a whole has faced its trials in the spirit of its father Avraham, and countless individuals have proved by their acts that Avraham's love of God was also in their hearts. Avraham heeded God's call to leave his home and family, just as his descendants today leave hearth and home and stand up to many trials as worthy sons of his. They do not lose confidence in their God though they suffer hunger and sorrow, want and distress, and they still introduce every newborn male child into Avraham's covenant, not with a sigh, but with delight and joyful celebration.

ה**עֲשָׂרָה נִסִּים נַעֲשׂוּ לַאֲבוֹתֵינוּ בְּמִצְרַיִם
וַעֲשָׂרָה עַל הַיָּם. עֶשֶׂר מַכּוֹת הֵבִיא
הַקָּדוֹשׁ בָּרוּךְ הוּא עַל הַמִּצְרִיִּים בְּמִצְרַיִם וְעֶשֶׂר עַל
הַיָּם:**

5 Ten miracles were wrought for our fathers in Egypt and ten at the sea. Ten plagues did the Holy One, blessed is He, bring upon the Egyptians in Egypt and ten at the sea.

*   *   *

In our holy tongue, trials (נסיונות) and miracles (נסים) are related both etymologically and semantically. Avraham's trials, the נסיונות of the last mishnah, and the נסים performed for his descendants, which are the subject of this mishnah, are profoundly connected to each other and both are directly related to the עשרת מאמרות, the ten utterances by which the world was created. They themselves were the foundation for the עשרת הדברות, the ten Divine commandments that we heard at Sinai. When Egypt, the most powerful nation in the ancient world—the world that had been called into existence with ten utterances—disavowed its Creator and rejected His moral law by brutally oppressing God's people, the Father of all mankind caused His creation to act against its established nature. Mankind needed to be reminded of God's existence.

Each of the ten plagues in Egypt was a distinct disruption of nature which punished the Egyptians in ten stages of suffering. These paralleled the ten stages of Creation, each a powerful manifestation of the sovereignty of the Creator Whom they denied and Whose Law would soon be revealed on Sinai. "If this, My Divine covenant, were not day and night, I would not have created the laws of heaven and earth" (*Yirmeyahu* 33:25). That is to say, when the Divine moral law is trampled upon, heaven and earth, air and water, the whole universe revolts against this violation, and thus proclaims that God is Lord and Master of nature and man. The reawakening of the whole earth to an acknowledgment of God was therefore the aim and purpose of Yisrael's suffering in Egypt. The event had been revealed to Avraham centuries before: "And He said unto Avraham, 'Know for certain that your seed will be strangers in a land that is not theirs, and will serve them, and be afflicted by them for four hundred years. And also that nation whom they shall serve, I will judge and afterwards they [your children] will emerge with great wealth' " (*Bereshith* 15:13-14).

Avraham's last and most difficult trial, the sacrifice of Yitzchak, is directly related, the Sages say, to the miracle performed at the sea for his descendants. "Rabbi Chiyya bar Yosei in the name of Rabbi Meyasa said: In reward for the two halves of wood that our father Avraham 'split for the burnt offering,' ויבקע עצי עולה (*Bereshith* 22:3), he merited that the Holy One, blessed is He, divided the sea, as it is said, ויבקעו המים, 'the waters were split' (*Shemoth* 14:21)" (*Midrash Rabbah Bereshith* 55:8).

This mishnah specifies ten plagues and ten miracles in Egypt, and another ten miracles and ten plagues at the sea. The Torah does not specifically tell us that our fathers had miracles performed for them in Egypt, nor that ten plagues again befell the Egyptians by the sea. The Rambam says that every time our fathers in Egypt were spared a plague, that was in itself a miracle. The fact that this mishnah mentions the miracles before mentioning the plagues, however, is probably to teach us that the material and spiritual elevation of our fathers was just as much a purpose of the plagues as was the demoralization of the Egyptians.

Rabbi Wessely answers a number of questions that occur to us as we read about the division of the Red Sea (*Shemoth* 14). What was the significance of the utter darkness that separated the Egyptians from the Israelites? "And the angel of God, who went before the camp of Yisrael, journeyed and went behind them; and the column of the cloud went from before them and stood behind them. And it came between the camp of Egypt and the camp of Yisrael, and it was a cloud and darkness [to them], but it gave light by night [to these]"(*Shemoth* 14:19-20; see also *Yehoshua* 24:7). That was the beginning of the miracle at the sea. Because of the darkness, the Egyptians were not aware of the upheaval that had begun around them. A pillar of fire might well have kept the Egyptians from reaching the Israelites, for by its light they would have seen the danger before them and fled.

The next question that occurs to us is: Why did it happen that the Lord first made the sea dry land, and afterwards divided the waters (*Shemoth* 14:21)? Logically, the land could only become dry once the waters were divided. The answer is that the sea bed rose when Moshe stretched forth his rod, heaved itself upward from the depths until it reached the level of the dry land on both banks. The waters so displaced would naturally be expected to flood both camps, but the Song of the Sea that follows in the Torah tells us, "With a blast of Your nostrils the waters were piled up, the floods stood upright" (*Shemoth* 15:8). This unnatural sequence of events explains why the Egyptians did not realize that they were marching down into the sea: the sea bed was now on a level with the shore. Besides, they could not see the walls of water that unnaturally towered over them because of the abnormal darkness surrounding them. In addition, the column of fire that preceded the Israelites, and which was also blotted from their vision by the darkness, had already dried the sea bed under their feet.

It is now clear to us why the Torah says ויבואו...בתוך הים, "They came into the sea," and not ירדו לים, "They went down into the sea." This also explains why the division of the waters followed the appearance of dry land in the midst of the sea. When morning came, the Egyptians saw with horror that they were on the bottom of the sea, and then God sent the mighty storm-wind, the thunder and lightning to upset their chariots and to overwhelm them with panic and fear. At this point God told Moshe to stretch out his rod again and the dry land suddenly collapsed to its former depth, but, only that part that supported the Egyptians! That is why the Torah tells us, "the sea returned...and the Lord overthrew the Egyptians in the midst of the sea" (ibid. 14:27-28); these were two separate actions. It also explains the double description in the Song of the Sea, "The earth swallowed them up" and "He cast them into the sea": some were killed in the earth tremor and some by the tidal force. When we read verse 29, which recounts for the second time that the Israelites continued walking on dry land, passing between two walls of water, we understand that the Torah is telling us that this occurred while the Egyptians were drowning behind them in the same sea!

Our Sages say that when our ancestors left Egypt and saw the sea before them and their oppressors behind them, they thought that the only choices they had were to jump into the sea and drown, to surrender to the Egyptians and return to slavery, or to stand fast and fight to the last man. No one envisioned the miracles that did occur. Should we not remember this every day of our own lives? Surely we can draw great comfort during difficult times by remembering that God watches over every human being with love and that He is our only hope of salvation. The Sages who arranged our daily prayers placed great emphasis on the remembrance of this miracle. Every day in our *Shacharith* prayers, just before we say the *Shemoneh Esreh*, we recall the miracles at the sea, intentionally linking those great miracles with the miracles granted to each of us every day by God.

עֲשָׂרָה נִסְיוֹנוֹת נִסּוּ אֲבוֹתֵינוּ אֶת־
הַקָּדוֹשׁ בָּרוּךְ הוּא בַּמִּדְבָּר, שֶׁנֶּאֱמַר
וַיְנַסּוּ אֹתִי זֶה עֶשֶׂר פְּעָמִים וְלֹא שָׁמְעוּ בְּקוֹלִי:

6 Ten times did our fathers try the Holy One, blessed is He, in the wilderness, as it is said, "Now they have tried Me ten times and have not listened to My voice" (*Bemidbar* 14:22).

* * *

The Talmud lists these ten trials as follows: twice by the sea, twice when they were short of water, twice with the *man* (manna), twice with the quails, once with the golden calf and once in the desert of Paran with the spies (*Erachin* 15). When Yisrael saw the sea in front of them and their enemy behind them, when the miracle of the division of the sea had not yet happened, Yisrael did not trust in God. They expressed their despair to Moshe: "Because there were no graves in Egypt, have you taken us away to die in the wilderness?" (*Shemoth* 14:11). Even when the sea was already divided and they were crossing over, they were still rebellious (*Tehillim* 106:7). They were afraid that their pursuers could reach the other bank too, and were not reassured until they saw the sea throw up the bodies of their oppressors.

Yisrael had hardly moved away from the seashore when the people began to grumble because there was no drinking water at Marah (*Shemoth* 15:22-24). Their newly-affirmed trust in God crumbled before its first test. And when they were given the *man*, the wonderful food from Heaven, some went to look for it on the Shabbath and some, on the weekdays, set aside a portion for the next day, not trusting in God to provide it afresh each day and a double portion for the Shabbath. The people not only asked for bread but also for meat, and this request was granted as well; it was even granted when they requested it a second time (*Shemoth* 16:3; *Bemidbar* 11:4). These transgressions were followed by their making a golden calf to worship and finally by the rebellion of the spies. Only now did those rebelling against God's leadership approach their final doom. God had shown consideration for their despondency; now, however, when they failed the tenth and final test, they were condemned to forty years' wandering and to death in the desert.

All ten trials took place during the first year and a half after the *bnei Yisrael* left Egypt. The forty years in the desert were to be an education for Yisrael, and the period of the trials was only the beginning of their apprenticeship. With each step they took, the direct and miraculous care of God became more manifest. Their repeated rebelliousness was not, therefore, directed at God, but against Moshe and Aharon who had led them out of Egypt. As anxious as they were to be released from slavery, they were not so eager to leave Egypt; it had become their home. Loyalty to a homeland is apparently inherent in human nature. The people probably did not even consider their desire to return to Egypt a direct rebellion against God. They did not doubt that He had broken the might of the Egyptians and had liberated them from oppression, but the exodus from Egypt and their passage through the desert seemed to them to be Moshe's work.

Their faith was strong after the occurrence of the miracles at the sea, but it wavered as soon as they lacked food and water. They may have thought that if it were really God's will for them to leave Egypt, they would not have had to suffer want. They had, reluctantly, followed Moshe, but only because they felt supported by God; when they thought they were being denied the means of sustenance, they protested what they thought was the absence of God. Moshe therefore said, יי עם היתם ממרים, "You have been rebellious"—not against, but "with God" (*Devarim* 31:27). Even in rebellion, they were עם יי, "with God." This more indulgent interpretation of our fathers' behavior in the desert is also found in Tanna devei Eliyyahu (ch. 23):

> "During my wanderings I once met an old man who said to me, 'Master, our generations are better than the generations of those who came out of Egypt. During the time of Moshe, they had only the Torah, but we have the Torah, the Prophets and the other Writings.' I answered him, 'This is not so, for the generations since the destruction of the first Temple and the

building of the Second Temple had the Torah, the Prophets and the other Writings and also the discussions linked to the words of the Torah (דברי פלפול), and yet they were not as perfect as those who came out of Egypt, for, of those who came out of Egypt it is said, "Go and announce it to the ears of Yerushalayim saying: Thus says the Lord: I remember the devotion of your youth... How you went after Me in the wilderness, in a land that was not sown" (*Yirmeyahu* 2:2).' "

זְ עֲשָׂרָה נִסִּים נַעֲשׂוּ לַאֲבוֹתֵינוּ בְּבֵית
הַמִּקְדָּשׁ. לֹא הִפִּילָה אִשָּׁה מֵרֵיחַ בְּשַׂר
הַקֹּדֶשׁ, וְלֹא הִסְרִיחַ בְּשַׂר הַקֹּדֶשׁ מֵעוֹלָם, וְלֹא
נִרְאָה זְבוּב בְּבֵית הַמִּטְבְּחַיִם, וְלֹא אֵרַע קֶרִי לְכֹהֵן
גָּדוֹל בְּיוֹם הַכִּפּוּרִים, וְלֹא כִבּוּ הַגְּשָׁמִים אֵשׁ שֶׁל־
עֲצֵי הַמַּעֲרָכָה, וְלֹא נִצְּחָה הָרוּחַ אֶת־עַמּוּד הֶעָשָׁן,
וְלֹא נִמְצָא פְסוּל בָּעֹמֶר וּבִשְׁתֵּי הַלֶּחֶם וּבְלֶחֶם
הַפָּנִים, עוֹמְדִים צְפוּפִים וּמִשְׁתַּחֲוִים רְוָחִים, וְלֹא
הִזִּיק נָחָשׁ וְעַקְרָב בִּירוּשָׁלַיִם מֵעוֹלָם, וְלֹא אָמַר
אָדָם לַחֲבֵרוֹ צַר לִי הַמָּקוֹם שֶׁאָלִין בִּירוּשָׁלַיִם:

7 Ten miracles were wrought for our fathers in the Temple: No woman miscarried because of the aroma of the sacrificial meat; the sacrificial meat never turned rancid; no fly was ever seen in the slaughterhouse of the temple; no unclean accident ever befell the High Priest on the Day of Atonement; the rain never extinguished the fire of the woodpile on the altar; the wind did not prevail over the column of smoke that rose from the altar; no disqualifying defect was ever found in the *Omer*, in the two *Shavuoth* loaves or in the showbreads; the people stood closely pressed together and yet found ample space to prostrate themselves; no snake or scorpion ever did injury in Yerushalayim, and no man ever said to his fellow, "There is too little room for me to lodge overnight in Yerushalayim."

* * *

These are just ten of all the miracles which, the Talmud tells us, took place in the Temple (*Yoma* 21a). The reason why our mishnah restricts the miracles to these ten may be found in the apparently extra word לאבותינו, "for our fathers." All miracles linked with the Temple had the purpose of manifesting God's continual Presence at that consecrated place chosen by Him; these ten miracles were particularly intended to honor our forebears as well. "Rabbi Pappa said to Abbaye, 'How is it that miracles were performed for former generations and for us miracles are not performed?' He replied, 'Former generations were ready to sacrifice their lives for the sanctity of God's Name' " (*Berachoth* 20a). Present generations have lost their belief and trust in God. When we are taught about intervention of the Divine will in the destiny of man, we shake our heads in doubt and disbelief, dismissing as legend and fancy all that occurred to our forefathers. Yet, the same people who do not trust in God expect miracles to be performed for them by chance. At the gambling tables, at the stock exchange, they hope that fortune will smile upon them; they hope for a miracle, but do not believe in miracles. Thousands upon thousands of our ancestors witnessed God's miracles. They were totally aware of God's miraculous rule because of His intervention in their lives, but they themselves did not ask for miracles, modestly considering themselves unworthy. As it is said, אין סומכין על הנס, "You must not rely on miracles" (see *Shabbath* 32a).

THE AROMA OF THE SACRIFICIAL MEAT. Our Sages knew that it is dangerous to the health of a pregnant woman not to satisfy her craving for a particular kind of food, and they therefore permitted such a woman to eat meat even on Yom Kippur. We are told here that the delicious aroma of the roasting sacrificial meat in the Temple, meat which was forbidden to all but the priests, never caused a pregnant woman to miscarry. We learn from this that שלוחי מצוה אינן ניזוקין, "those who are engaged in performing a duty commanded by God will suffer no harm" (*Pesachim* 8b), and we have seen this to be true not only in the days of the Temple but also in later Jewish history.

NO FLY WAS EVER SEEN. The next two miracles are related. Raw meat for the sacrificial offerings was not always roasted and consumed immediately, yet it never turned rancid, even in the hot summers of Yerushalayim, and it never attracted flies. This happened not once or twice, but regularly. We must draw the conclusion that decay and impurity (which draw flies) could not exist in the sanctified aura of the Temple. Similarly, if the human body is called by the Sages מקדש מעט, "a miniature sanctuary," because of the holy Divine soul living within it, we understand that we can keep impurity and decay away from ourselves to the extent that we guard the sanctity of our bodies. If sanctity has such power over earthly weakness, imagine the influence it has on a person who is completely devoted to guarding it.

NO UNCLEAN ACCIDENT. The next miracle connects the pure body to the pure mind. The high priest banished all impurities from his body, his heart and his mind and achieved such a degree of sanctity that no priest was ever disqualified from performing the Yom Kippur service in the Temple because of personal impurity. How then can this maxim possibly apply to us? Every Jew is endowed with the priestly vocation by God, every place sanctified to God is like the Temple, and every day of our life is a call for us to do *teshuvah* as we do on Yom Kippur, to renew our faith and trust in God. If every day is a Day of Atonement, each one of us can merit the miracle—if he is worthy of it.

THE FIRE OF THE WOODPILE. The elements of fire and water usually cannot coexist; one or the other must be overcome. The Divine fire that fell from Heaven and remained on God's altar, from the consecration of Shelomo's Temple until King Menashe removed it, was not an ordinary kind of fire. "Five things were reported about the fire on the pile of wood: it lay quiescent like a lion, it was as clear as sunlight, its flame was of solid substance, it devoured wet wood like dry wood, and it had no smoke arising from it" (*Yoma* 21b).

THE WIND DID NOT PREVAIL. What then are we to learn from that column of smoke that rose steadily from the offerings on the altar in the Temple, undisturbed by the strongest gusts of wind? What is lighter, more unsubstantial, more incapable of offering resistance than rising smoke? And what is stronger than the gale that uproots trees and topples buildings? Yet the wind halted, ineffectual, before the pillar of smoke rising heavenward from God's altar. For thousands of years, storms have rushed in upon Yisrael, yet they have never succeeded in altering the direction of the rising flame of its faith and its Law. This is a miracle that all the world can attest to today, just as thousands of eyes beheld the straight column of smoke in the Temple.

NO DISQUALIFYING DEFECT. Less visible but no less miraculous, was the uncontaminated purity of the *omer*, the two Shavuoth loaves and the showbreads, year after year, as long as the Temple stood. All three offerings had to be prepared in advance of the Festival, and if so much as a weevil touched them they could not be used for the offering nor could they be replaced on the Festival itself. But contamination was never found in them; this could only have occurred with Divine protection. The *omer*, the Shavuoth loaves and the showbreads are the symbolic representation of our daily bread, which is in turn the symbol of human life. As offerings in the Temple, they were intended to make us fully aware that not only our lives, but also our sustenance, are under special Divine care. To keep this awareness fresh in our minds with every piece of bread we eat, the wise King Shelomo initiated נטילת ידים, the ritual washing of our hands prior to eating bread.

Originally, this institution was only intended for sacrifices and sacred gifts; applying it to the mundane eating of bread raises our daily bread to the level of sanctification. Thus the Jewish hand that brings a slice of bread to the mouth must always be pure. God watched over the bread of the Sanctuary; the Jew himself must accomplish the miracle of keeping his daily bread free from contamination, both for himself and for his family. He can sanctify it by acknowledging with his blessing that it is not human intelligence, but the Divine intelligence of God, "which brings forth bread from the earth." This transforms every Jewish home into God's temple, every table into God's altar and every slice of bread into God's gift. Thus the Jew becomes a priest who has learned from God's miracles in the Temple to protect his מקדש מעט, the miniature sanctuary of his home, from contamination.

THE PEOPLE STOOD CLOSELY PRESSED TOGETHER AND YET FOUND AMPLE SPACE TO PROSTRATE THEMSELVES. This was a public miracle that could not be explained in a natural way. We know that at the time of Shelomo's Temple, there were four times as many Jewish souls as there were at the time of the exodus from Egypt (i.e. 2,400,000). The space in the Temple measured only 135 square cubits. The fact that such a small space easily held so many people during the three pilgrim Festivals was a miraculous phenomenon and we know this because every visitor to the Temple witnessed it. Bertinoro tells us, "The miracle would happen at the moment when everyone prostrated himself: four cubits suddenly separated each person from his fellow, so that no one could hear the other person confessing his sins." How did it become customary that sins were confessed on the three pilgrim Festivals? Rabbi Moshe Sofer, in his Torah commentary, points out that the laws of space were completely suspended when a person or object of unusual holiness existed. We find, for example, that the Holy Ark never occupied any space in the Sanctuary. The people who were standing in the Temple closely pressed together knew that as long as they felt this closeness they had not yet reached the highest level of holiness, that weaknesses and defects still adhered to them and rendered them unworthy of the miracle. This awareness urged them to confess their sins and repent, and then the miracle would occur: the law of space was suspended as soon as all prostrated themselves in homage to God.

In a figurative sense, we see that this miracle still happens today. When all people stand up and oppose one another, there is never enough room for everyone; but when each individual gives way to the next man, all find a place. It is ironic that our fathers managed to earn their daily bread in the narrow ghettos into which they were crowded, and yet had time to maintain their spiritual life, to learn and fulfill the Divine Torah; our generation, however, enjoys the freedom of the whole world but complains that the world is too narrow, competition too great, the fight for existence too severe to allow study of the Torah and fulfillment of its precepts! We find here a direct parallel to the miracle of space referred to in this mishnah. Every commandment we keep, every sin we avoid is a prostration, a surrender, a suppression of our own ego in honor of and in homage to God. The Jew who closes his business on the Shabbath has placed himself and his earning power at the feet of his Father in Heaven for more than twenty-four hours. Without submission there is "no room"—that is to say, without subordination to God there can be no spiritual development.

IN YERUSHALAYIM. The ninth and tenth miracles mentioned in this mishnah were not restricted to the Temple area, but extended to the entire city of Yerushalayim. None of the pilgrims who came up to pray, to sacrifice and repent, to carry out Divine service, were ever poisoned by the snakes and scorpions which abounded there. Nor did they ever have to sleep in the street! Everybody knew in advance, before setting out for Yerushalayim, that he would enjoy a miracle of hospitality and fraternity that has never happened anywhere else, before or since. Hundreds of thousands of travelers were accommodated in good fellowship. Those were the miracles that happened in the Temple but reached far beyond its boundaries. The miracles performed for our fathers are also a guarantee for us, their descendants, if we will only remain worthy and faithful to the teachings of our fathers.

עֲשָׂרָה דְבָרִים נִבְרְאוּ בְּעֶרֶב שַׁבָּת בֵּין הַשְּׁמָשׁוֹת, וְאֵלּוּ הֵן, פִּי הָאָרֶץ, פִּי הַבְּאֵר, פִּי הָאָתוֹן, הַקֶּשֶׁת וְהַמָּן וְהַמַּטֶּה וְהַשָּׁמִיר, הַכְּתָב וְהַמִּכְתָּב וְהַלּוּחוֹת. וְיֵשׁ אוֹמְרִים, אַף הַמַּזִּיקִין וּקְבוּרָתוֹ שֶׁל מֹשֶׁה וְאֵילוֹ שֶׁל־אַבְרָהָם אָבִינוּ. וְיֵשׁ אוֹמְרִים, אַף צְבָת בִּצְבָת עֲשׂוּיָה:

8 Ten things were created at twilight on the [first] Shabbath eve: The mouth of the earth, the mouth of the well, the mouth of the ass, the rainbow, the *man* (manna), the staff, the *shamir*-worm, the written characters, the writing and the Tablets. Some say also the destructive spirits, the grave of Moshe and the ram of our father Avraham. Others say also the tongs which are made with tongs.

* * *

"The mouth of the earth" is that which swallowed up Korach and his associates; "the mouth of the well" is the one that appeared in the desert for our fathers throughout their forty-year odyssey; "the mouth of the ass" is that which confounded Bilam in front of all his entourage; "the rainbow" is the sign by which God promised Noach that He would never again flood the world; "the *man*" is the Divine bread which was provided daily in the desert for forty years; "the staff" is that of Moshe, through which he performed the miracles that God commanded; "the *shamir*" is a small worm that can burrow through stone and was used for cutting, smoothing and polishing the altar stones and repairing the *ephod* of the High Priest; "the written characters, the writing and the Tablets" refer to the two stone Tablets of the Covenant; "the destructive spirits" cannot be perceived through ordinary human senses; "the grave of Moshe" cannot be found although its location is specified exactly; "the ram of our father Avraham" is the one which replaced Yitzchak for the sacrifice; "the tongs" are those which first came into being in order to make all the others possible, and which are therefore ascribed to special intervention by God.

TEN THINGS WERE CREATED AT TWILIGHT ON THE SHABBATH EVE. This mishnah deals not with miracles but with entities created by God and specifies precisely when they were created. Why? Is it imaginable that Avraham's ram and Bilam's ass were alive from the time of the creation of the world? Perhaps we can best understand this if we examine briefly what we call the laws of natural science. For thousands of years man has observed nature and recorded whatever phenomena he has been able to perceive. Thus we know just about all there is to know about what the perceivable material elements can do. We know nothing, however, about how or why they behave as they do. We must say, therefore, that there is a higher world of forces which defies our own perception. The following example will illustrate this.

We see and understand that rainfall can be beneficial or destructive to the earth and its processes. We know, too, that various natural phenomena can affect the rainfall in accordance with certain natural laws and thus we can "predict" rain. Nevertheless, we are clearly told in chapter 26 of Vayyikra, "And it will come to pass if you will hearken to the voice of the Lord, your God, to observe to do all His commandments...the Lord will open for you His good treasure, the heavens, to give the rain of your land in its season... But it shall come to pass if you will not hearken to the voice of the Lord your God...the heavens that are overhead shall be brass and the earth that is under you shall be iron. The Lord will make the rain of your land to powder and dust..." This reminds us that in spite of all our knowledge of meteorology, we really do not know why rain is provided or withheld by God; we know only that it is dependent on man's moral behavior and that the seat of its control is in a higher world order.

The Shabbath, the Sages tell us, was the concluding creation of the material world and the initial creation of that world of higher forces. In our lower world, the so-called natural laws prevail, but in that higher world the rules are supernatural and they are known only to God, the Creator of all worlds. Proof of this is found in the following examples: Ordinarily, fire burns and water flows, yet fire did not burn Chananyah, Mishael and Azaryah, and the waters of the Red Sea stood aside to allow the Israelites to pass through and receive God's Law. These examples are well-known to us as miraculous demonstrations that Divine rule can upset the "natural" course of things on earth.

However, the mishnah does not say "ten miracles," but "ten things" were created at twilight on the Shabbath eve. When fire stops burning and water stops flowing, when what appear to us as miracles occur, it is because we note a deviation from the laws of nature as far as we know them. In reality, however, our natural laws operate as a result of forces operating in the higher world order according to God's wisdom and they function, or can be suspended as required, to serve God's purposes. Just as God created the natural characteristics belonging to all things in the six days of Creation, in the same way He created the opposite characteristics to be called forth whenever God's cause on earth required them. מאת יי היתה זאת היא נפלאת בעינינו, "This is the Lord's doing. It is marvelous in our eyes" (*Tehillim* 118:23). From the point of view of God and His world order, things that we regard as miracles are really quite natural. The ten things or entities mentioned in this mishnah were not merely opposite or negative qualities but entirely new creations. They were brought into being, like all material things, in the six days of Creation, but since they represent the Divine Presence on earth in a remarkable way, they only belong partly to the material, created-in-six-days-world, and partly to the higher world to which the Shabbath gives its character. Thus they were created "at twilight on the Shabbath eve."

Miracles are proof that God can at any time suspend the laws of earthly nature, of the ordinary course of the world, when it is required by the higher order of things for which the world on earth was called into existence. The ten things that are the subject of this mishnah have existed since the beginning of the world, in a state that bridges the lower, material and the higher, spiritual worlds. We only became aware of them when the moment for which they were intended had arrived. The mouth of the earth, in which Korach, his associates and all their belongings were swallowed up, was not an earthquake or a geological fault. Had it been either of these, the fissure would have outlasted the catastrophe and left some sign in the crust of the earth. To punish Korach with Divine justice, however, the earth opened, swallowed him and closed up again, without leaving a trace. The ability of the earth to open and reseal itself was created at the end of the six days of Creation; it is, therefore, a characteristic of the earth but one that was perceived only on the occasion of Korach's catastrophe. This information may be derived from the description of the event in the Torah. It is called פיה, "its mouth," to indicate that it was a permanent feature of the earth that only then became known, having been concealed before. Ordinarily, the creation of such a feature for the earth was unnecessary for earthly purposes. When Divine authority was called into question by the rebel Korach in front of the entire nation, its purpose was fulfilled.

The mouth of Miryam's well, that served our people in the desert, was hidden within a rock and only became visible when Moshe tapped it with his staff. Then it opened up, provided God's people and their flocks with water, and closed again. It therefore does not resemble other wellsprings that flow out from between rocks. This was a unique creation, also created at the conclusion of the six days, for the purpose of serving God's cause on earth when it was required. The mouth of the ass, too, was given the ability to speak at the conclusion of the six days of Creation, but none of its kind ever did so until the moment chosen by God had come. A child has speaking organs from birth, but he does not begin to use them until a chosen time, which can be different with each child. In the same way, God prepared the animals when the first of each kind was created, each to be ready to carry out His purpose.

It is more difficult to explain the fourth work of twilight creation, the rainbow. We know that the rainbow was first observed after the Flood, and that it is a natural phenomenon which occurs when the rays of the sun are refracted and reflected by rain clouds. Why does the Sage list it together with the ten things that were not like the other miracles, but came into existence with the creation of the world? The Torah first mentions rain and its relation to vegetation in Bereshith 2:5-6. These verses clearly state that the original irrigation of the earth was from mist rising up from beneath the earth's surface and not from rain. The formation of rain is first reported at the beginning of the Flood. It is possible that it had not rained until then, and that all the earth was moistened like Egypt, which was known to have obtained its humidity from the Nile without rain. "And it will come to pass when I bring clouds over the earth and the bow is seen in the cloud that I will remember My covenant..." (*Bereshith* 9:14). Thus the rainbow is admirably suited to serve as the Divine guarantee that the whole earth will not be destroyed through a flood a second time. It appears to us as an optical phenomenon that was created like all other material objects, but it was perceived only later, when it fulfilled the higher purpose for which it was intended.

We know that the *man*, like the rainbow, was also a natural product of creation. But the *man*, just like Moshe's staff, the *shamir*-worm, and the Tablets with their characters, was withdrawn from earthly existence when its purpose had been fulfilled. They all exist today but we cannot perceive them.

We are not sure what the destructive spirits mentioned in this mishnah really are. According to one opinion, they are beings formed from fire and air (only two of the four elements comprising man) and are therefore not perceptible with our senses. They exist in the intermediate world, between the material earth and the spiritual realm, and that is why they were created in the hour between the work of Creation and the Shabbath. The Sages tell us that their purpose is to carry out Divine retribution for human errors and weaknesses.

The last of the ten things named in this mishnah seems different from all the others, in that it does not serve a higher purpose and does not relate to the higher realm. The tongs are a material tool of man intended only to help him in his everyday life on earth, his world of working and doing. What can the Sages be telling us when they emphasize the importance of this earthly world and man's work in it? From the beginning of the saying, we might think that the emphasis is placed upon the dividing line between the Shabbath and the weekday in order to point out the superiority of the spiritual world of the Shabbath. That is why the Sages mention the tongs, a tool of man, to tell us that both worlds have equal merit. The same Divine hand which opened the mouths of the earth and the ass, which wrote the covenantal promise both in stone and in the firmament, also provided bread from Heaven and the first tool for man to use.

ט שִׁבְעָה דְבָרִים בְּגֹלֶם וְשִׁבְעָה בְּחָכָם.
חָכָם אֵינוֹ מְדַבֵּר לִפְנֵי מִי שֶׁגָּדוֹל מִמֶּנּוּ
בְּחָכְמָה וּבְמִנְיָן, וְאֵינוֹ נִכְנָס לְתוֹךְ דִּבְרֵי חֲבֵרוֹ,
וְאֵינוֹ נִבְהָל לְהָשִׁיב, שׁוֹאֵל כָּעִנְיָן וּמֵשִׁיב כַּהֲלָכָה,
וְאוֹמֵר עַל־רִאשׁוֹן רִאשׁוֹן וְעַל־אַחֲרוֹן אַחֲרוֹן, וְעַל
מַה־שֶּׁלֹּא שָׁמַע אוֹמֵר לֹא שָׁמַעְתִּי, וּמוֹדֶה עַל־
הָאֱמֶת, וְחִלּוּפֵיהֶן בְּגֹלֶם:

9 There are seven traits which mark an immature
man and seven traits [which mark] a wise man. The
wise man does not speak ahead of one who is greater
than he in wisdom and years [or disciples]; he does
not interrupt the speech of his companion; he is not
hasty to answer; he asks questions keeping to the
subject and answers to the point; he speaks of the first
thing first and the last thing last; regarding that
which he has not heard he says: I have not heard this;
and he acknowledges the truth. The reverse of all
these traits marks the immature man.

*　　*　　*

When our holy writings mention a חכם (wise man), this refers to a
man wise in Torah and a man who not only knows what is written
in the Torah, but also acknowledges it by carrying out its commandments. The Jewish חכם is not so much distinguished by his
knowledge as by the utilization of this knowledge to refine his
mind and heart. His deed serves his thought, his mind works on
his character, and his whole life is the embodiment of his learning. The unfortunate division between teaching and living, between theory and practice, is not known in a *chacham*. Similarly,
the term גלם does not mean an ignorant man or, what is the same
thing for many, an uncultured person. A *golem* is, however, a
person who may even master Torah learning, but it does not

master him; that is, he does not show it in his actions. There is only one truth, the truth of mind and heart together, and this is what makes a man wise.

THE WISE MAN DOES NOT SPEAK AHEAD OF ONE WHO IS GREATER THAN HE IN WISDOM AND YEARS. Greater wisdom does not mean simply greater sagacity or greater erudition; the Sage does not refer to man's ability to merely add to his store of knowledge. When our Sages spoke of חכמה (wisdom), they spoke of חכמת התורה (the wisdom of the Torah). This wisdom comprises the subordination of mind and heart, word and deed, to the statutes of the Torah. This wisdom cannot be attained with human reason and intelligence for it belongs to God, Who alone may bestow it. The meaning of this mishnah thus becomes clear: The only way to acquire wisdom is to learn the words of the Torah—to learn its Divine commandments and prohibitions as they are outlined in the Written Law and explained in greater detail in the Oral Law, and to live in accordance with them. If respect for a sage were only a sign of good manners, there would be no need to teach it here. It is a commandment of the Torah— והדרת פני זקן, "and honor the face of the old man" (*Vayyikra* 19:32). "Greater in years," although the expression refers to "number," may indicate either greater experience acquired through the years, or a greater number of students. In any case, the main point is that one is obligated to show consideration for a sage whose knowledge of the Torah is greater than one's own.

HE DOES NOT INTERRUPT THE SPEECH OF HIS COMPAN-ION. A truly wise man will only start to speak after his companion has finished. "He is not hasty to answer." He does not flaunt his own versatility by deviating from the subject; he knows how to ask pertinent questions "and answers to the point." The *golem* does not ask in order to learn the answer to his question, but to place himself in a flattering light. The wise man carefully arranges his discourse with "the first thing first and the last thing last" so as to transmit it clearly to his listeners. This is of particular importance in learning Torah. In asking how Yisrael acquired the Oral Law, the Sages inquire כיצד סדר משנה, "What is the order of the Mishnah?" (*Eruvin* 54b). If anything in his discourse remains unclear, he does not gloss over it, but admits willingly that he does not know: "I have not heard this." This characteristic manifests the moral perfection of a wise man, which is so much greater than that of most men. In the writings of our Sages we repeatedly find the remark, דבר זה איני יודע לפרש, "I do not know how to explain this matter." The truly wise man is interested only in discovering the truth, not in outsmarting his companions. He is not only ready to admit his own ignorance, but he will readily admit his own mistakes, which is even more admirable. In all cases, "he acknowledges the truth." We know that Moshe *Rabbenu* stated publicly that he had erred and named his brother Aharon as the one who taught him to discover and correct the error (*Avoth of Rabbi Nathan* 37:12).

Our holy language has a wealth of expressions for fools and scoffers in their different manifestations, graded according to their distance from the path of truth: שוטים, סכלים, לצים, רשעים, חוטאים, כסילים, אוילים and more. The term *golem*, however, is the one used in this mishnah, and we can look for its meaning in the way it is used in other mishnayoth. For example, in Kelim 12:6, it refers to implements of metal which lack the final polish. We understand, therefore, that a *golem* is someone who has acquired a partial knowledge of Torah but is not yet able to subordinate his mind and his temperament to its wisdom. He is still immature and his practice falls short of his theory. One can imagine a *golem* who has more theoretical knowledge than a *chacham*; he may be a "walking encyclopedia," able to expound on any subject, but his knowledge does not inspire his actions and he will remain a *golem* despite all his knowledge. On the other hand, a person may very well have mastered only a small measure of Torah knowledge, but if that knowledge controls all his thoughts and desires, all his inclinations and passions, so that his whole life faithfully mirrors his learning, then he is a *chacham*, the wise man of whom the mishnah speaks.

שִׁבְעָה מִינֵי פְרְעָנֻיּוֹת בָּאִין לָעוֹלָם עַל־
שִׁבְעָה גוּפֵי עֲבֵרָה. מִקְצָתָן מְעַשְּׂרִין
וּמִקְצָתָן אֵינָן מְעַשְּׂרִין רָעָב שֶׁל־בַּצֹּרֶת בָּא מִקְצָתָן
רְעֵבִים וּמִקְצָתָן שְׂבֵעִים, גָּמְרוּ שֶׁלֹּא לְעַשֵּׂר רָעָב שֶׁל
מְהוּמָה וְשֶׁל־בַּצֹּרֶת בָּא, וְשֶׁלֹּא לִטּוֹל אֶת הַחַלָּה
רָעָב שֶׁל־כְּלָיָה בָּא:

10 Seven kinds of punishments come into the world for seven kinds of transgressions: (1) If some tithe and others do not, there will be a famine from drought and some will suffer hunger while others will have plenty; (2) if all cease to tithe there will be a famine from social unrest (panic) and drought; (3) if all cease to separate the [priest's] portion from their dough there will be a famine of extermination.

*   *   *

The first three kinds of famine are described in this mishnah. In the first type of famine mentioned, which is the lightest of the seven afflictions, some suffer and some do not. Many people therefore jump to the conclusion that the sole cause of famine in the world is the unequal distribution of wealth. When famine occurs, contemporary statesmen seek its causes in economic and social trends, unlike our Sages who know what causes different degrees of famine, as well as what causes all the other natural calamities that devastate large sectors of society. These disasters do not spring from superficial political, economic or social developments. The Sages call natural calamities פורענניות, "Divine retribution" or "punishments," a word which is semantically connected to the word פרעון, "settlement of debts." Therefore we may say that שבעה מיני פורעניות are seven kinds of Divine settlements exacted from man which are especially called into existence because of seven kinds of transgressions. This mishnah teaches us that when a general disaster occurs, we must look within ourselves and examine our own behavior to find the cause and try to correct it.

Increasingly severe types of famine are caused by Yisrael's failure to observe the commandments to tithe (מעשר) and to separate from the dough (הפרשת חלה) before baking bread. Now this may seem to us a very harsh penalty, but we must not forget that these are the commandments for which the universe was created (שנקראין ראשית—see *Midrash Rabbah, Parashah* 1:4, on the first word in the Torah). How can tithing and separating the dough be considered the purpose of Creation? These *mitzvoth* remind the Jew, in the fullness of his material wealth and pleasure, Who is responsible for it all; they elevate his daily use of the products of the earth to a higher level of awareness of God, thus strengthening his devotion to and reverence for God. It behooves us therefore to examine the laws surrounding these two commandments. As we know, the fields of the Holy Land may be cultivated for six consecutive years, but must lie fallow during the seventh. Landowners must tithe their produce at the end of each year and give this to the tribe of Levi, the caretakers of the Temple. This is מעשר ראשון, "the first tithe." מעשר שני, "the second tithe," is to be taken at the end of the first, second, fourth and fifth years as an additional tithe. The second tithe is also taken at the end of the third and sixth years, but it is given to the poor and is called therefore מעשר עני, "the poor man's tithe." Still another portion of the harvest must be set apart after the grain has been milled and made into dough, just before it is baked into bread; that is הפרשת חלה, to be given to the priests. This tithe, "taking *challah*," is the only one of all the tithes which applies outside of the Holy Land, albeit in a less stringent manner than in the Land.

The tithes are intended to counteract the dangers inherent in having great wealth. The first tithe, given every year, forces the Jew to remember those who own no land themselves and are entirely occupied with the nation's spiritual needs; the second tithe forces the Jew to sanctify his own portion in the sacred surroundings of the Temple in Yerushalayim; the third tithe forces him to remember all those who are less fortunate than he; and the fourth tithe recognizes the servants and representatives of God in His Sanctuary. Mankind was given the whole earth to plant and to harvest and to enjoy, but Yisrael alone was given God's own land to work, and therefore to accept special responsibilities as well. By raising all their mundane tasks and duties to a higher spiritual and moral level, Yisrael will carry out its Divine mission, to raise the spiritual and moral level of the entire world. If men counteract these Divine purposes, frantically holding on to their prosperity (which is in any case provided by God), if they show no feeling for enriching and refining themselves, and if they ignore the distress of their starving brethren, then God also keeps back His precious gifts—His rain, His sunshine, His blessing—and the consequence is "famine from drought," where the poor will be severely afflicted and the middle class will cease to exist.

FAMINE FROM SOCIAL UNREST...FAMINE OF EXTERMINATION. The crops do not fail in this case, but human greed causes an imbalance in society. The wealthy people abuse their privileges, and manipulate the economy in order to amass even greater wealth for themselves, and the poor begin to suffer immediately, even in the midst of abundance. As the evil spreads and the level of morality slackens further, the fabric of society disintegrates, business and commerce are corrupted, social upheaval is rampant and the entire populace suffers. When the women, too, become negligent in keeping up their obligations and give way to temptation (ed. note: taking challah is traditionally, although not exclusively, performed by women), then evil invades the home, society becomes sick and the entire community will literally be destroyed.

וְ**א**דֶבֶר בָּא לָעוֹלָם עַל מִיתוֹת הָאֲמוּרוֹת
בַּתּוֹרָה שֶׁלֹּא נִמְסְרוּ לְבֵית דִּין וְעַל פֵּרוֹת
שְׁבִיעִית. חֶרֶב בָּאָה לָעוֹלָם עַל עִנּוּי הַדִּין וְעַל עִוּוּת
הַדִּין וְעַל־הַמּוֹרִים בַּתּוֹרָה שֶׁלֹּא כַהֲלָכָה:

11 (4) Pestilence descends upon the world to exe-
cute those death penalties mentioned in the Torah
which may not be carried out by a court of justice, and
for those transgressions involving the fruits of the
seventh year. (5) The sword comes into the world
because of the delay of justice, the perversion of justice and those who teach distortions of the traditional
Law.

*   *   *

Disease, plagues, pestilence, or what we call epidemics, are now
attributed to bacteria, viruses and other investigable causes. The
Sages, however, look beyond these immediate causes and tell us
that the existence of the disease and its carrier is due to our own
immoral behavior. Disease, plague and pestilence, the Sages
teach us, are but the messengers of death. When man commits
capital transgressions (whose only expiation can be death), disease may become the messenger which executes the judgment.

DEATH PENALTIES MENTIONED IN THE TORAH WHICH
MAY NOT BE CARRIED OUT BY A COURT OF JUSTICE. These
may refer to transgressions for which a human court of justice
would decree a death sentence (מיתה בידי אדם) but not actually
carry it out, in which case the sinner would remain *de facto*
unpunished. They may also refer to transgressions deserving
death, but whose punishment has to be Divinely executed
(מיתה בידי שמים). The Gemara shows us how death asserts itself
according to the transgression that it is intended to expiate:

Rabbi Yosef said, and likewise Rabbi Chiyya taught, that
from the day the Temple was destroyed, although the

Sanhedrin ceased to function, the four modes of execution remained in force. Were they not stopped, though? The sentences of execution did not cease [to be decreed], but the executions were no longer carried out by man; the appropriate type of death was henceforth dealt out by God. Someone who would have been condemned to stoning either falls from a roof [and dies] or a wild beast tramples him; one who would have been condemned to burning either falls into a fire or is bitten by a snake; one who would have been condemned to decapitation is either apprehended by the government or is attacked by robbers; one who would have been condemned to strangulation either drowns in a river or dies of a quinsy.

(*Sotah* 8b)

Since death through pestilence is not mentioned in this passage from the Gemara, we understand that it is a form of punishment that only God Himself metes out. Moreover, God's messenger visits palace and cottage alike, and the doctor's art is powerless to halt it.

The modern trend to abolition of capital punishment is opposed by the ancient Biblical statute which condemns to death one who murders. Our Tradition declares that capital punishment exists for all time but its enforcement entails such complicated conditions that it is only rarely applicable. It exists *de jure*, and a murderer must therefore be prepared to receive the death sentence; *de facto*, however, it has hardly ever been applied by Jewish courts. A public which opposes all capital punishment on principle shows more sympathy for the murderer than for his innocent victim. Our values have become twisted, and human life is no longer respected as it should be. God sends communicable diseases into the world and everyone is equally endangered; this teaches us the equal value of every human life. The prophet says, "I will make [the weakest] man (אנוש) more rare than fine gold, and [the accomplished] man (אדם) [more rare] than the pure gold of Ophir" (*Yeshayahu* 13:12). In our day, dead metal is considered more precious than living man. Everyone complains about overpopulation and competition. Machines become more like human beings and human beings seem more like machines. Intelligence, wealth and appreciation of life seem limited to an ever-smaller circle in a widening battle of races and classes. The fight to accumulate wealth at the expense of others is a most unsuitable basis on which to develop an understanding of man's ultimate value.

THOSE TRANSGRESSIONS INVOLVING THE FRUITS OF THE SEVENTH YEAR. To protect ourselves from the madness of this unnatural struggle and to keep alive the knowledge that we are all, without exception, living on God's soil, we have been given the institution of the Sabbatical year, a whole year when the entire nation of Yisrael proclaims the quality of man and his utter dependence on the Owner of all the earth and its produce.

THE SWORD COMES INTO THE WORLD BECAUSE OF THE DELAY OF JUSTICE, THE PERVERSION OF JUSTICE AND THOSE WHO TEACH DISTORTIONS OF THE TRADITIONAL LAW. Today more than ever before, violence and armed force are increasing, justice is thwarted at every turn and we see the actualization of the first part of Esav's legacy: "By your sword shall you live" (*Bereshith* 27:40). But the verse continues: "and you shall serve your brother." Esav's sword of violence is meant to serve Ya'akov's voice of justice. "How can that be," you will ask, "when we all know that the rule of law and the rule of the sword are diametrically opposed?" The mishnah therefore attempts to explain the wisdom of our Sages as follows:

Violence is certainly not preferable to law and order, even though "might" at times, seems to make "right." The sword of violence is called into existence in the world when justice is perverted. The "world" the Sages refer to here is the Jewish world—the Jewish nation—and justice must be served in the Jewish nation according to God's Law. It is when God's Law is ill-served that Esav's sword will be called upon.

King David preferred punishment by disease to punishment by the sword, because the former comes directly from God while the latter is in the hands of man. "And David said to Gad, 'I am in a great strait; let us fall now into the hands of the Lord, for His mercies are great; and let me not fall into the hands of man.' So the Lord sent pestilence upon Yisrael..."(*Shemuel* II, 24:14-15).

As we have seen repeatedly in the commentaries, every word the Sages use has significance. We may ask ourselves, therefore, why the Sages say "sword" and not "war" here. Although the one is symbolic of the other, they are not really identical. War can be waged without a blow being struck, the sword can be employed without war being declared and an armed peace is still the lesser of two evils. As long as politics and diplomacy, rather than justice and right, decide the fate of nations, the sword will have to be retained. Indeed, as long as the nations do not recognize God's Law as supreme, this will be so. "As for His ordinances (משפטים), they do not know them" (*Tehillim* 147:20). Rabbi Hirsch explains that not only are all the other nations ignorant of the חוקים, those statutes which are unable to be understood but which help the Jew to stay within the required bounds of morality and sanctity, but they are even ignorant of the משפטים, those ordinances which appeal to human reason and are universally accepted as good for society. The nations believe that law is a variable, a social factor which can be determined by the views of any given society at any given time, based on what they see as their needs. That is why the law and social order of other nations are constantly changing and have no enduring basis.

יב חַיָּה רָעָה בָּאָה לָעוֹלָם עַל שְׁבוּעַת שָׁוְא
וְעַל חִלּוּל־הַשֵּׁם. גָּלוּת בָּא לָעוֹלָם
עַל־עֲבוֹדָה זָרָה וְעַל־גִּלּוּי עֲרָיוֹת וְעַל־שְׁפִיכוּת
דָּמִים וְעַל־שְׁמִטַּת הָאָרֶץ:

12 (6) Wild beasts come into the world because of
vain oaths and the profanation of the Divine Name.
(7) Exile comes to the world because of idolatry, immorality, murder and [the transgression of] the Sabbatical year.

*   *   *

שבועת שוא, "a vain oath," is to be distinguished from שבועת שקר, "a
false oath." If someone swears that wood is stone, that is a false oath,
but if someone swears that wood is wood then he has sworn in vain.
This vain oath is the subject of the third commandment and the
verse contains both the injunction and the penalty: "You shall not
take the Name of the Lord in vain, for the Lord will not hold him
guiltless who takes His Name in vain" (*Shemoth* 20:7). However, in
the Gemara, חיה רעה, "the wild beast," is mentioned also as the
penalty both for שבועת שקר, a false oath, and for the desecration of
the Shabbath (*Shabbath* 33a). The Torah tells us that after the Flood,
all the beasts of the earth would fear man (see *Bereshith* 9:2), not
because of man's strength, but because of the Divine light that
shines from every man's countenance when he truly walks in God's
pathways (see *Shabbath* 151b). If this spark is extinguished, if this
Divine light is dimmed, then the animals will lose their fear of man
and beasts of prey will enter the world. When God's majesty is
violated by human beings through false or even vain oaths, by the
desecration of the Shabbath, or profanation of the Divine Name,
then God's blessing is withdrawn and beasts of prey roam at will.

Some commentators are of the opinion that this mishnah refers
to man's degrading himself to a bestial state by profaning sacred
things on earth. According to this opinion, the difficult expression,
חיה רעה באה לעולם, "Wild beasts come into the world," would then be
adequately explained, for beasts of prey are not created by perjur-

ers and Shabbath-breakers, but already exist in the world.

The Divine Name is sometimes profaned even without an oath. Practically everything we do either sanctifies or desecrates the Name of God. "What constitutes profanation? Rav answered, 'If, for example, I take meat from the butcher and do not pay him at once'" (*Yoma* 86a). Postponing payment causes a loss to the seller, which is dishonest, and dishonesty is a desecration of God Who has founded His world on law and justice.

So far, we have described "the wild beast" as a beast of prey. Today beasts of prey are not too commonly seen in the civilized parts of the world; unfortunately, however, desecration of the Shabbath and profanation of God's Name are only too frequently seen. Even though the literal translation of חיה רעה is "evil beast," it is by no means certain that the evil beast is necessarily the strongest, the wildest or the most vicious animal. A scientist would tell us the opposite, in fact—that the physical strength of small animals is comparatively greater than that of large ones. "Wherever you will find the greatness of God, there you will also find His humility" (*Megillah* 31a). The most destructive creatures are not hyenas and tigers at all, but bacteria and viruses. Insects of many kinds devastate our fields far more effectively than all the beasts of the forest.

EXILE COMES TO THE WORLD BECAUSE OF IDOLATRY, IMMORALITY, MURDER AND [THE TRANSGRESSION OF] THE SABBATICAL YEAR. Exile has meant the loss of God's Temple, the devastation of the Holy Land and the necessity to live among hostile nations. Worse than famine and disease, worse than the sword and the wild beast, exile is really the worst punishment we can suffer. Yet exile has been a means of preserving the awareness of God and His Law through all times and in all countries, as well as a means of keeping the nation itself from annihilation. Although dispersed to every corner of the globe, Jews have found refuge with other Jews in other countries and have established vital communities. The prophet Yirmeyahu asked the question just before the first exile to Bavel (Babylonia):

> Who is the wise man who can understand this, and who is he
> to whom the mouth of the Lord has spoken, that he may
> declare it? Why is the Land perished and laid waste like a

wilderness, so that no one passes through?

The answer is:

> Then the Lord said, Because they have forsaken My Law which I set before them, and have not hearkened to My voice, neither walked in it. But they have walked after the stubborness of their own hearts and after the pagan gods which their fathers taught them. Therefore, thus says the Lord of Hosts, the God of Yisrael: Behold, I will feed this people with wormwood and give them water of gall to drink. I will scatter them among the nations whom neither they nor their fathers have known.
>
>   (*Yirmeyahu* 9:11-15).

God gave us a country to live in according to His Law, the Torah. If we break that Law, we forfeit our country. God's Law, considered simply, can be classified in three categories: duties toward God, duties toward ourselves, and duties toward our fellowmen. Through idol worship we disavow our duty toward God, through immorality we degrade our Divine souls, and through murder we violate our honorable relationship with other men. These are captial crimes; we are not allowed to commit them even to save our lives.

Yisrael, on their own, in their own country, saw only the glittering, tempting surface of the belief in false gods. When they paid the sad price of exile and lived among the idol-worshipers, they discovered the empty, vulgar essence of idol worship and realized the magnitude of their sin and folly. The worship of strange gods can best be countered by banishment to the nations that indulge in this kind of worship. The sanctity of the Holy Land will not tolerate immorality. For this reason the original inhabitants of Cana'an were expelled (*Vayyikra* 18:24-28). The expiatory power of exile has undoubtedly been effective in countering the cardinal sins—for idol worship ceased among the Israelites after the first exile to Bavel, murderers are rarely to be found among Jews anywhere in the world, and immorality is generally less prevalent among Jews. Similarly, the price we have paid for ignoring our duty to allow the soil of the Holy Land to rest in the Sabbatical year is clearly expulsion from the Land.

וג בְּאַרְבָּעָה פְּרָקִים הַדֶּבֶר מִתְרַבֶּה,
בָּרְבִיעִית וּבַשְּׁבִיעִית וּבְמוֹצָאֵי שְׁבִיעִית
וּבְמוֹצָאֵי הֶחָג שֶׁבְּכָל־שָׁנָה וְשָׁנָה. בָּרְבִיעִית מִפְּנֵי
מַעְשַׂר עָנִי שֶׁבַּשְּׁלִישִׁית, בַּשְּׁבִיעִית מִפְּנֵי מַעְשַׂר
עָנִי שֶׁבַּשִּׁשִּׁית, בְּמוֹצָאֵי שְׁבִיעִית מִפְּנֵי פֵּרוֹת
שְׁבִיעִית, בְּמוֹצָאֵי הֶחָג שֶׁבְּכָל־שָׁנָה וְשָׁנָה מִפְּנֵי גֶּזֶל
מַתְּנוֹת עֲנִיִּים:

13 Four times [in the seven-year cycle] pestilence increases: [it happens] in the fourth year, in the seventh year, at the conclusion of the seventh (that is, in the eighth year) and at the conclusion of the Festival of Sukkoth every year. In the fourth year, because the tithe was not given to the poor in the third year; in the seventh year because the tithe was not given to the poor in the sixth year; at the end of the seventh year because of transgressions involving the fruits of the seventh year; and at the conclusion of the Festival of Sukkoth every year because the poor were deprived of their rightful gifts.

*　　*　　*

At the beginning of mishnah 10, we were reminded of the Torah's instructions for planting the soil of the Holy Land in seven-year cycles, and for the division of tithing into three-year intervals for the poor (מעשר העני). Now we are reminded of the מתנות עניים, "the rightful gifts to the poor," which consist of the gleanings of the harvest that have fallen to the ground or have been left in the corners of the field. Likewise, any produce that grows by itself during the seventh year is considered ownerless and therefore the poor may take as much as they wish. The Torah commands property-owners to give these gifts to the poor because without such a reminder, a wealthy man is likely to forget about the poor. If the wealthy neglect their duty, then God will bring famine to the country so that the wealthy will have to share the hunger of the poor. If, even then, the wealthy man hardens his heart and cares purely for himself and his own family, then God will bring pestilence on top of famine to teach him, and us, that all the wealth in the world cannot buy protection from Divine retribution. The Sages regard withholding the poor man's tithe and the poor man's gifts as crimes worse than those which caused the Flood (*Midrash Tehillim* 12).

יד אַרְבַּע מִדּוֹת בָּאָדָם. הָאוֹמֵר שֶׁלִּי שֶׁלִּי
וְשֶׁלְּךָ שֶׁלָּךְ זוֹ מִדָּה בֵּינוֹנִית וְיֵשׁ אוֹמְרִים
זוֹ מִדַּת סְדוֹם, שֶׁלִּי שֶׁלָּךְ וְשֶׁלְּךָ שֶׁלִּי עַם הָאָרֶץ,
שֶׁלִּי שֶׁלָּךְ וְשֶׁלְּךָ שֶׁלָּךְ חָסִיד, שֶׁלִּי שֶׁלִּי, וְשֶׁלְּךָ שֶׁלִּי
רָשָׁע:

14 There are four types of character among men:
the one who says, "what is mine is mine, and what is
yours is yours" is an average type, but some say that
this is the characteristic of Sedom (Sodom); the one
who says, "what is mine is yours and what is yours is
mine" is an ignoramus; the one who says, "what is
mine is yours and what is yours is yours" is a saintly
man; and the one who says, "what is yours is mine and
what is mine is mine" is a lawless man.

*　　*　　*

The word אדם (man) comes from אדמה (the earth), and man is
tied to the material wealth of the earth by the strings of possession. Nothing characterizes a man as well as the way he deals with
his possessions: does he possess them or do they possess him?
This mishnah says that the first type of character is an average
one, a man who gives charity and tithes his produce exactly as
much as the Law says he must, but no more. The additional
duties of גמילות חסדים, "lovingkindness and good deeds," are not
ordered according to a fixed measure (אין להם שעור), so his true
character is revealed by how he allocates the nine-tenths left to
him after the required tenth is taken. Thus the average person
says, "What is mine is coming to me, so why should I share it?"
This is the mentality of strict justice untempered by mercy or
compassion. This is the harsh justice characteristic of the people
of Sedom, which led to terrible injustice, and finally, to extinction
by the hand of God. Avraham was destined to father a "great and
mighty nation...[because he would] command his children and
his household after him to keep the way of the Lord, to do

righteousness and justice" (*Bereshith* 18:18-19). Righteousness is placed before justice in the verse.

The character who says, "What is mine is yours and what is yours is mine," has to be an ignoramus, because if there is no longer a difference between mine and yours, then private property is forbidden and that is communism! This mentality can also lead to cold-blooded, shrewd opportunism, the expectation of a material return for the smallest service performed for someone else. This type is a striking contrast to the unselfish, righteous person who says, "What is mine is yours and what is yours is yours," or in other words, "Whatever is mine is at your disposal and I do not expect anything from you in return." This is the principle of חסד, doing good for its own sake without thinking of recompense. The lawless character who says, "What is yours is mine and what is mine is mine," is not even satisfied with being recompensed for his services—he wants only to take and never to give. "A lawless man borrows and never repays his debt, but a righteous man deals generously and gives" (*Tehillim* 37:21). The lesson we should learn here is that everything we have in this world is on loan to us for the sole purpose of benefiting God's world according to His Law. No person exists for himself alone; the more he has been given, the more is expected of him. On the other hand, the less the צדיק receives from this world, the more the world is indebted to him. Thus it is said of Rabbi Chanina ben Dosa: "Every day a Divine voice goes forth from Mount Chorev and proclaims, 'The whole world is sustained for the sake of My son Chanina, yet Chanina subsists on a few carobs from one Shabbath eve to the next' " (*Berachoth* 17b).

טו אַרְבַּע מִדּוֹת בְּדֵעוֹת. נוֹחַ לִכְעוֹס וְנוֹחַ
לִרְצוֹת יָצָא הֶפְסֵדוֹ בִּשְׂכָרוֹ, קָשֶׁה
לִכְעוֹס וְקָשֶׁה לִרְצוֹת יָצָא שְׂכָרוֹ בְּהֶפְסֵדוֹ, קָשֶׁה
לִכְעוֹס וְנוֹחַ לִרְצוֹת חָסִיד, נוֹחַ לִכְעוֹס וְקָשֶׁה
לִרְצוֹת רָשָׁע:

15 There are four types of temperament [among men]: one who is easy to provoke and easy to pacify— his loss disappears in his gain; one who is hard to provoke and hard to pacify—his gain disappears in his loss; one who is hard to provoke and easy to pacify is a saintly man; and one who is easy to provoke and hard to pacify is a lawless man.

*   *   *

The passion of anger is the subject of many admonitions and lessons from the Sages. It is one of the most common human weaknesses, but strangely enough, it is not regarded as a weakness by those who succumb to it. The man does not exist who is never provoked to anger; not only can man be angry once in a while, but he ought to become angry at times. Moreover, one who is incapable of feeling anger and cannot be aroused to indignation by a wrong is usually not capable of appreciating beauty either. Indeed, even God, the Holy One, blessed is He, has shown us His wrath. "God is the righteous Judge, and God is angered every day. And if man does not repent, He will sharpen His sword, He will bend and aim His bow. He will also prepare for him weapons of death, and use His arrows which He made sharp" (*Tehillim* 7:12-14). You, too, should become angry when you see evil being done. When you do grow angry, however, beware of two things: do not thirst for revenge and do not maintain your ire too long. "Be angry but do not sin!" (*Tehillim* 4:5). Let your anger be brief, like the lightning—רגע וכמה זעמו? זועם בכל יום, ואל, God also grows angry, as it were, but only for an instant (*Berachoth* 7a). Try not to be stirred to anger too easily, too often, or for trivial reasons, and above all, never act in anger. Listen to the words of the Sages:

> As to every man who becomes angry—if he is a Sage, his wisdom departs from him; if he is a prophet, his prophecy departs from him.
>
> *(Pesachim* 66b)

> A stone is heavy and the sand weighty; but a fool's anger outweighs them both.
>
> *(Mishlei* 27:3)

> It is sensible for a man to be slow to anger, and it is his glory to overlook a transgression.
>
> (ibid. 19:11)

The mishnah speaks of four degrees of anger. It is not especially meritorious to recognize people's good qualities and appreciate their virtues. On the other hand, it is indeed praiseworthy to tolerate the weaknesses of others and to forgive their errors. Our goal should be to emulate the truly pious: be slow to anger and quick to forgive. Even if we tend to lose our temper, it is always better to relent quickly. Nothing renders us more worthy of God's indulgence and mercy than the indulgence and mercy we show to others. And even if you are slow to become angry, by retaining your anger long after the event you will corrode your own character. This trait also reveals a certain amount of egotism. The ultimate degree of anger, exemplified by a volatile temperament which flares up easily and is also difficult to placate, reveals not only an evil person but a frustrated, unhappy one as well.

טז אַרְבַּע מִדּוֹת בְּתַלְמִידִים. מָהִיר לִשְׁמוֹעַ
וּמָהִיר לְאַבֵּד יָצָא שְׂכָרוֹ בְּהֶפְסֵדוֹ, קָשֶׁה
לִשְׁמוֹעַ וְקָשֶׁה לְאַבֵּד יָצָא הֶפְסֵדוֹ בִּשְׂכָרוֹ, מָהִיר
לִשְׁמוֹעַ וְקָשֶׁה לְאַבֵּד זוֹ חֵלֶק טוֹב, קָשֶׁה לִשְׁמוֹעַ
וּמָהִיר לְאַבֵּד זוֹ חֵלֶק רַע:

16 There are four types of students: one who is quick to learn and quick to forget—his gain disappears in his loss; one who is slow to learn and slow to forget—his loss disappears in his gain; one who is quick to learn and slow to forget—this is the best portion; one who is slow to learn and quick to forget—this is the worst portion.

* * *

We are students who learn all our lives, or at least we should be. Even if it were possible to learn everything worth learning, it would still be our duty to continue learning, for that is an end in itself. In the case of one who forgets everything as quickly as he learns it, he loses as much as he gains; perhaps, however, his effort will eventually be repaid and he will train his mind. "Rava said: By all means, one should learn even though one is liable to forget" (*Avodah Zarah* 19a). A student who is not gifted must expend a great deal of time and effort in learning, but he will be compensated in full: he will retain his knowledge. Once a student said to his more brilliant companion, "The difference between us is only a small piece of candle that I keep burning longer than you in order to complete my studies." Only the truly gifted can learn easily, expend little effort, and remember everything. Some versions of the text say that this type of student is a חכם, "a wise one," rather than that he has a חלק טוב, "the best portion." It is most likely that Rava's advice, to learn even though you may forget, really applies to the type of student who has the worst portion—slow to learn and quick to forget—because any student's success is ultimately dependent on God. If we do not meet with great immediate success, our efforts will be doubly rewarded, for לפום צערא אגרא, "The reward is according to the effort" (*Avoth* 5:28).

וַ אַרְבַּע מִדּוֹת בְּנוֹתְנֵי צְדָקָה. הָרוֹצֶה
שֶׁיִּתֵּן וְלֹא יִתְּנוּ אֲחֵרִים עֵינוֹ רָעָה בְּשֶׁל-
אֲחֵרִים, יִתְּנוּ אֲחֵרִים וְהוּא לֹא יִתֵּן עֵינוֹ רָעָה
בְּשֶׁלּוֹ, יִתֵּן וְיִתְּנוּ אֲחֵרִים חָסִיד, לֹא יִתֵּן וְלֹא יִתְּנוּ
אֲחֵרִים רָשָׁע:

17 There are four traits characterizing those who
give charity: one who wants to give but does not want
others to give—he looks grudgingly towards others;
one who wants others to give but will not give himself—he is miserly; one who gives himself and wants
others to give, also, is saintly, [but] one who will not
give himself, and does not want others to give either,
is wicked.

*   *   *

The act of giving to charity is used in this mishnah as a measure
of morality, just as anger and wealth are used in the previous
ones. The act of giving is meaningless in itself if the donor gives
with the wrong motives. Giving charity is no more the sign of a
good heart than paying taxes. The word we are accustomed to
translate as "charity" —צדקה—literally means "doing one's duty,"
so that wherever Jewish Law prevails, everyone is obligated to
give צדקה and may even be forced to do so. Gifts to the poor must
therefore not be regarded as alms but rather as dutiful donations,
and a poor man must not be considered a beggar. Thus, a person
who gives to the poor but resents it or is jealous when others give,
is not really compassionate and does not really care about the
poor. His donations are merely the fulfillment of a duty and a
display of selfishness to boot. Similarly, the man who allows
others to practice charity, but refuses to do so himself, also shows
a lack of true feeling for the poor. He may even encourage others
to help the poor, but he resents having to give from his own

wealth. The true צדיק acknowledges his own obligations and also tries to help others acknowledge theirs. In either case, his motivation is to provide properly for the poor; he is a *tzaddik*, a pious person. It is sad but true that even among supposedly humane and philanthropic men, we find the all-too-common attitude that the poor will always be poor and that they probably should remain so. This attitude is immoral and wicked.

יח אַרְבַּע מִדּוֹת בְּהוֹלְכֵי בֵית הַמִּדְרָשׁ.
הוֹלֵךְ וְאֵינוֹ עוֹשֶׂה שְׂכַר הֲלִיכָה בְּיָדוֹ,
עוֹשֶׂה וְאֵינוֹ הוֹלֵךְ שְׂכַר מַעֲשֶׂה בְּיָדוֹ, הוֹלֵךְ וְעוֹשֶׂה
חָסִיד, לֹא הוֹלֵךְ וְלֹא עוֹשֶׂה רָשָׁע:

18 There are four types among those who attend the house of study: one who attends but does not practice [what he has learned]—he will receive the reward for attending; one who practices [what he has learned] but does not attend [the house of study]—he will receive the reward for practicing; one who attends and also practices is saintly; and one who neither attends nor practices is wicked.

*   *   *

The Torah is the living soul of the Jewish people; it is a pillar which rests on the pedestal of the *beith ha-midrash*. The distinctiveness of the Torah is especially revealed in the Oral Law, that knowledge which was originally transmitted from generation to generation by word of mouth. Although the Oral Law was written down in the course of time, it cannot be studied exclusively from books even today. A thorough knowledge of the Torah requires the active association of students with teachers, and that is the purpose of the *beith ha-midrash*.

THOSE WHO ATTEND THE HOUSE OF STUDY. This expression means, in fact, the whole Jewish community. In the time of the Mishnah, establishing a *beith ha-midrash* was regarded as more important than building a *beith ha-kenesseth* (a synagogue). The Torah that is learned in the *beith ha-midrash* sets the standards for the service to be carried out in the synagogue. While prayer is an expression of the heart, the words of the Torah are aimed at the mind. The combined force of thoughts and feelings, of Torah and prayer, of *beith ha-midrash* (learning) and *beith ha-kenesseth* (doing) has preserved in Yisrael a unique acuity of intellect and warmth of heart to this very day. This harmonious cooperation of head and heart is a manifestation of God's splendor which illuminates the lives of all those who daily go from the synagogue to the house of study. "Rabbi Levi bar Chiyya said: When a man goes from the synagogue to the house of study and occupies himself with the Torah, he is worthy of having the Divine Presence rest upon him" (*Berachoth* 64a).

The extent of Jewish learning, at the time that the Assyrian military forces threatened to subjugate the Holy Land, is described to us in the Talmud.

> The yoke of Sancheriv was destroyed on account of the oil of King Chizkiyyahu which burned in the synagogues and academies. What did the king do? He planted a sword by the door of the houses of study and proclaimed, "He who will not study the Torah will be pierced with this sword." They searched from Dan to Be'ersheva and not one unlettered person was found; from Gevath to Antiferas, no boy or girl, no man or woman was found who was not thoroughly versed in the laws of cleanliness and uncleanliness [the difficult laws of the Torah].
>
> (*Sanhedrin* 94b)

Those who built and attended houses of study were accustomed to the constant and stimulating exchange of ideas among themselves. They continually heard instructive admonishment from the masters of the *beith ha-midrash*. This increased their fortitude and gave them strength for the constant battle against frivolity and sin. "If this repulsive wretch meets you, drag him to the *beith ha-midrash*" (*Sukkah* 52b). The remarkable spirit emanating from the *beith ha-midrash*, throughout the sorrowful centuries of exile, preserved Yisrael in its dispersion; it is described by Rabbi Hirsch in his commentary on the verse, יי אלהי ישועתי יום צעקתי בלילה נגדך, "*Hashem*, God of my salvation, I have cried out by day, at night I am before You" (*Tehillim* 88:2). All day long the Jew struggled for his bread, pitted his strength against his persecutors, and suffered derision, scorn and malice from the nations. At the end of the day, he returned to his home, to his beloved family, to his fellow Jews, to his books and his house of study and prayer, and to communion with God. Only at night could he communicate with like-minded companions and find knowledge and understanding, comfort and courage; the words of his great ancestors gave him strength and inspiration to carry out the mission assigned him by God. In this spirit the Jew worked with his brethren and built a communal life based on order and right. When the itinerant pedlar laid down his bundle of wares at night, he also put aside his burden of troubles. He stood proudly as a man among men before his God Who had "set him free"; he savored spiritual bliss. The mob that baited him by day had no understanding of his spiritual pleasures. Indeed, it hardly suspected their existence.

ONE WHO ATTENDS AND ALSO PRACTICES. The Jew who not only tries to perfect himself by learning devotedly, but also goes daily to the *beith ha-midrash* and exerts a favorable influence over others, is the most praiseworthy of men.

יט אַרְבַּע מִדּוֹת בְּיוֹשְׁבִים לִפְנֵי חֲכָמִים,
סְפוֹג וּמַשְׁפֵּךְ מְשַׁמֶּרֶת וְנָפָה; סְפוֹג
שֶׁהוּא סוֹפֵג אֶת־הַכֹּל, וּמַשְׁפֵּךְ שֶׁמַּכְנִיס בְּזוֹ וּמוֹצִיא
בְזוֹ, מְשַׁמֶּרֶת שֶׁמּוֹצִיאָה אֶת־הַיַּיִן וְקוֹלֶטֶת אֶת
הַשְּׁמָרִים, וְנָפָה שֶׁמּוֹצִיאָה אֶת־הַקֶּמַח וְקוֹלֶטֶת
אֶת־הַסֹּלֶת:

19 There are four types of men who sit before the Sages: a sponge, a funnel, a strainer and a sieve. A sponge absorbs everything; a funnel lets in at one end and lets out at the other; a strainer lets the wine pass through and retains the sediment; and a sieve lets out the coarse meal and retains the fine flour.

* * *

It is not sufficient to go to the house of study; you must also sit before the Sages. The word *yeshivah* is derived from the root ישב (sit), referring to the group-learning of many students together, but the Hebrew word implies more than just sitting down to study. It means sitting down and seriously learning the subject. As we have already learned: מרבה ישיבה מרבה חכמה, "The more study, the more wisdom" (*Avoth* 2:8). Thus the Talmud teaches that *yeshivah* is not only the institution where Torah is studied, but also the study itself when it is done diligently.

> The people of Alexandria asked Rabbi Yosei ben Chanina, "What must a man do to become wise?" He answered them, "Let him engage in much study and restrict his business."
>
> (*Niddah* 70b)

Resh Lakish said, "If you see a student to whom his studies are as hard as iron, it is because he has failed to systematize them...What is the remedy? Let him study more diligently." Thus Resh Lakish made it his practice to repeat his studies forty times over, corresponding to the forty days during which the Torah was given, and only then would he come before Rabbi Yochanan.

(Ta'anith 8a)

In this sense, we should all sit before the Sages. We should try to absorb carefully all the wisdom they impart, without intruding our own faulty reasoning or biased opinions. And later, we should not selfishly keep their instruction to ourselves but pass it on to others. Although the sponge needs help in passing on that which it has absorbed, and the funnel needs no help but receives more than it can transmit, nevertheless, a ray of Torah wisdom passed on from one person to another is a spiritual bond; it joins teacher to pupil, master to disciple, companion to companion, and above all, the past to the present. A disciple who truly understands the deeper truths he has learned but also recognizes the limitations of his own disciples, is like the strainer: he serves only the clear wine to his disciples. He may be considered a superior teacher. The sieve, however, represents the most accomplished disciple: he is so superior morally that he can separate the coarse meal from the pure refined flour by himself. Elisha ben Avuyah, the only Torah Sage in our history who disavowed the Torah, had a disciple even greater than himself: Rabbi Meir. Rabbi Meir could not renounce his teacher, and hoped to the end that he would repent. Still, we must ask ourselves how Rabbi Meir could have learned from such a teacher. Only a disciple of the highest moral character, like Rabbi Meir, could succeed in absorbing only wisdom and no damaging influences.

כָּל־אַהֲבָה שֶׁהִיא־תְלוּיָה בְדָבָר בָּטֵל
דָּבָר בְּטֵלָה אַהֲבָה, וְשֶׁאֵינָה תְלוּיָה
בְדָבָר אֵינָה בְּטֵלָה לְעוֹלָם; אֵיזוֹ הִיא אַהֲבָה שֶׁהִיא־
תְלוּיָה בְדָבָר זוֹ אַהֲבַת אַמְנוֹן וְתָמָר, וְשֶׁאֵינָה
תְלוּיָה בְדָבָר זוֹ אַהֲבַת דָּוִד וִיהוֹנָתָן:

20 Love which depends upon a specific cause will
cease once the cause is no longer there, but love
which is not dependent upon a specific cause will
never cease. Which love was dependent upon a specific cause? The love of Amnon and Tamar. And
which love did not depend upon any cause? The love
of David and Yonathan.

*   *   *

We read in the Torah and say in our daily prayers, שמע, "Hear!,"
followed by ואהבת, "and you shall love..." In Pirkei Avoth, "learning" is also followed by "love." This can only refer to the pure,
unselfish love of learning that draws Jews of all ages and abilities to
the *beith ha-midrash* and induces them to learn from the words of our
Sages. Torah knowledge, sought for its own sake and for no selfish
reasons, is what brings us the blessings listed in the next chapter.
The Sages explain love of God and His Torah in terms of human
love so that we may understand it better. Unselfish and lasting love
cannot really be explained. If we are able to name the reason why
we love a particular person, then our concern is not for that person
but for ourselves. Even if we think we love a person for his wonderful spiritual qualities, like a teacher, that is not the pure love we are
talking about. Pure love consists of complete devotion to the beloved
object with no expectation of that love being returned nor of deriving
any benefit from it. It does not arise from any cause, it is not based
on outward attraction and charm, and it is of unlimited duration. It
lasts as long as the person is alive, and even beyond the grave.

    A good example of this is the love of parents for their chil-
dren. Even when the child does not live up to the parents' expec-

tations, the parents do not cease to love him. Similarly, it is comforting to know that we are God's children, and that our own
weaknesses and faults will not cause Him to withdraw His love
from us. However, when we base our love of God on something
specific that He has granted us, like wealth, beauty, good health,
or having children, then even this love of God will probably not
last. It will disappear as soon as we are deprived of the wealth, the
beauty, the good health or the children. Likewise, a person who
loves God on account of His omnipotence, His omniscience, His
many acts of grace, or indeed any other reason, is actually engaging
in worship and not love. The love of God which is commanded to us
in the Torah: ואהבת את יי אלוהיך בכל לבבך ובכל נפשך ובכל מאדך, "You
shall love the Lord your God with all your heart, with all your soul
and with all your might" (*Devarim* 6:5), is an emotion that should
be like the love between parents and children, without relation to
God's greatness or blessings. It is an ideal achieved by few people;
our father Avraham was one of those few and he was called, אהבי,
"one who loved Me" (*Yeshayahu* 41:8).

The example of Amnon and Tamar, described in Shemuel II,
13, shows us how easily a person in love may delude himself.
Amnon felt a great passion for Tamar and thought it was love,
but when his passion was satisfied through cunning and force, his
so-called love turned into hatred even stronger than the love had
been. A perfect example of pure, unselfish love, independent of
external stimulus, is the love between Yonathan and David described in Shemuel I, 18. The first verse of this passage provides
a key to the secret of pure love: ויהי ככלתו לדבר אל שאול ונפש יהונתן
נקשרה בנפש דוד ויהבו יהונתן כנפשו, "And it came to pass when he had
finished speaking to Shaul, and the soul of Yonathan was knit
with the soul of David, and Yonathan loved him like his own
soul." Yonathan's love for David was as unblemished as the feeling we each have for our own soul. This love does not spring
from external causes; it is natural and eternal. A man will instinctively stake everything to save his own soul. The same expression
describes Ya'akov's love for Binyamin: ונפשו קשורה בנפשו, "And his
soul was knit with his soul" (*Bereshith* 44:30). That is the meaning
of the words ויאהבו כנפשו. Such is the love that man ought to feel
for his Creator. Such love can only be found together with wisdom, justice and fear of God, and is, in itself, a blessing from God.

כָּל מַחֲלֶקֶת שֶׁהִיא לְשֵׁם שָׁמַיִם סוֹפָהּ כא
לְהִתְקַיֵּם וְשֶׁאֵינָהּ לְשֵׁם שָׁמַיִם אֵין סוֹפָהּ
לְהִתְקַיֵּם; אֵיזוֹ הִיא מַחֲלֶקֶת שֶׁהִיא לְשֵׁם שָׁמַיִם זוֹ
מַחֲלֶקֶת הִלֵּל וְשַׁמַּאי, וְשֶׁאֵינָהּ לְשֵׁם שָׁמַיִם זוֹ
מַחֲלֶקֶת קֹרַח וְכָל-עֲדָתוֹ:

21 Every controversy which is in the name of
Heaven will in the end achieve a lasting result, and
every controversy which is not in the name of Heaven
will in the end have ephemeral results. Which controversy was in the name of Heaven? The controversy
between Hillel and Shammai. And which controversy
was not in the name of Heaven? The controversy of
Korach and his followers.

* * *

What we have just learned about love applies in the same way to
controversy. The outcome of a controversy that is conducted with
pure motives will be of enduring value, and just as all love is not
necessarily praiseworthy, all controversy is not necessarily reprehensible. "There is a time for loving and a time for hating"
(*Koheleth* 3:8).

IN THE NAME OF HEAVEN. It is characteristic of Jewish
thought that when Heaven is mentioned, reference to God is
intended. We Jews know that the whole earth is full of the same
Divine glory that radiates from Heaven, yet the voice of God
Himself came to them from out of the fire and the cloud at Sinai:
"You have seen that I spoke to you from Heaven" (*Shemoth*
20:19). Heaven remains God's but the earth was given to man. All
the heavenly bodies, every ray of sunlight and each drop of rain
proclaim the presence of God. Therefore, the more that Jews
were deprived of earthly possessions through the years, the more
whole-heartedly they turned to Heaven, to the Name of the One
Who revealed His Law to them.

Our holy tongue has several words besides מחלקת that express conflict and dispute: ריב, מצה, מדון. The root of the word מחלקת, "controversy," means a division or separation leading in different directions; thus a difference of opinion leads to a division. The result of such a difference of opinion, if it is truly intended for the sake of Heaven, will lead to the attainment of truth and will ultimately benefit both sides. Such a controversy is not really a conflict because the difference of opinion is not about the essence of the matter, nor does the difference impair the good personal relations between the contenders. This is what Rabbi Chiyya means when he teaches, "Even father and son, master and disciple, who study Torah at the same gate, become enemies of each other, yet they do not stir from there until they come to love each other" (*Kiddushin* 30b). The emphasis in this lesson is on the word "gate," that is, the gate of Heaven, where all those who act in the Name of Heaven will finally come together in peace.

The differences of opinion between Hillel and Shammai are cited as examples of this type of controversy. "Rabbi Abba stated in the name of Shemuel: For three years there was a dispute between *beith* Shammai and *beith* Hillel, the former asserting that the *halachah* was in agreement with their views, and the latter contending that the *halachah* was in agreement with theirs. Then a Divine voice was heard, announcing, 'The utterances of both are words of the living God, but the *halachah* is in agreement with the rulings of *beith* Hillel' " (*Eruvin* 13b). When Hillel and Shammai, or Abbaye and Rava, or two *Rishonim* or two *Acharonim*, differed in the interpretation of a law, there was never the slightest doubt on either side regarding the binding force of the law itself.

The commentators find it strange that two contending parties are mentioned as an example in the case of Hillel and Shammai, but only one party is mentioned in the example of Korach. A deeper study of the controversy will solve this question.

Korach was ambitious and resented Moshe's unselfishness. He was not only intent on usurping Moshe's position of leadership; he wanted to get rid of him altogether, and he needed his followers to act as a court of law which would sentence Moshe officially. Korach easily convinced his followers that Moshe deserved the death sentence, and they decided unanimously against Moshe. According to Jewish legal procedure, however, a unanimous judgment in favor of the death sentence shows that the panel is biased and that renders the sentence invalid. In the end, therefore, Korach himself had to render a dissenting opinion in Moshe's favor. Although Korach was forced into a controversy with his followers, there was really no difference of opinion between them.

Rabbi Yitzchak Arama, the author of the commentary Akedah, explains the mishnah this way: "Any controversy conducted for God's sake is aimed at preservation, and any controversy not conducted for God's sake is not aimed at preservation." This concept gives us a standard of values with which we can determine whether a controversy is moral or immoral, constructive or destructive. When you enter a controversy to correct something you believe is wrong, it is certainly meritorious on your part, whether it is a political or a religious matter. Take care, however, that you understand clearly beforehand what should replace that which will be destroyed if your efforts are successful. If you cannot create something new and better, then you are fighting for the pleasure of destruction, which is clearly not for the sake of Heaven.

כב כָּל־הַמְזַכֶּה אֶת־הָרַבִּים אֵין חֵטְא בָּא עַל־
יָדוֹ וְכָל־הַמַּחֲטִיא אֶת־הָרַבִּים אֵין־
מַסְפִּיקִין בְּיָדוֹ לַעֲשׂוֹת תְּשׁוּבָה. מֹשֶׁה זָכָה וְזִכָּה
אֶת־הָרַבִּים, זְכוּת הָרַבִּים תָּלוּי בּוֹ, שֶׁנֶּאֱמַר צִדְקַת יְיָ
עָשָׂה וּמִשְׁפָּטָיו עִם־יִשְׂרָאֵל. יָרָבְעָם בֶּן־נְבָט חָטָא
וְהֶחֱטִיא אֶת־הָרַבִּים, חֵטְא הָרַבִּים תָּלוּי בּוֹ,
שֶׁנֶּאֱמַר עַל־חַטֹּאות יָרָבְעָם אֲשֶׁר חָטָא וַאֲשֶׁר
הֶחֱטִיא אֶת־יִשְׂרָאֵל:

22 One who leads the multitude to righteousness shall cause no sin; but one who leads the multitude to sin will not be given the means to repent. Moshe was righteous and led the multitude to righteousness, so the merit of the multitude was ascribed to him, as it is said, "He performed the righteousness of God and His ordinances remained with Yisrael" (*Devarim* 33:21). Yarovam, the son of Nevat, sinned and led the multitude to sin. The sin of the multitude was ascribed to him, as it is said, "Because of the sins of Yarovam who sinned and caused Yisrael to sin" (*Melachim* I, 15:30).

*　　*　　*

In the last mishnah we were taught that controversy may be desirable at times, as long as its object is constructive and for the sake of Heaven. This mishnah directs us to the next step: in addition to upholding and preserving the Name and Laws of God, we ought to make them known to others. It is our duty to practice the commandments, but doing so is doing no more than our duty. Encouraging others to join us in doing good will discharge far more than just our personal obligations. We are all children of one Father. If one of us acts irresponsibly, others will be affected by it. We are even more answerable for a wrong done with our knowledge when we might have prevented it with a word of warning or encouragement. "Whoever can prevent his household from committing a sin, but does not, is held responsible for the sins of his household; if he can prevent his fellow citizens and does not, he will be held responsible for the sins of his fellow citizens; if the whole world, he will be held responsible for the sins of the whole world" (*Shabbath* 54b). We pray daily that God will protect us from "sin, transgression and iniquity and keep us from passion, temptation and error." Helping others to do good is a guarantee that our request will be granted. "And they that turn the many to righteousness [will shine] as the stars forever and ever" (*Daniyyel* 12:3). They stand forever as beacons to the generations that follow after them. Among the many teachers and prophets in Yisrael's history, our first and greatest was Moshe. He dedicated his life to enlisting Yisrael in the service of God and he succeeded so well, despite many adversities, that God's Torah is known as תורת משה, "Moshe's Torah," to this very day. Spreading God's Law was by no means an easy task, but he persevered.

This mishnah contrasts the tranquil, majestic leadership of Moshe with the turbulent kingship of Yarovam. Moshe's teachings extend forward into eternity; the good that Moshe did can never be revoked by any temporal event. Yarovam's achievements were ephemeral; his crimes can never be offset by repentance.

אמר לרשע צדיק אתה יקבהו עמים יזעמוהו לאמים: ולמוכיחים ינעם ועליהם תבוא ברכת טוב, "The one who says to the wicked, 'You are righteous' — the nations will curse him...[but] he who reproves others, they will fare well" (*Mishlei* 24:24-25). When you know that someone is doing something wrong and you keep silent, you are in effect condoning his evil and you deserve to be cursed with all the curses of the Torah. When you reprove your friend, however, and encourage him to repent, it will be well with you. Furthermore, when he accepts the reproof, it will be well with both of you, for the verse says עליהם, "they" will fare well. Moshe admonished his contemporaries, they accepted the reproof for life, and that is why they also received the blessing from God. King Shelomo said, "The ear that receives the reproof for life is wise and may be considered like Moshe's contemporaries" (*Midrash Yalkut Devarim* 793).

כג כָּל־מִי שֶׁיֶּשׁ־בּוֹ שְׁלֹשָׁה דְבָרִים הַלָּלוּ הוּא מִתַּלְמִידָיו שֶׁל־אַבְרָהָם אָבִינוּ, וּשְׁלֹשָׁה דְבָרִים אֲחֵרִים הוּא מִתַּלְמִידָיו שֶׁל־בִּלְעָם הָרָשָׁע. עַיִן טוֹבָה וְרוּחַ נְמוּכָה וְנֶפֶשׁ שְׁפָלָה מִתַּלְמִידָיו שֶׁל־אַבְרָהָם אָבִינוּ, עַיִן רָעָה וְרוּחַ גְּבוֹהָה וְנֶפֶשׁ רְחָבָה מִתַּלְמִידָיו שֶׁל־בִּלְעָם הָרָשָׁע. מַה בֵּין תַּלְמִידָיו שֶׁל־אַבְרָהָם אָבִינוּ לְתַלְמִידָיו שֶׁל־בִּלְעָם הָרָשָׁע. תַּלְמִידָיו שֶׁל־אַבְרָהָם אָבִינוּ אוֹכְלִין בָּעוֹלָם הַזֶּה וְנוֹחֲלִין הָעוֹלָם הַבָּא, שֶׁנֶּאֱמַר לְהַנְחִיל אֹהֲבַי יֵשׁ וְאֹצְרֹתֵיהֶם אֲמַלֵּא. אֲבָל תַּלְמִידָיו שֶׁל־בִּלְעָם הָרָשָׁע יוֹרְשִׁין גֵּיהִנֹּם וְיוֹרְדִין לִבְאֵר שַׁחַת, שֶׁנֶּאֱמַר וְאַתָּה אֱלֹהִים תּוֹרִדֵם לִבְאֵר שַׁחַת, אַנְשֵׁי דָמִים וּמִרְמָה לֹא־יֶחֱצוּ יְמֵיהֶם, וַאֲנִי אֶבְטַח־בָּךְ:

23 Whoever possesses the following three attributes is a disciple of our father Avraham, and whoever possesses the three opposite traits is a disciple of the lawless Bilam: a good eye, a humble spirit and an undemanding soul, these are the characteristics of the disciples of Avraham; an evil eye, a haughty spirit and a demanding soul are the characteristics of the disciples of Bilam. What difference is there between the disciples of Avraham and the disciples of Bilam? The disciples of Avraham enjoy this world and inherit the World to Come, as it is said, "That I may cause those who love me to inherit everlasting wealth and I shall fill their treasuries" (*Mishlei* 8:21). The disciples of Bilam, on the other hand, inherit *Gehinnom* and descend into the pit of destruction, for it is said, "You,

God, will bring them down into the pit; men of murder and deceit shall not live out half their days; but I
will go on trusting You" (*Tehillim* 55:24).

*   *   *

Our father Avraham was called upon, as his name indicates, to be
the spiritual father of a multitude of nations, אב המון גוים. Yet in
his time, with his steadfast faith and high standards of morality,
he stood alone in the world and had to search out like-minded
companions from among the people around him. Bilam, likewise, preached to the people among whom he lived. Yet those
who hearkened to Avraham and those who gravitated to Bilam
were not the same at all. In Avraham's day, as in ours, wherever
benevolence is practiced and modesty is cherished, there
Avraham's disciples gather; wherever envy and arrogance assert
themselves, there Bilam's curse upon mankind still prevails.

A GOOD EYE. This is said of someone who sees everything
optimistically, who believes in man's inherent goodness and humanity. This type of outlook ought to be applied in judging your
fellowman, in business dealings and in all circumstances of your
life. The good eye sees that learning God's Law is of prime
importance, and relies upon the truth of our Tradition; it has
אמונת חכמים, "trust in the Sages," which is one of the essential
requirements for acquiring Torah knowledge. Remember how
highly Rabbi Eliezer ben Hurkanos valued a good eye (*Avoth*
2:13).

A HUMBLE SPIRIT AND AN UNDEMANDING SOUL. A per-
son who controls the strivings and passions of his mind and heart
to such an extent that they never stray from God's path has
רוח נמוכה; he does not show anger even when it is permissible to;
he shows consideration and respect to all men, even the most
humble, and disregards his own honor completely. This humility
of spirit generates a degree of modesty which we call נפש שפלה,
"an unpretentious, undemanding soul." Throughout Avraham's life
he demonstrated these three qualities. He accepted God's instruction to leave his home and go to a strange country; he did it with
good will and forbearance; and he faced each of the ten trials of

his life with the same benevolence and humility. In his relationship with his nephew Lot, and in his hospitality to strangers and travelers, he acted as a servant does for a master. Without thought for himself, he interceded in the face of God's wrath to save the degenerate inhabitants of Sedom and Amorah (Sodom and Gomorrah), and he refused to take any spoils of war.

AN EVIL EYE, A HAUGHTY SPIRIT AND A DEMANDING SOUL. Let us now consider the opposite traits. The person with an evil eye looks unkindly at everyone; he is skeptical and critical when anyone tries to teach him something. He distrusts and belittles everything and eventually even turns against God Himself. Since he trusts no one else, he becomes egotistical, haughty and covetous, desiring more and more possessions and pleasures. The only goals of a רוח גבוהה (haughty spirit) and a נפש רחבה (demanding soul) are self-aggrandizement and the satisfaction of תאוה (desire) by means of the קנאה (envy) expressed by an עין רעה (evil eye). The tale of Bilam's attempts to curse Yisrael shows us clearly how deeply his mind and heart were influenced by these three vices. First, his evil eye rested maliciously on God's people moving along in peace. He was powerless to curse them, but would not admit it because of his immoderate pride. His craving for riches so completely corrupted him that all of Balak's rewards could not satisfy his greed, and finally he tried to corrupt God's people as well.

WHAT DIFFERENCE IS THERE BETWEEN THE DISCIPLES OF AVRAHAM AND THE DISCIPLES OF BILAM? This question is not about their characters, for that difference was pointed out in the first part of the mishnah. The Sage asks now about their respective destinies. The answer shows us that the true measure of a person's worth has nothing to do with his material success or failure in life, but is based only on his rectitude and goodness. "For God gives to a man who is good in His sight, wisdom, and knowledge and joy; but to the sinner He gives the urge to gather and amass—in order that he may give it to him who is good before God. This also is vanity and vexation of spirit" (*Koheleth* 2:26).

The righteous man enjoys חכמה ודעת ושמחה, "wisdom and

knowledge and joy," even though God's path is difficult to follow. The sacrifices he makes do not seem like hardships to him for he derives no satisfaction from forbidden pleasures. He is satisfied with whatever God grants him; in the enjoyment of the simple things of this world, he tastes some of the happiness of the World to Come. The future world is the better and more enduring one, but happiness and contentment may be enjoyed in the temporal one as well. Bilam's followers, on the other hand, are frantically attached to this world, but they do not even enjoy it. Their every desire for honor, wealth and pleasure may be granted, but each concession generates a multitude of insatiable new desires, rendering them even more discontent with what they already have. Their overindulgence in pleasure and passion completely expunges the next world from their future, for these passions are in reality the executors of the Angel of Death, gathering his victims into his arms before their time.

[THEY] SHALL NOT LIVE OUT HALF THEIR DAYS. The Midrash tells us that Bilam, for all his cleverness, talent and glib tongue, lived only to the age of thirty-four (*Yalkut Shimoni, Bemidbar* 31). Perhaps the saddest part of the inheritance he left to his disciples was his envy of Yisrael, for he said, "Who has counted the dust of Ya'akov...? Let me die the death of the upright and let my last end be like his" (*Bemidbar* 23:10).

כד יְהוּדָה בֶּן־תֵּימָא אוֹמֵר, הֱוֵה עַז כַּנָּמֵר
וְקַל כַּנֶּשֶׁר רָץ כַּצְּבִי וְגִבּוֹר כָּאֲרִי
לַעֲשׂוֹת רְצוֹן אָבִיךְ שֶׁבַּשָּׁמָיִם:

24 Yehudah ben Teima says: Be as firm as a leopard, light as an eagle, swift as a stag and mighty as a lion to do the will of your Father in Heaven.

*   *   *

The Arba'ah Turim, which is the basis of our Shulchan Aruch, has this maxim at the head of the list of our obligations, a sure indication of its importance. In this work, *Rabbenu* Ya'akov ben Asher explains that these are the four ways to serve the Creator, blessed is He. "Be as firm as a leopard" is first because this is the most important. When you want to perform a commandment but fear that people will laugh at you, face up to your detractors firmly, boldly and unashamedly and do not allow them to interfere with your duty. As Rabbi Yochanan ben Zakkai says: "If only your fear of God were as great as your fear of men of flesh and blood" (*Berachoth* 28b), and as King David says, "I will speak of Your testimonies before kings and not feel ashamed" (*Tehillim* 119:46)—which he did, never ceasing to study the Torah even when he was hiding among the heathens who laughed at him. The lightness of eagles in flight, continues *Rabbenu* Ya'akov, suggests the height of man's gaze, for just as the eagle rises high into the air, so should man's eyes always be raised in order to avoid seeing evil. Sin begins with what the eye sees, then the heart desires it and finally the limbs carry out the deed. The might of lions refers to the heart, for the fervency shown in the service of the Creator springs from the heart, and God urges you to strengthen your heart for His service. The swiftness of stags suggests strong, active limbs, and it therefore means that your legs should hasten to do good.

King David includes all three—legs, heart and eyes—in his prayer: "Make me go along in the path of your commandments, for therein do I delight. Incline my heart to Your testimonies and not to covetousness. Turn my eyes from beholding vanity, quicken me in Your ways" (*Tehillim* 119:35-37). The verbs used by the Psalmist are very significant. David prays for help in turning away his eyes from vanity because it is surely easier to avoid sin if you do not even see temptation in your path. However, that is not always possible; David therefore prays that he will be able to control the inclination of his heart after he has seen temptation.

The firmess of the leopard implies persistence and consistency, as it is said, "A lion out of the forest slays them, a wolf of the desert spoils them, a leopard lies in wait over their cities, every one that goes out from there is torn to pieces" (*Yirmeyahu* 5:6). Other animals satisfy their needs as they chance upon game, but the leopard will lie in wait with untiring vigilance and perseverence. "As a leopard will I watch by the way" (*Hoshea* 13:7). Yehudah ben Teima cites the most characteristic quality of each beast—the quality which enables each to excel and to rise far above the other animals in a specific way. Each of these four traits listed, however—firmness, aspiration, fleetness, and strength—is relative to the purpose for which it is used. We should therefore not only make use of each of these qualities, but we must also refine each to its maximum strength; we must reach higher and farther, go faster and try more persistently to carry out God's will.

כ**ה** הוּא הָיָה אוֹמֵר, עַז פָּנִים לְגֵיהִנֹּם וּבוֹשֶׁת
פָּנִים לְגַן־עֵדֶן. יְהִי רָצוֹן מִלְּפָנֶיךָ יְיָ
אֱלֹהֵינוּ וֵאלֹהֵי אֲבוֹתֵינוּ שֶׁיִּבָּנֶה בֵּית הַמִּקְדָּשׁ
בִּמְהֵרָה בְיָמֵינוּ וְתֵן חֶלְקֵנוּ בְּתוֹרָתֶךָ:

25 He would say: The impudent are destined for
Gehinnom (punishment in the World to Come), the
shamefaced for *Gan Eden* (reward in the World to
Come). May it be Your will, Lord our God and God of
our fathers, that the *Beith Ha-Mikdash* be rebuilt
speedily in our days and grant us our portion in Your
Torah.

* * *

In this mishnah, Yehudah ben Teima takes one of the traits
mentioned in the last mishnah and warns us about turning it
from a virtue into a sin. Firmness of purpose (עז) may become
impudence (עז פנים) and is often so obvious that it can be detected
just by looking at a person's face (פנים). Rabbi Wessely comments
that the face not only mirrors the soul, it also symbolizes the soul.
An impudent person turns his firmness into a weapon, ostensibly
aimed at others, but actually aimed against his own, better self.
Korach's impudent attack on Moshe repudiated his own inner
knowledge of the truth. The words of a righteous person, who
always acts for the sake of Heaven, will always be in harmony
with his behavior and beliefs.

Another trait that may be virtuous or sinful, depending upon
whether it is rooted in modesty or in vanity, is בושה (shame) or
בישנות (bashfulness). The addition of the word פנים (face) enables
us to understand clearly that the Sage is warning us about false
shyness and extolling the shamefacedness that characterizes reverence for God. The person who is more worried about his honor
than about what his teacher is saying, never learns anything (see
Avoth 2:6); the person who is ashamed of fulfilling a commandment in public because he thereby reveals that he is an observant

Jew, desecrates the Name of God. This is false shame; it springs from vanity and ambition and, bowing to the mistaken opinion of the public, it eschews good deeds and invites misbehavior. *Gan Eden* is not for such as these, says Yehudah ben Teima. True shame, such as that which Yosef felt in his hour of temptation, is shame before one's own soul, shame before God Himself. The Sages equate this type of shamefacedness with reverence for God, and maintain that it reveals the spark of Divine splendor that rests within every Jewish soul. The Talmud tells us, "It was taught, 'That the fear of Him may be before your faces that you sin not' (*Shemoth* 20:17), means that shame leads to the fear of sin; others say [it means that] one who experiences shame will not easily sin, and one who is not shamefaced certainly does not have ancestors who were present at Mount Sinai" (*Nedarim* 20a).

10-16-99
Rabbi — Jews)
have not changed
much.

כ הוּא הָיָה אוֹמֵר, בֶּן־חָמֵשׁ שָׁנִים לַמִּקְרָא,
בֶּן־עֶשֶׂר שָׁנִים לַמִּשְׁנָה, בֶּן־שְׁלֹשׁ עֶשְׂרֵה
לַמִּצְוֹת, בֶּן־חֲמֵשׁ עֶשְׂרֵה לַגְּמָרָא, בֶּן־שְׁמוֹנֶה
עֶשְׂרֵה לַחֻפָּה, בֶּן־עֶשְׂרִים לִרְדּוֹף, בֶּן־שְׁלֹשִׁים לַכֹּחַ,
בֶּן־אַרְבָּעִים לַבִּינָה, בֶּן־חֲמִשִּׁים לְעֵצָה, בֶּן־שִׁשִּׁים
לְזִקְנָה, בֶּן־שִׁבְעִים לְשֵׂיבָה, בֶּן־שְׁמוֹנִים לִגְבוּרָה,
בֶּן־תִּשְׁעִים לָשׁוּחַ, בֶּן־מֵאָה כְּאִלּוּ מֵת וְעָבַר וּבָטֵל
מִן הָעוֹלָם:

26 He would say: At five years [the age is reached for the study of] the Scriptures, at ten the Mishnah, at thirteen the *mitzvoth*, at fifteen the Gemara, at eighteen marriage, at twenty a livelihood, at thirty strength, at forty insight, at fifty good counsel, at sixty old age, at seventy a hoary head, at eighty special strength, at ninety the weight of years, at one hundred as if already dead and departed from this world.

* * *

Rabbi Yehudah ben Teima concludes the previous mishnah with the prayer that God grant us our share in His Torah. In this mishnah, he lists all the stages that man lives through in his realization of that prayer. There is no more reliable standard for measuring the individual stages of life than the Torah. With bent back, the ninety-year-old man contemplates the same Torah that the erect five-year-old studies at his school desk. Is there another book, another subject on earth, in which early youth and old age can both be absorbed with the same devotion and interest? "Rabbi Yehoshua ben Levi said: One who teaches his grandson Torah is regarded as if he had received it from Mount Sinai, for it is said, 'and you shall make them known to your sons and your sons' sons,' which is followed by 'that is the day that you stood before the Lord your God in Chorev" (*Devarim* 4:9-10, cited in *Kiddushin* 30a).

This mishnah is rich in golden rules. Since the precise time to begin teaching a child is not clearly stated, the Sages deduce that the first stage of instruction ought to be modified according to the health of the child (see *Kethubboth* 50a). Obviously if the child's fifth year has been appointed for beginning to study the written Torah, then lessons in the alphabet, in reading, and so on, must have preceded it. Rav, in fact, advises a well-known teacher of young children not to accept a pupil under the age of six (ibid.). The Torah, and later the Sages as well, attach great value to the instruction of children at home by their parents and grandparents. The duty of parents to teach their children was taken so seriously by the Jewish people that there were not even schools until the time of Rabbi Yehoshua ben Gamla, who first opened one to enable orphans to learn Torah along with other children. The existence of schools did not then, and does not now, exempt a father from the duty of teaching his child, or at least introducing him to, the Torah. When a child begins to speak, his first babble ought to be directed to Torah. Whatever else a Jewish father may teach his child, the first truth to impress upon him is that the Torah which Moshe handed down to us is the most precious heritage of the congregation of Ya'akov: תורה צוה לנו משה מורשה קהלת יעקב (*Devarim* 33:4; see *Sukkah* 42a).

A Jewish school builds on the foundation laid by parents. The harmonious link between the school and the home, so highly recommended by modern pedagogues, has always been a natural development in the Jewish world; every Jewish father is his child's first teacher and the school works hand in hand with him in continuing and perfecting his efforts. The Jewish child learns first that there is a God Who created Heaven and earth; that He formed man and then revealed His Law to him; and that this Law has a decisive effect on his own destiny whether he fulfills it or not. The child must be taught to learn from and model himself after the great figures in our history: Avraham, Yitzchak, Ya'akov, Yosef, Moshe and Aharon. The Jewish child is taught to feel as though he himself participated in the exodus from slavery in Egypt, accepted the Torah in the freedom of the desert, accompanied the wanderers in the desert up into the Promised Land, and saw the high walls and fortresses of the enemy kings fall before the might of God. The prophets speak to his youthful soul in thundering voices, but with comforting words; the sounds of David's harp touch his heart; Shelomo's wisdom enlightens his mind; and the history of his people unfolds before him in a vivid panoply of joy and tragedy, of loyalty and apostasy. In the first stage of his studies, which should be begun at the age of five according to this mishnah, he learns about all that God has done for man and for His people.

When the child progresses to the Mishnah at the age of ten, that does not mean that his occupation with the written Torah ceases. Studies in Mishnah and Gemara demand a thorough knowledge of the written word of God, to which they refer over and over again as they clarify and explain it. The word משנה (*mishnah*) is composed of the same letters as the word נשמה (*neshamah*), and from this we learn that the study of Mishnah is in harmony with the human soul. By the age of thirteen, a boy has long been familiar with the yoke of the commandments—not through sermons and moralizing, but through the daily, living example of his parents and teachers. They accustom him to the duties of Divine service from his earliest years. When he becomes *bar mitzvah*, however, he himself is obligated to practice the *mitzvoth* and knows that he is now personally responsible for their fulfillment. The study of Gemara, begun at the age of fifteen, is a positive influence on the development of his intellect and refines his spirit and character in every respect. For centuries, more than two thousand illustrious Sages contributed to this gigantic work, which includes the whole of the Oral Law and its myriad applications to concrete cases in life. There is no sphere of human knowledge or endeavor which is not dealt with in the Gemara. Its spiritual content is so potent that it can immunize youth against sin, for "the light in it returns every man to the right path" (Introduction to *Eichah Rabbathi* 2), and its study has enabled our people to find consolation in the saddest situations and the darkest times.

Nurtured by its spirit, filled with its view of life, the Jewish boy at the age of eighteen begins to think about finding his life's companion and founding a "house in Yisrael," a Jewish home and family. With the same fervor and love that he devoted to his study of the Law, the Torah Jew now joins himself to his chosen one, the עקרת, "the root and principle," the princess of his newly-founded home. The Jewish wife is a symbol of the happiness and unity of the Jewish family. The secret of the happiness of the Jewish marriage, which is the foundation and strength of that home, lies in the strict observance of Jewish Law. The Jew sanctifies his union with the words, "Behold, you are consecrated unto me, according to the Law of Moshe and Yisrael." At the age of twenty, the young husband must now seek to provide for his family's material needs. Unfortunately most twenty-year-olds today fritter away these important years and remain bachelors. When they do marry, much later in life, and begin to raise a family, the age differential between the parent and child is so great that the father has difficulty in understanding his son's needs and the son seems always to be disturbing his father's tranquillity. But כחצים ביד גבור כן בני הנעורים, "Children raised in one's youth are as arrows in the hand of a mighty man" (*Tehillim* 127:4).

"Our ancestors regarded the Torah as their main occupation and their work as incidental, and were successful in both" (*Berachoth* 35b). Their spiritual training, their devotion to Scripture, Mishnah and Gemara illuminated their minds, and also gave them the strength and capacity to achieve material goals. The strength of the thirty-year-old man, the insight of the forty-year-old and the sagacity of the fifty-year-old who were educated and well-versed in Torah according to the methods of our forefathers, can easily be matched against the products of any modern educational method. With the gift of old age, God bestows upon us the power to finally master passion and sensuality. The charms and pleasures of the world no longer attract and tempt us and we may devote all our thoughts and hopes to the Torah and to God, as the Psalmist says: כל היום היא שיחתי, "It is my meditation all the day" (*Tehillim* 119:97). Life's goals, from earliest childhood through golden youth and mature age, are the same as that of wonderful old age: אשרי ילדותנו שלא ביישה זקנתנו, "Happy is our childhood when it does not shame our old age" (*Sukkah* 53a).

כז בֶּן בַּג בַּג אוֹמֵר, הֲפָךְ־בָּה, וַהֲפָךְ־בָּה
דְכֹלָּא־בָה, וּבָה תֶּחֱזֵה וְסִיב וּבְלֵה בָה
וּמִנָּה לָא תָזוּעַ, שֶׁאֵין לְךָ מִדָּה טוֹבָה הֵימֶנָּה:

27 Ben Bag Bag says: Pore over it again and again,
for everything is contained in it; look into it, grow old
and gray over it, and do not depart from it, for there
is no better pursuit for you than this [the Torah].

* * *

We have just learned that our lifelong occupation with the
study and practice of Torah is the most significant factor linking
early youth and old age. This mishnah expresses that same
thought in Aramaic, the popular language at the time. The word
הפך does not have the same meaning in Aramaic as it does in
Hebrew. It means "to turn over" in Hebrew but "to study inten-
sively" in Aramaic; likewise, דכלה בה can mean either "because
everything is contained in it," or "a totality is contained in it."
There is no area of knowledge or behavior that is not acknowledged in the six hundred and thirteen commandments of the
Torah. Other disciplines are fragmentary or specialized, one
branching off from another, and it is difficult to master more
than one at the same time. The Torah, however, is comprehensive and all-embracing, as this verse shows us when it says of the
Divine Torah: לכל תכלה ראיתי קץ רחבה מצותך מאד, "I have seen an
end to every endeavor, but Your commandment is exceedingly
broad in scope" (*Tehillim* 119:96).

There are traditionally fifty aspects to the Torah, called
חמשים שערי בינה, "the fifty gates leading to true insight." Our
teacher Moshe, who received the secrets of the Torah from the
Almighty Himself, was privy to only forty-nine of these gates; one
remained closed to him. The Talmud tells us that although wisdom is traditionally associated with King Shelomo, for he was the
wisest of all men, nevertheless Shelomo longed to resemble
Moshe. But a Divine voice objected, saying, "There has never
again been a prophet in Yisrael like Moshe" (*Rosh Hashanah* 21b).

We learn from this that Shelomo's wisdom, the highest degree of human wisdom, was still only human and subject to error; perfect knowledge, Divine wisdom, was disclosed only to Moshe, and that is תורת משה, "the Torah of Moshe." Thus we know that the Torah contains the whole universe, it is the master plan for the management of heaven, earth and everything else that was called into existence. "The Torah says, 'I was the tool of the Holy One, blessed is He.' When an earthly king builds a palace, he does not normally build it according to his own inspiration but according to that of an architect. And even the architect does not build it entirely from inspiration but he has his parchments and books upon which to base his plan. Thus the Holy One, blessed is He, cast His glance upon the Torah and the world was created. The Torah says, 'For the beginning God created' (*Bereshith* 1:1), and this beginning is the Torah, as it is said, 'God made me as the beginning of His way' (*Mishlei* 8:22)" (*Midrash Yalkut Mishlei* 942).

LOOK INTO IT. Only the Torah gives us the correct perspective on worldy matters because the Torah is the master plan for the management of the whole universe as well as for the management of our personal lives. Look into it superficially and it seems impossible to carry out God's instructions in this world. How is it possible to keep the Shabbath properly in a world that never rests for a moment? How is one to be conscientiously honest in such a complicated marketplace that invites dishonesty? Only the awareness that we live בעלמא די ברא כרעותיה, "in a world created and preserved by His will" (*Kaddish* prayer), allows us to pronounce daily: יתגדל ויתקדש שמה רבה, that "God's great Name will be praised and sanctified through us" (ibid.). Only because the Jew accepts the world as his raw material to work upon for the realization of God's Law, can he happily attempt to carry out God's instructions. Ever mindful of his duty, the observant Jew will not encounter obstacles in his path—שומר מצות לא ידע דבר רע (*Koheleth* 8:5), and will have an incorruptible, unprejudiced outlook on life.

GROW OLD AND GRAY OVER IT AND DO NOT DEPART FROM IT. It is true that learning Torah is a difficult task. It demands strenuous and unstinting diligence. Remember, however, that its truth reaches far beyond this temporal state, outlasts death and is so transcendent that it will only be revealed to us in its full glory in the World to Come. " 'When you walk it shall lead you'—in this world; 'when you sleep it shall watch over you'—in death; and 'when you awake it shall talk with you'—in the hereafter" (*Mishlei* 6:22, cited in *Sotah* 21a).

FOR THERE IS NO BETTER PURSUIT FOR YOU THAN THIS. More than one thousand years passed between Moshe and Malachi, the first and the last prophets, and among the last words of the last prophet were: זכרו תורת משה עבדי, "Remember the Law of Moshe, My servant" (*Malachi* 3:22). We know that even the best books of science become antiquated after twenty years; the Torah, the Book of books, will never be out of date. It is applicable in every age, and it can be said to anticipate every civilization. How can we not, therefore, but solemnly resolve to remain faithful to the living word of God and to pass it on to our children?

בֶּן־הֵא הֵא אוֹמֵר, לְפֻם צַעֲרָא **כח**
אַגְרָא:

28 Ben He He says: The reward is according to the effort.

*   *   *

From the very first mishnah of this tractate, we have been taught the overriding importance of studying the Torah received at Sinai by our teacher Moshe; we have been enriched by the treasures of worldy wisdom and ineffable knowledge imparted to us by the Sages in order to help us in living our lives to perfection— or at least to attempt it. Although this is not easy, it is possible if we employ all our moral strength and constantly strive to correct all our bad habits throughout our lifetime. Lest we become discouraged by the weight of such a task, this last mishnah reassures us: One who tries very hard and acquires even a small part of the Torah may expect a greater reward than one who effortlessly learns a great deal. The moral and spiritual gain which comes to us from any Torah study is a reward in itself!

Contemporary reason requires labor to be paid for in terms of how much is produced, not in terms of the amount of effort involved in the production; labor itself and its recompense are definitively separated. The wisdom of our Sages not only connects the two and makes one dependent on the other, but elevates labor to a privilege for the worker and its reward to a privilege for the employer. However, it is not the sociological aspect of capital that concerns our Sages, but rather the Jew's spiritual and moral progress in general, and his Torah study in particular. This mishnah purports to teach us that what we learn with great effort remains our inalienable possession, while that which we acquire easily vanishes with great ease. There is a saying attributed to the same author in the Talmud which makes the meaning of this even more precise: "Ben He He said to Hillel: 'Then shall you again discern between the righteous and the wicked, between one that serves God and one that serves Him not' (*Malachi* 3:18). Is not the 'righteous' the same as 'the one that serves God,' and 'the wicked' the same as 'one that serves Him not'? Hillel answered: 'One that serves Him' and 'one that serves Him not' [both] refer to those who are perfectly righteous; but one that repeats his chapter a hundred times is not to be compared with one who repeats it one hundred and one times" (*Chagigah* 9b). Rashi explains that although both are righteous, the latter has served God more. The passage continues: "Eliyyahu said to Ben He He, though some say, to Rabbi Eliezer: What is the meaning of the verse, 'Behold I have refined you but not as silver. I have tried you in the crucible of poverty' (*Yeshayahu* 48:10)? It teaches that the Holy One, blessed is He, reviewed all His good qualities in order to give them to Yisrael, and He found only poverty" (ibid.). If poverty is a crucible for the refinement of virtues, then how brightly must glow the pure gold of the Jewish virtues!

> Rabbi Shimon ben Yochai says: The Holy One, blessed is He, gave Yisrael three precious gifts, and all of them were given only through suffering. They are: the Torah, the Land of Yisrael and the World to Come. How do we know this about the Torah? Because it is said, 'Happy is the man whom You chasten, O Lord, and teach him Your Law' (*Tehillim* 94:12). About the Land of Yisrael? Because it is written, 'As a man chastens his son, so the Lord, your God, chastens you' (*Devarim* 8:5), and after that it is written, 'For the Lord your God brings you into a good land' (ibid. 8:7). About the World to Come? Because it is written (*Mishlei* 6:23), 'For the commandment is a lamp and the teaching is a light, and reproofs of instruction are the way of life.'
>
> (*Berachoth* 5a)

Convinced that our reward in life will depend on how hard we strive to live according to the Torah, our rabbis and sages gratefully accepted their lot in life and became shining and noble examples for all who followed after them. "Rabbi Yochanan said: Why is Yisrael likened to an olive tree? To tell you that just as the olive produces its oil only after receiving a pounding, so Yisrael returns to the right way only after suffering" (*Menachoth* 53b).

* * *

This mishnah is the last one of the fifth chapter of Tractate Avoth. What is called the "sixth chapter" of the Sayings of the Fathers comprises additional maxims of the Sages in the language of the Mishnah.

Perek Six

שָׁנוּ חֲכָמִים בִּלְשׁוֹן הַמִּשְׁנָה בָּרוּךְ שֶׁבָּחַר בָּהֶם
וּבְמִשְׁנָתָם:

The Sages taught [this chapter] in the style of the
Mishnah. Blessed be He who chose them and their
teaching.

*   *   *

The last chapter of this collection comprises the *baraytha* called
פרק קנין תורה, "The Acquisition of the Torah." It contains lessons
on how we can obtain the Torah for ourselves. Although it is a
baraytha, it is written in the idiom of the Mishnah. The introduc-
tory words, שנו חכמים, "Our Sages taught," reminding us of the
Aramaic equivalent of the familiar Talmudic expression תנו רבנן,
convey the idea that the wisdom of the Sages is not only transmitted in the subject matter of their lessons but also in the words they
so carefully chose. The purity and clarity of their language, the
accuracy of their diction, the sparsity of expression and systematic
arrangement of vast material, all these external factors lent their
language, the language of the Mishnah, great individuality and
earned for their work the accolade of משנה, "Second," after the
Written Law. Furthermore, the morals taught by our Sages, the
wisdom they preach, and the virtues they extol are neither abstract philosophical goals nor utopian ideals. They are part of the
lives and surroundings of the Sages themselves. כגון אנא, "act as I
do," Rabbi Yochanan and Rav said, when they wanted to teach the
meaning of *kiddush Hashem* and *chillul Hashem* (*Yoma* 86a).

"What is meant by 'applied righteousness'?" the Sages ask.

The answer is not a learned treatise on righteousness, but the simple statement: "...[One who] does right as Abba Chilkiyyahu. [Who]'speaks truth in his heart'? [One who speaks] like Rabbi Safra. [Who]'swears to his own detriment and does not change [his vow]'? [One who acts] like Rabbi Yochanan. [Who] 'takes not a bribe against the innocent'? [One] like Rabbi Yishmael ben Rabbi Yosei" (*Makkoth* 24a on *Tehillim* 15:2-5). The Sages were fully aware that the activity to which they had dedicated their whole lives, learning God's Law, could not be an original, creative task, but only a protective and preservatory one. All their intellectual skill was devoted exclusively to protecting and preserving the Divine wisdom entrusted to their care, as it is said, ושמרתם את משמרתי, "Guard that which I have given over to you to keep" (*Vayyikra* 18:30). They devoted every breath of their lives to the fulfillment of this task (see *Yevamoth* 21a).

רַבִּי מֵאִיר אוֹמֵר, כָּל־הָעוֹסֵק בַּתּוֹרָה
לִשְׁמָהּ זוֹכֶה לִדְבָרִים הַרְבֵּה. וְלֹא עוֹד
אֶלָּא שֶׁכָּל־הָעוֹלָם כֻּלּוֹ כְּדַי הוּא לוֹ, נִקְרָא רֵעַ,
אָהוּב, אוֹהֵב אֶת־הַמָּקוֹם, אוֹהֵב אֶת־הַבְּרִיּוֹת,
מְשַׂמֵּחַ אֶת הַמָּקוֹם, מְשַׂמֵּחַ אֶת הַבְּרִיּוֹת,
וּמַלְבַּשְׁתּוֹ עֲנָוָה וְיִרְאָה וּמַכְשַׁרְתּוֹ לִהְיוֹת צַדִּיק
חָסִיד יָשָׁר וְנֶאֱמָן, וּמְרַחַקְתּוֹ מִן־הַחֵטְא וּמְקָרַבְתּוֹ
לִידֵי זְכוּת, וְנֶהֱנִין מִמֶּנּוּ עֵצָה וְתוּשִׁיָּה בִּינָה
וּגְבוּרָה, שֶׁנֶּאֱמַר לִי עֵצָה וְתוּשִׁיָּה אֲנִי בִינָה לִי
גְבוּרָה, וְנוֹתֶנֶת לוֹ מַלְכוּת וּמֶמְשָׁלָה וְחִקּוּר דִּין,
וּמְגַלִּין לוֹ רָזֵי תוֹרָה וְנַעֲשֶׂה כְּמַעְיָן שֶׁאֵינוֹ פוֹסֵק
וּכְנָהָר הַמִּתְגַּבֵּר וְהוֹלֵךְ, וְהֹוֶה צָנוּעַ וְאֶרֶךְ רוּחַ
וּמוֹחֵל עַל־עֶלְבּוֹנוֹ, וּמְגַדַּלְתּוֹ וּמְרוֹמַמְתּוֹ עַל־כָּל
הַמַּעֲשִׂים:

1 Rabbi Meir says: Whoever occupies himself with
the Torah for its own sake merits many things. Moreover, the whole world is indebted to him; he is called
friend, beloved; he loves God, he loves mankind; he
gladdens God, he gladdens men. It [the Torah]
clothes him in humility and fear [of God]; it enables
him to become just, pious, honest and faithful; it
keeps him far from sin and brings him close to virtue.
Through him the world enjoys counsel and sound
wisdom, insight and strength, as it is said, "Counsel
and wisdom are mine, I am insight, I have strength"
(*Mishlei* 8:14). It gives him sovereignty and dominion
and discerning judgment; to him its secrets are revealed; and he becomes like an unceasing fountain
and like a river that flows on with ever-increasing

vigor, and he becomes modest, patient and forgiving. It makes him great and exalted over all things.

*   *   *

Only a man who devotes himself to the Torah for its own sake, and not in order to excel or to gain honor or other advantages from it, will earn many blessings. The Torah mentions some of these blessings, which include long life, fertility, livelihood, sustenance, wealth, honor, preservation from danger, and more, and thus Rabbi Meir need not enumerate them here. The Sages teach that man was created for the benefit of the entire creation as well as for the pleasure and delight he himself can enjoy from God and His splendid creation. The fulfillment of all true delight, however, can only take place in the World to Come, and the only way that man can prepare himself for it, is by learning and doing precisely what God requires of him in this world. In other words, the means to arrive surely at his final, permanent, ideal abode are accessible to man only during his life on earth. The Sages find this truth in the verse: ושמרת את המצוה ואת החקים ואת המשפטים אשר אנכי מצוך היום לעשותם, " 'You will therefore keep the commandments and the statutes and ordinances which I command you today, to do them.' Today you will do them, but not tomorrow; today you will do them so that tomorrow you may reap the reward" (*Eruvin* 22a on *Devarim* 7:11). Since man was placed in this world only to fulfill God's will, his foremost obligation is to understand what that will is, as it is explained in the Torah. The world was not created in order to provide a laid table for man, at which he can feast and enjoy himself lightheartedly; it was created in order to provide the blossoms and fruit which man may bind into a wreath, as it were, as an offering for the glorification of God.

THE WHOLE WORLD IS INDEBTED TO HIM. The practical realization of God's Law presupposes the possession of some material means. The *mitzvah* of *tzitzith* for example, requires a garment; a *mezuzah* needs a lintel, the *mitzvoth* of *shemittah*, *yovel*, *terumah*, *ma'aser* and *pe'ah* need cultivated fields. The Torah, however, promises the means to fulfill the *mitzvoth* to those who perform them. "If you walk in My statutes, then you will have rain at the right time" (*Vayyikra* 26:3). Then you will be provided with ample means for the fulfillment of God's Law. Thus, the world that God created is placed at the service of those whose guiding principle is performing His will. A Jew who occupies himself totally with Torah, with no ulterior motive, is considered a partner of God in Creation. Knowledge of Torah and the fulfillment of the *mitzvoth* provide the reciprocal means whereby man enriches himself and enriches his environment simultaneously.

HE IS CALLED FRIEND, BELOVED. The Torah teaches the Jew to love and revere God. This love and reverence is a selfless attachment and it is the means through which he himself acquires good attributes in the image of God: justice, piety, righteousness and faithfulness. Armed with these attributes, he can keep sin at bay and practice all the virtues in which the Lord delights. Such virtues can only act and be acted upon for the general good, and all men will benefit from his good advice, his wisdom, his insight and his integrity. The blessings he receives from the wellspring of Torah flow forth from him in turn like a fountain, causing truth to flourish and to serve mankind. Thus he reaches an exalted height of spiritual and moral greatness.

בָּ אָמַר רַבִּי יְהוֹשֻׁעַ בֶּן־לֵוִי, בְּכָל־יוֹם וָיוֹם
בַּת־קוֹל יוֹצֵאת מֵהַר חוֹרֵב וּמַכְרֶזֶת
וְאוֹמֶרֶת אוֹי לָהֶם לַבְּרִיּוֹת מֵעֶלְבּוֹנָהּ שֶׁל־תּוֹרָה,
שֶׁכָּל־מִי שֶׁאֵינוֹ עוֹסֵק בַּתּוֹרָה נִקְרָא נָזוּף, שֶׁנֶּאֱמַר
נֶזֶם זָהָב בְּאַף חֲזִיר אִשָּׁה יָפָה וְסָרַת טָעַם. וְאוֹמֵר,
וְהַלֻּחֹת מַעֲשֵׂה אֱלֹהִים הֵמָּה וְהַמִּכְתָּב מִכְתַּב
אֱלֹהִים הוּא חָרוּת עַל־הַלֻּחֹת, אַל תִּקְרָא חָרוּת
אֶלָּא חֵרוּת שֶׁאֵין לְךָ בֶּן־חוֹרִין אֶלָּא מִי שֶׁעוֹסֵק
בְּתַלְמוּד תּוֹרָה, וְכָל־מִי שֶׁעוֹסֵק בְּתַלְמוּד תּוֹרָה
הֲרֵי זֶה מִתְעַלֶּה שֶׁנֶּאֱמַר וּמִמַּתָּנָה נַחֲלִיאֵל
וּמִנַּחֲלִיאֵל בָּמוֹת:

2 Rabbi Yehoshua ben Levi said: Every day a Heavenly voice comes forth from Mount Chorev proclaiming these words: "Woe to mankind for contempt of the Torah!" Whoever does not labor in the Torah is considered rebuked, for it is said, "Like a golden ring in a swine's snout is a beautiful woman who turns aside from discretion" (*Mishlei* 11:22). And it is said, "And the tablets are the work of God and the writing is the writing of God, engraved upon the tablets" (*Shemoth* 32:16). Do not read *charuth* (engraved) but *cheruth* (freedom), for no man is free but one who labors in the study of the Torah. The one who labors in the study of the Torah will be exalted, as it is said, "from *Mattanah* (gift of God) to *Nachaliel* (inheritance of God) and from *Nachaliel* to *Bamoth* (the high places)" (*Bemidbar* 21:19).

* * *

A careful study of the passages in the Talmud which mention a בת קול reveals that there is a בת קול מן השמים which is an actual voice, perceived as Divine and emanating from Heaven, and a בת קול, which is not described as directly emanating from Heaven and is usually the echo of another voice. The בת קול mentioned here by Rabbi Yehoshua seems to refer to the reverberation of the Divine voice that announced God's Law to Yisrael at Mount Chorev. That voice, it is said, never ceases: "These words were spoken by the Lord to your whole assembly on the mount, from out of the fire, the cloud and the thick darkness, a loud voice that will never cease. He wrote them on two tablets of stone and gave them to me" (*Devarim* 5:19). We must understand that that voice is the Divine call of God which first directed our people to open their minds and hearts to true knowledge and correct behavior, to law and justice, to human love and dignity. That voice has never, since then, stopped reminding us of God's truths. That voice has been translated into nearly three hundred languages, it has traversed continents and oceans and reached out to all nations, but the greater part of mankind has still not heard it.

That voice will continue to resound, therefore, until its mission is fulfilled. Not even God's own people, Yisrael, has listened to it carefully enough. The sound of that voice was impressed on stone and then on parchment and will "speak" to anyone who reads the holy Scriptures and tries sincerely to understand. The sacred sound of that בת קול continues to speak to every faithful member of God's people, proving that the One Who once gave us the Torah is the One Who still gives it to anyone prepared to accept it. A sage like Rabbi Yehoshua ben Levi can hear this voice from Chorev clearly; but he also hears another voice, a voice of woe that echoes when mankind shows contempt for the Divine voice. Our people show contempt for this voice when they cease to labor in the Torah; they show contempt when they continue to neglect the Torah even though they suffer infirmity and illness, poverty and famine, war and destruction. "And God said: If you will only hearken diligently to the voice of the Lord your God and will do that which is right in His eyes... I will put none of the diseases upon you which I have put upon the Egyptians, for I am the Lord that heals you" (*Shemoth* 15:26). The reponsibility is therefore Yisrael's own; when they turn their backs on the Torah, they are rebuked by God.

The prophets were fond of comparing Yisrael to the vine which produces the choicest fruits to gladden the heart of man and his Creator. But if the vine, Yisrael, does not produce its exquisite fruit, which is Yisrael's constant devotion to the Torah, it has not fulfilled its purpose, and is of no use to anyone. When Yisrael spurn their Divinely appointed vocation, they are of no use to themselves nor to anyone else. What is more, when they neglect the Torah, they lower themselves to such a level that the Sage compares them to a swine who absurdly wears a golden nose-ring and to an immodest woman whose depravity travesties her beauty. Let those who think that freedom means release from the discipline of the Torah, not be deceived. Not only does devotion to the Torah free a man truly, as we learned in earlier chapters, but it elevates him to the highest rank and status possible; it remains the most precious heritage which he can leave to his children. Although it is a gift from God, when a man is able to master the Torah by thorough study, it becomes his own possession, an inheritance of far greater value than any material achievement.

זַ הַלוֹמֵד מֵחֲבֵרוֹ פֶּרֶק אֶחָד אוֹ הֲלָכָה
אַחַת אוֹ פָסוּק אֶחָד אוֹ דִּבּוּר אֶחָד אוֹ
אֲפִילוּ אוֹת אַחַת צָרִיךְ לִנְהָג בּוֹ כָּבוֹד, שֶׁכֵּן מָצִינוּ
בְּדָוִד מֶלֶךְ יִשְׂרָאֵל שֶׁלֹּא לָמַד מֵאַחִיתֹפֶל אֶלָּא שְׁנֵי
דְבָרִים בִּלְבָד קְרָאוֹ רַבּוֹ אַלוּפוֹ וּמְיֻדָּעוֹ, שֶׁנֶּאֱמַר
וְאַתָּה אֱנוֹשׁ כְּעֶרְכִּי אַלּוּפִי וּמְיֻדָּעִי. וַהֲלֹא דְבָרִים
קַל וָחֹמֶר, וּמַה דָוִד מֶלֶךְ יִשְׂרָאֵל שֶׁלֹּא לָמַד
מֵאַחִיתֹפֶל אֶלָּא שְׁנֵי דְבָרִים בִּלְבָד קְרָאוֹ רַבּוֹ
אַלּוּפוֹ וּמְיֻדָּעוֹ, הַלוֹמֵד מֵחֲבֵרוֹ פֶּרֶק אֶחָד אוֹ הֲלָכָה
אַחַת אוֹ פָסוּק אֶחָד אוֹ דִּבּוּר אֶחָד אוֹ אֲפִילוּ אוֹת
אַחַת, עַל־אַחַת כַּמָּה וְכַמָּה שֶׁצָּרִיךְ לִנְהָג בּוֹ כָּבוֹד,
וְאֵין כָּבוֹד אֶלָּא תוֹרָה, שֶׁנֶּאֱמַר כָּבוֹד חֲכָמִים יִנְחָלוּ
וּתְמִימִים יִנְחֲלוּ טוֹב. וְאֵין טוֹב אֶלָּא תוֹרָה, שֶׁנֶּאֱמַר
כִּי לֶקַח טוֹב נָתַתִּי לָכֶם תּוֹרָתִי אַל־תַּעֲזֹבוּ:

3 One who learns from his companion a single
chapter, a law, a verse, a saying, or even one single
letter, must give him honor. For so, we find, did
David, king of Yisrael, who learned only two things
from Achithofel yet called him his master, his guide
and his intimate friend, as it is said, "You are a man
equal to me, my guide and my intimate friend"
(*Tehillim* 55:14). Now may we not infer: if David, king
of Yisrael, who had learned only two things from
Achithofel, called him his teacher, his guide and his
intimate friend, how much more ought one to honor
one's companion, from whom one learns one chapter,
one law, one verse, one saying or even only one single
letter. And honor is only Torah, as it is said, "The wise
shall inherit honor...and the observant shall inherit
good" (*Mishlei* 3:35 and 28:10). And only the Torah is

perfectly good, as it is said, "I have given you good doctrine, forsake not My Torah" (*Mishlei* 4:2).

*   *   *

The first two sayings in the *baraytha* emphasize the transcendent value of the Torah to the Jewish people and to the world, and it follows that those scholars and teachers who expound its meaning are themselves raised to a transcendent category. The Talmud tells us that the commandment את יי אלהיך תירא, "You shall fear the Lord your God" (*Dĕvarim* 6:13), extends to Torah scholars as well (*Pesachim* 22b). Indeed, Rabbi Elazar ben Shammua taught us in the fourth chapter that our reverence for our teacher ought to be like our reverence for God (*Avoth* 4:15). Nevertheless, it is doubtful whether this mishnah refers to teachers at all. First, the Sages clearly say הלומד מחברו, "one who learns from his companion," and then לנהג בו כבוד, "must give him honor," but this is generally understood as an outward show of esteem rather than the unreserved respect and total reverence implicit in the word ירא. In addition, the Sages specify quantities of knowledge, from a chapter down to a letter. Why do they not mention the larger division, a tractate? The commentary Midrash Shemuel explains that learning from one letter up to one chapter is considered to be Torah learned from a companion, but that anything larger than a chapter confers the status of master upon the teacher.

The reference to Achithofel, therefore, is instructive in two ways. Whether Achithofel taught him two, three or more chapters, or only one single letter, King David expressed his honor for whatever bit of Torah he taught him. Thus the inference of the mishnah is valid. Only the amount of respect King David gave to Achithofel was dependent on how much he had learned from him, but the principle of respect itself applies to even one letter learned. Secondly, although Achithofel was officially only David's advisor (יועץ—*Shemuel* II, 15:12) and Ira Ha-Ya'iri was his teacher (ibid. 20:26; see *Mo'ed Katan* 16b) and David was King of Yisrael, nevertheless David honored Achithofel with the title of "my teacher"—even after the latter betrayed him by joining Avshalom's rebellion.

What were the two things that David owed to Achithofel's instruction? Tradition is not quite clear on this point. According to the commentary on Avoth attributed to Rashi, Achithofel once found David engaged in learning Torah alone, and he pointed out to him that the Torah should always be studied with a companion to correct one's mistakes. "What shall I do?" David asked. "Let us jointly explore the sweet Divine mystery, let us learn together," Achithofel answered, as it is said, "We took sweet counsel together" (*Tehillim* 55:15). Another time, Achithofel saw David enter the House of God alone and, after questioning him about it, counseled him to enter it with the crowd, as it is said, "In the House of God we walked with the throng" (ibid.). According to the Midrash Yalkut Shemuel (142), David learned two other things from Achithofel. The first is that Achithofel reminded David that the Holy Ark may be carried only on the shoulders. The second is as follows: Upon laying the foundations for the *Beith Ha-Mikdash*, David accidentally released the flood waters that flowed under the earth's crust, and they threatened to inundate the world. David knew that if God's Name were written on a piece of clay and thrown into the waters, it would contain the flood, but he hesitated because he knew that the Name would thereby be obliterated and it is forbidden to erase God's Name. Achithofel brought proof that the threat of danger outweighed the prohibition.

house of the sanctuary

midrash — stories

ד

כָּךְ הִיא דַרְכָּהּ שֶׁל־תּוֹרָה, פַּת בְּמֶלַח
תֹּאכֵל וּמַיִם בִּמְשׂוּרָה תִּשְׁתֶּה וְעַל
הָאָרֶץ תִּישָׁן וְחַיֵּי צַעַר תִּחְיֶה וּבַתּוֹרָה אַתָּה עָמֵל.
אִם־אַתָּה עֹשֶׂה כֵּן אַשְׁרֶיךָ וְטוֹב לָךְ, אַשְׁרֶיךָ בָּעוֹלָם
הַזֶּה וְטוֹב לָךְ לָעוֹלָם הַבָּא:

4 This is the way of the Torah: To eat bread with
salt, to drink water by measure, to sleep upon the
ground, to live a life of hardship while studying the
Torah diligently. If you do this, then "you will be
happy and it shall be well with you" (*Tehillim* 128:2);
"you will be happy"—in this world, and "it shall be
well with you"—in the World to Come.

*　　*　　*

It cannot be that the Sages expect a Torah student to renounce all
the blessings of a good life. Indeed, we have learned from other
sayings that such privation is not a duty and may even be a
transgression. At best it is a great responsibility for someone to
reject the permissible enjoyments of this world. We have also
learned that total occupation with the Torah for its own sake
brings honor. This mishnah takes us a significant step forward,
teaching us that the Torah can be a substitute for other pleasures,
to a person who has only bread and salt to eat, for he does not feel
at all deprived. The refreshing well of the Torah quenches the
thirst of a man whose poverty denies him tasty beverages to
drink; the Torah cradles the head of one who is forced to sleep
upon the ground. Suffering and grief, illness and death, family
worries and social pressure are all eased by wholehearted devotion to the Torah.

IF YOU DO THIS. The Dubnow *maggid*, in his work Ohel
Ya'akov, explains these words with a parable:

Two young men attended a *yeshivah* and shared all the privations of *yeshivah* life. Finally one of them decided to go into

business while the other continued to learn Torah. After many years, the student, who by now had a wife and children whom he supported with a modest salary, heard that his friend had become the proprietor of one of the largest firms in the capital. He decided to travel to the capital and call upon his former friend.

He found his friend surrounded by many employees, salesmen, and customers, all of whom were waiting to speak to him—the head of the firm—in person. The businessman greeted his old friend warmly and took him at once into his private office. "You will be my guest," he said. "As you can see, many people are waiting to speak to me now, but I hope to be free later and you must come back so that we can lunch together at my home and have a long talk."

The student returned at the appointed hour and saw even more visitors than before. Nevertheless, the businessman took his friend home, introduced him to his family and promised to return quickly. As the hours passed, the wife told the guest with embarrassment that their mealtimes were always irregular because her husband was so busy. At long last the host appeared, apologizing tiredly for the long delay.

After they had eaten and conversed for a while, the guest said to his host, "I cannot imagine that you are happier now, with all your fortune, than you were when we lived in an attic and were happy when we had only bread and onions to satisfy our hunger. What good is your fortune to you if you cannot find time to enjoy it?" "You are mistaken," his friend replied with a smile. "There is nothing more pleasant for a businessman than to have so many business engagements that he has not even time to eat. I doubt that I can convince you, but I am sure that if you were a businessman yourself, you would understand; my words will never convince you."

Who will believe that a bit of bread and salt and a little water, and only the floor to sleep upon, will not only assure us of a place in the World to Come, but will even make us happy in this temporal world as long as we are totally absorbed with the Torah? The Sages therefore challenge us to put it practically to the test. "If you do this," then you will understand how true it is. Hardship, far from being a reason to give up the Torah, is, on the contrary, the greatest stimulus to remain faithful to it. As it is said, "If Your Torah had not been my delight, I would have perished in my affliction" (*Tehillim* 119:92).

ה אַל־תְּבַקֵּשׁ גְּדֻלָּה לְעַצְמְךָ וְאַל־תַּחְמוֹד כָּבוֹד יוֹתֵר מִלִּמּוּדֶךָ וְאַל־תִּתְאַוֶּה לְשֻׁלְחָנָם שֶׁל מְלָכִים, שֶׁשֻּׁלְחָנְךָ גָּדוֹל מִשֻּׁלְחָנָם וְכִתְרְךָ גָּדוֹל מִכִּתְרָם וְנֶאֱמָן הוּא בַּעַל מְלַאכְתְּךָ שֶׁיְּשַׁלֶּם לְךָ שְׂכַר פְּעֻלָּתֶךָ:

5 Do not seek greatness for yourself and do not covet more honor than is in keeping with your learning; and do not yearn for the table of kings; for your table is greater than theirs and your crown is greater than theirs, and your employer can be relied upon to pay you the reward for your work.

*   *   *

In keeping with the general theme of this chapter, this mishnah continues to expound the overriding importance of learning for its own sake. It is hard to imagine that a man who strives to be moral, pious and learned, knowing what great blessings will accrue to him, needs to be repeatedly warned about not seeking power and honor. This may be explained by comparing this mishnah with the verse ואתה תבקש לך גדלות אל תבקש, "And do you seek great things for yourself? Do not seek them" (*Yirmeyahu* 45:5). "Great things" refers to the gift of prophecy and the verse is God's answer to Yirmeyahu's disciple, Baruch ben Neriyyah, who asked for this gift. Even when one is worthy of receiving special gifts from God, as Baruch ben Neriyyah probably was, one should not presume that one ought to, or expect to, receive them. We have seen that one of the greatest rewards of learning for its own sake is the revelation of the secrets of the Torah—ומגלין לו רזי תורה (*Avoth* 6:1). The highest degree of wisdom that man is capable of attaining is רוח הקדש (Divine inspiration), of which prophecy is but one manifestation. Still, being worthy of it does not assure its bestowal. Often, external factors which are beyond the individual's control, like the worthiness of the whole generation, are also taken into account. The gift of prophecy can only be granted by God, it cannot be sought after, and, like other forms of spiritual greatness, it is exhibited more by those who shy away from it than by those who seek it. Moshe *Rabbenu* feared to raise his eyes lest he behold God's glory; King David said, "I did not reach for things too great or things too wonderful for me" (*Tehillim* 131:1).

DO NOT COVET MORE HONOR. Honor, too, is a quality that may not be sought after, but is a blessing that comes to us when we do God's will joyfully. Our pure faith in His Torah transforms itself into true honor. King Shelomo said, "The wise shall inherit honor" (*Mishlei* 3:35); that is, if we strive after Torah wisdom, we are sure to be honored by others. Honor, however, is considerably different from the greatness imparted by the Divine spirit through prophecy. Those few who were granted Divine inspiration were speaking, as it were, for God. The psalms of David and the holy writings of Shelomo are evidence of this extraordinary phenomenon: רוח יי דבר בי ומלתו על לשוני, "The spirit of God spoke through me and his word was on my tongue" (*Shemuel* II, 23:2). The wisest Torah scholar does not even say that. When Asaf prayed: בעצתך תנחני ואחר כבוד תקחני, "[first] guide me with Your counsel and afterward lead me to honor" (*Tehillim* 73:24), he was asking for Divine assistance in sustaining his faith and carrying out the commandments, but he was still asking for honor in the end. We conclude then that honor—the true honor that comes from learning for its own sake—is not only permissible but even praiseworthy. That is why the Sages do not say merely, "Do not covet honor," as they would if they had been speaking of ordinary honor. What is prohibited here is striving for honor יותר מלמודך, beyond the measure of your acquired knowledge of the Torah; the measure of your honor must and will be linked to the measure of your Torah learning. To covet honor is to be jealous of your companion's achievements, and that is worldly honor. Only the Omniscient, blessed is He, knows who truly deserves the reward; the measuring rod is not whether one has learned more or less, but rather whether one has worked harder or has, perhaps, purer motives than another. Honor must come of itself and worrying about one's status will not advance it.

DO NOT YEARN FOR THE TABLE OF KINGS. This warning seems just as unnecessary as the previous one, for anyone who is satisfied with a bit of bread and salt and the bare necessities of life. It is just as unlikely that a devoted Torah scholar would expect to be supported by others in a kingly lifestyle. We are all obligated to help support devoted Torah students, but even one who supports himself with ease must realize that his sustenance depends on the Eternal just as much as anyone else's. We need not be jealous of the lavish lifestyle of people who have waiters and butlers and pages; if we serve God as we should, our table will be laid by God Himself. "He gives food to those who fear Him" (*Tehillim* 111:5). The Sages conclude that not only will your table be superior, but your achievements (crown) will also be greater; your final reward for devotion and deprivation can be more assured.

> You prepare a table before me in the presence of my enemies; You have anointed my head with oil; my cup flows over. May goodness and mercy follow me all the days of my life, and I shall dwell in the house of the Lord forever.
>
> (*Tehillim* 23:5-6)

גְדוֹלָה תּוֹרָה יוֹתֵר מִן־הַכְּהֻנָּה וּמִן־
הַמַּלְכוּת, שֶׁהַמַּלְכוּת נִקְנֵית בִּשְׁלֹשִׁים
מַעֲלוֹת וְהַכְּהֻנָּה בְּעֶשְׂרִים וְאַרְבַּע, וְהַתּוֹרָה נִקְנֵית
בְּאַרְבָּעִים וּשְׁמוֹנָה דְבָרִים. וְאֵלּוּ הֵן, בְּתַלְמוּד,
בִּשְׁמִיעַת הָאֹזֶן, בַּעֲרִיכַת שְׂפָתָיִם, בְּבִינַת הַלֵּב,
בְּשִׂכְלוּל הַלֵּב, בְּאֵימָה, בְּיִרְאָה, בַּעֲנָוָה, בְּשִׂמְחָה,
(בְּטָהֳרָה), בְּשִׁמּוּשׁ חֲכָמִים, בְּדִקְדּוּק חֲבֵרִים,
בְּפִלְפּוּל הַתַּלְמִידִים, בְּיִשּׁוּב, בְּמִקְרָא, וּבְמִשְׁנָה,
בְּמִעוּט סְחוֹרָה, בְּמִעוּט דֶּרֶךְ אֶרֶץ, בְּמִעוּט תַּעֲנוּג,
בְּמִעוּט שֵׁנָה, בְּמִעוּט שִׂיחָה, בְּמִעוּט שְׂחוֹק, בְּאֶרֶךְ
אַפַּיִם, בְּלֵב־טוֹב, בֶּאֱמוּנַת חֲכָמִים, בְּקַבָּלַת
הַיִּסּוּרִין, הַמַּכִּיר אֶת־מְקוֹמוֹ, וְהַשָּׂמֵחַ בְּחֶלְקוֹ,
וְהָעוֹשֶׂה סְיָג לִדְבָרָיו, וְאֵינוֹ מַחֲזִיק טוֹבָה לְעַצְמוֹ,
אָהוּב, אוֹהֵב אֶת־הַמָּקוֹם, אוֹהֵב אֶת־הַבְּרִיּוֹת,
אוֹהֵב אֶת־הַצְּדָקוֹת, אוֹהֵב אֶת־הַמֵּישָׁרִים, אוֹהֵב
אֶת־הַתּוֹכָחוֹת, וּמִתְרַחֵק מִן־הַכָּבוֹד, וְלֹא־מֵגִיס
לִבּוֹ בְּתַלְמוּדוֹ, וְאֵינוֹ שָׂמֵחַ בְּהוֹרָאָה, נוֹשֵׂא בְעוֹל
עִם־חֲבֵרוֹ, וּמַכְרִיעוֹ לְכַף זְכוּת, וּמַעֲמִידוֹ עַל־
הָאֱמֶת, וּמַעֲמִידוֹ עַל־הַשָּׁלוֹם, וּמִתְיַשֵּׁב לִבּוֹ
בְּתַלְמוּדוֹ, שׁוֹאֵל וּמֵשִׁיב, שׁוֹמֵעַ וּמוֹסִיף, הַלּוֹמֵד
עַל מְנָת לְלַמֵּד, וְהַלּוֹמֵד עַל־מְנָת לַעֲשׂוֹת, הַמַּחְכִּים
אֶת־רַבּוֹ, וְהַמְכַוֵּן אֶת־שְׁמוּעָתוֹ, וְהָאוֹמֵר דָּבָר בְּשֵׁם
אוֹמְרוֹ. הָא לָמַדְתָּ כָּל־הָאוֹמֵר דָּבָר בְּשֵׁם אוֹמְרוֹ
מֵבִיא גְאֻלָּה לָעוֹלָם, שֶׁנֶּאֱמַר וַתֹּאמֶר אֶסְתֵּר לַמֶּלֶךְ
בְּשֵׁם מָרְדְּכָי:

6 Torah is greater than priesthood or royalty, for
royalty is acquired with thirty qualifications and the

priesthood with twenty-four, while the Torah is acquired by forty-eight. And these are they: by study, by attentive listening, by ordering one's speech, by an understanding and discerning heart, by awe, by reverence, by humility, by cheerfulness, by attending wise men, by communicating with colleagues, by discussion with students, by seriousness, by knowledge of the Scriptures and of the Mishnah, by moderation in business, in society, in pleasure, in sleep, in entertainment, and in laughter, by patience, by a good heart, by trust in the Sages and by acceptance of suffering. A person who knows his place, who rejoices in his portion, who fences off his words, who claims no merit for himself; he is loved, loves God, loves mankind, loves justice, loves rectitude and loves reproof; he keeps far from honor, does not boast of his learning, does not delight in giving decisions; he shares the burden of his fellowman, judges him favorably, leads him to truth and peace, is composed in his study; he asks and answers, listens and adds to his learning; he studies in order to teach and in order to do, he makes his teacher wiser, learns his lesson with precision and repeats a saying in the name of the one who said it. For so you have learned: Whoever quotes something in the name of the person who said it brings deliverance to the world, for it is said, "And Esther told it to the king in the name of Mordechai" (*Esther* 2:22).

*   *   *

The thirty prerogatives of royalty and the twenty-four of the priesthood are listed in the Talmud (*Sanhedrin* ch. 2 and *Chullin* 133b), but even so, it is clear that even all fifty-four of them together do not surpass the least important prerequisite of ac-

quiring the Torah as your own. The characteristics inherent in
the Torah itself are referred to as דברים (things) while the priesthood and royalty are said to enjoy מעלות (advantages). What do
we learn from this? That the Torah has sublime value even
though, or perhaps because, it does not confer worldly advantages. People who covet the privileges of kingship do not really
wish to assume its responsibilities. The external honors that accompany royal or priestly status are, in a way, necessary compen-
sations for the burdens. In no way can the yoke of Torah be
compared to this. The yoke of Torah is imposed in early youth
and does not let up until man draws his dying breath; it accords
no dispensation, no intermission, no retirement; it must be
learned, taught and practiced for a lifetime. The forty-eight qualities required of its devotees are anything but advantages in the
eyes of most men, involving as they do continuous renunciation.
It is clear from the fact that so many men have devoted themselves to it and continued to do so with no expectation of awards,
titles or gain, that the Torah is valued for itself.

BY STUDY. It is doubtful whether there is another people,
anywhere on earth, for whom the idea of learning is so current,
so widespread and so intrinsic to their nature as for the Jewish
people. Even an accomplished rabbi is regarded as a *talmid
chacham*, a "wise student." When companions sit down together to
study, they sit down to learn; the master does not only teach his
students, he learns with them. It is this unreserved devotion to
learning that is the first step on the way to acquiring the Torah.

BY ATTENTIVE LISTENING. How does one approach the
vast sea of material to be learned? You cannot just read the Torah
as you read a newspaper or a book. Any one of the five senses, in
fact, is merely a portal through which knowledge may enter your
spirit. In addition to seeing what is written, you must hear it too,
and not in a low rapid mumble, but distinctly enunciated. The
Sages do not say בשמיעה, "by listening," but בשמיעת האוזן, "by
hearing with the ear" that has the ability to weigh what has been
heard. The word אוזן (ear) is related to the word מאזנים (scales)
and thus we are expected to consider and weigh carefully from all
points of view what we hear before we accept it. The ear is said to

be more objective in its transmission of information than the eye, which is selective and thus more subjective.

BY ORDERING ONE'S SPEECH. If you wish to acquire Torah, you must use not only your eyes and ears but also your שפתים (lips). The commentators differ slightly in their interpretations of this phrase. It may be that this refers to the technique of repeating the text aloud when we learn, as the Sages have taught elsewhere. When thought is carried to the lips it reinforces the memory. Orderly speech also implies that you must organize the material and learn it in the correct order; you will surely remember it better that way. Moreover, moving your lips will focus your attention. This same idea is expressed in the Talmud: "Is it not written, ערוכה בכל ושמורה, 'ordered in all things and sure' (*Shemuel II* 23:5)? That is, if it [Torah learning] is arranged with all your two hundred and forty-eight limbs, it will be assured, and if not it will not be assured" (*Eruvin* 54a). The Torah can be acquired only when every organ is occupied with it, thus altering one's essentially sensual nature and adapting it to the demands of Torah. When the hand that would have reached out in vengeance is extended in brotherly love, when the foot that would have rushed headlong into places of entertainment and diversion turns rather toward the *beith ha-midrash*, then the Torah will surely be yours to possess. The hardest of all the organs to subordinate wholly to the dictates of the Torah are the lips. The commentators connect this *baraytha* with the following Talmudic passage: "ושננתם, 'and you shall teach them diligently,' means that the words of the Torah in your mouth should be clear and precise; if anyone asks you a question, you should not be in doubt about how to answer him but be able to answer immediately" (*Devarim* 6:7, cited in *Kiddushin* 30a).

BY AN UNDERSTANDING AND DISCERNING HEART. Several versions of this part of the *baraytha* have been handed down: שכלות הלב, בינת הלב, כונת הלב, and שכול הלב. All the readings interpret this as a mental rather than a physical act. כונה refers to the direction of your thoughts, and suggests that complete concentration should be your goal in learning; בינה as we have already learned (*Avoth* 3:21), connotes the intellectual integration and assimilation of knowledge; שכול and שכלות relate more to the spiritual perception and absorption of knowledge which must result in its practical application. We need all of these levels of mental activity in order to acquire Torah wisdom. Learning Torah is an art in itself. We are taught: "It is said, 'Son of man, behold with your eyes, and hear with your ears, and set your heart upon all that I shall show you' (*Yechezkel* 40:4). From this we can conclude that although the Sanctuary could be seen with the eyes and measured with the hand, it nevertheless required the careful attention of the eye, ear and heart; how much more so is this necessary for understanding the words of the Torah, which resemble mountains hanging by a hair!" (*Midrash Yalkut Yechezkel* 380).

BY AWE, BY REVERENCE. These two attributes are primarily required of us in our attitude toward God but they are also necessary in our relationship to the teacher who transmits His word to us. Our teacher is the link that joins us to the living chain reaching down to us from Sinai.

BY HUMILITY, BY CHEERFULNESS. An honest fear of God and respectful reverence for our teacher will naturally regulate our opinion of ourselves, and of our own abilities, to properly modest proportions. Humility is the next indispensable quality needed to acquire Torah. Personal humility will not only shield us from intemperance, presumption and error; it will also imbue in us a feeling of security and strength which will enable us to accept the yoke of Torah with good cheer and true joy and, as we learn it, teach it to others and practice it ourselves.

BY ATTENDING WISE MEN, BY COMMUNICATING WITH COLLEAGUES, BY DISCUSSION WITH STUDENTS. Once more, our attention is drawn to the living quality of Torah knowledge. It is intended for life and can only be acquired by living it. These three requirements are all dependent upon our relationship with our contemporaries, with whom we attempt to live this life to the best of our abilities. Therefore, learn from doing, not only from study. Learn from observing what your teachers do, as well as from what they teach; personal contact with learned men is in-

valuable instruction in itself. Talk things over with your companions and colleagues and you will each see the errors of the other
so that, together, you will arrive at a better understanding of
what you are studying. The best proof by far of your own knowledge is whether you can transmit it to your students—a bright
student will encourage you to analyze the subject in greater
depth, while a slow student will ask you to explain it with greater
clarity. This is like the Jewish tenet which holds that a poor man
performs a greater act of kindness than his benefactor, in accepting the latter's gift; this idea may be applied to spiritual as well as
material giving.

BY SERIOUSNESS. The quality which the Sages called ישוב
has been variously interpreted. The word is used in some places
in the Gemara to mean the acquisition of any practical knowledge
which will further help a man to survive in the marketplace,
further social welfare, or make the world a more civilized place to
live in. וכל שאינו לא במקרא ולא במשנה ולא בדרך ארץ אינו מן הישוב,
"One who has not learned the Written Law, nor studied the Oral
Law, nor has a worldly occupation, does not contribute to civilization" (*Kiddushin* 40b). In other places, the word seems to mean
"circumspection" or even "thoroughness," that is, ישיבה: sitting
long at one's studies. It seems sensible to relate it, in this
mishnah, to the acquisition of practical knowledge, whether scientific or manual. We know that the Sages considered no knowledge too alien to learn, nor any craft too menial to earn their
living by. Since learning Torah is the highest aim in life, anything that helped them to survive in the world was of importance only insofar as it furthered their ultimate goal. This
attribute was even more admirable, then, when the skill (for
example, knowledge of science) was one which could help
them in probing the deeper meaning of the Torah as well as in
earning their living.

BY KNOWLEDGE OF THE SCRIPTURES AND OF THE
MISHNAH. It may seem strange to see that the Bible and the
Mishnah are counted as prerequisites to acquiring the Torah,
since after all, they are the Torah. However, we must remember
what the Sages taught us earlier: "At five years the Scriptures, at

ten the Mishnah..." (*Avoth* 5:26). Without a foundation in the Written Law we cannot hope to begin to learn the Oral Law; the reverse is also true—without studying the Oral Law we will never fathom the Written Law. Scripture and Mishnah are the foundations of the Torah, which is life itself.

BY MODERATION. The next six qualities the Sages list demand the use of moderation and self-control in worldly matters. (In spiritual matters, the qualities we are instructed to employ in acquiring Torah have no limit.) There are some spheres of activity in everyday life which are necessary and permitted although we ought not to indulge in them to excess. Work hard and honestly "in business" in order to support yourself and your family, but spare as much time as you can for study; do your best to help and honor others "in society," but do not join them in immorality or crime; enjoy some "pleasure and entertainment" in life, but be neither wanton nor ascetic; "sleep" and "laughter" are important, but do not be either an idler or a buffoon. The detrimental effect of immoderation in these six spheres of conduct will slacken our minds and bodies and prevent us from absorbing the wisdom of the Torah. We Jews would, perhaps, prefer to enjoy the world to its fullest and indulge in its pleasures. Compliance with the laws of the Torah compels us to forego that indulgence. We traditionally say, after learning each chapter of the Sayings of the Fathers: "[God]...wished to confer a favor upon Yisrael; therefore he gave them the Torah..." How did God do us a "favor" by giving us the Torah? When we are so occupied with *mitzvoth* that we have no time left for vain pleasures and idle pastimes, we will keep ourselves pure and strong, and then we will fulfill our life's goal and the Torah will truly become ours.

BY PATIENCE. The term ארך אפים, "long-suffering," is first used in the Torah by Moshe to describe God's patience toward His sinful people, Yisrael. Just as we are taught to aspire to and emulate the other attributes of God, the Sages teach us to imitate His quality of patience. In all our relationships with our fellow-man, whether as student, companion, child, parent or stranger, patience means consideration, respect and selflessness. Allow for the differences in temperament between people and it will help you to restrain your impatience.

BY A GOOD HEART. We have learned that a good heart will guide us along the right path in life (*Avoth* 2:13). The Sages now tell us that even by applying the qualities of diligence in our studies and moderation in our behavior, neither will benefit us unless we combine it with a good heart. Good does not mean weak and malleable, but rather kind and steadfast; a good heart must be strengthened and trained to incline in the right direction. Rashi explains that וייטב לבו, "and his heart was merry" (*Ruth* 3:7) means that Boaz was happy because he occupied himself with the Torah. When the hearts of all Yisrael will be filled with Torah once again, as when our fathers stood at the foot of Mount Sinai כאיש אחד בלב אחד, "as one man with one heart" (Rashi, *Mechilta* on *Shemoth* 19:2), then shall we be able to reach exceptional spiritual heights. Only because our fathers' hearts were dedicated and true did the entire nation reach the unsurpassed spiritual level which led them to call out as one: נעשה ונשמע, "We shall do [what God has said] and then we shall hear [the explanation]" (*Shemoth* 23:8).

BY TRUST IN THE SAGES AND BY ACCEPTANCE OF SUFFERING. It is not accidental that these two qualities are placed one after the other. The uncomplaining acceptance of pain and affliction is proof of man's implicit trust in God. The Talmud tells us how important it is to accept suffering. Rabbi Akiva said, "Suffering is precious." Rabbi Eliezer asked, "Akiva, how do you know this?" Rabbi Akiva quoted, " 'Menashe ruled for fifty-five years in Yerushalayim...and he did that which was evil in the eyes of the Lord' (*Melachim* II, 21:2). Would the pious Chizkiyyah have taught Torah to the whole world and not to his only son, Menashe? Of course not! But all of Chizkiyyah's teaching was in vain, and only suffering brought Menashe to repentance" (*Sanhedrin* 101a).

Torah scholars are considered God's representatives, as it were, who interpret His word for us. Consequently, we must revere them and place our trust in their words. את יי אלהיך תירא, לרבות תלמידי חכמים, " 'You shall revere the Lord your God,' includes Torah scholars" (*Devarim* 6:13, cited in *Pesachim* 22b). Where there is reverence, there is trust—trust and faith. Because of this commandment, *Rabban* Gamliel tried to keep his academy free of disciples whose deeds were not consistent with their words, for as future teachers of Torah, they would have to be worthy of their students' trust (*Berachoth* 28a). אפילו שיחת חולין של תלמידי חכמים צריכה תלמוד, "Even the ordinary conversation of Torah scholars is worth study" (*Sukkah* 21b). Our *Amoraim*, great sages themselves, used to accompany their teachers everywhere to learn both from their words of instruction as well as from their behavior in every kind of situation. גדולה שימושה יותר מלמודה, "The application of Torah in deed is greater than its study" (*Berachoth* 7b). Our trust must therefore be twofold: trust in the personal character of the sage and trust in his wisdom. How has our generation detached itself so thoroughly from this attribute? Disrespect shown to Torah scholars by our youth is by far the most serious flaw of our generation, yet it is one of the easiest to correct.

A PERSON WHO KNOWS HIS PLACE. The commentators note a difference in syntax at this point in the *baraytha*. Here the subject of the saying changes from character traits to the Torah student. Rabbi Shemuel of Ozedah explains that it is a rare person who can acquire more good traits than those mentioned up to this point. To know your place means to know yourself. How hard that is! Few people are capable of assessing the true value of their achievements, uninfluenced by flatterers and unswayed by the crowd. It is a natural tendency to overestimate one's achievements; self-criticism is a very difficult skill to acquire. On the other hand, this saying is also a warning against being overly modest. The Midrash says that עיניך יונים, "Your eyes are like doves" (*Shir Ha-Shirim* 1:15, 4:1) means that just as the dove knows, as soon as she enters the dovecote, which is her nest and which are her chicks, the same applies to the disciples who sit in three rows before the Sages—each one knows his rank (*Shir Ha-Shirim Rabbah, Parashah* 4:2).

WHO REJOICES IN HIS PORTION. In life, this trait and the one that precedes it are found together. When you can honestly

assess your own capability and attainments you will not only be
able to assess your colleagues' capacities accurately, but you will
also rise above jealousy. Men's abilities are not equal. The great
teachers of the Gemara must be our models: they generously
praised their colleagues' successes. We have read these words
before: "Ben Zoma said: Who is rich? One who rejoices in his
portion" (*Avoth* 4:1). A Torah scholar who devotes all his energy
to his learning is surely in great need of feeling this kind of
satisfaction. The Torah was given to a generation of our people
which did not know the worry of acquiring earthly goods. Our
fathers in the desert lived on Heavenly bread and drank water
from a miraculous well. For forty years, their only concern was to
learn the revealed Torah so thoroughly that it would become
מורשה קהלת יעקב, "the eternal heritage of the congregation of
Ya'akov" (*Devarim* 33:4). Today, when a disciple sits down to
learn Torah, he must try to keep his mind free of all material
concerns. Just as we ban all weekday worries when the Shabbath
begins, we should forget all our business worries when we start to
learn. You can only do this if you accept your station in life and
are satisfied with the blessings you have been given.

WHO FENCES OFF HIS WORDS. We have seen this phrase
before, as well: "Make a fence around the Torah" (*Avoth* 1:1), and
"Tithes are a fence around wealth" (*Avoth* 3:17). Rashi tells us that
to fence off words means to protect them. Thus, when a scholar
fences off his words, he is protecting them by proving them
beyond any doubt; this assures that his words, which are really his
teacher's words, are valid for all time. This attribute, therefore, is
also related to the quality of trust in the words of our Sages.

WHO CLAIMS NO MERIT FOR HIMSELF. This is a warning—
be satisfied with whatever you have of material things; do not,
however, become self-satisfied when you surpass others in spiritual attainments. True knowledge is so difficult to acquire that it is
a goal which can never be achieved in practice. The Sages caution
us not to become complacent and smug: "The more wisdom, the
more vexation; the greater the knowledge, the greater the sorrow" (*Koheleth* 1:18) and "I have seen that all things have a
limit, but Your commandment is broad beyond measure"

(*Tehillim* 119:96). Through natural talent or a good memory, we may acquire an extensive understanding of the Torah, but a certain degree of discontent with the level of our achievement is indispensable.

HE IS LOVED. Who does not want to be loved? Yet surprisingly few people are liked by all. To gain friends requires unselfishness and humility. When you accept the teachings of the Torah and try to live in its spirit, you will naturally curb your selfish impulses and steer clear of pride and arrogance. The true sage neither prides himself of his knowledge nor looks down upon one who knows less than he; he does not even hold himself aloof from ordinary people. A Torah scholar who wants to be a recluse, isolated from others, will lack the qualities necessary for understanding certain parts of the Torah; he will also lack the ability to apply the Law to his own time and circumstances with wisdom. The great teachers of our Mishnah and Gemara earned their livelihood in the most varied occupations and they were able to discuss a wide range of subjects with first-hand knowledge. They tried to place themselves in the position of their fellowmen in order to understand them better, and thus they were all greatly beloved by the people. No matter how erudite you may be, emulate the behavior of the Sages and people will love and honor you; as an unexpected reward, you will find that others will volunteer to do tedious tasks for you so that you can devote your time and strength to even greater achievements in learning Torah.

[HE] LOVES GOD. Love is true if it stands firm even when it is not returned, and even when it is repaid with malice. King Shelomo said, "Love forgives all transgressions" (*Mishlei* 10:12). We have learned that love must not be dependent on anything (*Avoth* 5:20). Our love of God should be so completely independent of any secondary factor, such as reward or punishment, that it is unshakeable. Iyyov showed this kind of love in his saddest hour: "Though He slay me I put my trust in Him" (*Iyyov* 13:15); his true love of God overcame his great grief and consoled him. The *baraytha* says that this true love of God is necessary in order to acquire a complete knowledge of the Torah. The Torah scholar must love God if he wishes to learn Torah לשמה, "for its own sake." If he truly loves and reveres God, he will be devoted to His Torah with the same love and reverence. The Torah comprises so many lessons for life, its scope is so broad and its topics so manifold that a student might become too attached to one subject that appeals to him and neglect other, no less important, matters. One who devotes himself to the study of the Torah out of love will study the whole Law with the same devotion, every part of it being equally important to him.

[HE] LOVES MANKIND. It seems that every nation has its poor and its wealthy, and no country has ever succeeded, despite many attempts, in eradicating poverty. We must infer from this that poverty and its companion, discontent, will never disappear from society. The Torah revealed to us long ago that poverty is an eternal problem. It also told us how to cope with it, for what is poverty but the unequal distribution of wealth on earth. "There shall be no needy among you"—this is a promise made to Yisrael—"if only you will listen to the voice of the Lord your God..." (*Devarim* 15:4,5). If, however, we do not fulfill the *mitzvoth* wholeheartedly, then "the poor shall never cease out of the Land, therefore I command you: You must open your hand to your poor and needy brother in your Land" (ibid. 15:11). This, then, is the remedy; if we give help gladly and recognize all poor men as our brethren, then the affliction of poverty will shrink. The Torah wants us to enjoy life—ושמחת, "and be happy" (ibid. 26:11)—but we should always include the stranger, the widow and the orphan in our rejoicing and festivity. If we but heed the words of the Torah, we can solve our serious social problems: Believe in God's omnipotence and goodness and love your fellowman; you will thus eradicate class hatred and mitigate suffering.

[HE] LOVES JUSTICE [AND]...RECTITUDE. Although some commentators translate the word צדקות as "charity," it seems more in keeping with the spirit of the *baraytha* to see it as the plural of צדקה, "justice" or "righteousness," as it is said, כי צדיק יי צדקות אהב ישר יחזו פנימו, "For the Lord is righteous, He loves righteousness, the upright will behold His face" (*Tehillim*

11:7). The plural term צדקות can be explained in the same way as the Talmud explains the verse צדק צדק תרדוף, "Justice, justice, shall you follow" (*Devarim* 16:20). It is extremely difficult for a human judge to be completely impartial; he must employ perseverance and discretion. A judge is not always obligated to pass a sentence; often an amicable settlement or a reconciliation will serve justice better than strict adherence to the law. There is only one kind of justice, but it may assume different forms (see *Sanhedrin* 32b). To be a judge, one must know more than the law; one must also know how to interpret and apply the law. One can do this properly only through a full understanding of what both parties are saying and what they really want. When David wished to praise God Who loves justice, he used the plural form: צדקות, to show us that God's justice is not one-sided, but satisfies all the parties. The meaning of צדקות in the verse from Tehillim then, is its meaning in this mishnah, and that kind of justice is naturally followed by a love of rectitude.

[HE] LOVES REPROOF. The mishnah again uses the plural form, this time in reference to reproof: תוכחות. This, the Midrash Shemuel explains, is because two ways of reproving are meant here. The Torah student should not only want to admonish others; he should also be grateful when others show him his own shortcomings. The mishnah places love of reproof between love of rectitude and keeping far from honor. We learn from this that someone who really loves rectitude cannot ignore the sinful behavior of others and will reprimand them, in a suitable manner, when necessary. And someone who studies the Torah with pure intentions, not for personal honor or glory, loves the truth so much that he will encourage anyone who is able to point out his shortcomings. The Gemara tells us that Rabbi Yochanan was overwhelmed with grief when Reish Lakish died. The Rabbis selected Rabbi Eliezer ben Pedath to be his companion and help him overcome his grief. Rabbi Eliezer would respond to Rabbi Yochanan's every remark with these words: "There is a *baraytha* which supports you." Rabbi Yochanan's despair thus increased, for he missed the constant criticism of his statements by Reish Lakish, which had always led them both to a fuller understanding of the Law (*Bava Metzia* 84a).

If our intention is really to help our companions or neighbors when we admonish them, then we must do it in the right way. The Torah places the commandment הוכח תוכיח את עמיתיך, "You shall surely rebuke your fellowman," after the commandment לא תשנא את אחיך בלבבך, "You shall not hate your brother in your heart" (*Vayyikra* 19:17). Our reprimand will achieve results only if it is offered without anger and contempt toward the person, even though we abhor the sin itself.

> Rabbi Tarfon said: I wonder whether there is anyone is this generation who accepts reproof, for if you tell someone to remove the splinter from between his teeth, he tells you to remove the beam from between your eyes! (See Rashi's explanation.) Rabbi Elazar ben Azaryah said: I wonder if there is one person in this generation who knows how to reprove! Rabbi Yochanan ben Nuri said: I call Heaven and earth to witness that Akiva was often punished because I used to complain against him before *Rabban* Gamliel, and he only showered all the more love upon me, to make true what has been said: "Do not reprove a scorner, lest he hate you; reprove a wise man and he will love you" (*Mishlei* 9:8).
>
> (*Erachin* 16b)

HE KEEPS FAR FROM HONOR. This quality bridges the two sections of the *baraytha*. Until now, the Sages have advised us which character traits would contribute to our becoming successful Torah students. The rest of the qualities are related to study itself. A man who has truly acquired the Torah recognizes his limitations and knows that he will never master the entire body of sacred knowledge. He therefore does not bask in the praise and honor that others accord him for his accomplishments. He "does not boast of his learning," for there is always one more precept to master; he "does not delight in giving decisions," for he knows there are others wiser than he. Yet, if a companion asks him for help in rendering a decision, or if no one else is available to assist in reaching a decision in a matter of the Law, then the Torah scholar will not refuse to give a decision; thus "he shares the burden of his fellowman."

Ideal cooperation between men is necessarily based on their attitudes toward each other, and here we are told how a Jew should relate to his fellowman. He "judges him favorably," say the Sages, and does not find fault with him because he holds a different opinion; he "leads him to truth and peace" by being understanding and considerate of his weaknesses and is not offended when his companion corrects his errors. "[He] is composed in his study." Do not pester your teacher with questions as soon as they occur to you; try first to solve the problem yourself. "[He] listens and adds to his learning." Study well the questions asked of the great Torah scholars in the past, and their answers to those questions, and you will find a wealth of knowledge. Furthermore, if one "studies in order to teach and in order to do"— in other words, as if you had to explain the subject thoroughly to someone else or had to teach someone else precisely how to carry out the Law—with this study method you will greatly expand your own knowledge. At the same time, you will find yourself seeking more detailed explanations from your own teacher. This is how the student "makes his teacher wiser," too. Do not, however, confuse your own interpretations with what your teacher has taught; a good student "learns his lesson with precision."

[HE] REPEATS A SAYING IN THE NAME OF THE ONE WHO SAID IT. The last admonition is the high point of the *baraytha*. It is, in fact, so important that the Gemara tells us in three different places that when a teacher repeats a lesson in the name of the one who taught it to him, he brings redemption to the world. It is so important that the Sages remind us again, in this mishnah, to be sure we mention the name of the teacher who has taught us what we are teaching. In this way the great teachers of the Mishnah and the Gemara still live among us when we meet them in the Talmud. "Rabbi Yehudah said, in the name of Shemuel, 'I shall dwell in Your tent in [both] the worlds' (*Tehillim* 61:5). How is it possible to dwell in two worlds? What David meant was: 'Lord of the world, may it be Your will that Torah will be repeated in my name in this world.' Thus Rabbi Yochanan said in the name of

Rabbi Shimon bar Yochai: Every *talmid chacham* whose words of Torah are repeated in this world, his lips will move in his grave" (*Yevamoth* 96b-97a).

We have now seen that the sixth *baraytha* has said practically everything there is to say on how to make the Torah our own permanent possession. This *baraytha* is followed by another six, which glorify the Torah in such poetic terms that very few of our own words need to be added.

ד גְּדוֹלָה תוֹרָה שֶׁהִיא נוֹתֶנֶת חַיִּים
לְעוֹשֶׂיהָ בָּעוֹלָם הַזֶּה וּבָעוֹלָם הַבָּא,
שֶׁנֶּאֱמַר כִּי־חַיִּים הֵם לְמֹצְאֵיהֶם וּלְכָל־בְּשָׂרוֹ
מַרְפֵּא, וְאוֹמֵר רִפְאוּת תְּהִי לְשָׁרֶּךָ וְשִׁקּוּי
לְעַצְמוֹתֶיךָ, וְאוֹמֵר עֵץ־חַיִּים הִיא לַמַּחֲזִיקִים בָּהּ
וְתֹמְכֶיהָ מְאֻשָּׁר, וְאוֹמֵר כִּי לִוְיַת־חֵן הֵם לְרֹאשֶׁךָ
וַעֲנָקִים לְגַרְגְּרֹתֶיךָ, וְאוֹמֵר תִּתֵּן לְרֹאשְׁךָ לִוְיַת־חֵן
עֲטֶרֶת תִּפְאֶרֶת תְּמַגְּנֶךָּ, וְאוֹמֵר כִּי בִי יִרְבּוּ יָמֶיךָ
וְיוֹסִיפוּ לְּךָ שְׁנוֹת חַיִּים, וְאוֹמֵר אֹרֶךְ יָמִים בִּימִינָהּ
בִּשְׂמֹאולָהּ עֹשֶׁר וְכָבוֹד, וְאוֹמֵר כִּי אֹרֶךְ יָמִים
וּשְׁנוֹת חַיִּים וְשָׁלוֹם יוֹסִיפוּ לָךְ:

7 Great is the Torah, for it confers life upon those who fulfill it, both in this world and in the World to Come, as it is said, "For they [the teachings of the Torah] are life to those who find them, and a healing to his entire flesh" (*Mishlei* 4:22). And it says, "It shall be a healing to your body, and marrow to your bones" (ibid. 3:8). And it says, "It is a tree of life to those who grasp it, and its supporters are praiseworthy" (ibid. 3:18). And it says, "They are a garland of grace for your head, and necklaces for your neck" (ibid. 1:9). And it says, "It will give to your head a garland of grace; a crown of glory it will deliver to you" (ibid. 4:9). And it says, "Indeed through me [the Torah] your days shall be increased and years of life shall be added to you" (ibid. 9:11). And it says, "Lengthy days are at its right, and at its left are wealth and honor" (ibid. 3:16). And it says, "For lengthy days and years of life, and peace shall they add to you" (ibid. 3:2).

* * *

The sixth *baraytha* taught us that acquiring the Torah is greater than both the priesthood and the kingship; here we learn that our acquisition of the Torah assures us of a happy life in both this world and in the World to Come.

חַ רַבִּי שִׁמְעוֹן בֶּן־יְהוּדָה מִשׁוּם רַבִּי שִׁמְעוֹן
בֶּן־יוֹחַאי אוֹמֵר, הַנּוֹי וְהַכֹּחַ וְהָעֹשֶׁר
וְהַכָּבוֹד וְהַחָכְמָה וְהַזִּקְנָה וְהַשֵּׂיבָה וְהַבָּנִים נָאֶה
לַצַּדִּיקִים וְנָאֶה לָעוֹלָם, שֶׁנֶּאֱמַר עֲטֶרֶת תִּפְאֶרֶת
שֵׂיבָה בְּדֶרֶךְ צְדָקָה תִּמָּצֵא, וְאוֹמֵר תִּפְאֶרֶת
בַּחוּרִים כֹּחָם וַהֲדַר זְקֵנִים שֵׂיבָה, וְאוֹמֵר עֲטֶרֶת
חֲכָמִים עָשְׁרָם, וְאוֹמֵר עֲטֶרֶת זְקֵנִים בְּנֵי בָנִים
וְתִפְאֶרֶת בָּנִים אֲבוֹתָם, וְאוֹמֵר וְחָפְרָה הַלְּבָנָה
וּבוֹשָׁה הַחַמָּה כִּי־מָלַךְ יְיָ צְבָאוֹת בְּהַר צִיּוֹן
וּבִירוּשָׁלַיִם וְנֶגֶד זְקֵנָיו כָּבוֹד. רַבִּי שִׁמְעוֹן בֶּן־מְנַסְיָא
אוֹמֵר, אֵלוּ שֶׁבַע מִדּוֹת שֶׁמָּנוּ חֲכָמִים לַצַּדִּיקִים,
כֻּלָּם נִתְקַיְּמוּ בְּרַבִּי וּבְבָנָיו:

8 Rabbi Shimon ben Yehudah says in the name of Rabbi Shimon ben Yochai: Beauty, strength, wealth, honor, wisdom, old age, hoary age, and children— these befit the righteous and befit the world, as it is said, "Ripe old age is a crown of splendor; it can be found in the path of righteousness"(*Mishlei* 16:31). And it says, "The splendor of young men is their strength and the glory of old men is hoary age" (ibid. 20:29). And it says, "The crown of the wise is their wealth" (ibid. 14:24). And it says, "The crown of the aged is grandchildren, and the splendor of the children is their fathers" (ibid. 17:6). And it says, "The moon will grow pale and the sun be shamed, when the Lord of Hosts will reign on Mount Tzion and in Yerushalayim, and glory will be before His elders" (*Yeshayahu* 24:23). Rabbi Shimon ben Menasya said: These seven qualities that the Sages attributed to the righteous were all realized in Rabi and his sons.

ט אָמַר רַבִּי יוֹסֵי בֶּן־קִסְמָא, פַּעַם אַחַת
הָיִיתִי מְהַלֵּךְ בַּדֶּרֶךְ וּפָגַע בִּי אָדָם אֶחָד
וְנָתַן־לִי שָׁלוֹם וְהֶחֱזַרְתִּי לוֹ שָׁלוֹם. אָמַר לִי, רַבִּי
מֵאֵיזֶה מָקוֹם אָתָּה, אָמַרְתִּי לוֹ מֵעִיר גְּדוֹלָה שֶׁל
חֲכָמִים וְשֶׁל־סוֹפְרִים אָנִי. אָמַר לִי, רַבִּי רְצוֹנְךָ
שֶׁתָּדוּר עִמָּנוּ בִּמְקוֹמֵנוּ וַאֲנִי אֶתֵּן לְךָ אֶלֶף אֲלָפִים
דִּינְרֵי זָהָב וַאֲבָנִים טוֹבוֹת וּמַרְגָּלִיּוֹת, אָמַרְתִּי לוֹ,
אִם אַתָּה נוֹתֵן לִי כָּל־כֶּסֶף וְזָהָב וַאֲבָנִים טוֹבוֹת
וּמַרְגָּלִיּוֹת שֶׁבָּעוֹלָם אֵינִי דָר אֶלָּא בִּמְקוֹם תּוֹרָה,
וְכֵן כָּתוּב בְּסֵפֶר תְּהִלִּים עַל יְדֵי־דָוִד מֶלֶךְ יִשְׂרָאֵל
טוֹב לִי תוֹרַת פִּיךָ מֵאַלְפֵי זָהָב וָכָסֶף. וְלֹא עוֹד,אֶלָּא
שֶׁבִּשְׁעַת פְּטִירָתוֹ שֶׁל אָדָם אֵין מְלַוִּין לוֹ לְאָדָם לֹא
כֶסֶף וְלֹא זָהָב וְלֹא אֲבָנִים טוֹבוֹת וּמַרְגָּלִיּוֹת אֶלָּא
תוֹרָה וּמַעֲשִׂים טוֹבִים בִּלְבָד, שֶׁנֶּאֱמַר בְּהִתְהַלֶּכְךָ
תַּנְחֶה אֹתָךְ בְּשָׁכְבְּךָ תִּשְׁמוֹר עָלֶיךָ וַהֲקִיצוֹתָ הִיא
תְשִׂיחֶךָ. בְּהִתְהַלֶּכְךָ תַּנְחֶה אֹתָךְ בָּעוֹלָם הַזֶּה,
בְּשָׁכְבְּךָ תִּשְׁמוֹר עָלֶיךָ בַּקֶּבֶר, וַהֲקִיצוֹתָ הִיא
תְשִׂיחֶךָ לָעוֹלָם הַבָּא. וְאוֹמֵר לִי הַכֶּסֶף וְלִי הַזָּהָב
נְאֻם יְיָ צְבָאוֹת:

9 Rabbi Yosei ben Kisma said: Once when I was
walking on the road, a certain man met me. He
greeted me and I returned his greeting. He said to
me, "Rabbi, from what place are you?" I said to him,
"I am from a great city of scholars and sages." He said
to me, "Rabbi, would you be willing to live with us in
our place? I would give you thousands upon thousands of golden dinars, precious stones and pearls." I
replied, "Even if you were to give me all the silver and

gold, precious stones and pearls in the world, I would dwell nowhere but in a place of Torah." And so it is written in the book of Tehillim by David, King of Yisrael: "I prefer the Torah of your mouth above thousands in gold and silver"(*Tehillim* 119:72). Furthermore, when a man departs from this world, neither silver, nor gold, nor precious stones nor pearls escort him, but only Torah study and good deeds, as it is said, "When you walk, it shall guide you; when you lie down, it shall guard you; and when you awake, it shall speak on your behalf" (*Mishlei* 6:22). "When you walk, it shall guide you"—in this world; "when you lie down, it shall guard you"—in the grave; "and when you awake, it shall speak on your behalf"—in the World to Come. And it says, "Mine is the silver and Mine is the gold, says the Lord of Hosts" (*Chaggai* 2:8).

* * *

Earthly possessions are undeniably a source of pleasure both for the learned and the pious as well as for most people in this world. Yet the possession of Torah is of so much greater value than all other possessions that the Sages warn us not to imperil our Torah studies for the sake of acquiring wealth and worldy goods. All the verses which are brought to support this admonition resound with praise of the Torah.

ךַ חֲמִשָּׁה קִנְיָנִים קָנָה לוֹ הַקָּדוֹשׁ בָּרוּךְ
הוּא בְּעוֹלָמוֹ וְאֵלוּ הֵן. תּוֹרָה קִנְיָן אֶחָד,
שָׁמַיִם וָאָרֶץ קִנְיָן אֶחָד, אַבְרָהָם קִנְיָן אֶחָד, יִשְׂרָאֵל
קִנְיָן אֶחָד, בֵּית הַמִּקְדָּשׁ קִנְיָן אֶחָד. תּוֹרָה מִנַּיִן,
דִּכְתִיב יְיָ קָנָנִי רֵאשִׁית דַּרְכּוֹ קֶדֶם מִפְעָלָיו מֵאָז.
שָׁמַיִם וָאָרֶץ מִנַּיִן, דִּכְתִיב כֹּה אָמַר יְיָ הַשָּׁמַיִם כִּסְאִי
וְהָאָרֶץ הֲדוֹם רַגְלָי אֵי־זֶה בַיִת אֲשֶׁר תִּבְנוּ־לִי וְאֵי־
זֶה מָקוֹם מְנוּחָתִי. וְאוֹמֵר מָה רַבּוּ מַעֲשֶׂיךָ יְיָ כֻּלָּם
בְּחָכְמָה עָשִׂיתָ מָלְאָה הָאָרֶץ קִנְיָנֶךָ. אַבְרָהָם מִנַּיִן,
דִּכְתִיב וַיְבָרֲכֵהוּ וַיֹּאמַר בָּרוּךְ אַבְרָם לְאֵל עֶלְיוֹן
קֹנֵה שָׁמַיִם וָאָרֶץ. יִשְׂרָאֵל מִנַּיִן, דִּכְתִיב עַד־יַעֲבֹר
עַמְּךָ יְיָ עַד יַעֲבֹר עַם־זוּ קָנִיתָ. וְאוֹמֵר לִקְדוֹשִׁים
אֲשֶׁר בָּאָרֶץ הֵמָּה וְאַדִּירֵי כָּל־חֶפְצִי בָם. בֵּית
הַמִּקְדָּשׁ מִנַּיִן, דִּכְתִיב מָכוֹן לְשִׁבְתְּךָ פָּעַלְתָּ יְיָ
מִקְדָּשׁ אֲדֹנָי כּוֹנֲנוּ יָדֶיךָ. וְאוֹמֵר וַיְבִיאֵם אֶל־גְּבוּל
קָדְשׁוֹ הַר זֶה קָנְתָה יְמִינוֹ:

10 Five possessions did the Holy One, blessed is He, acquire for Himself in His world, and they are: Torah, one; Heaven and earth, one; Avraham, one; Yisrael, one; the Holy Temple, one.

From where do we know this about the Torah? Since it is written, "The Lord acquired me [the Torah] at the beginning of His way, before His works in time of old" (*Mishlei* 8:22).

From where do we know this about Heaven and earth? Since it is written, "So says the Lord. The Heaven is My throne and the earth is My footstool; what house can you build for Me and where is the place of My rest?" (*Yeshayahu* 66:1). And it says, "How abundant are Your works, O Lord; with wisdom You made them all; the earth is full of Your possessions" (*Tehillim* 104:24).

From where do we know this about Avraham? Since it is written, "And he blessed him and said: blessed is Avram of God the Most High, Who acquired Heaven and earth" (*Bereshith* 14:19).

From where do we know this about [the people of] Yisrael? Since it is written, "Until Your people passes through, O Lord, until it passes through, this people You acquired" (*Shemoth* 15:16). And it says, "But for the holy ones who are in the earth, they are the noble ones in whom is all My delight" (*Tehillim* 16:3).

From where do we know about the Holy Temple? Since it is written, "Your dwelling place which You, O Lord, have made; the sanctuary, my Lord, that Your hands established" (*Shemoth* 15:17). And it says, "And he brought them to His sacred boundary, to this mountain which His right hand acquired" (*Tehillim* 78:54).

* * *

The Holy One, blessed is He, made five things especially for Himself in this world. The first, the Torah, was already in existence before the world was created; the other four—the miraculous signs in the heavens and on the earth, Avraham's activities, Yisrael's place in history and the Holy Temple (both while it existed and even after it was destroyed)—are all additional elements which were to assist in making God's Law, as laid down in the Torah, the guide and molder of all men.

יא כֹּל מַה־שֶּׁבָּרָא הַקָּדוֹשׁ בָּרוּךְ הוּא
בְּעוֹלָמוֹ לֹא בְרָאוֹ אֶלָּא לִכְבוֹדוֹ, שֶׁנֶּאֱמַר
כֹּל הַנִּקְרָא בִשְׁמִי וְלִכְבוֹדִי בְּרָאתִיו יְצַרְתִּיו אַף
עֲשִׂיתִיו. וְאוֹמֵר, יְיָ יִמְלֹךְ לְעֹלָם וָעֶד:

11 All that the Holy One, blessed is He, created in
His world, He created solely for His glory, as it is said,
"All that is called by My name, indeed, it is for My
glory that I have created it, formed it, and made it"
(*Yeshayahu* 43:7). And it says, "The Lord shall reign
forever and ever" (*Shemoth* 15:18).

*   *   *

The object of the creation of the world will be attained when, one
day, all of mankind will learn to appreciate the gracious gift of
the Torah to the world. Then, all the creatures in all the world
will glorify the Creator, and "Many nations will go and say: We
want to go up to God's mountain, to the House of the God of
Ya'akov, and He will teach us His ways, and we will walk in His
paths. For out of Tzion shall go forth the Torah and the Word of
the Lord from Yerushalayim" (*Michah* 4:2).

רַבִּי חֲנַנְיָא בֶּן־עֲקַשְׁיָא אוֹמֵר, רָצָה הַקָּדוֹשׁ בָּרוּךְ
הוּא לְזַכּוֹת אֶת־יִשְׂרָאֵל לְפִיכָךְ הִרְבָּה לָהֶם תּוֹרָה
וּמִצְוֹת, שֶׁנֶּאֱמַר יְיָ חָפֵץ לְמַעַן צִדְקוֹ יַגְדִּיל תּוֹרָה
וְיַאְדִּיר:

Rabbi Chananya ben Akashya says: the Holy One,
blessed is He, wished to confer a favor upon Yisrael;
therefore He gave them Torah and *mitzvoth* in abundance, as it is said, "It pleased the Lord for the sake of
its [Yisrael's] righteousness, to make the Torah great
and glorious" (*Yeshayahu* 42:21).

*   *   *

These words are traditionally repeated after learning each of the
six chapters of the Sayings of the Fathers. Now that we have
carefully studied them all, we find Rabbi Chananya ben
Akashya's words affirmed: the Torah is our greatest blessing.